DNA AND OTHER POLYMORPHISMS IN FORENSIC SCIENCE

DNA and Other Polymorphisms in Forensic Science

Henry C. Lee, Ph.D.
Chief Criminalist and Director
Connecticut State Police
Forensic Science Laboratory
Meriden, Connecticut

R. E. Gaensslen, Ph.D.
Professor and Director
Forensic Sciences Program
University of New Haven
West Haven, Connecticut

YEAR BOOK MEDICAL PUBLISHERS, INC.
CHICAGO • LONDON • BOCA RATON • LITTLETON, MASS.

1 2 3 4 5 6 7 8 9 0 YR 94 93 92 91 90

Library of Congress Cataloging-in-Publication Data

DNA and other polymorphisms in forensic science / [edited by] Henry C. Lee, R. E. Gaensslen.
p. cm.
Includes bibliographical references.
ISBN 0-8151-5348-1
1. DNA fingerprints. 2. Forensic pathology—Technique. I. Lee, Henry C. II. Gaensslen, R. E. (Robert E.)
[DNLM: 1. DNA—analysis. 2. Forensic Medicine. W 750 D629]
RA1057.55.D63 1990
614′.1—dc20 89-22592
DNLM/DLC CIP
for Library of Congress

Sponsoring Editor: Richard Wallace
Associate Director, Manuscript Services: Frances M. Perveiler
Production Project Coordinator: Gayle Paprocki
Proofroom Supervisor: Barbara M. Kelly

ADVANCES IN FORENSIC SCIENCES

Titles in the series include:

Forensic Serology
Instrumental Analysis
DNA and Other Polymorphisms in Forensic Science

CONTRIBUTORS

Dwight E. Adams, Ph.D.
DNA Unit
Scientific Analysis Section
Laboratory Division
Federal Bureau of Investigation Headquarters
Washington, D.C.

Michael L. Baird, Ph.D.
Lifecodes Corporation
Valhalla, New York

Ivan Balazs, Ph.D.
Lifecodes Corporation
Valhalla, New York

Bruce Budowle, Ph.D.
Research Scientist
Federal Bureau of Investigation Forensic Science Research and Training Center
FBI Academy
Quantico, Virginia

Professor Doctor René Bütler
Zentrallaboratorium
Blutspendienst SRK
Bern, Switzerland

Catherine C. Comey, Ph.D.
Research Scientist
Federal Bureau of Investigation Forensic Science Research and Training Center
FBI Academy
Quantico, Virginia

Robert P. Erickson, M.D.
Director, Division of Pediatric Genetics
Professor of Pediatrics and Human Genetics
Department of Human Genetics
The University of Michigan Medical School
Ann Arbor, Michigan

Steven M. Fletcher, Ph.D.
Home Office Forensic Science Service
Central Research Establishment
Aldermaston, England

Lisa Forman, Ph.D.
Scientist, Cellmark Diagnostics
Division of Imperial Chemical Industries, Ltd.
Germantown, Maryland

Daniel D. Garner, Ph.D
Laboratory Director, Cellmark Diagnostics
Division of Imperial Chemical Industries, Ltd.
Germantown, Maryland

George Herrin, Jr., Ph.D.
Staff Scientist, Cellmark Diagnostics
Division of Imperial Chemical Industries, Ltd.
Germantown, Maryland

Paul L. Huang, M.D., Ph.D.
Cardiac Unit
Department of Medicine
Harvard Medical School
Massachusetts General Hospital
Boston, Massachusetts

Philip L. Huang, M.D., Ph.D.
Department of Neurology
Massachusetts General Hospital
Boston, Massachusetts

Mia Kirnbauer
Institut für Blutgruppenserologie der Universität Wien
Wien, Austria

Terry A. Landers, Ph.D.
Molecular Biology Research and Development
Bethesda Research Laboratories
Life Technologies Incorporated
Gaithersburg, Maryland

Sylvia Lee-Huang, Ph.D.
Professor of Biochemistry
Department of Biochemistry
New York University Medical Center
New York, New York

Professor Doctor of Medicine Wolfgang Mayr
Director, Institut für Transfusionsmedizin der Fakulät
Rheinisch-Westfälischen Technischen Hockschule Aachen
Aachen, Federal Republic of Germany

Carl R. Merril, M.D.
U.S. Public Health Service
National Institutes of Health
National Institute of Mental Health
Bethesda, Maryland

Kevin McElfresh, Ph.D.
Lifecodes Corporation
Valhalla, New York

Shannon J. Odelberg, Ph.D.
Postdoctoral Research Associate
Department of Human Genetics
The University of Utah School of Medicine
Salt Lake City, Utah

Moses S. Schanfield, Ph.D.
Laboratory Director
Analytical Genetic Testing Center
Denver, Colorado
Associate Professor
Department of Pediatrics (Medical Genetics)
Emory University
Atlanta, Georgia

Ray White, Ph.D.
Co-Chairman and Professor
Department of Human Genetics
The University of Utah School of Medicine
Salt Lake City, Utah

Michal Witt, M.D., Ph.D.
Visiting Scientist
Department of Human Genetics
The University of Michigan Medical School
Ann Arbor, Michigan

PREFACE

It is altogether appropriate that Volume 3 of this series return to coverage of forensic serology, which was the subject of the premiere volume. Progress in the field of molecular biology over the past decade or so has recently led to the application of DNA polymorphism analysis in forensic serology. This development, among the most novel and exciting in forensic sciences in this century, promises to revolutionize the forensic serology field. This volume thus contains a number of chapters written by some of the world's leading authorities on DNA polymorphisms and their applications in forensic serology. We believe this is the first forensic science book to treat this subject in detail, and we trust that forensic scientists, medical and legal professionals, students and other interested readers will find it valuable.

As exciting as the advent of DNA polymorphism analysis is in forensic serology, there will nevertheless be a period of development and implementation, during which current methods will continue to be used exclusively in many laboratories. In addition, many samples reaching the forensic laboratory will not be amenable to DNA analysis for a variety of reasons, and these samples will continue to be analyzed using more traditional methods and genetic marker systems. Accordingly, it is equally appropriate that this volume contain chapters that review several important serological subjects apart from DNA polymorphisms. The HLA system remains a mainstay of parentage testing. There are also reviews of two important serum group marker systems seldom treated in extensive reviews, the Ag polymorphism of human low density lipoproteins and the immunoglobulin allotypes. These systems may offer information on sera and bloodstains that is unobtainable using other systems or methods. An extensive review of ELISA technology, and its recent applications in forensic serology, completes the volume. A number of laboratories are beginning to develop routine methods for immunoglobulin allotyping. Others are in the process of implementing ELISA procedures for species identification and ABH and Lewis grouping. The technique offers not only increased sensitivity, and increased specificity taking advantage of monoclonal antibodies, but the potential for increased automation in testing.

We take this opportunity to thank all the contributors to this volume who have labored diligently to produce an informative and useful product. We thank the editorial staff at Year Book Medical Publishers for their efforts in producing this latest volume of the series, and for making the transition to a larger publisher smooth and unobtrusive for us and our contributors. And not least, we thank Margaret and Jacqueline for their love and unending patience with us and our work schedules.

Henry C. Lee, Ph.D.
R. E. Gaensslen, Ph.D.

CONTENTS

Chapter 1

DNA Polymorphism and Forensic Identification

Paul L. Huang, M.D., Ph.D.
Philip L. Huang
Sylvia Lee-Huang, Ph.D.

INTRODUCTION

Recent developments in recombinant DNA technology offer specific tools in human gene and disease mapping as well as in forensic identification. The forensic analysis of DNA is perhaps the most significant advance in modern crime solving and law enforcement. It can enable the identification of an individual based on molecular evidence left at the scene of the crime: a drop of blood, a semen stain, or even a single hair. Because of its unique specificity, forensic DNA analysis is also referred to as "DNA typing" or "DNA fingerprinting."

The most common approach of forensic DNA typing is restriction fragment length polymorphism (RFLP) analysis. This process involves the extraction of DNA from the biological samples collected, digestion of the DNA with restriction enzymes, resolution of the restriction fragments by agarose gel electrophoresis, transfer of the DNA from the gel to a membrane support, hybridization of the DNA with labeled probes, and identification of a specific pattern by autoradiography. The recently developed technique of polymerase chain reaction (PCR) provides a means for effective in vitro cloning and amplification of subanalytical quantities of specific regions of DNA molecules. Together, these techniques will revolutionize the power and accuracy of forensic identification.

In this chapter we shall review the structure of DNA and genes, and then present some of the techniques used in molecular biology. Next, we will present an overview of recent developments in DNA biotechnology and molecular biology that are particularly relevant to forensic DNA typing. Finally, we will discuss some practical aspects of DNA work and how PCR technology will be useful.

STRUCTURE OF DNA

Historical Perspective

Although it was known that all living cells contain nucleic acids and proteins, it was not until the early 1950s that it became clear that genetic information is encoded in the sequence of DNA. The structure of DNA, as worked out by Watson and Crick,[1,2] consists of a long linear chain of bases. There are four such bases, known as A, G, T, and C. It is the sequence of these bases in DNA which encodes genetic information.

Crick first expressed the "central dogma" of molecular biology[3]: DNA may be copied to make more DNA in a process known as replication; short stretches of DNA may be copied into RNA in a process known as transcription; and certain RNA molecules, known as messenger RNA, can direct the synthesis of proteins based on the genetic information encoded in the process of translation. The genetic code consists of three base combinations in the sequence of DNA or RNA that are known as codons. Each three bases code for a particular amino acid in the sequence of a protein. A gene consists of one or several stretches of DNA, in which the sequence of the DNA determines the sequence of the protein encoded by that gene.

Since the time of Watson and Crick, the story has become more complex as we have learned more about the structure of genes. Not all genes are continuous; some are broken up. Stretches of DNA which code for proteins (called exons) are separated by stretches of DNA which do not (called introns or intervening sequences).[4] In fact, the introns within some genes have been shown to serve as exons coding for other genes. Some genes do not code for proteins; they may code for structural RNAs. Much of the DNA in the genome does not appear to code for genes at all; the function of these areas is not yet known.

Basic Structure of DNA

Deoxyribonucleic acid (DNA), the genetic material of all living organisms, is found in chromosomes in the nuclei of cells. DNA is a polynucleotide, or a polymer made up of individual deoxyribonucleotide units. A single deoxyribonucleotide unit is made up of three components (Fig 1–1,A): a sugar, a nitrogenous base, and a phosphate. The sugar and phosphate groups are involved in the backbone structure of the DNA molecule, whereas the bases carry the genetic information.

The sugar in a deoxyribonucleotide is deoxyribose; the "deoxy" denotes that the sugar lacks an oxygen atom at the C-2 position of ribose. The nitrogenous base can be a purine or a pyrimidine. The purines are adenine (A) and guanine (G), and the pyrimidines are thymine (T) and cytosine (C). Their structures are shown in figure 1b. The unique part of the DNA molecule is the sequence of the four kinds of bases (A, G, T, and C). The bases are attached to the deoxyribose by an N-glycosidic linkage between the C-1 carbon atom of the sugar, and the N-9 nitrogen atom of the purine or the N-1 nitrogen atom of the pyrimidine.

The sugar phosphate backbone of DNA is shown in Figure 1–2. Each sugar has two hydroxyl (-OH) groups, one each at the 3' and 5' positions. The 3'-OH group of one sugar is linked to the 5'-OH group of the adjacent sugar by a phosphodiester

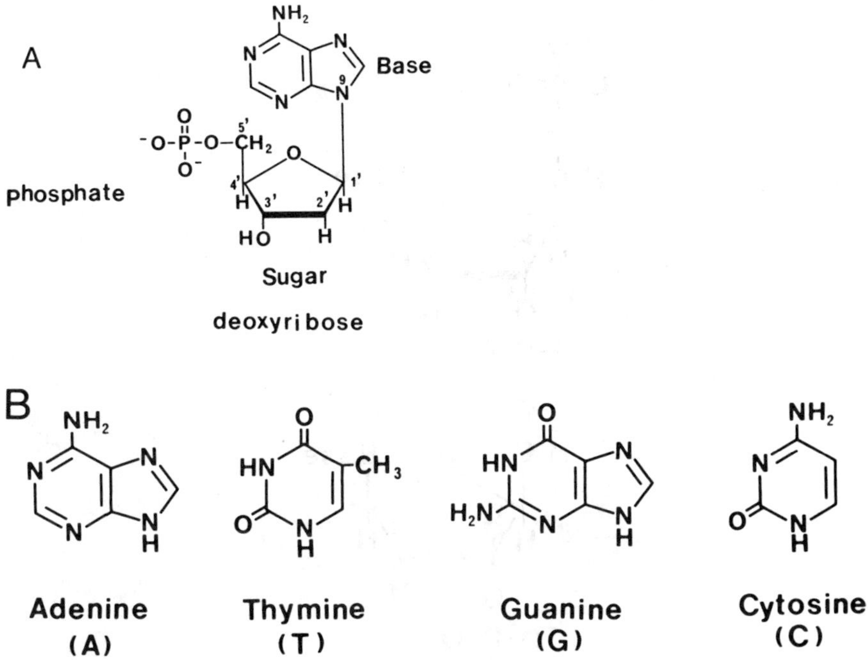

FIG 1–1.
Structure of deoxyribonucleotides. **A,** the structure of a deoxyribonucleotide, showing the sugar, nitrogenous base, and phosphate group and **B,** the structures of adenine, thymine, guanine, and cytosine.

bond. Because of this, DNA has directionality. Conventionally, the DNA sequences is written from right to left, where the first base has a free 5'-OH group, and the last base has a free 3'-OH group. The sequence is thus written "5' to 3'."

Secondary Structure of DNA

The sequence of the bases in DNA is known as primary structure. Secondary structure refers to interactions between the bases in DNA. DNA actually consists of two polynucleotide chains, known as strands, arranged parallel to one another, and in opposite orientation. The sequence of one of the strands determines the sequence of the other strand. The two strands are held together by hydrogen bonds between the bases. Because of their steric properties, A is always paired with T, and G is always paired with C (Fig 1–3). The two strands of DNA are complementary to each other.

DNA is "double-stranded" when the two strands are linked by hydrogen bonds. The hydrogen bonds are weak; they may be stabilized by increasing salt concentrations, and they may be weakened by increasing temperature. Above a certain temperature, the hydrogen bonds are too weak to hold the two strands together, and they dissociate

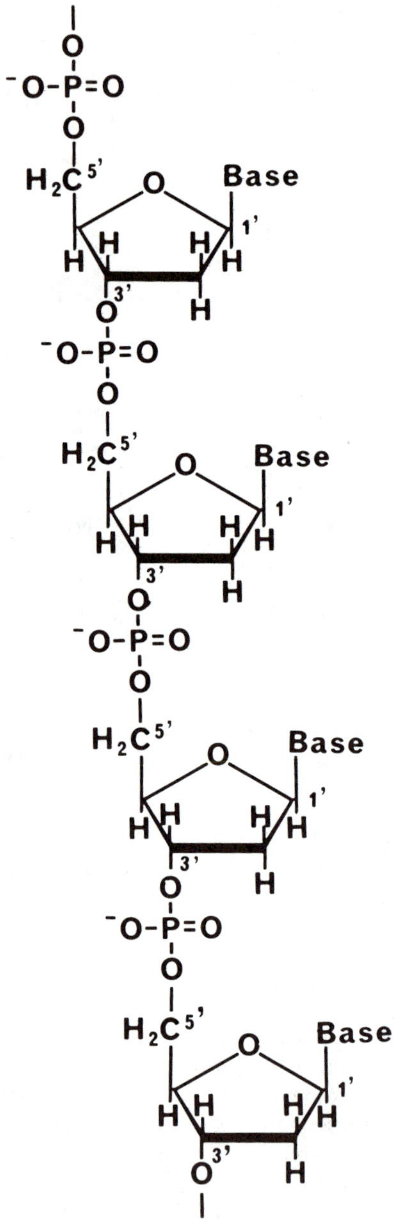

FIG 1–2.
Structure of the sugar-phosphate backbone of DNA. The deoxyribonucleotides are attached to one another by means of phosphodiester linkages between the 3'-OH of one nucleotide and the 5'-OH of the next nucleotide.

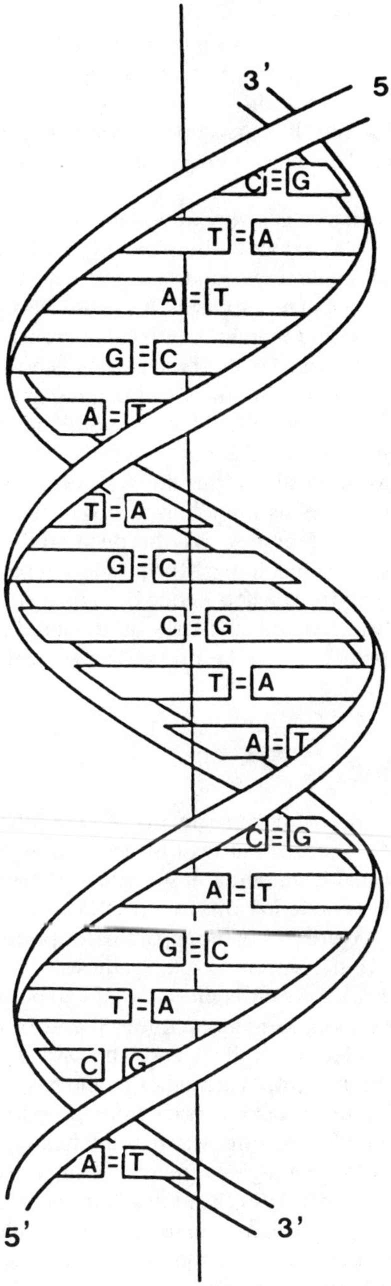

FIG 1–3.
Structure of DNA, showing base-pairing between the two strands. The sugar-phosphate backbones of the two strands are indicated by the ribbons. Base pairing is shown between the two complementary strands. Together, the strands form a double helix.

or come apart. The strands themselves may not be damaged, since the phosphodiester bonds linking the individual deoxyribonucleotides in the strands are much stronger than the hydrogen bonds. If the temperature is brought back down, DNA strands can come back together and form hydrogen bonds in a process known as annealing, renaturation, or hybridization. Of course, one DNA strand can only anneal or renature with a strand that is complementary. Otherwise, hydrogen bonds cannot be formed all along the strand.

Base pair complementarity is a very important concept. It is the basis by which cells can replicate their DNA. A double-stranded DNA molecule is enzymatically "unzipped" to give two complementary strands, each of which directs the synthesis of a new DNA molecule complementary to itself. It is how DNA is transcribed into RNA. A segment of DNA which codes for an RNA molecule is transiently dissociated to allow synthesis of complementary RNA. Finally, base pairing is how information in the RNA is translated into synthesis of protein. In assembling the amino acids which make up a protein, the codons in messenger RNA base pair with transfer RNA molecules which each carry the appropriate amino acid.

Base pair complementarity also forms the basis of many of the techniques used in molecular biology. DNA that is immobilized onto solid supports, such as nitrocellulose sheets or nylon membranes, may be denatured so that it is primarily in single-stranded form and is available for hybridization. A particular DNA probe, or a known piece of DNA, may be labelled either by radioactivity or by enzyme-linked color reagents, and hybridized with the DNA on the solid support. The probe will detect sequences complementary to the probe. These techniques will be described in detail later.

Structure of a Gene

A gene consists of one or more segments of DNA whose sequence encodes a particular RNA molecule. There are at least three different kinds of RNA molecules: messenger RNAs, ribosomal RNAs, and transfer RNAs. Messenger RNAs are the intermediates through which genetic information in DNA is translated into the structure of proteins, ribosomal RNAs are part of the apparatus for protein synthesis, and transfer RNAs carry amino acids to the site of protein synthesis.

A model of a gene is shown in Figure 1–4. The gene is flanked on either side by other DNA. By convention, sequences at the 5' end of the DNA are said to be upstream from sequences located at the 3' end. The DNA segments encoding a gene, or its exons, may be separated from each other by introns, or intervening sequences (IVS). The number and size of introns varies from gene to gene. For example, the human alpha globin gene has 2 introns, whereas the human alpha collagen gene has 50 introns. Often, the non-coding regions are much longer than the coding sequences. An exact copy of the stretch of DNA, including introns, is transcribed into an RNA molecule within the nucleus. This precursor RNA molecule is then spliced into a mature RNA molecule by the removal of the introns. The mature RNA is then allowed to leave the nucleus and enter the cytoplasm, where it will function as messenger RNA, transfer RNA, or ribosomal RNA.

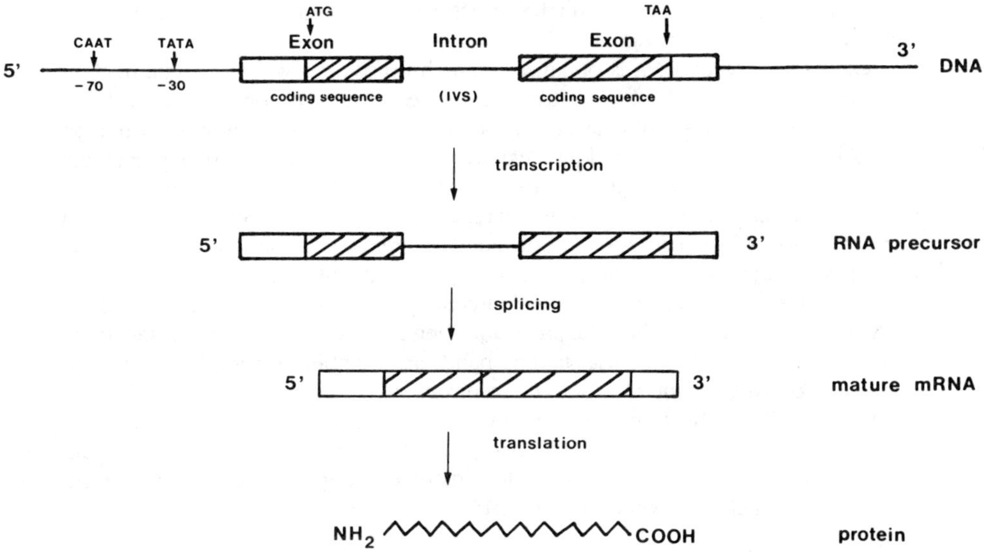

FIG 1–4.
Model of a gene. The gene sequence in DNA is shown. The regulatory "TATA box" and "CAAT box" are located upstream from the gene. In this gene, the two exons are separated by an intron. The gene is transcribed to yield a precursor RNA molecule, which is then spliced to yield a mature mRNA. The hatched areas represent protein coding regions. The blank areas in the RNA molecules represent 5' and 3' untranslated regions.

Eukaryotic genes have regulatory sequences at their 5' flanking regions similar to those found in prokaryotic genes. The first of these is located about 25 to 30 base pairs (bp) upstream from the RNA start site. It is the promotor site for RNA polymerase and consists of a consensus sequence TATAAA. It is also called the "TATA box," or the Goldberg-Hogness box. Next, there is a "CAAT box" found about 70 to 90 bp upstream.[5] The expression of a given gene may be stimulated also by enhancer sequences located up to many thousands of base pairs from the actual starting point of the gene. The triplet ATG at the 5' end of the gene is the initiation signal for protein synthesis on messenger RNA. ATG is the codon which specifies the amino acid methionine. At the 3' end of the coding region of a gene, there is a triplet TAA, TAG, or TGA. These are called termination codons because they are signals to terminate protein synthesis. They do not code for any amino acid.

There are long stretches of DNA which have no known function. They do not appear to code for proteins or RNA molecules. Some of these stretches contain many copies of particular DNA sequences known as repetitive regions. These regions give rise to "satellite bands" in reassociation kinetics because they reanneal faster than single-copy sequences. Thus, they are called "satellite DNA." Because they do not appear to be critical to life processes, there may be a great deal of variability in the number of these repeated regions, and in the areas where they are located. The existence of these non-coding stretches of DNA is the key to some of the techniques used in forensic DNA typing.

On a larger level, DNA is organized into chromosomes within the cell nucleus. Each somatic human cell contains 46 chromosomes; 23 chromosomes are contributed by each parent. DNA is visible as chromosomes only during cell division, or mitosis. The exact way in which long, double-stranded DNA molecules are tightly packaged into compact chromosomes is still unknown, but this packaging serves to allow the two copies of each DNA molecule to segregate cleanly to different poles of the cell during division. Chromosomes may be stained by Giemsa stain, and each chromosome produces a distinctive banding pattern, allowing its identification.

Chromosomes have structures called centromeres which divide them into two arms. The arms may be called the short and long arms, or they may be designated p and q, respectively. The Giemsa staining bands are numbered from the centromere outwards, so that the band closest to the centromere is band 1. The band furthest out is called "ter," for the terminal band. Genes may be localized to their particular location on a chromosome. The terminology involves naming the chromosome number, the arm, and the band number.[6,7] For instance, the gene coding for the insulin gene resides on chromosome 11, band p15.

RESTRICTION MAPPING OF DNA

Restriction Endonucleases

Restriction endonucleases were discovered by Arber, and by Smith and Nathans.[8] These endonucleases, or restriction enzymes, recognize specific base sequences of 4 to 8 base pairs (bp) in double-stranded DNA, and cleave a phosphodiester linkage in each strand in this region. These enzymes are found in a wide variety of bacterial and fungal organisms. Their major biological function is to degrade foreign DNA for self-protection. The organism's own DNA is not cleaved, because the sites recognized by its own restriction enzymes are modified by a process called methylation.

Over 90 restriction enzymes have been purified, characterized, and made available commercially. Their names consist of a 3- or 4-letter abbreviation for the host organism, a designation of strain (if necessary), and a Roman numeral (if several restriction enzymes are produced). For example, EcoRI is the first restriction enzyme produced by *Escherichia coli*, strain RY13.

The restriction sites recognized by some common restriction enzymes and their source microorganisms are summarized in Table 1–1.[9] A striking characteristic of most of the restriction sites is that they are palindromic. That is, they read the same on one strand as they do on the complementary strand. For example, the sequence recognized by Eco R1 is

↓
5' GAATTC 3'
•
3' CTTAAG 5'
↑

TABLE 1–1.
Commonly Used Restriction Endonucleases*

<table>
<tr><th>Microorganism</th><th>Enzyme</th><th>Recognition Site</th></tr>
<tr><td>Acinetobacter calcoaceticus</td><td>Acc I</td><td>GT|$^{AG}_{CT}$AC</td></tr>
<tr><td>Anabena variabilis</td><td>Ava I</td><td>C|PyCGPuG</td></tr>
<tr><td></td><td>Ava II</td><td>G|G$^{A}_{T}$CC</td></tr>
<tr><td>Arthrobacter luteus</td><td>Alu I</td><td>AG|CT</td></tr>
<tr><td>Bacillus amyloliquifaciens</td><td>Bam HI</td><td>G|GATCC</td></tr>
<tr><td>Bacillus caldolyticus</td><td>Bcl I</td><td>T|GATCA</td></tr>
<tr><td>Bacillus globigii</td><td>Bgl I</td><td>GCCNNNN|NGGC</td></tr>
<tr><td></td><td>Bgl II</td><td>A|GATCT</td></tr>
<tr><td>Bacillus stearothemophilus</td><td>Bst EII</td><td>G|GTNACC</td></tr>
<tr><td>Brevibacterium albidum</td><td>Bal I</td><td>TGG|CCA</td></tr>
<tr><td>Caryophanon latum L</td><td>Cla I</td><td>AT|CGAT</td></tr>
<tr><td>Desulfovibrio desulfuricans</td><td>Dde I</td><td>C|TNAG</td></tr>
<tr><td>Diplococcus pneumoniae</td><td>Dpn I</td><td>GA|TC</td></tr>
<tr><td>Escherichia coli RY13</td><td>Eco RI</td><td>G|AATTC</td></tr>
<tr><td>Escherichia coli R245</td><td>Eco RII</td><td>|CC$^{A}_{T}$GG</td></tr>
<tr><td>Fusobacterium nucleatum D</td><td>Fnu DII</td><td>CG|CG</td></tr>
<tr><td>Haemophilus aegyptius</td><td>Hae III</td><td>GG|CC</td></tr>
<tr><td>Haemophilus aphrophilus</td><td>Hpa II</td><td>C|CGG</td></tr>
<tr><td>Haemophilus haemolyticus</td><td>Hha I</td><td>GCG|C</td></tr>
<tr><td>Haemophilus influenzae Rd</td><td>Hind III</td><td>A|AGCTT</td></tr>
<tr><td>Haemophilus influenzae Rf</td><td>Hinf I</td><td>G|ANTC</td></tr>
<tr><td>Haemophilus parainfluenzae</td><td>Hpa I</td><td>GTT|AAC</td></tr>
<tr><td></td><td>Hpa II</td><td>C|CGG</td></tr>
<tr><td>Klebsiella pneumoniae OK8</td><td>Kpn I</td><td>GGTAC|C</td></tr>
<tr><td>Microcoleus species</td><td>Mst I</td><td>TGC|GCA</td></tr>
<tr><td>Moraxella bovis</td><td>Mbo I</td><td>|GATC</td></tr>
<tr><td>Proteus vulgaris</td><td>Pvu I</td><td>CGAT|CG</td></tr>
<tr><td></td><td>Pvu II</td><td>CAG|CTG</td></tr>
<tr><td>Providencia stuartii 164</td><td>Pst I</td><td>CTGCA|G</td></tr>
<tr><td>Serratia marcescens</td><td>Sma I</td><td>CCC|GGG</td></tr>
<tr><td>Streptomyces achromogenes</td><td>Sac I</td><td>GAGCT|C</td></tr>
<tr><td></td><td>Sac II</td><td>CCGC|GG</td></tr>
<tr><td>Streptomyces albus G</td><td>Sal I</td><td>G|TCGAC</td></tr>
<tr><td>Streptomyces aureofaciens</td><td>Sau I</td><td>CC|TNAGG</td></tr>
<tr><td>Streptomyces tubercidicus</td><td>Stu I</td><td>AGG|CCT</td></tr>
<tr><td>Thermus aquaticus YT1</td><td>Taq I</td><td>T|CGA</td></tr>
<tr><td>Xanthomonas badrii</td><td>Xba I</td><td>T|CTAGA</td></tr>
<tr><td>Xanthomonas holcicola</td><td>Xho I</td><td>C|TCGAG</td></tr>
<tr><td>Xanthomonas malvacearum</td><td>Xma III</td><td>C|GGCCG</td></tr>
</table>

*Recognition sites are given from 5' to 3', and only one strand is given. | = the point of cleavage; N = any of the four bases; Py = the pyrimidines T or C; Pu = the purines A or G. Where there are two bases, the restriction enzyme recognizes either one. A detailed review of restriction endonucleases is presented in Roberts.[9]

The enzyme will cut the DNA molecule at each place that this restriction site appears. The cleavage sites are indicated by arrows. On each strand, the enzyme cleaves the phosphodiester bond between the G and the A, on the 5' side of the axis of symmetry denoted by a dot.

Some enzymes cleave both strands at the same point, leaving blunt ends. Others make cuts which are offset, producing sticky or cohesive ends, which are so-named because a resulting DNA fragment is able to hybridize by base pairing with any other fragment generated by the same restriction enzyme. Offset cutting may result in a longer strand with either a free 5' or 3' end, called an overhang.

Restriction endonucleases have two major applications. First, they enable the cleavage of DNA into specific fragments that are more readily analyzed and manipulated than the parent molecules. They are essential for the analysis of chromosomal structure, the sequencing of DNA, the isolation of genes, and the creation of specific sites in DNA for molecular cloning. Second, they provide a new and extremely powerful means for analyzing genetic diversity. In the human genome, base alterations may eliminate pre-existing restriction enzyme sites or create new ones. The presence of differing numbers of repetitive sequences may also cause variability in the length of restriction fragments. Variability in restriction fragment lengths created by either of these mechanisms is inherited in a simple Mendelian fashion. These restriction fragment length polymorphisms (RFLP) serve as characteristics which may be used to identify one individual from another.

Gene Mapping

Restriction endonuclease mapping, also known as gene mapping, has become a major tool for genetic analysis. In this technique, DNA is treated with a particular restriction enzyme. The mixture of restriction fragments can be separated by gel electrophoresis. The electrophoretic mobility of a DNA fragment is inversely proportional to the logarithm of the number of base pairs within a certain range. Small DNA fragments, from a few base pairs up to about 1,000 base pairs, can be separated by polyacrylamide gels. Larger fragments, from a few hundred base pairs up to about 20,000 base pairs (20 kb) can be separated using 0.5% to 2.0% agarose gels. Chromosomes containing millions of nucleotides may be separated on agarose gels by the technique of pulsed-field electrophoresis. Once separated by gel electrophoresis, DNA fragments can be visualized by staining with ethidium bromide, a dye which fluoresces an intense orange color when it is bound to double-stranded DNA and is viewed by an ultraviolet light source. A photograph can be taken of the stained gel for record-keeping.

A restriction digest of a single piece of DNA separated by gel electrophoresis would yield a certain pattern on ethidium bromide staining. However, a restriction digest of total genomic DNA from a person would yield an uninterpretable smear on a stained gel. This is because the restriction digest would result in a vast number of different fragments of many different sizes. Restriction fragments containing a specific base sequence, however, can be identified clearly by hybridization to a small DNA segment containing its complementary sequence, known as a probe. DNA probes are usually labelled with the radioisotope ^{32}P for sensitive detection.

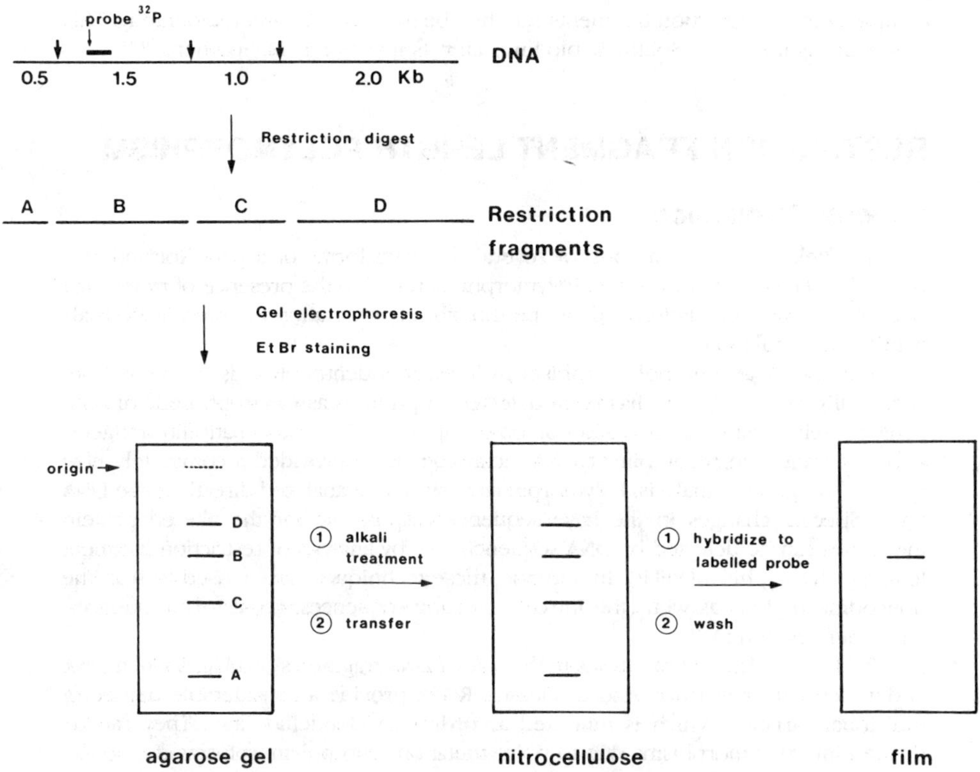

FIG 1–5.
Restriction mapping and Southern blot analysis. A DNA molecule with three restriction sites shown by *arrows* is digested into four separate fragments by the restriction enzyme. These fragments are separated by size by gel electrophoresis, and visualized by staining with ethidium bromide (EtBr). The gel is treated with alkali, and the DNA transferred to nitrocellulose. The location of the transferred bands on the nitrocellulose is shown, although ordinarily they would not be visible. The nitrocellulose blot is hybridized to a labelled probe, washed, and exposed to film. The probe shown in the original DNA molecule would bind only to fragment B.

Figure 1–5 shows the process of restriction mapping. A DNA molecule can be digested with restriction enzymes, whose sites are indicated by arrows. The resulting mixture of restriction fragments can be separated by gel electrophoresis, denatured to single-stranded DNA by alkaline treatment with 0.2 N NaOH, and transferred to a solid support (usually a sheet of nitrocellulose or a negatively charged nylon membrane). The support is then hybridized with a ^{32}P-labelled single-stranded DNA probe, and non-specific binding is removed by washing with buffers under conditions of decreasing ionic strength and increasing temperature. Under very stringent conditions, the DNA probe will bind only by hydrogen bonding to complementary DNA. The complementary restriction fragments can then be identified by autoradiography. This procedure is known as Southern blotting, after its inventor E. M. Southern.[10, 11]

RESTRICTION FRAGMENT LENGTH POLYMORPHISM

General Discussion

An allele is defined as one of several alternate forms of a gene located at a particular site on a chromosome. Polymorphism refers to the presence of more than one allele in the population and can be thought of as variation between individuals within the population.

The use of genetic polymorphism in forensic indentification is not new. Conventionally, polymorphism has been detected in proteins as electrophoretic or antigenic protein variants, such as ABO blood groups or HLA histocompatibility antigens. Recent advances in recombinant DNA technology have provided a completely new approach in genetic analysis. Polymorphism now can be analyzed directly at the DNA level. Specific changes in the base sequence responsible for the altered protein molecules can be detected by DNA sequencing or by analysis of restriction fragment length polymorphism (RFLP). In addition, these techniques can be used to scan the noncoding regions as well (the introns, flanking sequences, regulatory sequences, and other segments).

RFLPs are inherited variations in the size of DNA fragments produced when DNA is digested with restriction endonucleases. RFLPs provide a considerable degree of individual variation which is inherited according to Mendelian laws. They can be divided into polymorphisms due to point mutations and polymorphisms due to differences in hypervariable regions. The molecular basis for each of these will be described briefly here, and these polymorphisms will be discussed in detail in other chapters.

Point Polymorphism

Point polymorphism is caused by a single base substitution which results in the creation or elimination of a restriction site. A shorter or longer restriction fragment is thus generated by a restriction enzyme. RFLPs of this type have been observed within or near almost all of the human genes which have been analyzed thus far.

The molecular basis of point polymorphism is schematically diagrammed in Figure 1–6, using the beta-globin gene in sickle cell anemia as an example. Hemoglobin S (sickle cell) differs from normal hemoglobin A by a single amino acid change at the sixth position of the beta chain. A valine is present in hemoglobin S, where there is a glutamate in hemoglobin A. At the DNA level, the normal and sickle cell alleles differ by a single base substitution from A to T, changing the codon for glutamate in the normal gene (GAG) to a codon for valine in the sickle gene (GTG). This point polymorphism can be detected by the restriction enzyme Mst II, which recognizes the site CCTNAGG. A restriction site for Mst II that is present in a normal gene is

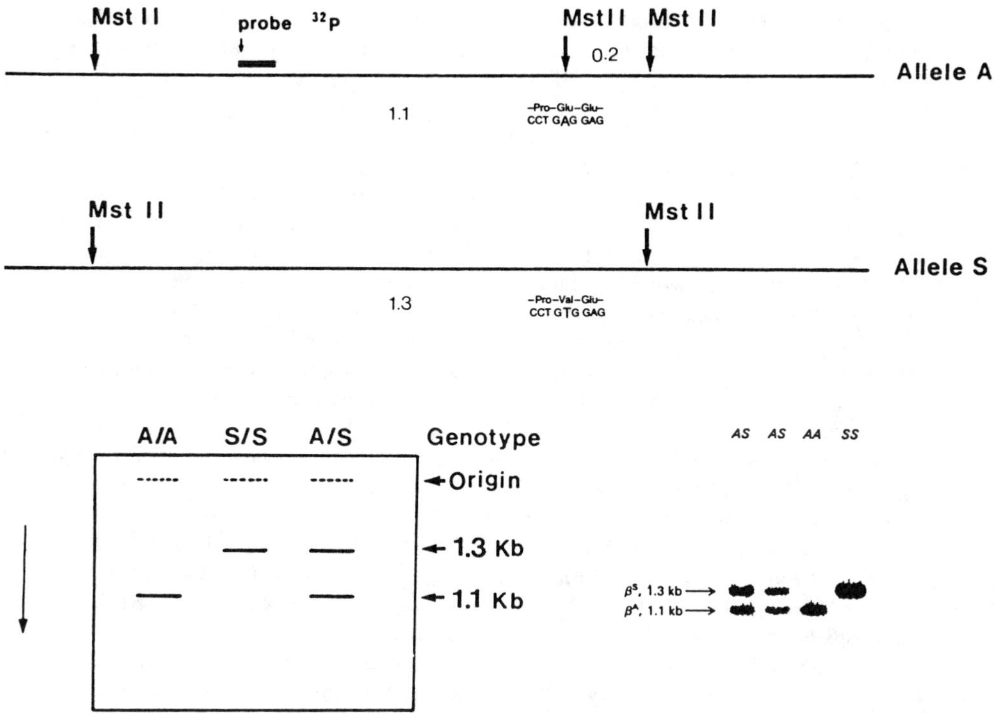

FIG 1–6.
Restriction fragment length polymporphism in sickle cell anemia. Two alleles of the beta globin gene are shown; allele A codes for normal globin, whereas allele S codes for sickle globin. The two alleles differ by the lack of an Mst II site in allele S. The appearance of a Southern blot is shown on the left, using a probe located within the normal 1.1 kb fragment. The genotype of the samples is shown over each lane. An autoradiogram of an actual blot is shown on the right.

eliminated in the sickle cell gene. Other Mst II restriction sites are the same for the two alleles. The two restriction fragments of lengths 1.1 and 0.2 kb in the normal gene are thus changed to a single fragment of 1.3 kb size in the sickle gene. In a stained agarose gel, bands arising from the restriction fragments would be obscured by the hundreds of thousands of other fragments from the rest of the DNA. Southern blotting with a probe located in the normal 1.1 kb fragment would detect this RFLP as a 1.1 kb fragment in the normal globin allele and a 1.3 kb fragment in the sickle allele. A heterozygous individual would demonstrate both alleles.

The RFLPs in the globin gene complex on chromosome 11 have been studied most extensively.[12] In the 60 kb DNA which makes up the gene cluster, at least 12 RFLP sites have been found. Of these, one is located in the beta globin gene coding region, one in a pseudogene, three within introns, and seven in the flanking regions. Sequence analysis of all these sites indicates that each results from a single base substitution. RFLPs in the beta globin gene cluster have been further grouped as "public" or "private." "Public" RFLPs are those found in all racial groups with a frequency of the least common allele greater than 5% in every racial group studied, whereas "private" RFLPs are those found only in African blacks. Nine out of the 13 RFLPs in the globin gene cluster are "public."

RFLP distribution can be random or non-random. If one RFLP site is found in 60% of the chromosomes examined in a particular population and a second RFLP site is found in 30%, the probability of both of their being found together on a particular chromosome would be $0.6 \times 0.3 = 0.18$, or 18%, if the sites were randomly associated. If the sites were non-randomly associated, then the probability of both RFLP sites being present together would be different. Non-random distribution is referred to as linkage disequilibrium. A given pattern of occurrences of RFLP sites for any chromosome is called a haplotype. Because of linkage disequilibrium, only a few haplotypes out of many possibilities are observed. For example, the 5 RFLP sites in the region upstream from the beta-globin gene could generate 32 possible haplotypes. However, only 3 haplotypes account for over 95% of normal chromosomes in Greek, Italian, and Asian Indian populations. Certain haplotypes are associated with specific mutations in particular populations.[13]

Because point mutation RFLPs generally have two alleles (either the presence or absence of a given restriction site), they are of limited utility in the absolute identification of individuals. However, they are very important for several reasons. First, these RFLPs have served as important genetic markers for inherited diseases. The genes responsible for Duchenne type muscular dystrophy[14] and Huntington's disease[15] have been located using RFLPs of this type. Furthermore, similar techniques are being used to study cystic fibrosis,[16] Alzheimer's disease, and von Recklinghausen's disease.[17] Second, the occurrence of linkage disequilibrium makes it possible to use RFLP haplotypes to determine whether or not two people are related. Whereas multilocus RFLP probes can determine with a high degree of accuracy whether two samples came from the same individual (see below), the complexity of the restriction fragment pattern makes it difficult to analyze whether the samples came from *related* individuals. In contrast, point mutation RFLPs are simpler and lack the absolute specificity of multilocus probes, but are much more useful for verifying or refuting alleged blood relationships. This type of analysis may prove extremely useful for legal cases involving paternity or immigration issues. Finally, the presence of specific haplotypes in certain races opens up the intriguing possibility of using DNA typing to determine the race of origin of a given sample.

Polymorphism in Hypervariable Regions

Hypervariable region polymorphism results from differences in the length of DNA in a region between fixed restriction sites. In Figure 1–7, three alleles are shown, and the restriction sites are designated by arrows. The boxed areas represent tandemly repeated units of DNA. Restriction digests would generate fragments of different sizes, depending upon the number of copies of repeat units. The appearance of these fragments on a Southern blot is shown below. Each individual's genotype consists of two alleles. Probes for RFLPs generated by hypervariable regions include those which recognize variable number tandem repeats (VNTR) at a single locus, and multilocus repeat probes.

Wyman and White[18] first reported a highly polymorphic locus in human genomic DNA not associated with any specific gene. They isolated a 16 kb fragment from a human genomic library in lambda phage Charon 4A. Hybridization of an Eco RI digest of total human genomic DNA with this fragment results in a high degree of RFLP. This

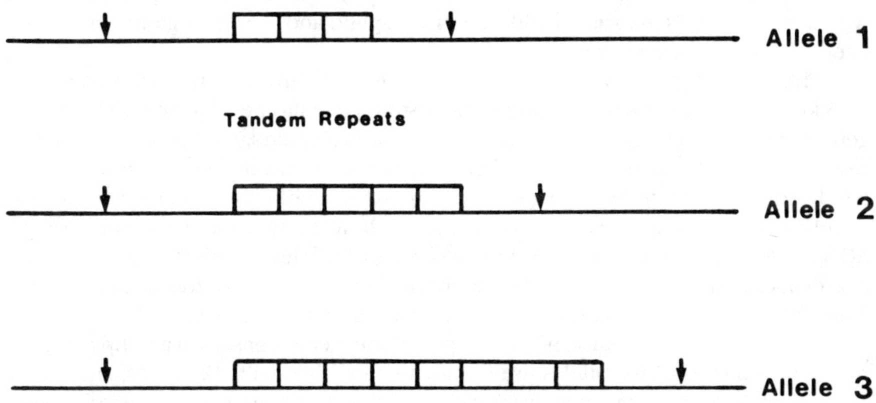

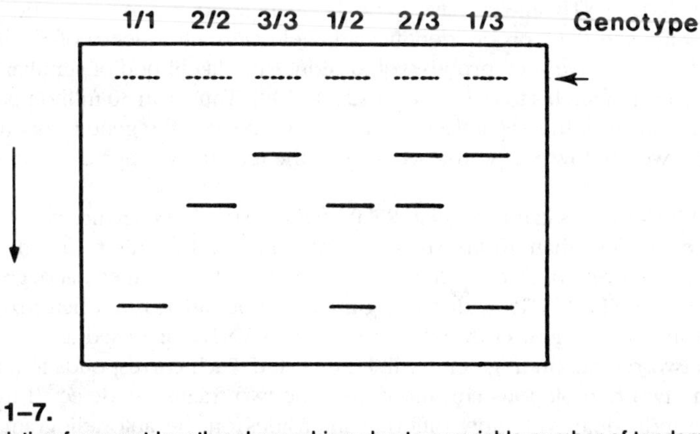

FIG 1–7.
Restriction fragment length polymorphism due to a variable number of tandem repeats. The boxed areas represent repeat units. The three alleles shown have 3, 5, and 8 copies of the repeat. The appearance of a Southern blot is shown. The genotype of the samples is shown over each lane.

locus is extremely variable; in the individuals studied, at least eight different alleles were found, and homozygotes accounted for less than 25% of the population. This high frequency of DNA sequence variation is the result of DNA rearrangements rather than single base substitution. The variation in restriction fragment lengths is due to the presence of a variable number of tandemly repeated DNA segments. Therefore, these regions are called variable number tandem repeats, or VNTRs. Subsequently, similar polymorphisms have been reported in the introns of the insulin gene by Bell et al,[19] in the Harvey ras oncogene by Capon et al,[20] and in the myoglobin gene by Weller et al.[21] RFLPs associated with the insulin gene and the alpha globin gene have been investigated extensively.

The insulin gene is located on the short arm of chromosome 11, in band p15. A 45 kb DNA segment which includes the insulin gene has been isolated. The insulin gene itself is 1.43 kb and contains two introns of 179 bp and 786 bp. A hypervariable region is found 360 bases upstream from the start of the insulin gene, with a sequence highly homologous to similar regions near the alpha globin gene. There are a variable number of tandemly repeated units, with a consensus sequence of 5'-ACAGGGGTGTGGG-3'. Three common classes of alleles of different lengths have been described. Class 1 alleles have approximately 40 copies of this sequence, class 2 alleles have 95 copies, and class 3 alleles have about 170 copies.

The hypervariable region near the alpha-globin genes consists of a 36 bp tandemly repeated sequence. Two alleles are found, a short allele with 32 copies, and a long allele with 59 copies. Further examination of this 36 bp repeat unit reveals that it contains two strongly homologous domains of 13 or 14 bp; these domains flank a region of 9 to 15 bp. These domains are also homologous to the hypervariable region near the insulin gene and the first intron of the zeta globin gene. The sequence of these domains and their homology is shown in Table 1–2.

Some VNTR sequences demonstrate such a high degree of polymorphism that they are heterozygous in all individuals tested. This makes them very useful for forensic identification. Most VNTR alleles have gene frequencies between 0.1% and 10%. Assuming that a given RFLP probe identifies an allele with a frequency of 5% in the population, the use of five such probes would reduce the likelihood of simultaneous occurrence of a set of alleles to $(0.05)^5$, or 3.125×10^{-7}. Thus, 1 in 30 million people has the given pattern of five separate VNTR alleles. Of course, the gene frequency of many alleles is well below 5%, so the accuracy of the technique may be substantially higher.

Certain VNTR probes can recognize RFLPs using restriction enzymes which generate fragments of less than 10 kb, such as Hinf I and Msp I. This means that the technique is useful even for samples in which the DNA has been somewhat degraded.

One problem with VNTRs is that recognition of both alleles in a heterozygous individual requires sufficient DNA for analysis. When VNTRs are used as probes, a maximum of two restriction fragments will be detected. Each corresponds to a locus on one of the two homologous chromosomes. The two fragments detected from a heterozygous individual will show different intensities on the autoradiogram. The slower-moving band is larger in size because it contains more copies of the repeats. It will hybridize with more probe molecules, and thus will exhibit stronger intensity on autoradiography. The faster-moving, smaller restriction fragment will demonstrate

TABLE 1–2.
A Comparison of Homologous Sequences in Hypervariable Repeated Units*

1 14 24 36
GGGGCACAGGTTGT (GAGGGTGCC) CGGGACGGCTTGT
or
Domain 1 (GAGAGGTGCC) Domain 2

	Sequence	Homology
Domain 1	GGGGCACAGGTTGT	10/14
Domain 2	CGGG ACGGCTTGT	
Domain 1	GGGGCACAGGT TGT	
Insulin	GGGG ACAGGGGTGT	12/14
Domain 2	CGGG AC GGCTTGT	10/14
Domain 1	GGGGCACAGGT TGT	
Zeta globin	GGGG ACAGTGAGGA	9/14
Domain 2	CGGG AC GGCTTGT	7/14
Insulin	GGGGACAGGGGTGT	10/14
Zeta globin	GGGGACAGTGAGGA	

*The sequence of the 36 base pair repeat unit in alpha globin is shown. Two homologous domains flank a central region shown in parentheses. The sequence of each of these two domains is compared with the other and with homologous sequences in the insulin gene and the first intron of the zeta globin gene. The number of homologous bases is shown.

a less intense band. In forensic analysis, if the quantity of a DNA sample is too small, the signal may be insufficient to pick up the light band, giving rise to misleading results. ^{32}P with high radiospecific activity should be used to label the probes; longer film exposure times, and the use of intensifying screens will also help to increase sensitivity.

In contrast to the VNTR probes, multilocus repeat sequence probes recognize restriction fragment length polymorphism in more than one location at the same time. Jeffreys et al[22] showed that a DNA probe based on a core sequence of the tandem repeats found in the hypervariable region of the myoglobin gene could detect many highly variable loci simultaneously. These multilocus repeat sequence probes essentially detect many individual VNTRs at the same time. RFLPs based on these multilocus probes have been termed "DNA fingerprinting."

Jeffreys' probes were derived from a 33 bp tandem repeat in the first intron of the human myoglobin gene, with the sequence:

5'-GACCGAGGTCTAAAGCTGGAGGTGGGCAGGAAG-3'

When this sequence was head-to-tail ligated and cloned, a 767 bp insert was obtained from one of the recombinants. This probe, known as pAV33.7, was used to detect RFLPs in Hinf I and Hae III digests of human genomic DNA. Both Hinf I and Hae III recognize a 4 bp restriction site not present in the 33 bp repeat, and they release minisatellites (fragments containing the repeats) with sizes which reflect the number of repeats.

Using pAV33.7, other probes were isolated and designated 33.1 to 33.15. The utility and specificity of these probes has been summarized by Jeffreys et al.[23] The repeat length of each minisatellite is usually half the length (33.5 and 33.15), the same length (33.3, 33.6, 33.10, and 33.11), or double the length (33.1 and 33.4) of the original 33 bp probe from the human myoglobin genes. This indicates that detection of the minisatellites depends not only on the core sequence in each of the repeats, but also on in-phase alignment between the sample and the probe. Based on this, a core sequence of 10 to 15 bp was established, consisting of a consensus sequence of GGGCAGGANG preceded by a 5 bp sequence common to most, but not all, repeats. This core probe detects an extremely polymorphic pattern using a Hinf I digest of human DNA.

Probe 33.15 and probe 33.6 have been successfully used for forensic analysis.[24] The probability of chance association giving rise to a specific pattern is 3×10^{-11} using probe 33.6. When both 33.6 and 33.15 probes are used, this number is reduced to 5×10^{-19}, making possible virtually absolute identification of individuals.

PRACTICAL ASPECTS OF DNA TECHNOLOGY

Isolation of DNA

DNA can be isolated from any cell which contains a nucleus. Human red blood cells do not contain nuclei, so DNA isolated from blood or bloodstains is really isolated from white blood cells. DNA can be damaged by enzymatic degradation by microorganisms or by conditions of extreme heat or radiation. Although it exists in lengths of millions of base pairs in the cell, DNA is broken down by the processes used in isolation. A good preparation of human genomic DNA can be expected to be of average size (20 kb to 100 kb) if specific precautions and great care are taken. Even then, the solution of DNA is likely to be extremely viscous and difficult to work with because of the lengths of the DNA. In general, DNA of sizes from several hundred base pairs to about 20 kb is the most convenient to handle in the laboratory. Most RFLP probes will work with starting DNA in this general size range. If DNA is degraded smaller than several thousand base pairs in size, RFLP analysis may not be possible. However, PCR amplification of such degraded DNA may yield sufficient quantities for other forms of analysis.

The isolation of DNA from cells involves suspending the cells in a solution containing a detergent such as SDS or Triton X-100 and treating them with a protease such as proteinase K, which will digest proteins. The DNA then can be separated from proteins and other cell components by extraction with a mixture of phenol and chloroform. Phenol is an organic solvent that forms a separate layer when mixed with an aqueous solution. It denatures proteins, and causes them to precipitate at the interface, leaving DNA and RNA in the aqueous solution. The nucleic acids then can be recovered by precipitation with ethanol in the presence of salt, at low temperatures. The nucleic acids can be centrifuged and will form a small pellet in the ethanol/water mixture. The pellet can be dried and resuspended in water, to yield a purified concentrated DNA solution.

Procedures for the isolation of DNA from likely forensic samples have been reported. Kanter et al[25] showed that 40 micrograms (μg) of DNA could be isolated from 1 ml of blood or from an equivalent 4.5 cm bloodstain, even after storage for 3 years. The DNA isolated was of a size greater than 20 kb, and yielded clear results when used in RFLP analysis. Only 10 μg of DNA is needed per lane. Jeffreys et al used 1 to 2 drops (30 to 100 μl) of blood to isolate sufficient DNA for analysis with their multilocus probes.

Giusti et al[26] have reported the isolation of DNA from sperm cells from vaginal washings and dried semen stains. Vaginal samples contain a large amount of DNA from the female which might obscure analysis of sperm DNA. Fortunately, sperm cells are rich in proteins with cross-linked sulfhydryl groups, so that vaginal cells can be lysed in SDS and proteinase K under conditions which leave sperm cells intact. The sperm cells may be separated by centrifugation, and they can then be lysed in the presence of the thiol-reducing agent, DTT.

Gill, Jeffreys, and Werrett[24] showed that DNA of high molecular weight could be isolated from 4 year-old bloodstains (60 μl equivalent), semen stains (20 μl equivalent) made on cotton cloth, and semen-contaminated vaginal swabs. They also isolated DNA from the roots of 15 freshly plucked hairs. The DNA isolated was sufficient for clear results using their multilocus fingerprinting probes.

Isolation of DNA from single hairs has not been very successful. Only the root of a hair contains DNA; the shaft does not contain any living cells. It has been estimated that 200 μg of DNA can be obtained from the root cells of a freshly plucked hair, while only 10 μg can be isolated from hair that has been shed.[27] The DNA obtained is also very often degraded. It is thus unlikely that samples of single hairs will be useful for RFLP analysis. However, Higuchi et al[27] have been able to use PCR to amplify short regions of DNA from single hairs. This technique is more amenable to mitochondrial DNA segments than to genomic DNA segments, since there are hundreds of copies of mitochondrial DNA per cell. However, RFLP analysis requires genomic DNA. The PCR-amplified DNA was usable in dot blot analysis and for direct DNA sequencing.

Polymerase Chain Reaction

A technique known as polymerase chain reaction, or PCR, has been developed.[28, 29] PCR is a process by which a certain segment of a small amount of DNA, an amount much less than that approachable by conventional techniques, can be amplified into a large quantity of that particular segment. However, it is necessary to know the structure of the DNA surrounding the segment of interest for the procedure to work. Hence, much as PCR has been likened to turning a needle in a haystack to a mountain of needles, one needs to have a magnet, or some way of specifically identifying the needle as opposed to the strands of hay. This specificity resides in the choice of the PCR primers used in the reaction.

In the PCR technique (Fig 1–8), DNA containing the sequence of interest is first

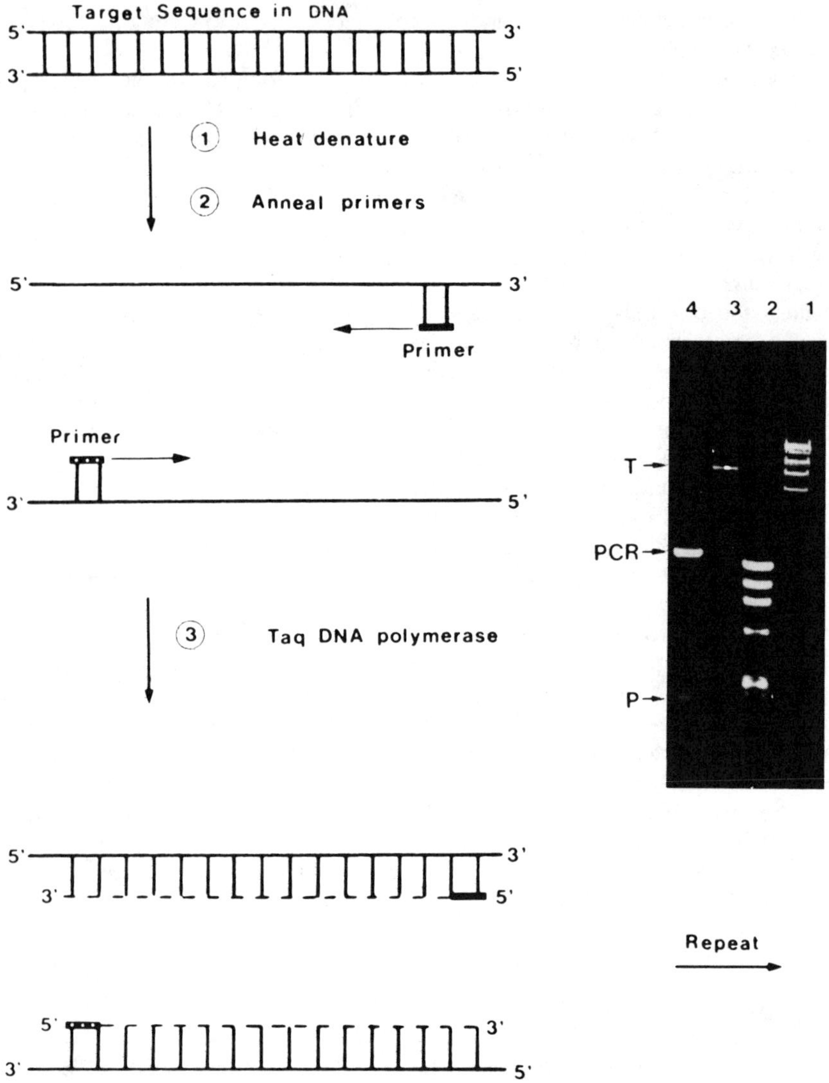

FIG 1–8.
Polymerase chain reaction. A double-stranded DNA molecule is held together by hydrogen bonds, indicated by the vertical lines. The DNA is heat denatured, and specific PCR primers are annealed to each strand. DNA polymerase is added, which catalyzes the synthesis of a new strand of DNA along each of the original strands. The process of heat denaturation, primer annealing, and polymerase reaction are repeated over and over, to amplify the yield of this specific segment of DNA.

In the *inset*, an ethidium bromide-stained gel is shown to demonstrate the result of a PCR reaction. Lanes 1 and 2 are molecular weight markers of Lambda DNA digested with Hind III and Phi X DNA digested with Hae III. Lane 3 shows a 7 kb fragment of a cloned human gene from the author's laboratory. This fragment is used as a template *(T)* for the synthesis of a 1.5 kb target sequence *(PCR).* Lane 4 shows an aliquot of the PCR reaction mixture, indicating the PCR product, and the primers *(P).*

denatured by heating, so that the hydrogen bonds between the two strands come apart. Then, specific PCR primers, or small segments of DNA complementary to the borders of the segment of interest, are used to hybridize to the strands. One primer hybridizes to the 3' end of the segment on one strand, and the other primer hybridizes to the 3' end of the segment on the opposite strand. In this way, the primers flank and define the segment to be amplified. DNA polymerase, an enzyme which catalyzes the replication of DNA, is then added. It starts at the primers and synthesizes a new strand of DNA along each of the old strands. Thus, the segment of DNA has been copied, and there is now twice as much of the DNA segment as before. The reaction mixture is then denatured by heating again, and the process is repeated, creating four times as much DNA segment. The procedure is repeated many times, to create a large quantity of the specific DNA segment. The yield of PCR is 2^n, where n is the number of times the reaction is cycled.

In earlier studies, the Klenow fragment of DNA polymerase from *E. coli* was used. It was necessary to add fresh enzyme at each cycle because the enzyme was denatured by the heating conditions used to denature the DNA at each step. Now, the PCR technique makes use of a DNA polymerase from the thermophilic bacterium *Thermus aquaticus*,[30] which lives in hot springs. This Taq polymerase is stable under heating conditions that denature the DNA, so the reaction can be cycled again and again in the same test tube using the same enzyme. A machine to automate this process has been developed by Cetus Corporation and Perkin Elmer.

One of the major advantages of PCR is that it enables amplification (from an extremely small quantity of DNA) of a specific sequence which does not even have to be in pure form. It has been used in the diagnosis of beta thalassemia,[31] sickle cell anemia,[22,32] and hemophilia.[34] PCR was used to isolate AIDS virus DNA from the blood cells of individuals who test positive for the antibodies to the AIDS virus, thereby showing that these individuals carry AIDS virus DNA, even though the virus itself could not be isolated.[35] In forensic medicine, PCR has been used in one case to prove that partially decayed organs buried with a person had not been switched in an attempt to hide the cause of death.[36]

The forensic applications of PCR are far-reaching. The amount of biological material available as evidence can be extremely small. Although DNA isolated from bloodstains, semen stains, and vaginal swabs has been used in RFLP analysis, it is apparent that the amount of evidence available approaches the very lowest limits of detection. PCR will be useful to amplify these minute quantities of DNA into much larger quantities for study, as long as the appropriate PCR primers for the region of interest are available.

If the DNA is not degraded, amplification by the PCR technique may be usable in RFLP analysis, with probes for available point polymorphism, VNTR polymorphism, or multilocus polymorphism. If the DNA has been degraded to sizes of less than 1,000 bases, PCR still will yield quantities sufficient for dot hybridization or even DNA sequence determination.

In dot hybridization, as used by Higuchi et al,[27,33] DNA segments corresponding to 242 bp of the human HLA histocompatibility antigen DQ-alpha were amplified from single human hair roots by PCR. Because the PCR products are of the same size, it is not necessary to subject them to restriction enzyme digestion or gel electrophoresis.

The DNA was immobilized onto nylon membranes in the form of dots, and hybridized with a very specific oligonucleotide probe for different alleles. The probe was hybridized and the blots washed under extremely stringent conditions, so that even a single base mismatch would cause the probe to wash off. The probes would bind only if they were entirely specific for the DQ-alpha allele contained in that hair. By determining the amount of each probe bound to each dot, they were able to assign HLA typing based on the single hair sample.

One advantage of the PCR reaction is that the yield of the DNA is so good that it is not necessary to use radioactive probes to achieve high sensitivity. Probes which may be labeled by enzyme-linked color reagents are sensitive enough, and have the advantage of being more stable and safer to work with. However, the probes currently available for dot blot hybridization do not have enough variability among individuals to be as useful as RFLP analysis in the identification of individuals.

DNA obtained by PCR analysis can also be sequenced. The techniques of DNA sequencing have been well worked out by Maxam and Gilbert,[37] and by Sanger et al.[38] New techniques in sequencing have been described recently.[39] This is the ultimate level of analysis of DNA polymorphism, for one can determine the exact sequence of a particular DNA segment from an individual.

CONCLUSION

In this chapter we have reviewed our current knowledge about the structure of DNA and genes, as well as some of the techniques used in molecular biology. DNA biotechnology has had a tremendous impact on our understanding of human variability and what makes each individual unique. We have increased our knowledge of gene organization and the genetic basis of certain inherited diseases.

In forensic science, the techniques of RFLP analysis using VNTR and multilocus probes now allow the virtually unambiguous identification of individuals based on vanishingly small amounts of biological evidence. PCR further lowers the limits of detection of DNA by orders of magnitude.

Those who wish to pursue topics beyond this review are encouraged to consult the texts by Stryer,[40] Darnell et al,[41] Alberts et al,[42] and Lewin[43] for additional background on DNA structure, function, and enzymology. The general topic of DNA polymorphism and chromosome mapping has been summarized by Gusella[44] and White.[45] Finally, specific techniques used in molecular biology are outlined in works by Maniatis et al,[46] Ausubel et al,[47] and Watson et al.[48]

REFERENCES

1. Watson JD, Crick FHC: A structure for deoxyribose nucleic acid. *Nature* 1953; 171:737–738.
2. Watson JD, Crick FHC: General implications of the structure of deoxyribonucleic acid. *Nature* 1953; 171:964–967.

3. Crick FHC: The genetic code: III. *Sci Am* 1966; 215:55–62.
4. Nevins JR: The pathway of eukaryotic mRNA formation. *Ann Rev Biochem* 1983; 52:441–466.
5. Gluzman Y, Shenk T: *Enhancers and Eukaryotic Gene Expression*. Cold Spring Harbor, New York, Cold Spring Harbor Laboratory, 1983.
6. *Paris Conference on Birth Defects*, 1971, 1972. Original Abstract Series 3, no 7.
7. Yunis JJ: High resolution of human chromosomes. *Science* 1976; 191:1268–1270.
8. Nathans D, Smith HO: Restriction endonucleases in the analysis and restructuring of DNA molecules. *Ann Rev Biochem* 1975; 44:273–293.
9. Roberts RJ: Restriction and modification enzymes and their recognition sequences. *Nucleic Acids Res* 1981; 9:75–96.
10. Southern E: Detection of specific sequences among DNA fragments separated by gel electrophoresis. *J Mol Biol* 1975; 98:503–517.
11. Southern E: Gel electrophoresis of restriction fragments. *Methods Enzymol* 1979; 68:152–176.
12. Antonarakis SE, Kazazian HH: Polymorphism and molecular pathology of the human beta-globin gene, in Brown EB (ed): *Progress in Hematology, XIII*. New York, Grune & Stratton, 1983, pp 49–73.
13. Kazazian HH, et al: Linkage of beta-thalassemia mutations and beta-globin gene polymorphisms with DNA polymorphisms in human beta-globin gene cluster. *Nature* 1982; 296:627–631.
14. Monaco AP, Kunkel LM: A giant locus for the Duchenne and Becker muscular dystrophy gene. *Trends in Genetics* 1987; 3:33–37.
15. Martin J, Gusella JF: Huntington's Disease. Pathogenesis and Management. *N Engl J Med* 1986; 315:1267–1276.
16. Nugent CE, Gravius T, Green P, et al: Prenatal diagnosis of cystic fibrosis by chorionic villus sampling using 12 polymorphic deoxyribonucleotide markers. *Obstet Gynecol* 1988; 71:213–215.
17. Martuza RL, Eldridge R: Neurofibromatosis. *N Engl J Med* 1988; 318:684–688.
18. Wyman AR, White R: A highly polymorphic locus in human DNA. *Proc Natl Acad Sci USA* 1980; 77:6754–6758.
19. Bell GI, Selby MJ, Rutter WJ: The highly polymorphic region near the human insulin gene is composed of simple tandemly repeating sequences. *Nature* 1982; 295:31–35.
20. Capon DJ, Chen EY, Levinson AD, et al: Complete nucleotide sequence of the T24 human bladder carcinoma oncogene and its normal homologue. *Nature* 1983; 302:33–37.
21. Weller P, Jeffreys AJ, Wilson V, et al: Organization of the human myoglobin gene. *EMBO J* 1984; 3:439–446.

22. Jeffreys AJ, Wilson V, Thein SL: Hypervariable minisatellite regions in human DNA. *Nature* 1985; 316:67–73.
23. Jeffreys AJ, Wilson V, Thein SL: Individual specific fingerprints of human DNA. *Nature* 1985; 316:76–79.
24. Gill P, Jeffreys AJ, Werrett DJ: Forensic application of DNA fingerprints. *Nature* 1985; 318:577–579.
25. Kanter E, Baird M, Shaler R, et al: Analysis of restriction fragment length polymorphisms in deoxyribonucleic acids (DNA) recovered from dried bloodstains. *J Forensic Sci* 1986; 31:403–408.
26. Giusti A, Baird M, Pasquale S, et al: Application of deoxyribonucleic acid (DNA) polymorphisms to the analysis of DNA recovered from sperm. *J Forensic Sci* 1986; 31:409–417.
27. Higuchi PG, VonBeroldingen CH, Sensabaugh GF, et al: DNA typing from single hairs. *Nature* 1988; 332:543–546.
28. Saiki RK, Gelfand DH, Stoffel S, et al: Primer directed enzymatic amplication of DNA with a thermostable DNA polymerase. *Science* 1988; 239:487–491.
29. Mullis KB, Faloona FA: Specific synthesis of DNA in vitro via a polymerase catalyzed chain reaction. *Methods Enzymol* 1987; 155:335–350.
30. Chien A, Edgar DB, Trela JM: Deoxyribonucleic acid polymerase from the extreme thermophile *Thermus aquaticus*. *J Bacteriol* 1976; 127:1550–1557.
31. Saiki RK, Scharf S, Faloona F, et al: Enzymatic amplification of beta globin genomic sequences and restriction site analysis for diagnosis of sickle cell anemia. *Science* 1985; 230:1350–1354.
32. Wong C, Dowling CE, Saiki RE, et al: Characterization of beta thalassemia mutations using direct genomic sequencing of amplified single copy DNA. *Nature* 1987; 330:384–386.
33. Saiki RK, Bugawan TL, Horn GT, et al: Analysis of enzymatically amplified HLA-DR alpha DNA with allele-specific oligonucleotide probes. *Nature* 1986; 324:163–166.
34. Kogan SC, Doherty M, Gitschier J: An improved method for prenatal diagnosis of amplified DNA sequence. *N Engl J Med* 1987; 317:985–990.
35. Ou GY, Kwok S, Mitchell SW, et al: DNA amplification for direct detection of HIV-1 in DNA of peripheral blood mononuclear cells. *Science* 1988; 239:295–297.
36. Marx JL: DNA fingerprinting takes the witness stand. *Science* 1988; 240:1616–1618.
37. Maxam AM, Gilbert W: A new method for sequencing DNA. *Proc Natl Acad Sci USA* 1977; 74:560–564.
38. Sanger F, Nicklen S, Coulson AR: DNA sequencing with chain terminating inhibitor. *Proc Natl Acad Sci USA* 1977; 74:5463–5467.

39. Johnston-Dow L, Mardis E, Heiner C, et al: Optimized methods for fluorescent and radiolabeled DNA sequencing. *Biotechniques* 1987; 5:754–765.
40. Stryer L: *Biochemistry*, 3rd ed. New York, W H Freeman & Company, 1988.
41. Darnell J, Lodish H, Baltimore D: *Molecular Cell Biology*. New York, Scientific American Books, 1986.
42. Alberts B, Bray D, Lewis J, et al: *Molecular Biology of the Cell*. New York, Garland Publishing, Inc, 1983.
43. Lewin B: *Genes*. New York, John Wiley & Sons, 1988.
44. Gusella JF: DNA polymorphism and human disease. *Ann Rev Biochem* 1986; 55:831–854.
45. White R, Lalouel J-M: Chromosome mapping with DNA markers. *Sci Am* 1988; 258:40–48.
46. Maniatis T, Frtisch EF, Sambrook J (eds): *Molecular Cloning: A Laboratory Manual*. Cold Spring Harbor, New York, Cold Spring Harbor Laboratory, 1983.
47. Ausubel F, Brent R, Kingston RE, et al: *Current Protocols in Molecular Biology*. New York, John Wiley & Sons, 1987.
48. Watson JD, Tooze J, Kurtz DT: *Recombinant DNA: A Short Course*. New York, W H Freeman & Company, 1983.

Chapter 2

Repetitive DNA: Molecular Structure, Polymorphisms, and Forensic Applications

Shannon J. Odelberg, Ph.D.
Ray White, Ph.D.

INTRODUCTION

Polymorphism at many loci is a feature of the human genome. Usually, polymorphism reflects single base-pair variation, yielding two possible alleles at a single locus. Some loci, however, exhibit structural differences based on the number of times a short DNA sequence is tandemly repeated. These loci are hypervariable in that several alternative alleles exist, each representing a different number of tandemly repeated units.

The discovery of these highly polymorphic loci has been primarily a product of the efforts of investigators who have developed linkage maps for the human genome. The concept of using DNA polymorphisms as genetic markers for the construction of a human linkage map was first suggested by Botstein et al.[1] Based on theoretical considerations, these authors estimated that more than 150 polymorphic loci would be required to construct a human linkage map spanning the entire genome. It was noted also that highly variable loci would be necessary for such a mapping project to become a practical reality. This map could then be used to localize other loci, e.g., loci that were harboring disease genes. Close linkage between a genetic marker and a disease locus provides a powerful tool for preventive medicine through the avenue of genetic counseling. The ascertainment of linkage is also a first step in the isolation and characterization of a gene that may cause disease.

Following this paradigm, the search began for highly polymorphic loci suitable for constructing linkage maps. The first locus of this nature was discovered by Wyman and White[2] using the arbitrary probe pAW101. Later, it was mapped to chromosome 14 and designated as *D14S1*.[3] Soon, other hypervariable loci were identified near coding regions, e.g., the 5' flanking region of the insulin gene,[4] the intergenic region between the zeta-globin gene and its pseudogene,[5,6] the zeta-globin pseudogene,[6,7] and the Harvey-*ras* oncogene.[8] These latter polymorphisms were found while studying individual genes and were not a consequence of a linkage mapping project.

Later, Jeffreys et al[9] significantly advanced these efforts. They observed partial homology among some highly polymorphic loci, allowing them to hybridize a single probe to numerous related loci under hybridization conditions of low stringency. This produced a complex banding pattern for each individual known as a 'DNA fingerprint' (this technique will be discussed in greater detail later in the chapter).

Building on the phenomenon of partial homology, Nakamura et al[10] constructed oligonucleotides from the known sequences of several hypervariable loci. By screening cosmid libraries of the human genome with the oligonucleotide probes and, in turn, using the positive cosmid clones as probes in restriction fragment length polymorphism (RFLP) analysis of random individuals, these investigators have been able to identify over 200 hypervariable loci (Y. Nakamura, personal communication, October 1988).

Jeffreys et al[9,11] were the first to recognize the vast potential of these loci in investigations involving personal identification, e.g., individualization of body fluid stains and parentage testing. The 'DNA fingerprint' patterns obtained from hybridization with two minisatellite probes were found to be an individualizing characteristic. Later, Gill et al[12,13] successfully applied the 'DNA fingerprinting' technique to the analysis of blood and semen stains, hair roots, and post-coital vaginal swabs. Odelberg[14] confirmed these results and, in addition, studied the long-term effects of temperature and humidity on the successful RFLP analysis of blood and semen stains. Other investigators[15–18] used probes that recognized single hypervariable loci (known as variable number of tandem repeats or VNTR loci) to analyze samples likely to be encountered in forensic casework. The usefulness of 'DNA fingerprinting' in parentage testing has been amply demonstrated,[19–21] while others have advocated the use of VNTR loci for this purpose.[22,23]

All of the highly polymorphic loci discussed in this section belong to a class of DNA known as repetitive DNA. There are two major categories of repetitive DNA: (1) interspersed repetitive DNA and (2) tandemly repeated DNA. Interspersed repetitive DNA consists of similar sequences that are scattered throughout the genome but are not found in tandemly repeated arrays. These interspersed units show a high degree of variation within a single genome and, therefore, have not been useful for personal identification. Tandemly repeated DNA is composed of long 'satellite' regions located near the centromeres and shorter 'minisatellite' DNA scattered throughout the genome. Numerous minisatellite loci exhibit length polymorphisms based on the number of times a particular segment of DNA is tandemly repeated. These loci (known as VNTR loci) are valuable for purposes of personal identification, such as individualization, parentage testing, and twin-zygosity studies. The hypervariable loci discussed in this chapter fall into this class of repetitive DNA.

The remaining portion of this chapter will focus on several aspects of repetitive DNA: its molecular structure and polymorphisms, and the statistical considerations necessary for its application to forensic biology.

INTERSPERSED REPETITIVE DNA

Interspersed repetitive DNA can be divided into two major categories: (1) short interspersed repetitive sequences (SINEs), and (2) long interspersed repetitive sequences (LINEs). In general, SINEs consist of DNA segments that are less than 500 base pairs long, while the repeating units in LINEs contain more than 5,000 base pairs.[24] These repetitive segments are interspersed singly throughout the genome and have not been found in tandem arrays. Recent evidence suggests that SINEs and LINEs are generally segregated from one another and occupy different regions of the chromosome (see below).[25]

SINEs

The predominant family of SINEs in primates is the *Alu* family. This family consists of a repeating unit of approximately 300 base pairs with an average sequence divergence of about 12.8% between individual members of the family.[26] Each repeat contains a single *Alu* I restriction site within its sequence. The copy number per haploid genome in humans has been estimated to be between 300,000 and 910,000.[27,28] Thus, the *Alu* family comprises between 3% and 9% of the total human genome. Other primates that have been studied seem to have fewer copies of the *Alu* sequence.[28]

Jagadeeswaran et al[29] proposed that the widespread dispersion of *Alu* family repeats was generated by a transposition mechanism involving self-primed reverse transcription of *Alu* RNA transcripts. Until recently, only indirect evidence supported this hypothesis: (1) *Alu* sequences are flanked by short, direct repeats characteristic of those observed following nonhomologous recombination; (2) the *Alu* repeat contains an internal split promoter and is readily transcribed in vitro by RNA polymerase III; (3) the 3' end of the repeat contains a poly(dA) segment; and (4) like all RNA polymerase III products, *Alu* transcripts contain a U-rich 3' end in the flanking regions of DNA, downstream from the repeating unit. Therefore, the U-rich end could loop back and anneal to the poly(A) region of the repeat, thus acting as a primer for reverse transcriptase. The cDNA copy then could be integrated into a new site at a break in the genome. Recently, direct evidence of *Alu* transposition in human lung cancer cells has been reported.[30] Fusion of UV-irradiated lung cancer cells with cells containing one copy of the *Ecogpt* gene demonstrated a transposition of an *Alu* sequence into the *gpt* gene. Although this indicates that some *Alu* sequences can behave as transposable elements under certain conditions, the mechanism for transposition is still uncertain.

There is evidence that *Alu* sequences may play a role in the replication of the human genome. A 14-base-pair sequence within the *Alu* repeat shows a high degree of homology with a segment of DNA known to be near the origin of replication in papovaviruses.[31] This segment of DNA contains the pentanucleotide GAGGC, which binds the T antigen (a requirement for SV40 replication).[32] Moreover, a 16-base-pair segment of the *Alu* repeat, covering most of the homologous 14-base-pair region, is necessary for plasmid replication in monkey COS-7 cells that have been transformed with a pBR322 plasmid containing a human *Alu* sequence.[32] Recently, it was shown that repeats of the *Alu* family reside mainly in GC-rich, structural regions of the chromosome known as the Reverse bands (R bands).[25] The DNA in R bands is replicated early during synthesis, possibly due to the putative role of *Alu* sequences.

Other families of SINEs exist in the human genome, for example, the NTS (nontranscribed spacer) family, originally identified in the nontranscribed spacer region of ribosomal DNA.[24] However, these families are not as ubiquitous as the *Alu* family.

LINEs

In contrast to the SINEs, only one family of LINEs has been found in each species studied.[33] In humans, this family is the L1*Hs* (or *Kpn*) family. The full-length repeat is greater than 6 kilobases; however, many of the individual members of the family are truncated—most missing the 5' end of the repeat.[33–35] The number of copies in the human haploid genome has been estimated to be as high as 107,000.[28]

Like the *Alu* family, L1*Hs* sequences are believed to have been generated through transpositional events involving self-priming and cDNA formation. Additionally, because of the long open reading frames within the 6-kilobase repeat, the presence of L1*Hs* transcripts in various cells, and the weak sequence homology with the polymerase domains of reverse transcriptases, it has been proposed that L1*HS* may encode a protein with reverse transcriptase activity.[35,36] If so, not only could certain L1*Hs* sequences encode a protein that could reverse-transcribe its own transcript, but the same protein could be responsible for polymerase activity that may be necessary for the observed *Alu* transpositional event discussed above.[30]

Recent evidence indicates that the LINEs exist mainly in the chromosomal regions subject to Giemsa/quinacrine staining (G/Q bands).[25] This is in contrast to the *Alu* family, whose sequences are located primarily in the region of the R bands. The G/Q bands are generally AT-rich and represent late-replicating DNA.

TANDEMLY REPEATED DNA

Satellite DNA

Through the years, the criteria that define satellite DNA have evolved rapidly. The first reports described satellite DNA as the minor fractions resulting from ultracentrifugation of genomic DNA on a CsCl density gradient.[37,38] Later, satellite DNA was also defined according to the reassociation kinetics of denatured DNA.[39,40] Highly repetitive DNA, such as satellite DNA, reassociates much more rapidly than single copy or moderately repetitive DNA. 'Hidden' satellite DNA was later discovered by ultracentrifugation on a Cs_2SO_4 density gradient in the presence of heavy metal ions such as Hg^{2+} or Ag^{+}.[41,42] The same effect was achieved on a CsCl gradient containing certain antibiotics.[43,44] More recently, the term 'satellite DNA' has been extended to describe long blocks of highly repetitive DNA sequences that are in a tandem array, regardless of their densities relative to the major fraction of DNA in the genome.[45,46]

Satellite DNA seems to be ubiquitous to all eukaryotic systems but absent in prokaryotes.[47] It is located primarily near the centromeres in the regions of heterochromatin, although some satellite DNA has been observed in other regions of the chromosomes.[47–49]

Human satellite DNA can be divided into several categories according to buoyant density: satellite DNAs I, II, III, IV, A, B, and C.[47] In addition, a type known as alphoid (or alpha) satellite DNA is electrophoretically characterized by a ladder of fragments that are multiples of a 340-base-pair unit following restriction endonuclease cleavage.[27,47] Satellite DNA appears to occupy less than 10% of the total human genome.[47]

Several biological functions for satellite DNA have been suggested: (1) binding proteins that are essential for centromeric functions, e.g., assembling the kinetochores which allow spindle attachment, holding daughter chromatids together during metaphase, and directing topoisomerases to the appropriate sites on sister-chromatids following replication[50]; (2) providing the sequences necessary for homologous chromosome pairing at meiosis and for general recognition of different chromosomes leading to the formation of a chromocenter[51]; and (3) influencing the frequency and position of recombinational events in the genome.[52]

Minisatellite DNA and VNTR Loci

Minisatellite DNA is a general term referring to short, tandemly repeated sequences of DNA that are dispersed throughout the genome. These sequences may or may not reveal length polymorphisms following digestion of genomic DNA with a restriction endonuclease.[9] The term 'minisatellite DNA' has been used to describe a family of related repeated sequences that give a complex banding pattern upon RFLP analysis[9,11] and also to describe a single polymorphic locus.[53] A more specific term, VNTR (variable number of tandem repeats) locus, refers to a single locus (usually hypervariable) containing alternative alleles. These alleles appear to be defined by the number of times a short DNA sequence is tandemly repeated.[10] By definition, length polymorphisms will always be generated following Southern blot analysis of a VNTR locus if an appropriate enzyme was chosen for the digestion. Therefore, a VNTR locus is equivalent to a single, polymorphic minisatellite DNA locus; however, not all minisatellite DNA loci qualify as VNTR loci.

Historical Background.—When *D14S1* was first identified by an arbitrary DNA probe, pAW101,[2] the authors did not know the molecular basis for the observed length polymorphism. This length variation is now known to reflect two separate polymorphisms.[54] The primary polymorphism is due to the number of times the 3-base-pair sequence $^{T}_{C}$GG is tandemly repeated. The minor polymorphism consists of a 60-base-pair repeating unit, with either 10 or 26 copies. Therefore, *D14S1* is properly classified as a VNTR locus or, more appropriately, as a pair of VNTR loci.

The molecular basis for VNTR polymorphisms was first described by Bell et al[4] following sequence analysis of the hypervariable region flanking the 5'-end of the human insulin gene. They found that the length polymorphism at this locus results from the variable number of times that a 14-base-pair sequence is tandemly repeated.

By hybridizing a pure repeat probe, constructed from a minisatellite located in the first intron of the myoglobin gene (a 33-base-pair repeat unit), to a human genomic library, Jeffreys et al[9] isolated eight clones, each containing a different minisatellite region of DNA. When tested by RFLP analysis under high stringency conditions, each clone hybridized to a unique minisatellite locus. Four of the eight loci exhibited polymorphisms and therefore qualify as VNTR loci. The other four loci revealed no polymorphism following Southern blot analysis of 14 unrelated British Caucasians and therefore cannot be classified as VNTR loci. Low stringency hybridization of probes 33.15 and 33.6, which respectively recognize two of the four polymorphic minisatellite regions, to Southern blots reveals complex banding patterns termed 'DNA fingerprints' (due to their apparent ability to discriminate between all unrelated individuals).[9, 11] These complex patterns are a result of cross-hybridization of the probe to several related minisatellite loci. Figure 2–1 compares the simple banding patterns obtained at a VNTR locus under conditions of high stringency to the complex 'DNA fingerprint' patterns.

Six of the most polymorphic loci that contribute to the complex 'DNA fingerprint' pattern have been cloned and characterized.[53, 55] Each of these represents a unique locus and thus meets the definitional requirements of a VNTR locus.

Recently, a technique was developed for the rapid identification and isolation of VNTR loci.[10] This method involves the construction of several synthetic oligonucleotides based on the published sequence data of known VNTR loci. In addition, oligonucleotides have been constructed from the known sequences of the X-gene region of the hepatitis B virus genome. This region, which is thought to be responsible for integration of the viral DNA into the host genome, contains similarities to the consensus sequence of the repetitive units found in the myoglobin family. These oligonucleotides are used as probes to identify related sequences in cosmid libraries of the human genome. Positive cosmid clones are hybridized to Southern blots of DNA from unrelated individuals to determine whether each recognizes a unique polymorphic locus. If several alleles are observed, or if polymorphism is revealed by digestion with more than one enzyme, the region is classified as a VNTR locus. The polymorphic region is localized further and subcloned into a plasmid vector.

The Molecular Basis for the Length Polymorphisms at VNTR Loci.—The molecular basis for the length polymorphisms found at VNTR loci is schematically represented in Figure 2–2. An allele at a particular locus is defined by the number of times a short DNA sequence is tandemly repeated. For example, the *D17S5* locus contains a repeating unit of 70 base pairs. A particular allele may contain two tandemly repeated copies of this 70-base-repair unit, while a different allele may have three tandemly repeated copies. Since the flanking regions surrounding the repeating units are highly conserved between the alternative alleles, the distance from these repeats to a particular restriction site in the flanking DNA is consistent between the different alleles (except for the rare occurrence of a point mutation). Therefore, the observed length polymorphisms reflect the variable number of repeating units and are not due to the presence or absence of a particular restriction site.

Sequence and Structure of VNTR Loci.—The individual repetitive units of known VNTR loci vary in length from only a few base pairs up to more than 70

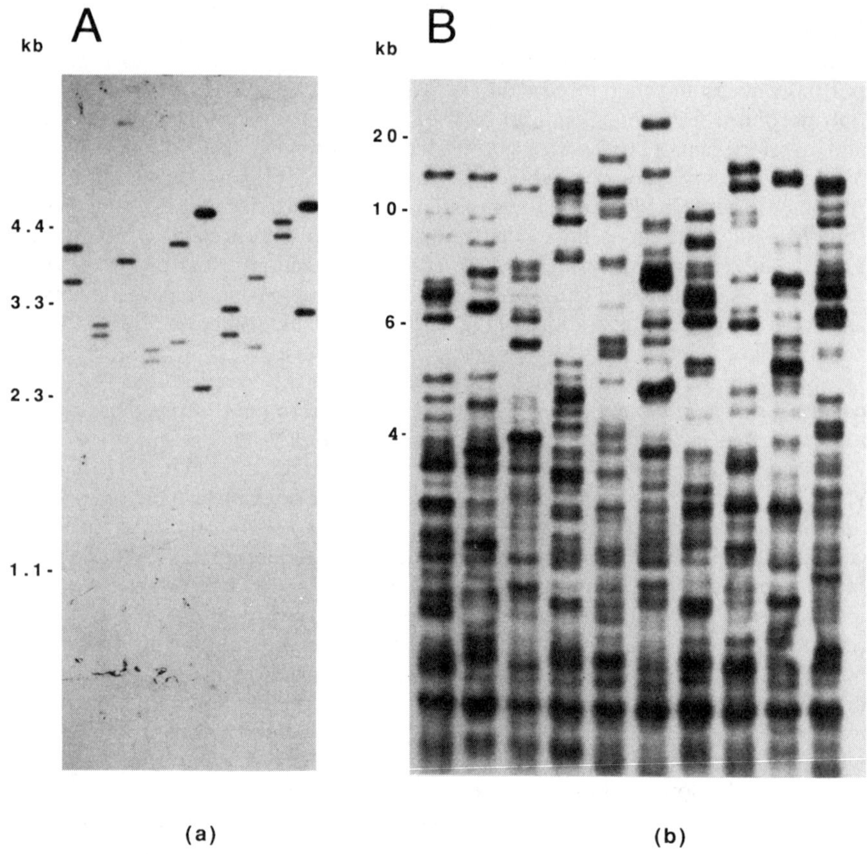

FIG 2–1.
A, ˜ 2 μg of genomic DNA from each of 10 unrelated individuals digested with *Hin*f I. Following Southern blotting, the membranes were hybridized with probe pYNH24. This probe recognizes the VNTR locus, *D2S44*. **B,** ˜ 10 μg of genomic DNA from each of 10 unrelated individuals [different individuals than those shown in **A**] digested with *Sau* 3A. Following Southern blotting, the membranes were hybridized with the minisatellite probe 15.1.11.4. (Courtesy of Dr. Alec J Jeffreys.)

base pairs. Most of the sequenced VNTR loci are GC-rich; however, a VNTR region associated with the apoB gene is composed almost entirely of the nucleotides deoxyadenylic acid and deoxythymidylic acid.[56] Some VNTR loci contain repeating units that are highly conserved at both the intra-allelic and inter-allelic levels (e.g., the 70-base-pair repeat of *D17S5*),[57] while others show a divergent repeating unit (e.g., the 30-base-pair repeat of *D2S44*).

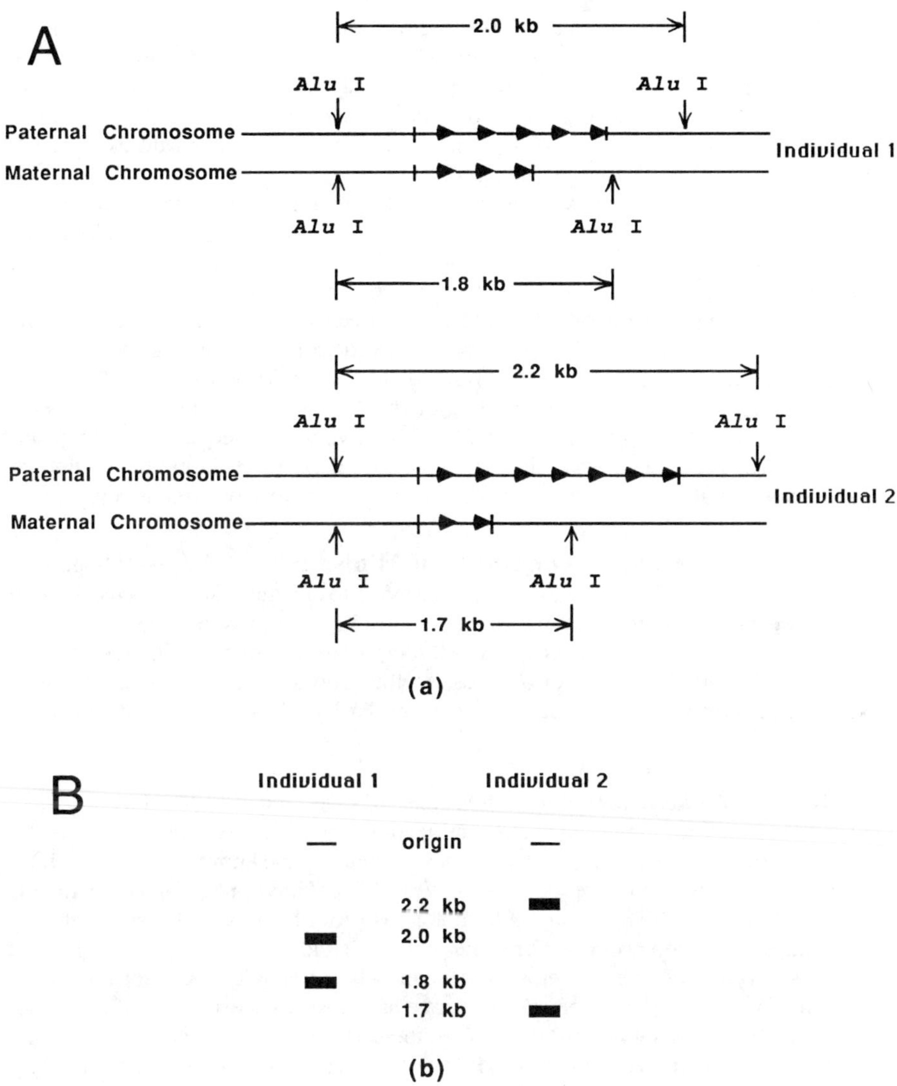

FIG 2–2.

A, a schematic diagram of a VNTR locus showing the number of repeating units and the *Alu* I restriction sites on each of the two homologous chromosomes from two different heterozygous individuals. Note that the differences in the length of the DNA segment between the restriction sites depend on the number of repeating units and not on the length of the flanking DNA, which is constant. **B,** the expected RFLP pattern from both individuals. *Side arrow* = repeating unit; *downward arrow* = *Alu* I restriction site.

Mechanisms for the Generation of Polymorphisms at VNTR Loci.— Recently, high mutation rates (up to 5.2% per gamete for the λMS1 locus) have been observed in some of the VNTR loci that contribute to the minisatellite 'DNA fingerprint' pattern.[58] It was proposed that unequal exchange at meiosis could be responsible for these mutations. Other possible mechanisms leading to the generation of length polymorphisms at VNTR loci include unequal sister-chromatid exchange at mitosis or polymerase slippage during replication.[9]

Wolff et al[57] have recently investigated in detail a mutation in which exactly one 70-base-pair repeating unit was deleted at the *D17S5* locus. The mutant allele was inherited from the mother. By sequencing both maternal alleles (polymorphisms in the base sequence were found in the flanking regions at both ends of these alleles) and the mutant allele in the offspring, the authors determined that the flanking regions surrounding the mutant VNTR allele were derived from only one of the mother's alleles, and were not a composite of both alleles as would be expected if unequal crossing-over at meiosis was responsible for the mutation. Possible mechanisms for the generation of this mutant allele include the following: (1) unequal sister-chromatid exchange; (2) DNA polymerase slippage during replication; (3) loop-out deletion by intrachromosomal recombination; (4) a double cross-over event; or (5) gene conversion.

Possible Biological Functions of Minisatellite DNA.—Although no particular biological function has yet been assigned to any minisatellite locus,* several roles have been hypothesized for these regions: (1) they may be hotspots for homologous recombination (especially VNTR loci); (2) some minisatellite loci may act as regulators of transcription; or (3) these loci may be involved in bringing the four homologous chromatids into register at meiosis. Each of these possible functions will be addressed in this section.

Hotspots for Recombination.—Jeffreys et al[9] suggested that VNTR loci may function as hotspots for homologous recombination. Two observations make this hypothesis attractive. First, the repeat sequences in many of the known VNTR loci exhibit weak homology to the *chi* sequence of *Escherichia coli* and phage lambda, which is involved in the RecBCD-pathway of homologous recombination.[59] Second, high mutation rates have been observed for some of the VNTR loci.[58] These authors suggested that unequal crossing-over at meiosis was the most likely explanation for the mutations. However, unequal sister-chromatid exchange at mitosis may explain a different mutation that has been studied in detail[57] (see the section entitled "Mechanisms for the Generation of Polymorphisms at VNTR Loci"). Moreover, the high degree of length polymorphism observed at these loci could be explained by unequal crossing-over.

Regulators of Transcription.—Some tandemly repeated units have been shown to be in vitro enhancers of transcription in other organisms. Examples include the

*A VNTR-like region has been found within the third exon of the BstNI-type loci of the human proline-rich protein (PRP) multigene family. See Lyons KM, Stein JH, Smithies O: Length polymorphisms in human proline-rich protein genes generated by intragenic unequal crossing over. *Genetics* 1988; 120:267–278.

72-base-pair repeat of the simian virus 40 (SV40)[60, 61] and the 73-base-pair repeat within the long terminal repeat of the murine Moloney sarcoma virus.[62] However, enhancement of transcription has not yet been demonstrated for VNTR loci.

Aligning Homologous Chromatids at Meiosis.—Sen and Gilbert[63] recently demonstrated that single-stranded DNA composed of short, G-rich segments will self-associate at physiological salt concentrations to form a four-stranded complex. Presumably these complexes are held together by Hoogsteen pairing between the guanine bases. These authors suggested that the self-association of G-rich sequences may be responsible for bringing the four homologous chromatids into register at meiosis. Most VNTR loci appear to be comprised of G-rich repeating units and therefore, by association, may assist in the alignment of the four homologous chromatids at meiosis.

STATISTICAL CONSIDERATIONS FOR FORENSIC BIOLOGY

This section will focus on the statistical analyses required when single-locus VNTR probes are used for personal identification. For a discussion on the statistical analyses of 'DNA fingerprint' patterns, the reader is referred to the paper by Jeffreys et al.[11] These two methods of analysis differ substantially as a consequence of the complexity of the 'DNA fingerprint' pattern that is obtained when hybridizing with probes that recognize multiple minisatellite loci. Because individual loci cannot be distinguished from the 'DNA fingerprint' pattern, the classical methods for determining relative allele frequencies cannot be used. For this reason, an alternative method for determining relative allele frequencies, based on band sharing, has been developed.[11, 53] However, this method assumes that all DNA fragments of a particular size originate from the same locus and are therefore the same allele—an assumption that may not be true. To determine the relative frequency of a particular 'DNA fingerprint' pattern within a given population, it is also necessary to assume: (1) that no linkage disequilibrium exists between the loci, and (2) that no two bands used in the analysis are alternative alleles at the same locus. In contrast, relative allele frequencies for a single VNTR locus are determined using the maximum likelihood estimate. This is accomplished by performing RFLP analysis on numerous unrelated individuals, counting the frequency for each distinguishable allele, and dividing by the total number of alleles in the analysis (= 2N, when N is the number of individuals tested).

Relative Allele Frequencies

Studies designed to estimate the relative allele frequencies for various VNTR loci have been published.[22, 23] Between two major studies, a total of ten VNTR loci were characterized: *D14S1, D17S5, D2S44, D9S7, D14S13, D19S20, D16S83, D1S74, D3S42,* and the Harvey-*ras* oncogene VNTR. Relative allele frequencies for the Caucasian population were obtained for all ten loci, while *D14S1* and the Harvey-*ras* oncogene VNTR were also characterized for the Hispanic and American black populations.[22]

A Priori Probabilities

Once allele frequencies are known, several a priori probabilities can be calculated which show the potential of each locus for various purposes related to personal identification (individualization, parentage testing, and twin-zygosity studies).

Probability of Matching.—The probability of matching (also known as the probability of nondiscrimination) is the a priori probability that two individuals selected at random from a given population will genotypically match at a particular locus or set of loci. This probability, P_M, is defined by the following formula:

$$P_{M_i} = \sum_{k=1}^{n} p_k^2$$

In this formula, n is the number of genotypes at the ith VNTR locus and p_k is the relative frequency of the kth genotype.[64] The smaller the value of P_M, the better the system is for individualization purposes. When a sample is genotyped at more than one locus, a joint probability of matching can be obtained easily if all the analyzed loci are statistically independent (i.e., they are not in linkage disequilibrium). This joint probability is simply the product of the P_M values for the individual loci. To illustrate the power of VNTR loci for individualization purposes, the joint matching probability for eight independent loci (*D17S5, D2S44, D9S7, D14S13, D19S20, D16S83, D1S74,* and *D3S42*) in the Utah Caucasian population is about 1.29×10^{-14}.[23] The sample sizes in this study were small, and three of the eight loci showed significant deviations from Hardy-Weinberg equilibrium; therefore, the above probability should be interpreted with caution. However, it does serve to illustrate the potential power of VNTR loci for purposes of individualization.

The probability of matching for two siblings can be calculated also. Obviously, the probability that two siblings are genotypically identical at a particular locus is much higher than that of two unrelated individuals. Nevertheless, the joint probability that two siblings genotypically match at all of the above eight VNTR loci is low—about 1.09×10^{-4}.[23] This probability is important in forensic work when a sibling in question is unavailable for genetic testing. It is also useful for determining the potential power of these loci for twin-zygosity studies.

Average Power of Exclusion.—The average power of exclusion is the a priori probability that a falsely-accused putative father will be excluded as the biological father of a particular child. The higher the probability, the better the genetic system is for parentage testing. This probability can be calculated for a trio when the genotypes of the alleged father, the mother, and the child are known, and can be calculated also for a parent/child duo. The general formulae for both of these situations are given below:

$$PE_{trio} = \sum_{i=1}^{n} P_i (1 - P_i)^2 + \sum_{i=1}^{n} \sum_{j=i+1}^{n} (P_iP_j)^2(3P_i + 3P_j - 4)$$

$$PE_{duo} = \sum_{i=1}^{n} P_i^2(1 - P_i)^2 + \sum_{i=1}^{n} \sum_{j=i+1}^{n} 2P_iP_j(1 - P_i - P_j)^2$$

P_i is the frequency of the ith allele and n is the number of alleles at the locus.[65] A computer program is necessary for calculating these probabilities for VNTR loci, because the number of alleles at each locus is numerous.

The joint power of exclusion for several independent loci is given by the following formula:

$$PE_{joint} = 1 - \Pi\,(1 - PE_{locus})$$

In this formula, PE_{locus} is the power of exclusion for each individual VNTR locus. The joint power of exclusion for the eight VNTR loci mentioned in the section regarding probability of matching is approximately 0.9999974 for the trio and 0.9998732 for the duo.[23] Thus, VNTR loci are extremely valuable markers for parentage testing. However, as previously mentioned, some VNTR loci have shown mutation rates up to 5.2% per gamete[58]; therefore, these particular loci should be avoided for parentage testing. Other loci, including those used in the above calculations, are useful in investigations of parentage, because they exhibit mutation rates that are much lower.

Statistical Evaluations Following RFLP Analysis

Individualization.—Assuming Hardy-Weinberg equilibrium, relative allele frequencies can be used to estimate genotype frequencies following RFLP analysis. These simple calculations are classical methods of population genetics. To determine the frequency of a heterozygote (usually an individual expressing two bands at a particular VNTR locus), the following formula is used:

$$\text{heterozygote freq.} = 2pq$$

Here p is the relative allele frequency of one of the fragments and q is the relative allele frequency of the other fragment. The frequency for a homozygote is simply p^2.

Assuming statistical independence of the VNTR loci (that is, no linkage disequilibrium), the product of the estimated genotype frequencies at each locus represents the joint frequency for the given set of genotypes. Table 2–1 gives the estimated frequency of the most common genotype in the Utah white population for each of the eight loci, and also the joint frequency for this set of genotypes. These data indicate that the most common set of genotypes should be present in about 2 out of every 100 billion white people. All other possible sets of genotypes are expected to be even rarer.

The probability that two or more individuals on earth have the most common set of genotypes can be estimated using the Poisson distribution:

$$P[X=x] = \frac{e^{-m}\, m^x}{x!}$$

TABLE 2–1.
Frequency of Most Common Genotypes

Locus	Enzyme	Frequency of Most Common Genotype*
D17S5	*Hinf* I	0.097
D2S44	*Hinf* I	0.005
D9S7	*Hinf* I	0.081
D14S13	*Hinf* I	0.023
D19S20	*Hinf* I	0.164
D16S83	*Alu* I	0.066
D1S74	*Alu* I	0.021
D3S42	*Hinf* I	0.178
All 8 systems jointly		3.61×10^{-11}

*Genotypic frequencies were calculated assuming Hardy-Weinberg equilibrium.

In this equation, x is the hypothetical number of individuals with a particular set of genotypes, and m is the expected number of individuals with this set of genotypes (i.e., m = [population of the earth] [joint frequency of the set of genotypes] = $[5 \times 10^9]\,[3.61 \times 10^{-11}] = 0.181$). In this case, x is assumed to be 0 or 1 as shown below:

$$P[X=0] = \frac{e^{-0.181}\,(0.181)^0}{0!}$$

$$P[X=0] = 0.834$$

$$P[X=1] = \frac{e^{-0.181}\,(0.181)^1}{1!}$$

$$P[X=1] = 0.151$$

To obtain the probability that two or more individuals on earth have the most common set of genotypes, the above values are added and subtracted from unity:

$$P[X>1] = 1 - (0.834 + 0.151)$$

$$P[X>1] = 0.015$$

It is even less probable that two or more individuals on earth share any other set of genotypes. Therefore, it appears that practical individualization of unrelated individuals can be achieved using this set of eight VNTR probes. However, it must be noted that the above calculations were based on data obtained from relatively small Utah white samples under the assumption of Hardy-Weinberg equilibrium. This sample cannot be considered representative of the world population; furthermore, three of the eight VNTR loci statistically deviated from Hardy-Weinberg equilibrium.[23] Therefore, these probabilities only serve to illustrate the potential power of VNTR loci for purposes of individualization and should not be construed as actual values.

Parentage Testing.—Two methods are commonly used to analyze data obtained in a paternity investigation; these are known as the paternity index and the probability of paternity. The paternity index is a likelihood ratio representing the probability that a putative father could be the biological father of a particular child, compared to the probability that a random man could be the biological father. The probability of paternity is based on Bayes' Theorem and requires an a priori probability in favor of paternity. This prior probability is usually assumed to be 0.5. Therefore, before testing it is assumed that the putative father has a 50% chance of being the biological father and a 50% chance of not being the true father. In most paternity tests, the mother is assumed to be the biological mother of the child.

Paternity Index.—The paternity index can be calculated for each VNTR locus separately or for all loci jointly. Assuming that X is the probability that the putative father could be the biological father of the child, and that Y is the probability that a random man could be the father of the child, the following rules can be followed to obtain the paternity index for a particular locus.

1. If possible, determine which allele the mother passed on to the child. The biological father must have passed on the allele not inherited from the mother. If the child is homozygous for a particular allele, then both the mother and the biological father must have passed the same allele to the child.
2. Determine whether the putative father possesses the obligatory paternal allele. If he does not, he is excluded as the father of the child (except for the possibility of a rare mutation). If he possesses the obligatory allele in the homozygous state, then $X = 1$. If he is heterozygous for the allele, then $X = 0.5$.
3. If the mother and child are both heterozygous and have the same genotype at a locus, it is impossible to determine which allele the mother passed to the child. Both possibilities are equally likely in that both have a probability of 0.5. A specific example will be used to illustrate the calculation of X. Assuming that the mother (M) has the genotype 1/2 (i.e., she has allele 1 on one chromosome and allele 2 at the same locus on the homologous chromosome), the child is also 1/2, and the alleged father (AF) is 1/4, then X would be calculated as follows: X = (M's chance of passing allele 1)(AF's chance of passing allele 2) + (M's chance of passing allele 2)(AF's chance of passing allele 1). Therefore, $X = (0.5)(0) + (0.5)(0.5) = 0.25$.
4. Y is calculated in a similar manner, except that relative frequencies of a particular allele are used in place of the chance the alleged father has of passing on a particular allele. To continue the above example, assume that allele 1 has a relative frequency equal to 0.15, allele 2 is equal to 0.10, and allele 4 equals 0.05. Therefore, $Y = (0.5)(0.10) + (0.5)(0.15) = 0.125$.
5. The paternity index for each locus is simply X/Y, while the joint paternity index, X_j/Y_j, for all independent loci tested is $\prod_{i=1}^{n} X_i/Y_i$, where X_i and Y_i are the X and Y values, respectively, for the ith locus, and n is the number of loci analyzed.

Probability of Paternity.—Once the joint paternity index has been calculated, the probability of paternity can be obtained easily with the following formula:

$$\text{Prob. of Paternity} = \frac{1}{1 + (Y_j/X_j)\,(y/x)}$$

In this formula, y is the prior probability that the putative father is not the biological father, while x is the prior probability that the accused is the biological father. This formula can also be applied to the analysis of data from a single locus. As previously stated, x and y are usually assumed to be 0.5, and therefore $y/x = 1$. The formula can be simplified as follows:

$$\text{Prob. of Paternity} = \frac{1}{1 + (Y_j/X_j)}$$

FUTURE ROLES ENVISIONED FOR VNTR LOCI IN FORENSIC BIOLOGY

In the future, the VNTR genotypes of perpetrators of violent crimes might be stored in a data base, similar to the system already established for fingerprints. This would allow law enforcement officials throughout the world to compare the genotypes of known criminals to the results obtained from RFLP analysis of evidence samples in order to implicate or eliminate an individual as the perpetrator of a particular crime. In addition, military personnel also might be routinely genotyped for identification purposes, and parents might choose to have the genotypes of their children stored in a data base to aid in the process of identification in cases of abduction.

REFERENCES

1. Botstein D, White RL, Skolnick M, et al: Construction of a genetic linkage map in man using restriction fragment length polymorphisms. *Am J Hum Genet* 1980; 32:314–331.
2. Wyman AR, White R: A highly polymorphic locus in human DNA. *Proc Natl Acad Sci USA* 1980; 77:6754–6758.
3. de Martinville B, Wyman AR, White R, et al: Assignment of the first random restriction fragment length polymorphism (RFLP) locus (*D14S1*) to a region of human chromosome 14. *Am J Hum Genet* 1982; 34:216–226.
4. Bell GI, Selby MJ, Rutter WJ: A highly polymorphic region near the human insulin gene is composed of simple tandemly repeating sequences. *Nature* 1982; 295:31–35.

5. Higgs DR, Goodbourn SEY, Wainscoat JS, et al: Highly variable regions of DNA flank the human α globin genes. *Nucleic Acids Res* 1981; 9:4213–4224.
6. Goodbourn SEY, Higgs DR, Clegg JB, et al: Molecular basis of length polymorphism in the human zeta-globin gene complex. *Proc Natl Acad Sci USA* 1983; 80:5022–5026.
7. Proudfoot NJ, Gil A, Maniatis T: The structure of the human zeta-globin gene and a closely linked, nearly identical pseudogene. *Cell* 1982; 31:553–563.
8. Goldfarb M, Shimizu K, Perucho M, et al: Isolation and preliminary characterization of a human transforming gene from T24 bladder carcinoma cells. *Nature* 1982; 296:404–409.
9. Jeffreys AJ, Wilson V, Thein SL: Hypervariable 'minisatellite' regions in human DNA. *Nature* 1985; 314:67–73.
10. Nakamura Y, Leppert M, O'Connell P, et al: Variable number of tandem repeat (VNTR) markers for human gene mapping. *Science* 1987; 235:1616–1622.
11. Jeffreys AJ, Wilson V, Thein SL: Individual-specific 'fingerprints' of human DNA. *Nature* 1985; 316:76–79.
12. Gill P, Jeffreys AJ, Werrett DJ: Forensic application of DNA 'fingerprints'. *Nature* 1985; 318:577–579.
13. Gill P, Lygo JE, Fowler SJ, et al: An evaluation of DNA fingerprinting for forensic purposes. *Electrophoresis* 1987; 8:38–44.
14. Odelberg SJ: *The Individualization of Physiological Fluid Stains and Postcoital Vaginal Swabs Using Restriction Fragment Length Polymorphisms* (dissertation). Medical College of Virginia, Virginia Commonwealth University, Richmond, Va, 1987.
15. Baird M, Kanter E, Shaler R, et al: Application of DNA polymorphisms to the forensic examination of dried blood stains, in Brinkmann B, Henningsen K (eds): *Advances in Forensic Haemogenetics*. Berlin, Springer-Verlag, 1986, pp 351–355.
16. Baird M, Giusti A, Balazs I, et al: Application of DNA polymorphisms to the forensic examination of semen, in Brinkmann B, Henningsen K (eds): *Advances in Forensic Haemogenetics*. Berlin, Springer-Verlag, 1986, pp 356–360.
17. Kanter E, Baird M, Shaler R, et al: Analysis of restriction fragment polymorphisms in deoxyribonucleic acid (DNA) recovered from dried bloodstains. *J Forensic Sci* 1986; 31:403–408.
18. Giusti A, Baird M, Pasquale S, et al: Application of deoxyribonucleic acid (DNA) polymorphisms to the analysis of DNA recovered from sperm. *J Forensic Sci* 1986; 31:409–417.

19. Jeffreys AJ, Brookfield JEY, Semeonoff R: Positive identification of an immigration test-case using human DNA fingerprints. *Nature* 1985; 317:818–819.
20. Helminen P, Ehnholm C, Lokki M-L, et al: Application of DNA "fingerprints" to paternity determinations. *Lancet* 1988; i:574–576.
21. Odelberg SJ, Demers DB, Westin EH, et al: Establishing paternity using minisatellite DNA probes when the putative father is unavailable for testing. *J Forensic Sci* 1988; 33:921–928.
22. Baird M, Balazs I, Giusti A, et al: Allele frequency distribution of two highly polymorphic DNA sequences in three ethnic groups and its application to the determination of paternity. *Am J Hum Genet* 1986; 39:489–501.
23. Odelberg SJ, Plaetke R, Eldridge JR, et al: Characterization of eight VNTR loci by agarose gel electrophoresis. *Genomics,* submitted for publication.
24. Singer MF: SINEs and LINEs: Highly repeated short and long interspersed sequences in mammalian genomes. *Cell* 1982; 28:433–434.
25. Korenberg JR, Rykowski MC: Human genome organization: Alu, Lines, and the molecular structure of metaphase chromosome bands. *Cell* 1988; 53:391–400.
26. Deininger PL, Jolly DJ, Rubin CM, et al: Base sequence studies of 300 nucleotide renatured repeated human DNA clones. *J Mol Biol* 1981; 151:17–33.
27. Singer MF: Highly repeated sequences in mammalian genomes. *Int Rev Cytol* 1982; 76:67–112.
28. Hwu HR, Roberts JW, Davidson EH, et al: Insertion and/or deletion of many repeated DNA sequences in human and higher ape evolution. *Proc Natl Acad Sci USA* 1986; 83:3875–3879.
29. Jagadeeswaran P, Forget BG, Weissman SM: Short interspersed repetitive DNA elements in eukaryotes: Transposable DNA elements generated by reverse transcription of RNA pol III transcripts? *Cell* 1981; 26:141–142.
30. Lin CS, Goldthwait DA, Samols D: Identification of Alu transposition in human lung carcinoma cells. *Cell* 1988; 54:153–159.
31. Jelinek WR, Toomey TP, Leinwand L, et al: Ubiquitous, interspersed repeated sequences in mammalian genomes. *Proc Natl Acad Sci USA* 1980; 77:1398–1402.
32. Johnson EM, Jelinek WR: Replication of a plasmid bearing a human *Alu*-family repeat in monkey COS-7 cells. *Proc Natl Acad Sci USA* 1986; 83:4660–4664.
33. Singer MF, Skowronski J: Making sense out of LINES: Long interspersed repeat sequences in mammalian genomes. *Trends Biochem Sci* 1985; 10:119–122.

34. Hattori M, Hidaka S, Sakaki Y: Sequence analysis of a KpnI family member near the 3' end of human β-globin gene. *Nucleic Acids Res* 1985; 13:7813–7827.
35. Scott AF, Schmeckpeper BJ, Abdelrazik M, et al: Origin of the human L1 elements: Proposed progenitor genes deduced from a consensus DNA sequence. *Genomics* 1987; 1:113–125.
36. Hattori M, Kuhara S, Takenaka O, et al: L1 family of repetitive DNA sequences in primates may be derived from a sequence encoding a reverse transcriptase-related protein. *Nature* 1986; 321:625–628.
37. Kit S: Equilibrium sedimentation in density gradients of DNA preparations from animal tissues. *J Mol Biol* 1961; 3:711–716.
38. Schildkraut CL, Marmur J, Doty P: Determination of the base composition of deoxyribonucleic acid from its buoyant density in CsCl. *J Mol Biol* 1962; 4:430–443.
39. Waring M, Britten RJ: Nucleotide sequence repetition: A rapidly reassociating fraction of mouse DNA. *Science* 1966; 154:791–794.
40. Britten RJ, Kohne DE: Repeated sequences in DNA. *Science* 1968; 161:529–540.
41. Nandi US, Wang JC, Davidson N: Separation of deoxyribonucleic acids by Hg(II) binding and Cs_2SO_4 density-gradient centrifugation. *Biochemistry* 1965; 4:1687–1696.
42. Skinner DM, Beattie WG: Cs_2SO_4 gradients containing both Hg^{2+} and Ag^+ effect the complete separation of satellite deoxyribonucleic acids having identical densities in neutral CsCl gradients. *Proc Natl Acad Sci USA* 1973; 70:3108–3110.
43. Peacock WJ, Brutlag D, Goldring E, et al: The organization of highly repeated DNA sequences in *Drosophila melanogaster* chromosomes. *Cold Spring Harbor Symp Quant Biol* 1974; 38:405–416.
44. Manuelidis L: A simplified method for preparation of mouse satellite DNA. *Anal Biochem* 1977; 78:561–568.
45. Pech M, Igo-Kemenes T, Zachau HG: Nucleotide sequence of a highly repetitive component of rat DNA. *Nucleic Acids Res* 1979; 7:417–432.
46. Lee TNH, Singer MF: Structural organization of α-satellite DNA in a single monkey chromosome. *J Mol Biol* 1982; 161:323–342.
47. Beridze T: *Satellite DNA*. Berlin, Springer-Verlag, 1986.
48. Kurnit DM, Maio JJ: Variable satellite DNA's in the African green monkey *Cercopithecus aethiops*. *Chromosoma* 1974; 45:387–400.
49. White R, Pasztor LM, Hu F: Mouse satellite DNA in noncentromeric heterochromatin of cultured cells. *Chromosoma* 1975; 50:275–282.
50. Watson JD, Hopkins NH, Roberts JW, et al: *Molecular Biology of the Gene*. Menlo Park, Calif, The Benjamin Cummings Publishing Co, 1987.

51. Brutlag D, Appels R, Dennis ES, et al: Highly repeated DNA in *Drosophila melanogaster. J Mol Biol* 1977; 112:31–47.
52. Miklos GLG, Nankivell RN: Telomeric satellite DNA functions in regulating recombination. *Chromosoma* 1976; 56:143–167.
53. Wong Z, Wilson V, Patel I, et al: Characterization of a panel of highly variable minisatellites cloned from human DNA. *Ann Hum Genet* 1987; 51:269–288.
54. Wyman AR, Mulholland J, Botstein D: Oligonucleotide repeats involved in the highly polymorphic locus D14S1. *Am J Hum Genet* 1986; 39:A226.
55. Wong Z, Wilson V, Jeffreys AJ, et al: Cloning a selected fragment from a human DNA 'fingerprint': Isolation of an extremely polymorphic minisatellite. *Nucleic Acids Res* 1986; 14:4605–4616.
56. Huang L-S, Breslow JL: A unique AT-rich hypervariable minisatellite 3' to the ApoB gene defines a high information restriction fragment length polymorphism. *J Biol Chem* 1987; 262:8952–8955.
57. Wolff RK, Nakamura Y, White R: Molecular characterization of a spontaneously generated new allele at a VNTR locus: No exchange of flanking DNA sequence. *Genomics* 1988; 3:347–351.
58. Jeffreys AJ, Royle NJ, Wilson V, et al: Spontaneous mutation rates to new length alleles at tandem-repetitive loci in human DNA. *Nature* 1988; 332:278–281.
59. Smith GR: Homologous recombination sites and their recognition, in Low KB (ed): *The Recombination of Genetic Material*. San Diego, Academic Press, 1988, pp 115–154.
60. Benoist C, Chambon P: *In vivo* sequence requirements of the SV40 early promoter region. *Nature* 1981; 290:304–310.
61. Gruss P, Dhar R, Khoury G: Simian virus 40 tandem repeated sequences as an element of the early promoter. *Proc Natl Acad Sci USA* 1981; 78:943–947.
62. de Villiers J, Schaffner W: A small segment of polyoma virus DNA enhances the expression of a cloned β-globin gene over a distance of 1400 base pairs. *Nucleic Acids Res* 1981; 9:6251–6264.
63. Sen D, Gilbert W: Formation of parallel four-stranded complexes by guanine-rich motifs in DNA and its implications for meiosis. *Nature* 1988; 334:364–366.
64. Fisher RA: Standard calculations for evaluating a blood-group system. *Heredity* 1951; 5:95–102.
65. Garber RA, Morris JW: General equations for the average power of exclusion for genetic systems of n codominant alleles in one-parent and no-parent cases of disputed perentage, in Walker RH, Duquesnoy RJ, Jennings ER, et al (eds): *Inclusion Probabilities in Parentage Testing*. Arlington, Va, American Association of Blood Banks, 1983, pp 277–280.

Chapter 3

The Use of Jeffreys' Multilocus and Single Locus DNA Probes in Forensic Analysis

George Herrin, Jr., Ph.D.
Lisa Forman, Ph.D.
Daniel D. Garner, Ph.D.

INTRODUCTION

Forensic scientists can now utilize the accuracy of DNA probe technology to help resolve many cases successfully. DNA testing enhances conventional serology because of the following characteristics. The first of these is the stability of the DNA molecule. Unlike proteins, which degrade in only days or months, DNA that it suitable for use in restriction fragment length polymorphism (RFLP) analysis can be isolated from samples which are several years old. The second advantage is the high degree of variability between individuals observed with these probes, which allows positive identification of sample donors. Protein analysis can exclude a suspect but cannot make a positive identification because of limited isozyme polymorphisms within each system. Using Jeffreys' multilocus or single locus DNA probes, 150 to 300 different band positions can be distinguished,[1] yielding an extraordinary level of polymorphism.

The two sets of related probes developed by Dr. Alec Jeffreys and his co-workers at the University of Leicester are used currently in forensic and paternity cases in both the U.S. and the U.K. The multilocus probes (MLP) 33.6 and 33.15 were the first set to be developed and analyzed for these purposes.[2–4] Several single locus probes (SLP) were then derived from the two multilocus probes,[5,6] four of which will be characterized below. These single locus probes have been effective in identifying biological fluids from victims and suspects, and in excluding possible suspects in forensic investigations.

In this chapter we describe the history and characteristics of the multilocus and single locus probes used at Cellmark Diagnostics (CMD). Additionally, we outline validation studies performed using these probes and criteria imposed on these probes to meet standards of forensic and legal responsibility.

VALIDATION

Validation testing was performed before the multilocus and single locus probes were used for casework. In order to assure that results were reliable, the probes had to exhibit three basic properties: (1) the same banding pattern had to be produced from the same individual regardless of source material; (2) environmental conditions could not change the position of bands in the banding pattern; and (3) the banding pattern obtained from a single individual at different times had to remain constant.

Validation for Paternity Testing

Two separate paternity validation studies were conducted to ensure that the results obtained with the Jeffreys multilocus probes 33.6 and 33.15 were consistent with the results obtained with more conventional blood group testing, enzyme grouping, and HLA typing. Independent validation of the multilocus probes has also been conducted for paternity tests.[7] The multilocus probes also have been used to establish relationships of children in the absence of samples from a parent when sufficient numbers of siblings were available for testing.[7,8]

In the first validation study, 28 mother/child/alleged father trios were tested using Jeffreys' multilocus probes. In 27 cases, the result obtained from DNA testing agreed with that obtained from blood group and enzyme analysis.[9] The discrepancy in the one case was traced to a sample handling problem between the two collaborating laboratories and was not an error in typing the samples. The second validation study involved examination of 191 paternity trios previously tested at the Memorial Blood Center of Minneapolis.[10] In this trial, 139 cases were found to be paternities and 49 were non-paternities. The DNA results agreed with those obtained from serum protein and enzyme markers. In 3 of the 191 cases, the alleged father was excluded by DNA testing, although protein and enzyme markers provided only a single indirect exclusion.

Reproducibility of Band Patterns

The results of a new technique must be reproducible before they can be relied upon in a forensic setting. Production of a DNA fingerprint from one sample by more than 50 U.K. and U.S. scientists in several hundred replicate tests demonstrated that the banding pattern obtained from both the 33.6 and the 33.15 probes could be reproduced in different laboratories and by different scientists. In addition, many of the paternity trios mentioned above were tested in duplicate or triplicate, with the same paternity/non-paternity decision being made each time.[11]

TABLE 3–1.
Effect of Moisture and Temperature on DNA From Stains

	Days Before Sample Degraded	
Temperature °C	Semen	Blood
0	8–10	3–4
4	8–10	2–3
23	6–8	1–2
30	6–8	1–2
37	4–5	1

Sample Types

The most common types of samples used for DNA testing are blood, semen, and various tissues. Studies have shown that DNA isolated from sperm cells, blood, hair roots, and various organ tissues from the same individual all yield the same DNA banding pattern.[6, 11–13] There has been no case of two samples from the same individual producing different DNA fingerprints in our experience, although tumors may produce a different DNA banding pattern compared with samples from an individual's normal tissue (A.J. Jeffreys, personal communication, 1989).

Gill et al[12] first demonstrated the use of Jeffreys' multilocus probes to examine actual forensic samples. DNA fingerprints from vaginal swabs and dried blood or semen stains were compared to the DNA fingerprints from whole blood from the donor individual. Banding patterns from the different sample sources were identical and unique to the individual's blood sample.

Sample Storage Conditions

In order for the DNA testing technique to prove practical, the storage conditions commonly used for forensic samples should have no effect on the results. Optimally, storage methods should reduce the possibility of DNA degradation, and several parameters have been studied which could affect the condition of the DNA isolated from samples.

Blood and semen stains were subjected to a variety of different conditions to determine the effects of moisture and temperature on the quality of the DNA isolated from them. All samples were kept moist for a varying number of days at the following temperatures: 0°C, 4°C, 23°C, 30°C, and 37°C.[13] The results are shown in Table 3–1. Similar results concerning degradation of samples exposed to moisture have been obtained by McNally et al.[14] In contrast, stains from a dry environment yielded DNA still suitable for testing after 3 years.[14] Dry storage dramatically increases the integrity of an intact DNA molecule. For example, a 9 year-old blood stain has yielded a sufficiently high molecular weight DNA to produce a banding pattern.[15]

The DNA banding pattern obtained from hair roots mounted in Permamount is identical to the pattern obtained from a blood sample from the same individual (L. Tonelli et al, unpublished results, 1988). DNA banding patterns also have been obtained from formalin-fixed and paraffin-embedded tissue (R. Cotton et al, unpublished results, 1988). DNA isolated from a variety of surfaces (including glass, paper, wood, plastic, floor tile, cloth, etc.) showed no changes in banding patterns as compared to control samples.[13,16–18] Intact high molecular weight DNA has been extracted from blood stored at temperatures up to 37°C for periods of up to 6 months and has been shown to be stable for 13 years when stored as a dry pellet.[19]

Stability of Band Pattern Over Time

In addition to testing DNA from one individual in several hundred replicate tests over a period of approximately 2 years, samples obtained from other individuals over a period of months also have demonstrated that the banding pattern remains constant for a given individual.[13] DNA banding patterns obtained from ambiguous dried blood and semen samples matched those obtained from fresh control samples.[12] A further study conducted at the British Home Office, using blind trial samples as old as 4 years, correctly identified and matched all appropriate samples.[20]

MULTILOCUS PROBES

Introduction

The multilocus probes were the first set of identification probes developed by Jeffreys et al.[1,2] Upon demonstration of Mendelian inheritance, the probes were used for identity testing in paternity and immigration casework.[8] Because of the high level of heterozygosity observed, the power of the multilocus probes for other forensic applications was quickly realized and utilized.[8,12]

Probe Isolation

The two multilocus probes were isolated from a human DNA genomic library using a synthetic DNA probe complementary to a portion of the human myoglobin gene. Of the 40 recombinants which tested positively with the human myoglobin probe, 8 were screened further for the following characteristics: high polymorphism, low possibility of rearrangement during isolation, and repeat sequence homogeneity. Two of the 8 positive recombinants, 33.6 and 33.15, satisfied all three of these conditions. First, both probes were shown to yield a highly polymorphic banding pattern, with DNA digested with the restriction enzyme Hinf1. The second requirement was met because the most commonly occurring allele in the population was the same size as the cloned fragment from the library, indicating that no rearrangement had taken place during the isolation procedure. Finally, the core repeat sequence of the polymorphic region was shown to vary by 0.7% ± 0.4% (from copy to copy) for 33.6 and 1.1% ± 0.5% for 33.15, indicating a very stable sequence between individuals.[2]

The basis for the many bands observed in a multilocus DNA "fingerprint" is the core, or repeated sequence. This sequence is present in many places throughout the genome and thus gives rise to the 20 to 30 bands per probe that can be visualized for one individual. The core sequence from which both the 33.6 and 33.15 probes are derived is GGAGGTGGGCAGGA$^{A}_{G}$G. The variation in this core sequence known to be present in the repeat unit of 33.6 is $(AGGGCTGGAGG)_3$ repeated 18 times. The 33.15 probe does not contain a trimer repeat unit but is composed instead of 29 tandem repeats of the sequence AGAGGTGGGCAGGTGG.[2–4]

Hybridization Conditions

The banding patterns obtained with the 33.6 and 33.15 probes are a result of using low stringency hybridization conditions.[2,3] Changes in the salt concentration and/or temperature (stringency) can affect the number of bands observed, but not the position of a particular band. The banding pattern observed will be replicated when the hybridization conditions are duplicated.

Sample Requirements in Forensics

Approximately 500 ng of DNA[5] are required for visualization of a DNA fingerprint with the 33.6 and 33.15 probes. This amount of DNA equals a bloodstain of about 50 μl (quarter-sized), a semen stain of about 5 μl (dime-sized), 0.5 to 1 g of tissue, or approximately 15 hair roots.[12,20,21] Because of these relatively large sample size requirements, the use of the multilocus probes is limited in the forensic arena.

Quality Control of Probes

Quality control procedures are essential in any forensic testing laboratory. This is especially true in light of the identification power which DNA probe technology affords. There are several elements of quality assurance in a DNA laboratory, including equipment maintenance, laboratory procedures, DNA probe quality, and independent quality control tests.

The first two of these considerations are handled through the periodic recording of equipment conditions (e.g., temperature records for all water baths) and extensive written procedures. The laboratory protocols require the presence of a witness at every step in the procedure where a sample transfer takes place. All of these procedures help to minimize the possibility of human error and to maximize the confidence level in the results.

The use of DNA probes in a forensic setting requires that the same conclusion be reached from identical samples using probes prepared from different lots of probe template which are processed in separate laboratories. The following procedure can be used to assure this condition is met. A nylon membrane, hybridized with a previous lot of the probes and for which the DNA fingerprint is known, is rehybridized with the new lot of probe. The DNA fingerprints from this test are compared with those produced previously. Although no discrepancies have been noted in such testing, any discrepancies would be investigated and corrected before the new lot is used for casework.

Band Sharing Between Unrelated Individuals

Calculation of the likelihood that two unrelated people have bands which comigrate at the same molecular weight (visualized by the band position on the autoradiogram) is an important factor in using DNA fingerprints for identification. This number (known as the percentage band sharing) was determined to be less than 25% for the 33.6 and 33.15 probes when considering unrelated individuals from northern Europe and the Indian subcontinent.[2, 21]

Subsequent work in the United States has shown the percentage band sharing for U.S. whites (252 individuals) to be less than 25% for both the 33.6 and 33.15 probes.[11] For U.S. blacks, the percentage band sharing was also determined to be less than 25% for both 33.6 and 33.15, with the average being very close to that observed for whites (D. Garner et al, unpublished results, 1988).

The percent band share is dependent on the size range in which bands are analyzed. Smaller-sized bands are more frequently shared among unrelated individuals in a population. For example, when bands larger than 10 kb are analyzed, the percent band share is less than 10%,[21] while fragments smaller than 3 kb are shared at a percentage above 25%.[2, 3] However, all bands apparently shared may not actually be the result of hybridization to the same piece of DNA from the same chromosomal locus. Instead, indistinguishable bands from different individuals could arise from fortuitous comigrations of nonallelic DNA fragments of identical sizes.[21]

Mutation Rates

The rate at which new bands appear in the population as a result of mutation does not play a role in cases of direct comparison between two samples from the same person. However, the mutation rate does need to be considered when determining family relationships. To arrive at the mutation rate of the multilocus probes 33.6 and 33.15, 27 documented paternity trios were studied. Only one of 240 bands counted in the children could not be assigned to either parent in the trio, resulting in a calculated mutation rate of 0.004.[2]

Statistical Evaluation of Data

The statistic derived for most serology testing depends on calculations made using observed frequencies for blood types and isozymes. Such a statistic has not been used with the 33.6 and 33.15 probes because, as described above, the band frequencies at any one position do not readily translate into allele frequencies for the multilocus probes. For this reason, the statistic derived for the data using the 33.6 and 33.15 probes must consider the likelihood that two unrelated individuals will produce a band of the same size. As discussed earlier, this percent band share has been experimentally determined to be less than 25% for both of the multilocus probes[2, 11, 21] (Garner et al, unpublished results, 1988) in several ethnic groups. As a conservative measure, a 25% band share is used in the calculations. If the observed percent band share between the parents is higher than 25% in a paternity case, this higher percentage is used in the calculations.

To determine the probability that two individuals would produce the same DNA pattern the following formula is used:

$$\text{Equation 1.} \quad P = 1/.25^{n}$$

In this equation, n is the total number of bands seen with the two probes and P is the probability of identical banding patterns.[8, 21] If $n = 30$ (an average number observed in actual casework), the probability of two individuals producing the same DNA banding patterns by chance would be 1 in 1.2×10^{18}. This infers that 1.2×10^{18} people would have to be tested before two people (except identical twins) with identical banding patterns would be located. This number is greater than the total number of people alive today (approximately 5.2×10^{9}) and is the basis for the claim that DNA fingerprinting is individual-specific. In determining paternity of a child, n is equal to the total number of bands observed in the child's DNA fingerprint which did not originate from the mother.

Legal Acceptance of Results

Results produced using the multilocus probes 33.6 and 33.15 have been used in both the U.K. and the U.S. court systems. In the U.K. they have been used to resolve immigration disputes,[8] rape, and homicide cases.[22] In the U.S., multilocus probe testing has been largely confined to paternity testing. Multilocus DNA fingerprint test results have been allowed in a criminal paternity case in North Carolina. After 1 year, no civil paternity cases have been to trial to challenge the DNA results. Many paternity suits have been resolved out of court after the alleged father acknowledged his responsibility on the basis of the DNA fingerprint test results.

SINGLE LOCUS PROBES

Introduction

Most DNA probes used for identification are single locus probes.[23–25] The primary difference between single locus and multilocus probes is that a single locus probe hybridizes to a specific, known location on a single chromosome. Each single locus probe will produce only one or two bands per individual. Individuals in which the DNA fragments from each chromosome in the chromosome pair are the same size are termed homozygotes. Individuals with two bands are termed heterozygotes, because the DNA fragments which result from each chromosome in a pair are of different lengths. The major advantages to using single locus probes rather than multilocus probes in forensic cases are that: (1) smaller quantities of DNA can be examined; (2) it is possible to interpret the banding patterns obtained from mixed stains; (3) interpretation of the banding patterns is easier; and (4) the probability of identification can be calculated using traditional models of population genetics.

Probe Isolation

The single locus probes discussed here were derived from the multilocus probes 33.6 and 33.15. The four probes used most commonly in our laboratory are designated MS1, MS31, MS43, and pλg3. The DNA fragment which comprises the insert of pλg3 was derived from the multilocus probe 33.15.[5] To isolate the fragment, human genomic DNA was digested with the restriction enzyme *Sau*3A and electrophoresed. Fragments of approximately 8.3 kb in length were isolated from the gel using electroelution. These fragments were then screened, after cloning into a lambda vector using 33.15 as a probe. The insert in λg3 was then isolated from one of four clones which hybridized to the 33.15 probe.

The remaining single locus probes were isolated by screening a lambda library of human genomic DNA pooled from 40 individuals with the 33.6 and 33.15 multilocus probes. Ten lambda constructs were isolated which hybridized to the multilocus probes. Further studies to investigate both the degree of heterozygosity and polymorphism of these constructs produced the final list of MS1, MS31, MS43, MS8, and MS32 probes. MS8 and MS43 were derived from 33.6, while the other three probes were isolated using 33.15.[6]

Hybridization Conditions

Prehybridization and hybridization conditions for single locus probes are described in Smith et al (*J. Forensic Sci,* in press). The lower salt concentration and higher temperature used with the single locus probes reduces the likelihood that these DNA probes will hybridize to sequences on the membrane which are not highly complementary.

Heterozygosity, Chromosome Assignment, and Size Range of Fragments

One important characteristic of a single locus probe is the degree of heterozygosity observed in the population. Probes with low heterozygosity will be less useful for identification purposes because many people will exhibit only a single, indistinguishable band. The degree of heterozygosity of the four single locus probes developed by Wong et al[5,6] was estimated at 98%, 99%, 94%, and 97% for MS1, MS31,

MS43, and pλg3, respectively. These values were determined for a northern European population.

As the number of different alleles detected by a probe increases, the discriminatory power of that probe increases. Using the single locus probes MS1, MS31, MS43, and pλg3, we have resolved between 75 and 150 alleles (i.e. different-sized bands) for each probe. This number agrees well with the estimates made by Wong et al.[6] These probes hybridize to alleles in the 2 to 24 kb size range.[6]

The single locus probes have been mapped to specific chromosomes and assigned human gene workshop symbols. The designations are D1S7, D7S21, D12S11, and D7S22 for MS1, MS31, MS43, and pλg3, respectively.[6]

Sample Size Required

The four single locus probes are able to detect DNA at levels approximately one-tenth of that required by the multilocus probes 33.6 and 33.15. This means that 20 to 50 ng of genomic DNA can produce a visible banding pattern.

The average-sized blood stain required for single locus probe (SLP) analysis is slightly smaller than a dime. The actual size of a stain needed to extract 20 to 50 ng of genomic DNA varies according to the white blood cell count of the individual and the permeability of the substrate material upon which the blood is found. Laboratory studies have repeatedly produced banding patterns from as little as 2 to 3 μl of whole blood. This would translate into a stain on white cotton of about the size of half a pencil eraser.[13]

The number of sperm in a semen stain is the determining factor for DNA testing of this fluid. Here, the average stain for which a banding pattern can be obtained is about half the size of a dime. Controlled studies have shown that 1 μl or less of semen can produce a visible banding pattern.[13]

The number of hair roots needed to isolate sufficient DNA to produce a banding pattern varies with the size and growth stage of the root. Banding patterns have been produced from single hair roots from all body areas using pulled or plucked hairs,[13] but it should be stressed that not all single hair roots will contain sufficient DNA to produce a banding pattern with the single locus probes.

The amount of tissue (i.e. organs, bone, skin) required to produce a banding pattern with the single locus probes is quite small. Bone fragments as small as 1 cm^3 usually will yield enough DNA for several tests. Soft tissue in quantities as small as 0.2 to 1.0 g should yield sufficient DNA if the tissue is not badly decomposed.

Mixed Stains

One of the great advantages of single locus probes is the ability to resolve stains resulting from the mixture of more than one individual's body fluids. For example, a panel or 'cocktail' of single locus probes can be used to positively identify all individuals involved in a multiple rape by comparing the evidentiary banding pattern with control samples from the suspects and the victim. By the sequential use of each single locus probe, the total number of people involved in the rape can be estimated, and each person's DNA banding pattern can be identified. The number of people involved can be estimated even without control samples, since it is known that each single locus probe will produce at most two bands per individual.

Several studies have been conducted to determine the levels at which a contaminating or minor constituent of a mixed stain could be detected. The first study used blood from two individuals. The blood of the first individual was kept constant, while progressively lower amounts of the second individual's blood were added. The lowest level at which this second blood sample could be detected was at 0.5% of the total sample.[13] A second study investigated the likelihood of identifying one mismatched hair when mixed with hairs from a second individual. Identification was routinely possible with as many as 10 hair roots from the second individual.[13]

Mutation Rates of the Four Probes

The mutation of alleles to new sizes is not considered when a direct comparison of two samples from the same individual is being performed. However, the mutation rate should be considered when parentage is being determined. Mutation of a single band in an offspring may result in a non-match between parent and offspring. For this reason, it is important to know the mutation rates of the probes being used, so that if there is a single mismatched band between child and either of the parents, a likelihood of this band being the result of an independent mutation in the child can be estimated. The mutation rates of the four probes MS1, MS31, MS43, and pλg3 have been estimated using known families by Jeffreys et al[1] and determining the number of unassigned bands which were observed with each of the four probes. These values are approximately 5%, 0.7%, 0.15%, and 0.3% for MS1, MS31, MS43, and pλg3, respectively.[1]

Quality Control of the Probes

Quality control of the single locus DNA probes requires that the same sample source give an identical banding pattern over time. Additionally, the purity of the DNA templates used to synthesize the probes themselves are checked through hybridization of the probe synthesized from the template to bacterial genomic DNA. The sensitivity levels of the probes are evaluated with each new lot, by hybridization to membranes with known amounts of DNA in a fashion similar to the quality control of the multilocus probes.

Methods of Use

Single locus probes can be used in two different ways: as a cocktail, or one at a time. A great deal of information can be obtained relatively quickly when the probes are combined in a cocktail. In cases where the single locus probes are being used to determine family relationships (when insufficient DNA is present for multilocus testing), there are several bands upon which to base the analysis so that a more rapid first assessment can be made. Single locus probes may be used individually also, by sequential hybridizations, exposures, and membrane strippings. This method of testing determines allelism at each locus, identifies which bands are inherited from each parent in parentage testing, and determines which probe produces each band in the banding pattern in direct comparison cases.

Population Data Bases

Like classical blood grouping, the analysis of results using single locus DNA probes requires the preparation of a population data base. Compilation of these data is a multi-step process. First, samples are obtained from unrelated individuals. DNA must be isolated from each sample and carried through the entire procedure, including restriction digestion, electrophoresis, and Southern blotting, hybridization with the desired probe, exposure of the nylon membrane to x-ray film, and analysis of the resulting data. Allele sizes are calculated using the equations of Elder and Southern.[26] The allele frequencies are stored in data bases corresponding to the probe and the racial group which produced the data. Data bases are being compiled on U.S. white, U.S. black, U.S. Oriental, U.S. Hispanic, U.S. Indian, northern European white, Near East Indian, and West Indian black populations.

Interpretation of Results

Interpretation of autoradiographs from single locus probe hybridizations is based on straightforward examination. In identity cases which directly compare two or more evidentiary samples, the banding patterns are measured and compared between the known and unknown samples. If all the bands in the known lane are present in the same position as those in the lane from the unknown, the conclusion that the DNA banding patterns match is made (Fig 3–1,A).

In cases when bands in the known sample are absent in the unknown sample (Fig 3–1,B), or when the unknown sample contains more bands than the known lane (Fig 3–1,C), additional factors must be considered. The first case (see Fig 3–1,B) can be explained by partial degradation of the starting DNA. This explanation is correct only if the band(s) missing in the unknown sample is of the highest molecular weight present in the known sample. In terms of molecular mechanisms, the average size of the fragments in the partially degraded DNA may be smaller than the size of the high molecular weight fragment present in intact DNA from the known sample. In such cases, the known banding pattern is reported to contain the banding pattern of the unknown. When all high molecular weight bands are present in the unknown sample and only lower molecular weight bands are missing, the differences in the banding patterns cannot be explained by partial degradation of the DNA from the unknown samples (see Fig 3–1,D).

The banding pattern from the unknown sample may contain more bands than the control sample. This may be due to the presence of more than one individual's DNA in the unknown sample (see Fig 3–1,C). Analysis of such banding patterns is

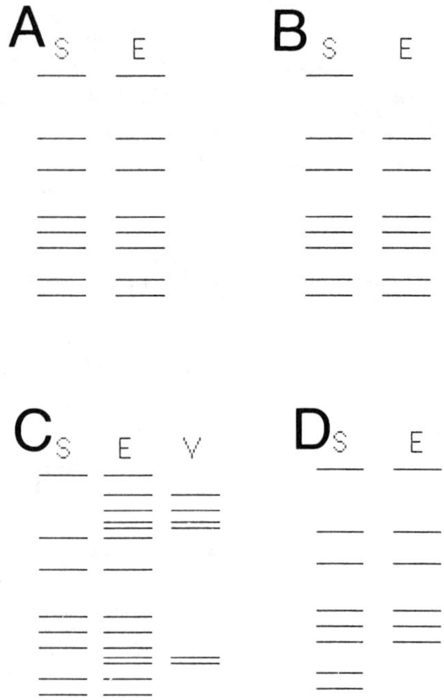

FIG 3–1.
Single locus cocktail banding examples. *V* = victim, *E* = evidence, *S* = suspect.

accomplished easily when the single locus probes are used sequentially. The one or two bands present in the known sample should be matched by corresponding bands in the lane from the unknown sample. An exclusion would be reported if the missing band(s) in the unknown sample could not be the result of degradation. If all bands in the known sample match, it is reported that the banding pattern from the unknown sample contains the banding pattern from the known sample.

Statistical Evaluation of Data

There are two different methods of calculating the frequency of a banding pattern in a population, depending upon whether the probes were used individually or as a cocktail. Because the four single locus probes are independently inherited (i.e., unlinked loci),[6] analysis is possible using either the combined or individual data measured. Both methods rely on counting bands and estimating the allele frequencies of those bands in a population.

The analysis of the data is dependent upon the resolution of the gel system being used. Studies measuring the accuracy of DNA fragment sizing have determined that band size resolution varies according to the greater than 20 kb fragments (R. Cotton et al, unpublished results, 1988). These resolution studies allow deviation estimates of the calculated fragment size from the actual fragment size. Fragment sizes are calculated using the algorithm described by Elder and Southern.[26]

The size of each fragment is determined in order to perform statistical analysis of allele frequencies for the single locus probes. The allele frequency of this fragment in the appropriate ethnic population is determined for each of the probes used in the cocktail and allele frequencies are summed as described below:

$$\text{Equation 2.} \quad \text{Band frequency} = \sum_{i=1}^{i=n} (\text{frequency with probe})_i$$

In this formula, n is the total number of probes used. The overall frequency for the cocktail generated banding pattern is calculated by computing the product of the band frequencies from Equation 2 as shown in Equation 3.

$$\text{Equation 3.} \quad 1/\text{Frequency} = \prod_{i=1}^{i=n} (\text{Band Frequency})_i$$

Here, n is the total number of bands observed. Overall frequencies for SLP cocktail banding patterns have been observed to vary from 1 in several thousand to 1 in several hundred million.

Data analysis for individual single locus probes is performed using the classical population genetics theory of Hardy-Weinberg in the same manner in which blood groups and enzyme frequencies are derived. The Hardy-Weinberg equation ($p^2 + 2pq + q^2 = 1$) is used to describe the frequency of a particular genotype in a population when the conditions of random mating, negligible mutation, migration, generational overlap, and an infinitely large population are met. The term of this equation that deals with heterozygotes is 2pq, where p and q are the frequencies of the two alleles. Since the heterozygosity of the single locus probes previously described is known to be high,[6] the 2pq term of the equation is used for all calculations. Individual single locus probes are used to generate a probability statistic based on the frequency of a phenotype in a population. The heterozygosity value (2pq) for the bands is calculated for each probe. Multiplying the heterozygosity values from the four probes and taking the inverse gives an estimate of the likelihood that two individuals would have the same DNA banding pattern. The equations for calculations when the single locus probes are used sequentially are shown below.

$$\text{Equation 4.} \quad p, q = \sum_{i=B-S}^{i=B+S} (\text{allele frequency})_i$$

B is the calculated fragment size, S is the resolution interval at that size as discussed above, and p and q are the frequencies of the DNA fragments.

$$\text{Equation 5.} \quad \text{Pattern frequency} = 2pq$$

If only 1 band was observed $q = 1$.

$$\text{Equation 6.} \quad 1/\text{Frequency} = \prod_{i=1}^{i=n} (\text{pattern frequency})_i$$

In these equations, n is the total number of probes used. The results produced using Equation 6 have been observed to vary between 1 in several hundred million to 1 in several trillion, depending on the alleles in question.

Legal Acceptance of Results

Test results using the Jeffreys single locus probes have been presented at trial in criminal cases in several states, including Maryland, Colorado, Florida, Texas, Ohio, Wisconsin, Michigan, Mississippi, Iowa, North Carolina, and Virginia. Additionally, results of DNA tests have been presented in Frye hearings in Arizona, New York, Indiana, Colorado, and Maryland. In each of these states, testimony as to the comparison of the DNA banding patterns between the unknown and known samples was accepted by the courts.

SUMMARY

The Jeffreys multilocus and single locus probes have been subjected to numerous validation experiments to demonstrate their effectiveness and reliability for forensic casework. The use of DNA probes in forensic testing opens new horizons for both the legal and scientific communities as never-before realized powers of identification become possible. Early indications point toward a general acceptance of DNA testing as a new and powerful tool in the resolution of criminal and paternity cases. As the technology progresses, it is likely that even greater sensitivity and discriminatory power will become available to the forensic scientist through DNA analysis.

REFERENCES

1. Jeffreys AJ, Royle NJ, Wilson V, et al: Spontaneous mutation rates to new length alleles at tandem-repetitive hypervariable loci in human DNA. *Nature* 1988; 332:278–281.
2. Jeffreys AJ, Wilson V, Thein SL: Hypervariable "minisatellite" regions in human DNA. *Nature* 1985; 314:67–73.
3. Jeffreys AJ, Wilson V, Thein SL: Individual specific "fingerprints" of human DNA. *Nature* 1985; 316:76–79.
4. Jeffreys AJ, Wilson V, Thein SL, et al: DNA "fingerprints" and segregation analysis of multiple markers in human pedigrees. *Am J Hum Genet* 1986; 39:11–24.
5. Wong Z, Wilson V, Jeffreys AJ, et al: Cloning a selected fragment from a human DNA "fingerprint": Isolation of an extremely polymorphic minisatellite. *Nucleic Acids Res* 1986; 14:4605–4616.

6. Wong Z, Wilson V, Patel I, et al: Characterization of a panel of highly variable minisatellites cloned from human DNA. *Ann Hum Genet* 1987; 51:269–288.
7. Odelberg SJ, Demers DB, Westin EH, et al: Establishing paternity using minisatellite DNA probes when the putative father is unavailable for testing. *J Forensic Sci* 1988; 33:921–928.
8. Jeffreys AJ, Brookfield JFY, Semeonoff R: Positive identification of an immigration test-case using human DNA fingerprints. *Nature* 1985; 317:818–819.
9. Rubenstein KR, Tonelli LA, Anderson MB, et al: Use of DNA "fingerprints" for identity determination: Comparison to traditional paternity testing methods-II. *J Forensic Sci*, in press.
10. Tonelli LA, Rubenstein KR, Anderson MB, et al: Use of DNA "fingerprints" for identity determination: Comparison to traditional paternity testing methods-I. *J Forensic Sci*, in press.
11. Garner DD, Herrin GL, Cotton RW, et al: Use of DNA "fingerprints" for identity determination: Reproducibility of the DNA fingerprinting[SM] technology. *J Forensic Sci*, in press.
12. Gill P, Jeffreys AJ, Werrett DJ: Forensic application of DNA 'fingerprints'. *Nature* 1985; 318:577–579.
13. Garner DD, Herrin G, Bergen A, et al: Increased sensitivity using the Jeffreys single-locus DNA probes. Abstracts of the 40th Annual Meeting of the American Academy of Forensic Sciences, 1988.
14. McNally L, Schaler R, Baird M, et al: Evaluation of DNA isolated from bloodstains exposed to UV light, heat, humidity and soil contamination. *J Forensic Sci*, in press.
15. Kuo M, Bashinski J, Vukovich K, et al: {*California Association of Crime Laboratory Directors*} DNA Committee Report #6, 1988.
16. McCabe ERB, Huang S, Seltzer WK, et al: DNA microextraction from dried blood spots on filter paper blotters: Potential applications to newborn screening. *Hum Genet* 1987; 75:213–216.
17. Kanter E, Baird M, Shaler R, et al: Analysis of restriction fragment length polymorphisms in deoxyribonucleic acid (DNA) recovered from dried blood stains. *J Forensic Sci* 1986; 31:403–408.
18. Baird M, Kanter E, Shaler R, et al: Application of DNA polymorphisms to the forensic examination of dried blood stains. *Adv Forensic Haemogenetics* 1986; 1:351–355.
19. Madisen L, Hoar DI, Holroyd CD, et al: DNA banking: The effects of storage of blood and isolated DNA on the integrity of DNA. *Am J Med Genet* 1987; 27:379–390.
20. Gill P, Lygo JE, Fowler SJ, et al: An evaluation of DNA fingerprinting for forensic purposes. *Electrophoresis* 1987; 8:38–44.

21. Jeffreys AJ: Highly variable minisatellites and DNA fingerprints. *Biochem Soc Trans* 1987; 15:309–317.
22. Schmitz A: Murder on Black Pad. *Hippocrates* Jan/Feb, 1988, 48–58.
23. Balazs I, Baird ML, Wexler K, et al: Characterization of the polymorphic DNA fragments detected with a new probe derived from the D14S1 locus. *Am J Hum Genet* 1986; 39:A229.
24. Wyman AR, White R: A highly polymorphic locus in human DNA. *Proc Natl Acad Sci USA* 1980; 77:6754–6758.
25. Nakamura Y, Leppert M, O'Connell P, et al: Variable number of tandem repeat (VNTR) markers for human gene mapping. *Science* 1987; 235:1616–1622.
26. Elder JK, Southern EM: Computer-aided analysis of one dimensional restriction fragment gels, in Bishop MJ, Rawlings CJ (eds): *Nucleic Acid and Protein Sequence Analysis: A Practical Approach*. Oxford, IRL Press, 1987, pp 165–172.

Chapter 4

Examination of Forensic Biological Evidence by DNA Print Analysis

Michael L. Baird, Ph.D.
Ivan Balazs, Ph.D.
Kevin McElfresh, Ph.D.

It is now possible to examine biological evidence in ways which allow one to identify the specific individual from whom it came. Traditional testing, including blood typing, HLA typing, and enzyme or protein typing, typically produces a level of identification of one in a few hundred, thus leaving the possible identification of many individuals with the same genetic characteristics. Advances in science now allow the analysis of the genetic material itself, deoxyribonucleic acid (DNA). All inherited differences, such as eye color, skin color, hair color, blood type, Rh type, PGM type, and HLA type, have their origins within the DNA molecule. Much of the DNA within different individuals is similar, resulting in similar gene products which make it possible to perform blood transfusions and organ transplantations with proper matching. There are also regions within the DNA which vary highly between individuals. Because everyone's DNA is different (except for that of identical twins), we are able to examine regions within it with probes ("identity genes"), and generate patterns which are characteristic of the person from whom the DNA came. An estimate of the frequency of occurrence of a person's DNA-PRINT pattern in a given population comes from an extrapolation from a data base. When the frequency of the occurrence of a combination of patterns exceeds that of the population, this provides overwhelming evidence that the pattern is individualistic.

SCIENTIFIC BACKGROUND

The scientific knowledge that currently forms the basis for DNA identity testing has accumulated since the late 19th century. Technological advances that have occurred during the last 25 years enable the DNA identity test to be performed efficiently and accurately. Biological research in the early 19th century resulted in the development of light microscopes and techniques for fixing and staining living tissues, allowing scientists to see into the cell and identify structures. With this ability, scientists were able to begin to understand how life reproduces itself, and to identify characteristics which are inherited. With the light microscope, it was possible to observe that every cell results from the growth and division of a parental cell into two daughter cells, and that every cell has within it a nucleus. By the 1860s, chromosomes had been identified as rod-like bodies inside the nucleus. The individual chromosomes within a cell could be distinguished by their shape and size and, for any given species, the number of chromosomes per cell was a constant, even number.

In 1865, the Austrian monk Gregor Mendel recorded his observations about the inheritance of such characteristics as color and shape in pea plants. He showed that these characteristics were controlled by hereditary factors, later called genes, and he defined laws of inheritance that bear his name. Mendel's first law, the principle of segregation, described how different forms of a characteristic (gene) are inherited such that an offspring is composed of characteristics from each parent. Mendel's second law, the principle of independent assortment, describes how characteristics (genes) which are on separate chromosomes are inherited independently. These observations and principles helped to establish the foundation of genetics.

The substance now known as deoxyribonucleic acid (DNA) was discovered in 1869 by the Swiss scientist Frederick Miescher. Using a DNA-specific purple dye which bears his name, in the 1920s the German chemist Robert Feulgen showed that DNA is found as a major component of the nucleus and is associated with the chromosomes. By 1944, through research conducted by Oswald Avery and colleagues of Rockefeller University in New York, it became known and broadly accepted that DNA is indeed the basic genetic material. This was confirmed by research announced in 1952 by Alfred Hershey and Martha Chase of Cold Spring Harbor, New York.

Meanwhile, physical chemists and x-ray crystallographers in the United States and Europe were studying the size and shape of the DNA molecule, and the spatial relationship of the atoms within it. Crystallographic analysis of DNA was begun in 1949 at Kings College, London, by physicists Maurice Wilkins and Rosalind Franklin, who produced remarkably detailed x-ray pictures of the DNA molecule. In the spring of 1953, the American scientist James Watson and the British scientist Francis Crick, working together at Cambridge University in England, announced their discovery that the structure of DNA is a double helix in which two chains of nucleotides (the building blocks of DNA) running in opposite directions, are held together by hydrogen bonds (a weak form of chemical bond) between pairs of centrally located bases. Each nucleotide contains a phosphate group, a sugar, and either a purine or a pyrimidine base (a ringed molecule containing carbon, nitrogen, and hydrogen). The four bases, adenine, guanine, thymine, and cytosine, are abbreviated using their first letter to make up the four-letter DNA alphabet, A, G, T, C. Furthermore, the adenine and thymine bases will only pair with one another and the guanine and cytosine bases will only pair with one another. Thus, in the double helix, adenine (A) is always hydrogen bonded to thymine (T), while guanine (G) is always hydrogen bonded to cytosine (C). Thus, the overall structure of DNA is that of a ladder, with the rungs of the ladder being formed by the base pairs. Accordingly, if the sequence of one half (chain) of the double helix is known, the other half (chain) can be determined from the base pairing principle. The sequence G-A-T-T-C-C-G will match (by complementary base pairing) the sequence C-T-A-A-G-G-C. The discovery of the structure of DNA made by Watson and Crick is recognized as one of the major scientific advances of the 20th century and these researchers were awarded the Nobel Prize for their efforts. In the years following the discovery of the structure of DNA, much effort has been directed toward gaining an understanding of the information present in the double helix. To this end, the initial experiments addressed specific genetic defects, and these now are applied to forensic identification.

In order for new scientific evidence to be introduced into testimony in a court trial, a number of criteria must be established. The decision made in the Frye case set the standard for the admission of novel scientific evidence. This decision calls for the general acceptance by the scientific community of the principles upon which the testing is based, plus the demonstration that the technique is reliable. As of this writing, DNA identification evidence has been introduced in 18 states in the U.S. by three different groups. One case from Florida has been reviewed and affirmed by an appellate court. Frye hearings have been held for most of the cases, and in no case has the DNA evidence not been allowed.

In order to show the acceptance and reliability of the DNA-PRINT test, both the scientific method and the laboratory performing the testing must be validated. The scientific method is validated in a number of ways. First, the protocol must be published in peer-reviewed journals by at least two different groups. This has been done for the DNA test by hundreds of publications by scientists around the world. The publication of Southern[1] in 1975 established the so-called "Southern blot" technology for the analysis of DNA. This publication is the cornerstone upon which all DNA testing is built. A review of the Citation Index shows that this article has been referenced thousands of times in other publications. The first report of a difference visualized at the DNA level by the Southern blot technology was by Kan and Dozy in 1978.[2] In this article, they described a DNA polymorphism associated with sickle cell anemia. DNA was cut with the restriction enzyme Hpa 1, separated by agarose gel electrophoresis, transferred by the Southern blot procedure, and hybridized with a DNA probe specific for the beta globin gene. When the autoradiograph was analyzed, DNA fragments of 7.6 kb and/or 13.0 kb (kilobase pairs) were observed. Individuals containing two normal beta globin genes most often had a 7.6 kb fragment (band), indicating that both number 11 chromosomes contained normal B^A genes. Individuals with two sickle cell anemia genes most often had only a 13.0 kb fragment, indicating that both number 11 chromosomes contained abnormal B^S genes (homozygous). Individuals with non-clinically severe sickle cell anemia trait often displayed both a 7.6 kb fragment and a 13.0 kb fragment (heterozygous), indicating that the beta globin genes on the two number 11 chromosomes were different. One chromosome 11 contained a normal B^A globin gene and the other chromosome 11 contained an abnormal sickle cell anemia B^S gene. With this information, it became possible to perform prenatal diagnosis for sickle cell anemia in cases in which each parent had sickle cell trait, and each was informative (heterozygous). In this situation, there is a 25% chance that the child will have sickle cell anemia. This type of testing required a pedigree analysis of other family members to help establish the linkage of the B^s gene with a specific fragment size. Because the change at the DNA level which causes the Hpa 1 polymorphism on the sickle cell anemia chromosome does not cause the sickle cell anemia gene defect, results are only suggestive of the genotype (the genes present). This same approach has been used for the diagnosis of a number of genetic diseases.[3] When this test is performed prenatally in cases in which the parents are both carriers, the genotype of the developing fetus can be determined, and therapeutic measures can be taken if the fetus is determined to be affected. The same protocol is used for the DNA identity test.

The probes that are used to examine polymorphic loci for the identity test also must be shown to obey the laws of genetics. This includes a demonstration of both Mendelian inheritance and adherence to the Hardy-Weinberg equilibrium. Mendelian inheritance, named after the published observations of the Austrian Monk Gregor Mendel in 1863, is shown by pedigree studies. Mendel observed the inheritance of color and shape characteristics in pea plants and showed how he could numerically predict the occurrence of specific characteristics in subsequent generations. His observations showed that traits assort independently of each other and segregate independently in subsequent generations. The probes used for the DNA-PRINT test have been mapped to specific regions on different chromosomes (single locus) and have been arranged relative to other known genes by linkage studies. Each DNA probe has been given a locus designation by the Human Gene Mapping Workshop which meets every 2 years. By tracing a DNA pattern through a three-generation pedigree, one with both sets of grandparents, parents, and offspring, estimates of recombination, mutation, and linkage can be obtained. Estimates of the Hardy-Weinberg equilibrium are derived from the same data. If there is no selective advantage to the presence of a particular DNA fragment, the occurrence of patterns is predictable according to the formula $p^2 + 2pq + q^2 = 1$, where p is the frequency of gene 1 and q is the frequency of gene 2. Stated in this form, the frequency of an individual with two copies of the same gene (homozygous) is determined by multiplying the frequency of the gene by itself. The frequency of individuals with both genes (heterozygous) is determined by multiplying the frequency of the two genes together, then multiplying by 2. If we let p be the frequency of gene A at 40%, and q be the frequency of gene B at 60%, then:

$$p^2 + 2pq + q^2 = (0.4)^2 + 2\,(0.4)\,(0.6) + (0.6)^2 = 0.16 + 0.48 + 0.36 = 1 = AA + 2AB + BB.$$

	A	B
A	AA	AB
B	BA	BB

Using the same formulation, the frequency of a pattern using DNA identity probes is defined as the product of 2 times each gene (DNA fragment) making up the pattern. Because most of the DNA probes which are used for determining identity are from regions of the DNA which do not code for any known function, it is unlikely that there is any selective advantage for a particular DNA fragment. This is perhaps why these regions have evolved into such a large number of different forms (alleles).

ADMISSIBILITY CRITERIA

In order for scientific evidence to be admissible in court, it is also essential to demonstrate that a given test is applicable to the sample types likely to be tested. Published studies exist for the analysis of DNA from liquid blood and dried blood,[4] semen, dried semen, and tissues.[5] The DNA pattern has been shown to be the same in different tissue sources taken from the same person. Pedigree studies have demonstrated that patterns generated with single locus probes are not likely to change over time. Tests of the effect of the environment on the integrity of DNA show that under laboratory-generated conditions of heat, humidity, or ultraviolet light, no adverse effects occur on the proper DNA patterns.[6] In addition, the substrate upon which blood and semen were deposited has no effect on obtaining the correct DNA pattern.[7] The major reason for not being able to obtain a DNA pattern from a stain with an adequate number of nucleated cells is bacterial or fungal contamination. If a sample remains in a moist environment after it is deposited, bacteria and/or fungi can grow, using the biological material as a food source. The DNA in these cells is thus susceptible to being broken down (degraded) by this process.

It is important to look for degraded DNA in specimens isolated from biological material to determine if bacterial or fungal action is evident. As long as there is undegraded (high molecular weight) DNA greater than 20 kb, the chances of obtaining a DNA-PRINT are good, because the presence of some degraded DNA does not affect the true pattern. However, it has been observed that as DNA becomes more and more degraded, the patterns of larger-sized DNA fragments are preferentially lost. Thus, from a sample of DNA that is partially degraded, it is possible to obtain results with some DNA probes but not with others, by virtue of the size range of fragments identified by the probes.

It is also important to identify any possible contribution of bacterial or fungal DNA fragments to the overall pattern. All bands must be accounted for in order to interpret the results. It has been reported that some bacterial sequences can react with DNA probes used for identification under low stringency hybridization. This reaction can be with the sequence which recognizes the polymorphism, or with the vector (plasmid) used to propagate the probe. The use of a DNA probe(s) which recognizes both bacterial DNA and plasmid DNA sequences helps to identify contaminating DNA sequences. In testing done at the Lifecodes Corporation, a DNA probe derived from the bacteria *Escherichia coli* that recognizes the ribosomal gene is used to identify the presence of bacterial DNA. Ribosomal DNA sequences code for the production of part of the ribosomes, the structures necessary for growth and production of bacterial proteins. Since the ribosomal genes have been shown to be conserved throughout most bacteria, this probe reacts with a wide variety of different bacteria. The bacterial DNA probe is not used as an insert, as are other DNA probes for identity, but is used with the vector (plasmid) present. Plasmids are autonomously replicating pieces of DNA which can reside in bacteria and can confer selective advantages, such as genes for resistance to antibiotics. Because plasmids modified for laboratory procedures are used routinely in recombinant DNA techniques, these sequences can react with plasmid sequences in DNA that is isolated from bacterial contaminated samples. Again, the identification of such sequences is essential for the final analysis. If the situation occurs in which a DNA fragment appears in the identical position with both an identity probe and a bacterial probe, then the results of that identity probe cannot be used. For example, if a pattern of two fragments of 4.43 kb and 3.52 kb was seen with an identity probe, and one fragment of 4.43 kb was seen with the bacterial/plasmid probe, it would be difficult to determine whether the true pattern for the identity probe was one or two bands. If plasmid contamination is evident, it usually is confined to a single region of the gel, commonly in the smaller size range, below 5.0 kb. It is also possible to introduce plasmid contamination into DNA preparations through solutions or pipetting devices. Therefore, it is important to keep these functions separate and to utilize the whole size range of DNA fragments for generating a pattern, so that even if one probe cannot be used, other probes which recognize different size classes can be used.

The laboratory performing the testing also must be shown to be valid before the introduction of results at trial. First, the scientific personnel present in the laboratory must be shown to possess the training and background necessary to conduct the tests and analyze the results. Because the recombinant DNA techniques currently employed are taught as part of college-level courses, most experienced laboratory personnel will hold at least a bachelor's-level degree. Since the interpretation of the results requires a background not only in recombinant DNA techniques, but also in population genetics and statistical analysis, the laboratory employee who performs this function will probably hold a doctorate-level degree.

The laboratory also must have a quality control program in place to ensure that the testing is administered correctly and to maximize the success rate. All reagents should be checked for conductivity (salt concentration) and pH level (acid/base), and an aliquot should be used on control samples before it is released for general consumption. All purchased components (enzyme, agarose, nucleotides) should be tested with known controls to ensure proper quality. The integrity of DNA that is isolated for analysis should be visually checked with 1% of the sample as undigested DNA by electrophoresis on a yield gel. Samples with no high molecular weight DNA visible on a yield gel are not likely to yield DNA-PRINT results, although they may be typed using the polymerase chain reaction (PCR) technique. The enzymatic digestion of high molecular weight DNA must be complete, because a partial digestion can lead to the presence of additional fragments of larger size than the true alleles (fragments). Commercially purchased enzymes should be checked by digestion of DNAs which produce known patterns. This can be accomplished by digestion of a bacterial, viral, or plasmid DNA which has been sequenced; that is, the linear order of nucleotides has been established. Thus, both the number and size of the fragments generated with a particular enzyme are known. It is also important to determine the activity of the commercially purchased enzyme. This is accomplished best by performing titration experiments, varying the enzyme to DNA ratio, and determining when a pattern consistent with partial digestion is observed. It should be noted also that genomic (total human) DNA may cut differently than bacterial, viral, or plasmid DNAs, and may require more units of enzyme to cut the same amount of DNA to completion. A unit of enzyme is defined as the amount of enzyme necessary to cut 1 μg of DNA in 1 hour in a 50 μl reaction at the appropriate temperature. All enzyme digestions should be performed using the conditions recommended by the manufacturer to eliminate cutting activity at sites other than the recognition site. Such minor activity, known as "star activity", can occur if salt and/or pH conditions are not optimal and can generate additional fragments smaller than the true alleles. Lastly, a control human DNA, for example a cultured cell line, should be tested with all new lots of enzyme and the hybridization pattern should be compared with previously generated patterns. This same DNA is included with all tests conducted on evidentiary samples and also helps to show that the proper sensitivity levels are maintained.

The completion of digestion can be checked by separating an aliquot (about 5%) of the digested DNA by electrophoresis, using a test gel. Visual examination after ethidium bromide staining allows one to determine whether the enzyme digestion appears complete. If a portion of the DNA remains in the high molecule weight region of the gel, relative to a control, the sample should be redigested by adding additional enzyme until the pattern appears consistent with complete digestion. The test gel DNA should be transferred to a nylon membrane. The test gel membrane can be tested to establish whether the unknown DNAs are of human origin or contain male DNA, and to confirm complete digestion by observing the presence of constant fragments in all DNA lanes.

Additional quality control steps are needed to ensure that the electrophoretic separation occurs correctly. A standard way by which to separate DNA by size is with agarose gel electrophoresis in a TAN buffer (40 mM Tris-HCl, pH 7.9; 20 mM sodium acetate; 2 mM EDTA). Under these conditions, the DNA fragments have a net negative charge and travel toward the position pole (cathode) when a direct electric current is applied across the gel. The distance that a fragment travels under these conditions is proportional to the log of the molecular weight. When plotted on semilog graph paper, a straight line should be observed over the size range one wishes to analyze for maximal resolution. This can be confirmed easily by the incorporation of a number of known size fragments into a single lane to act as a molecular size standard (ruler). This standard is also used to size the DNA fragments composing a pattern. In addition to checking an aliquot of new lots of agarose, a control DNA is included with each electrophoretic "run," and the pattern that is generated with each DNA probe system is checked. After electrophoresis is completed, the size-separated DNA fragments from the evidentiary material can be visualized as a smear with the fluorescent dye, ethidium bromide. A photograph of this can be taken to provide a permanent record. Visual examination of this picture helps to ensure that the electrophoretic separation was performed correctly. This is confirmed by the presence of visual size markers in addition to the overall pattern.

Another area where quality control is important involves the hybridization of the nylon membranes with labelled DNA probes. Whether one uses a radioactively labelled ^{32}P probe or a nonradioactively labelled probe, such as biotin, monitoring of the solutions and probe labelling are critical to maximize results. The solutions used for the prehybridization, hybridization, and washing need to be monitored before use. In addition, the temperature at which the hybridization and washing steps occur is critical for ensuring proper, high-quality results. The standard temperature for aqueous hybridization and washing is 65°C. Temperatures above this level can prevent a DNA probe from binding efficiently to its complementary sequences on the membrane, and lead to the appearance of faint bands or no bands at all. Temperatures below this level can cause a DNA probe to bind to other sequences on the filter which have partial homology with the probe, and result in the presence of additional bands. The addition of the control DNA on the filter allows one to confirm that these steps occurred properly.

If a filter is to be re-used to generate patterns with additional probes, one must ensure that the previous signal has been removed. Depending upon the membrane used, a typical procedure to remove ^{32}P–labelled probes relies on the action of a 50% formamide solution at 65°C. At this temperature, the probe is melted off the membrane in 30 to 60 minutes. This can be confirmed by exposing the stripped membrane to x-ray film. The membrane is then available for additional analysis. It is possible to leave the filter for 6 to 8 weeks to allow the ^{32}P-signal to decay (^{32}P half-life is 14.3 days). If a signal has not been completely removed after stripping, the residual bands can be accounted for by overlaying the x-ray films from the first and second probings. The only time this may cause problems is when the same-sized fragment was identified with two different probes.

Another important validation criteria for the laboratory is participation in blind trial proficiency programs. This allows an independent assessment of the performance of the laboratory personnel. One type of program involves the analysis of known samples for typing and possible matching. Also, the determination of fragment sizes should conform to the known resolution of the electrophoretic system being used. This can be accomplished by providing cultured cells from the American Tissue Culture Collection in Camden, New Jersey. Another way to accomplish this is through cultured cells from known pedigrees. Situations of paternity or non-paternity could be included in the testing program. In addition, calculations for identity or paternity should produce similar results, based on the standard deviation of the system.

The last important area for laboratory validation is the experience of the laboratory. The number of typings performed and the range of samples analyzed there are important issues. The requisite numbers are left to interpretation, but clearly the laboratory must demonstrate that a test can be completed successfully on the sample type undergoing analysis.

TEST PROCEDURE

The analysis of DNA from forensic samples is performed using the standard restriction fragment length polymorphism (RFLP) approach (Fig 4–1). The first step in the DNA analysis of a sample is the isolation of DNA from the sample. DNA is present in all cells that have a nucleus, which includes all cells except red blood cells. DNA is isolated from the white blood cells. There are about 5 picograms (trillionths of a gram) of DNA in each white cell nucleus and there are typically about 5 to 10 million white cells per 1 cc of liquid blood. Thus, it is possible to obtain a theoretical yield of 25 to 50 micrograms (millionths of a gram) from 1 cc of blood. A test can be performed with one microgram of DNA, although under ideal laboratory conditions 10 to 50 times less can be used routinely. DNA also can be isolated from blood stains as old as 7 years. The most critical factor in obtaining DNA from a blood stain appears

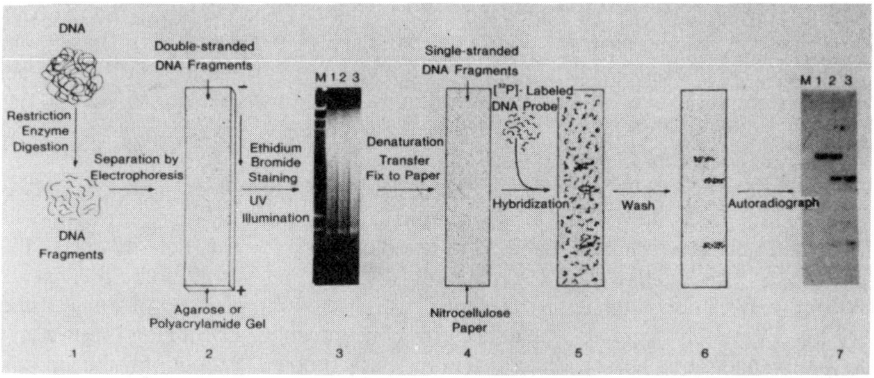

FIG 4–1.
Outline of the procedure used for restriction fragment length polymorphism (RFLP) analysis.

to be the storage conditions which occurred after the blood was deposited. The best DNA is obtained from stains which dried quickly. A stain left in a moist environment can grow bacteria which break down the cells, including the DNA. Initially, a blood stain can be soaked in an aqueous buffer to preserve the proteins and enzymes for analysis before the DNA is isolated.

DNA can be isolated also from sperm cells in liquid semen or semen stains. Sperm cells contain half as much DNA as do white cells. The sperm count from an ejaculant varies from a few million to hundreds of million per cc. Semen from a properly vasectomized male does not contain sperm and is not appropriate for analysis currently, although it may become possible in the future to analyze sloughed epithelial cells using amplification techniques. When DNA is isolated from a semen stain or vaginal swab, an initial procedure eliminates contaminating female epithelial cells by differential lysis. This ensures that the DNA pattern obtained is male-specific. This can be verified with a male-specific (Y-chromosome) probe to the DYZ1 locus.

DNA also can be isolated from other tissues including liver, heart, muscle, bone, dental pulp, spleen, kidney, and brain. From milligram amounts of tissue, large amounts of DNA can be isolated (as well as RNA in some cases). Studies have shown that DNA from different tissues obtained from the same person is the same at the loci used for identification. That is why it is possible, for example, to match a DNA pattern from the blood and semen of the same person. Therefore, even though each sperm within a person has a different organization of DNA due to recombination (crossing over) during the sperm production (meiosis), the overall pattern is that of the somatic cells.

The isolation procedure for DNA involves the treatment of a sample with a buffered aqueous solution (50 mM Tris, pH 7.0) containing a detergent SDS (sodium dodecylsulfate) and an enzyme (proteinase K) to break down the proteins that trap the DNA in the cells. Incubating this solution at 37°C to 65°C on a platform shaker and mixing it slowly for 2 to 4 hours is sufficient to liberate the DNA from the cells. The DNA is purified by extraction of the lysis solution with the organic solvents phenol and chloroform which partition the DNA into the aqueous phase, the proteins into the interphase, and the lipids into the organic phase. Once extracted, the aqueous DNA phase is dialyzed against 1 × TE (10 mM Tris, pH 7.0; 1 mM EDTA). The amount of nucleic acid isolated is determined by multiplying the concentration by the volume. The concentration is calculated by recording the optical density (O. D.) at 260 nm (ultraviolet wavelength light) using a spectrophotometer. A DNA concentration of 50 micrograms per 1 ml has an O. D. at 260 nm of 1.0.

An additional estimate of the amount of usable high molecular weight DNA is obtained by the analysis of 1% of the sample as undigested DNA by electrophoresis in a yield gel. After staining, usable DNA is indicated by material near the top of the gel greater than 20 kb. If the DNA is partially degraded, a test still can be performed, but more DNA needs to be analyzed than is indicated by the O. D. reading. If the DNA is completely degraded due to bacterial contamination, a DNA-PRINT test cannot be performed. The O. D. reading does not identify usable DNA, but only the amount of total nucleic acid (DNA plus RNA), and it also does not indicate if the DNA is of high molecular weight. The DNA in the yield gel can be hybridized with a human repeat sequence (Alu) to determine the amount of human DNA present.

The next step in the test is to cut the DNA with the restriction endonuclease Pst I. A restriction endonuclease is isolated from bacteria cells and cuts DNA at a specific sequence of bases. In bacteria cells, these enzymes play a role in protecting the bacteria from invasion by foreign DNA. The bacterial DNA is protected from the action of the enzyme by processes like methylation. The enzyme Pst I recognizes the sequence CTGCAG. The origin of the bacteria from which an enzyme is derived is coded into the enzyme name. For example, Pst I is from the bacteria *Providencia stuartii*. The first letter of the enzyme is the first letter of the genus name of the bacteria, and the second two letters of the enzyme are the first two letters of the species name. A wide variety of restriction endonucleases can be used to generate patterns that are useful for identification. Restriction enzymes can be purchased commercially from a number of different sources. Digestion conditions provided by the manufacturers should be followed to ensure complete digestion with no star activity (cutting by the enzyme at less specific sites). For example, Eco RI cuts at GAATTC, while Eco RI star cuts at AATT. One unit of an enzyme should cut 1 microgram of DNA to completion in 1 hour. Most enzymes work best at 37°C, although some require higher temperatures. Approximately five- to ten-fold excess units of Pst I are added routinely, with incubation performed for 2 hours at 37°C to ensure complete digestion.

After digestion, the DNA can be concentrated by precipitation, if necessary. Ammonium acetate is added to 0.3 M of final concentration, and then two volumes of absolute ethanol are added. After mixing thoroughly and cooling at −20°C, the DNA can be precipitated by centrifugation in a microcentrifuge. The DNA often can be seen as a whitish pellet on the wall or bottom of the microfuge tube. The ethanol is removed, and the DNA pellet is dried briefly and re-suspended in a small amount of buffer. An estimate of the extent of digestion can be obtained by the analysis of a portion of the sample (5%) by electrophoresis on a test gel. After staining, the pattern of DNA should look like a smear from the top of the gel to the bottom. If the proper pattern is not seen, additional enzyme can be added to redigest the sample until digestion appears complete. One must be careful not to add too much volume of enzyme solution to the DNA, because glycerol concentrations above 5% can cause some enzymes not to cut properly. Because most enzymes contain 50% glycerol for storage (this keeps the enzyme solution from freezing at −20°C), only 2.5 microliters of enzyme solution per 25 microliters of final volume can be added.

An analytical gel is run to separate the DNA fragments by electrophoresis for comparisons. A 30 cm, 0.9% agarose gel is used and is run for 65 hours at 17 volts to maximize resolution. After the DNA is transferred to a nylon membrane, a series of labelled DNA probes are applied (Table 4–1). The following DNA loci are presently examined by the DNA-PRINT test: D14S1,[8] DXYS14,[9] D17S79,[10] D2S44, D14S13,[11] 018S27, and HRAS.[12] In addition, labelled bacteriophage lambda and phiX174 are added during each hybridization to generate the size ladder. After hybridization in an aqueous solution at 65°C for 20 hours, the membranes are washed at 0.1 × SSC at 65°C, blotted dry, wrapped in plastic wrap, and placed in a cassette with x-ray film sandwiched between intensifying screens. The film is developed after an exposure of 1 to 7 days. An example of the results of the hybridization of a membrane with D2S44 plus DXYS14 is shown in Figure 4–2. The signal from hybridization can be removed by incubation of the membrane in a 50% formamide solution at 65°C for 45 minutes. The membrane is then ready for additional hybridizations. Alternatively, the signal from a hybridization can be allowed to decay (^{32}P half-life is about 14 days) for 4 to 6 weeks.

The allele frequency of the DNA fragments from the above-listed loci have been determined in Pst I digested DNA.[13,14] An example of the allele frequency for the D2S44 locus in three ethnic groups is shown in Figure 4–3. Fragment sizes are determined with a computer-assisted bit pad using formulae reported by Elder and Southern.[15] The frequency of an allele is calculated from the data base, assuming a continuous allele distribution for the loci examined.[16] Thus, because the polymorphic fragments examined at the loci result from a variable number of tandem repeats (VNTR), there are more alleles than can be resolved. Standard population genetic calculations are performed using the allele frequencies to arrive at a frequency of

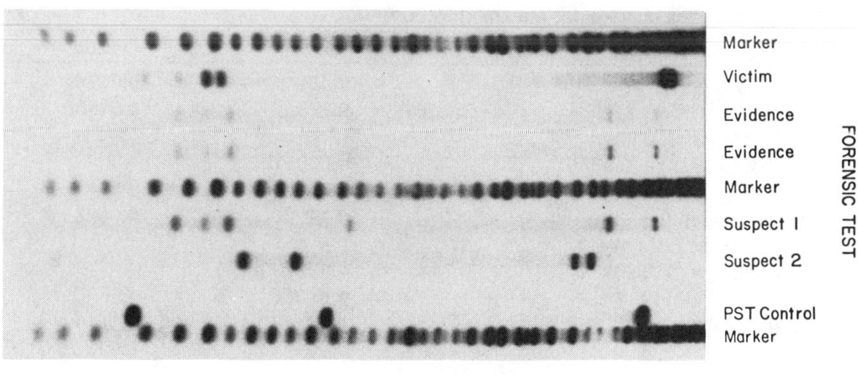

FIG 4–2.

Photograph of an autoradiograph of DNAs examined with ^{32}P-labelled probes recognizing the D2S44 (upper) and DXYS14 (lower) loci from bloods and evidence (vaginal swab) from a rape case. The three lanes labelled *"marker"* include bacteriophage lambda and phiX174 DNAs cut with various restriction endonucleases to generate a sizing ladder.

TABLE 4–1.
Lifecodes Identity Probes

Probe	Locus
pAC061	D14S1
pAC225	DXYS14
pAC255	D2S44
pAC256	D17S79
pAC257	D14S13
pAC222	HRAS
pAC404	D18527

occurrence for each locus. Because the loci are independent and apparently do not deviate from Hardy-Weinberg equilibrium, a cumulative frequency of occurrence is determined by multiplying the values for each locus together. A sample calculation is shown in Table 4–2. Probes which recognize other loci have been shown to be useful for identification. These include multilocus probes[17] and single locus probes derived from the multilocus pattern.[18]

The use of DNA RFLPs in the identification of forensic case material should revolutionize the analysis of biological evidence in that it will allow the exact determination of the source of the evidence. The impact of this type of scientific result on the courts, and in the legal community as a whole, will become evident in the near future. The DNA-PRINT is likely to replace the fingerprint as the benchmark for identification.

TABLE 4–2.
Examples of Calculations for Matching Pattern

		Size	Frequency
Genetic system 1:		12.53	0.0074
		9.27	0.03460
Ocurrence of pattern	1 −		
(2) × (0.0074) × (0.0346)	=	0.000512	
	=	1 in 1,953	
Genetic system 2:		5.14	0.0523
Occurrence of pattern	2 −		
(0.0523) × (0.0523)	=	0.0027352	
	=	1 in 366	
Genetic system 3:		4.79	0.0211
		3.30	0.0102
Occurrence of pattern	3 −		
(2) × (0.0211) × (0.0102)	=	0.0004304	
	=	1 in 2,323	
Occurrence of combined pattern			
(0.000512) × (0.0027352) × (0.0004304)	=	0.0000000006	
	=	1 in 1,660,475,700	

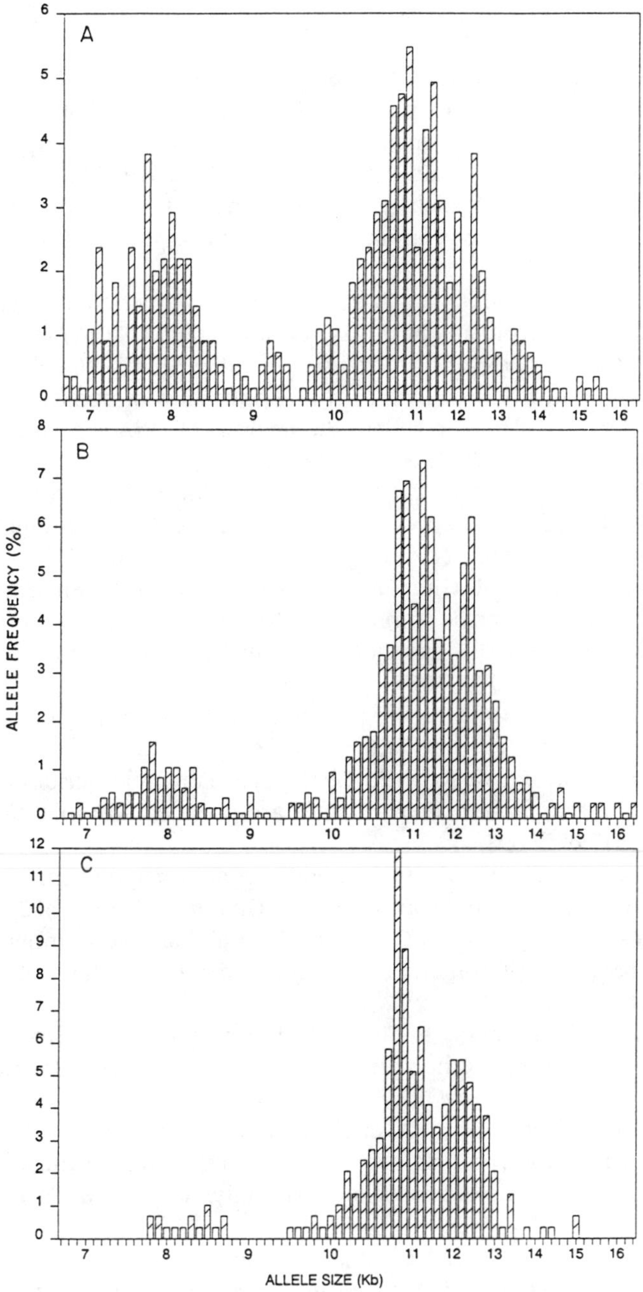

FIG 4–3.
Allele frequency distribution for the D2S44 locus with Pst I digested DNA from random North American people from three ethnic groups: **A,** American black. **B,** Caucasian. **C,** Hispanic.

REFERENCES

1. Southern E: Detection of specific sequences among DNA fragments separated by gel electrophoresis. *J Mol Biol* 1975; 98:503–517.
2. Kan YW, Dozy AM: Antenatal diagnosis of sickle cell anemia by DNA analysis of amniotic fluid cells. *Lancet* 1978; 2:910–912.
3. White R, Leppert M, Bishop D, et al: Construction of linkage maps with DNA markers for human chromosomes. *Nature* 1985; 313:101–105.
4. Kanter E, Baird M, Shaler R, et al: Analysis of restriction fragment length polymorphisms in deoxyribonucleic acid (DNA) recovered from dried bloodstains. *J Forensic Sci* 1986; 31:403–408.
5. Giusti A, Baird M, Pasquale S, et al: Application of deoxyribonucleic acid (DNA) polymorphisms to the analysis of DNA recovered from sperm. *J Forensic Sci* 1986; 31:409–417.
6. McNally L, Shaler R, Giusti A, et al: Evaluation of DNA isolated from human bloodstains exposed to ultra violet light, heat, humidity and soil contamination. *J Forensic Sci* 1989; 34:1059–1069.
7. McNally L, Shaler R, Giusti A, et al: The effects of the environment and drying surfaces on the stability of DNA for RFLP analysis in forensic casework: The use of casework samples from New York City. *J Forensic Sci* 1989; 34:1070–1077.
8. Wyman A, White R: A highly polymorphic locus in human DNA. *Proc Natl Acad Sci USA* 1980; 77:6754–6758.
9. Cooke H, Brown W, Rappold G: Hypervariable telomeric sequences from the human sex chromosomes are pseudoautosomal. *Nature* 1985; 317:687–692.
10. Nakamura Y, Lathrop M, O'Connell P, et al: A mapped set of DNA markers for human chromosome 17. *Genomics* 1988; 2:302–309.
11. Nakamura Y, Leppert M, O'Connell P, et al: Variable number of tandem repeat (VNTR) markers for human gene mapping. *Science* 1987; 235:1616–1622.
12. Fasano O, Taparowsky E, Fiddes J, et al: Sequence and structure of the coding region of the human H-ras gene from T24 bladder carcinoma cells. *J Mol Appl Genet* 1983; 2:173–180.
13. Baird M, Balazs I, Giusti A, et al: Allele frequency distribution of two highly polymorphic DNA sequences in three ethnic groups and its application to the determination of paternity. *Am J Hum Genet* 1986; 39:489–501.
14. Balazs I, Baird M, Clyne M, et al: Human population genetic studies of five hypervariable loci. *Am J Hum Genet* 1989; 44:182–190.

15. Elder J, Southern E: Measurement of DNA length by gel electrophoresis II: Comparison of methods for relating mobility to fragment length. *Anal Biochem* 1983; 128:227–231.
16. Morris J, Sanda A, Glassberg J: Biostatistical evaluation of evidence from continuous allele frequency distribution DNA probes in reference to disputed paternity and disputed identity. *J Forensic Sci*, 1989, in press.
17. Jeffreys A, Wilson V, and Thein S: Hypervariable "minisatellite" regions in human DNA. *Nature* 1985; 314:67–73.
18. Wong Z, Wilson V, Patel I, et al: Characterization of a panel of highly variable minisatellites cloned from human DNA. *Ann Hum Genet* 1988; 51:269–288.

Chapter 5

Mitochondrial DNA: A Possible Genetic Material Suitable for Forensic Analysis*

Bruce Budowle, Ph.D.
Dwight E. Adams, Ph.D.
Catherine C. Comey, Ph.D.
Carl R. Merril, M.D.

INTRODUCTION

Advances in recombinant DNA technology have provided the molecular tools to enable scientists to detect the extraordinary variability that exists among individuals at the level of their DNA. In fact, molecular biology techniques for typing DNA possess the potential to enable individualization of biological specimens. The technology holds the promise of affording the forensic serologist the ability to identify a specific body fluid or tissue donor to the exclusion of all other individuals. One approach that is already gaining widespread utilization for characterization of evidentiary materials is that restriction fragment length polymorphism (RFLP) technology. Presentations at scientific meetings[1–20] and in the literature[21–29] quickly are becoming replete with data defining and validating the application of RFLP analysis of forensic biological specimens. However, since the quality and quantity of DNA that is present in forensic evidentiary materials can be limiting, the RFLP methodology (in its present form) will not be the sole molecular biology technology employed for the characterization of evidentiary material.

*This is publication number 89–02 of the Laboratory Division of the Federal Bureau of Investigation. Names of commercial manufacturers are provided for identification only and inclusion does not imply endorsement by the Federal Bureau of Investigation.

A technique known as the polymerase chain reaction (PCR) method may resolve the difficulty of examining specimens which yield limited quantities of DNA. The PCR method, in which short target sequences of DNA can be quantitatively amplified to an analytical level,[30–34] obviously can be quite useful in a forensic context. Higuchi et al[35] have reported using PCR in concert with dot blot typing of alleles of the HLA-DQ alpha locus to genetically characterize hairs. To date, only the HLA-DQ alpha locus has been used in conjunction with PCR for forensic characterization, but additional genetic sites that might be amenable to PCR and subsequent analyses also could prove useful in this field.

Mitochondrial DNA (mtDNA) may be one of these candidates for forensic analysis of evidentiary material. It was suggested first by Merril[36] that mtDNA could serve as a useful marker(s) for the characterization of evidentiary material. The mtDNA is an extrachromosomal, circular piece of DNA which has been sequenced completely (16,569 base pairs)[37] and has had all genes mapped. The additional facts that mtDNA can occur in greater than 10,000 copies per cell, it is monoclonal, and it appears to be homogeneous within different tissues of an individual, make it desirable to pursue research into the possible forensic utility of this substance.

The purpose of this chapter is two-fold. The first goal, although not exhaustive, is to review for the forensic scientist some information regarding the interesting and unique characteristics of human mtDNA. Although some sections may not appear pertinent to the forensic serologist for the everyday application of molecular biology to the analysis of evidentiary material, the authors feel that it is important to provide this information on mtDNA. In this way, the forensic serologist will be more knowledgeable regarding the material he may be analyzing. More explicit information on each section can be obtained by reading the appropriate citations. The second purpose of this chapter is to define the research approaches presently underway by the authors to exploit mtDNA for genetic characterization.

The Mitochondrial Genome

Human mitochondria possess a genome separate from the nucleus. The mtDNA is a typical genome in that it is double-stranded, and the strands are oriented in an antiparallel fashion. However, in other respects, mtDNA is quite unlike the eukaryotic (nuclear) genome. The mtDNA is circular, naked, and much smaller (16,569 base pairs)[37] than human nuclear DNA (6×10^9 base pairs). The mtDNA double helix demonstrates strand bias, and by cesium chloride gradient centrifugation, the two strands can be separated based upon buoyant density. The heavy (H) strand is rich in G-T nucleotides compared with the light (L) strand. The mitochondrial genome is not self-sufficient; most proteins for the function and structure of mitochondria are encoded by the nucleus.[38–41] However, the mitochondrial genome does encode two ribosomal RNAs (12S and 16S), 22 tRNAs, and 13 significant reading frames (protein-encoding regions). The 13 significant reading frames are comprised of seven genes, termed unidentified reading frames (URF 1, 2, 3, 4, 4L, 5, and 6), that recently have been determined to encode subunits of respiratory chain NADH dehydrogenase,[38,42,43] and one URF-URFA6L-, which encodes a subunit of $H+$-ATPase.[42] The other five

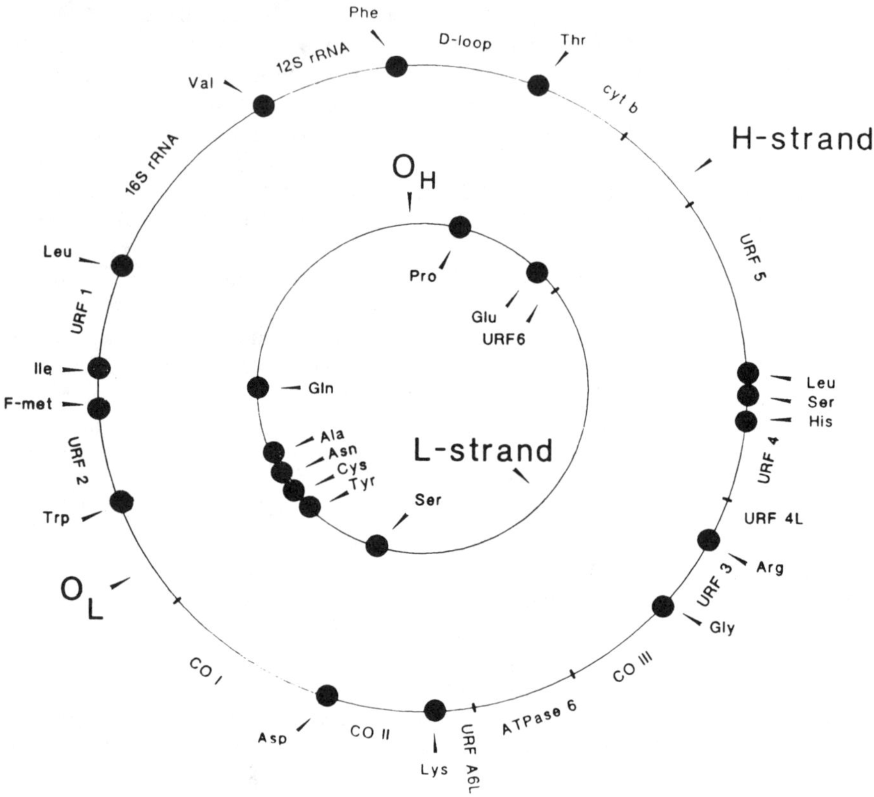

FIG 5–1.
A diagram of the basic gene map of the mitochondrial genome.

significant reading frames encode the subunits of cytochrome oxidase I, II, and III, cytochrome b component, and ATPase 6. Except for approximately 5% to 7% of the human mitochondrial genome which contains the D-loop (displacement loop) region, the mitochondrial genome is dedicated to genetic information. In other words, only a small portion of mtDNA is of a noncoding nature. The H strand contains the two rRNAs, 14 tRNAs, and 12 significant reading frame genes which are contiguous. There appear to be no or only a few nucleotides intervening between the genes on the H strand. The L strand contains the additional eight tRNAs and one significant reading frame (Fig 5–1). Further, there are no introns within the genes,[37] no 5' and 3' noncoding regions, and a lack of termination codons.[37,41,44–46] Thus, since mtDNA lacks many of the complex features of nuclear DNA, it is apparent that this genome is extremely compact, presenting itself as a model of genetic economy. An additional point of interest is that mtDNA is susceptible to strand breakage in the presence of alkali or ribonuclease. According to Grossman et al,[47] this phenomenon is due to the presence of 5 to 10 ribonucleotides covalently bound within the mitochondrial genome.

Replication

The mitochondrial genome must replicate to continue its existence in the eukaryotic cell. Replication is semiconservative, unidirectional, and asymmetrical. The origin of replication for H strand synthesis (O_H) is identified by the D-loop region.[48, 49] This noncoding region is characterized as a 680 nucleotide sequence, flanked by the $tRNA^{PHE}$ and $tRNA^{PRO}$ genes.[37, 50–53] The D-loop is a triplex structure formed by the synthesis of a short daughter H strand which remains stably associated with the parental L strand. Thus, the D-loop is a parental template (L strand) primed for H strand synthesis. Using the L strand as a template, replication of the H strand begins at the D-loop and continues in a clockwise direction. When the synthesis of the daughter H strand is two-thirds complete, the L strand origin of synthesis (O_L) is exposed on the displaced H strand. L strand synthesis begins and proceeds in the opposite direction.

Transcription

Since mtDNA lacks the regulatory mechanisms common to the eukaryotic genome, transcription has taken on unusual regulatory mechanisms. The promoters for transcription of the H and L strands are in the vicinity of the D-loop. The transcripts, which are co-linear to the DNA, lack extraneous DNA such as introns, leaders, and caps.[37, 41, 44–46] Although all transcripts of the H strand reside on one polycistronic message, there appears to be differential expression of the rRNA transcripts. The rRNAs are expressed in a 15- to 60-fold greater concentration than are mRNA transcripts of the H strand polycistronic message. However, the polycistronic message does not appear to account for the higher concentration of rRNA compared with mRNA. Rather, the increased production of rRNAs arises from a second transcription initiation site separated by less than 100 bases from the initiation site on the H strand that transcribes the polycistronic message.[54] One site is near the 5' end at the 12S rRNA gene and the other is 20 to 40 nucleotides upstream of the tRNA ^{PHE}gene.[54, 55] The two sites produce two functionally different transcripts which overlap the same region. The transcript which begins upstream from the $tRNA^{PHE}$ gene terminates at the 3' end of the 16S rRNA gene. This transcript is responsible for the increased expression of the rRNAs. The other transcription site produces a transcript containing the polycistronic message. In addition to the differential regulation of the two distinct transcripts, there is control of expression based upon the stability of the mature (processed) transcripts.

The L strand transcription rate is elevated two- to three-fold compared with the H strand, although its half-life is less.[46, 54, 56] Attardi[46] also has suggested that transcription of the L strand, which contains a large amount of noncoding DNA, may play a role in regulating the expression of H strand genes.

A striking feature of mitochondrial transcription is the tRNA punctuation. Given the lack of regulatory genetic information in the minimized mitochondrial genome, a mechanism had to develop to process the polycistronic message to yield mature RNAs. It appears that the tRNA genes, which flushly flank almost all rRNA and significant reading frame genes, provide a signal site for processing the polycistronic message.[37, 45, 52, 56, 57] There is precise endonucleolytic cleavage occurring before and after a tRNA sequence. Presumably, the formation of a cloverleaf structure by the tRNA sequences on the polycistronic message, while still attached to the DNA template, provides a structure which endonucleolytic enzymes can identify. Attardi[46] suggests that, while there are a few sites not flanked by tRNA genes, it is likely that secondary structures similar to that of tRNAs on the transcript provide sites for enzymatic processing.

Additionally, the RNAs are post-transcriptionally modified in a manner different than nuclear transcripts. All human mitochondrial transcripts, except for ND5 (URF5), cytochrome oxidase I, and cytochrome oxidase II lack a terminator codon[46] and terminate only in a U or a UA. Polyadenylation of the 3' end of the transcript completes the terminator codon (UAA).[37,45,52] Further, the 3' terminus CCA of tRNAs is added post-transcriptionally.[46]

Translation

The most interesting feature of the translation mechanism for the mitochondrial genome is that some codon assignments are at variance with the universal genetic code. It once was believed that the genetic code was the same throughout nature; this does not appear to be the case for mitochondria. In human mtDNA, the terminator codon UGA is read as tryptophan, and AUA, which normally codes for isoleucine, is read as methionine. In addition, AUG, AUU, AUC, and AUA can serve as initiator codons.[58–60] This divergence of the mitochondrial genetic code is believed to be the result of genetic drift or retrogressive evolution that occurred as a result of the relative lack of constraints placed on the mitochondrial genome. Mitochondria do not encode proteins involved directly in their own replication, transcription, translation, and structure.[38,40] According to Cann et al,[61,62] the translation apparatus is more free to be inaccurate because a small genome that codes for only 13 polypeptides can tolerate less accuracy. However, the human mitochondrial genome does encode all tRNAs necessary for translation of its 13 polypeptides. The wobble theory of Crick[63] postulated that a minimum number of 32 tRNAs would be necessary to read all 64 possible codons. Yet, there are only 22 tRNAs in the human mitochondrial genetic code-translation system. Thus, it appears that each tRNA can read two or four synonymous codons in humans. Plus, there is an absence of the AGG and AGA arginine codons in humans.[46] These phenomena support the need for only a minimum of 22 tRNAs. Again, the scheme appears to be in favor of reducing the mitochondrial genome to a minimum size. Thus, the less constrained translation system permits the interpretation of all codons with fewer tRNAs than are required for the nuclear genome.

Evolution

Wallace[64] has described a theory deducing the evolution of the mitochondria. Briefly, it is believed that the mitochondrion was originally a free-living bacterium which had developed an oxidative phosphorylation system for enhancing energy production. Predatory protoeukaryotes (inefficient energy cells) digested the energy source bacterium. Eventually, the bacterium evolved a mechanism to resist digestion within the protoeukaryote. Then, the cell developed a method to utilize the excess ATP of the bacterium. The rich cellular environment rendered many biosynthetic pathways unnecessary for the bacterium, and it was afforded a degree of protection.

Thus, a symbiotic relationship began. Through time, there was an exchange of genes between the mitochondrial genome and the eukaryotic genome. Eventually, the nuclear genome became more complex and sophisticated, while the mitochondrial genome became simpler. Presumably, the mitochondrial genetic code began to drift when only a few genes remained. The different genetic codes, the difference in the complexity of the genomes, the reduction in size of the mitochondrial genome to a minimum number of genes for oxidative phosphorylation and translation, and the lack of extraneous, noncoding DNA limit the mitochondrion from evolving further. Thus, mitochondria are at a genetic dead end, evolutionarily frozen.

In contrast to the minimized size and informational content and the simplified gene organization of mtDNA, it does possess an elevated rate of nucleotide sequence evolution. The substitution rate in mtDNA is an order of magnitude greater than nuclear single copy DNA.[65–68] The mutation rate of the rRNA genes is less than that of the significant reading frame genes, but is at least 10-fold higher than nuclear rRNA genes.[65, 66, 68–70] Approximately 25% to 30% of the mitochondrial genome appears to demonstrate an increased rate of nucleotide substitution. Sequence analyses[71–73] and restriction enzyme cleavage analyses[62] demonstrate that nucleotide substitutions are biased approximately 25-fold toward transitions (i.e., a purine substituted for a purine, or a pyrimidine substituted for a pyrimidine).[46, 61, 72] The higher rate of mutation observed for mtDNA may be due to several factors, including (1) exposure to endogenous DNA-damaging agents, (2) poor fidelity of the replicating and/or editing capacity of the mtDNA polymerase(s), (3) deficiencies in the mtDNA repair system, (4) ready fixation of mutations in mtDNA, and (5) fewer translational constraints.[38, 39, 66–68, 74]

Genetics

Several other unique characteristics of mtDNA are its maternal mode of inheritance (haploidy status), homogeneity within an individual (monoclonal nature), and lack of recombination. Giles et al[75] performed restriction fragment length polymorphism (RFLP) analysis on mtDNA from seven families. They were able to scan effectively 4% of the mitochondrial genome. There was no evidence of any paternal contribution of mtDNA. Further, Case and Wallace,[76, 77] using RFLP analysis of mtDNA derived from fibroblasts of a six-member, three-generation family, verified maternal inheritance for human mtDNA. This observation was not unexpected, since the mature egg contains 10^5 mitochondria, while sperm contain only approximately 50 mitochondria.[68, 78] Either the number of mitochondria in the egg simply overwhelms that of the sperm,[68, 79] or no sperm mitochondria are transferred to the zygote. However, the signal-to-noise ratio of the current molecular biology analytical methods is such that a minor paternal contribution cannot be ruled out.[68]

Of particular concern for the use of mtDNA in forensic analysis is whether or not mtDNA is homogeneous within an individual. Although there is a lack of fidelity and editing capacity mechanisms for mtDNA replication, there appears to be some system that maintains a homogeneous population of mtDNA within an individual.[80–83] Several lines of evidence support the observation of homogeneity. White and Bunn,[84] using RFLP analysis, demonstrated that mtDNA sequences do not change as human fibroblasts age. This observation suggests that efficient maintenance of mtDNA and/or elimination of damaged DNA occurs within the cell, although the mechanisms by which this occurs are unknown. A study by Monnat and Reay[83] also strongly supports the homogeneity of mtDNA. These researchers isolated mtDNA from the brain, heart, liver, kidney, and skeletal muscle of two individuals, cloned regions of cytochrome oxidase III and the D-loop, and subsequently sequenced the clones. The study demonstrated no nucleotide sequence between tissues within an individual. The results suggested that mtDNA sequence changes do not occur during organogenesis, and that somatic mutations of mtDNA in different tissues do not accumulate to detectable levels (1 out of 49,000 sequences). Again, due to the resolving capacity and sensitivity of the testing procedures, a small number of altered mtDNAs cannot be ruled out. However, when tests are chosen that dilute out low-level contributions of variability, minor alterations will not be identified. All that will be observed is the homogeneity of mtDNA from tissue to tissue within an individual. Finally, there has been only one report[85] (to be discussed later) on the mtDNA of diseased individuals in which sequence changes were observed. Even in the presence of mutagenic agents, there are no apparent sequence changes. Mita et al[86] demonstrated that extremely mutagenic agents had no effect on the base sequence of a portion of the D-loop region of mtDNA.

Recombination between mtDNA molecules does not appear to transpire.[68,87] This phenomenon contributes to the high rate of fixation of mtDNA mutations compared with nuclear DNA. The lack of recombination, and the high rate of sequence evolution of maternally inherited mtDNA make this DNA molecule a good candidate as a tool for evolution and genealogy studies. Numerous studies have identified human mtDNA polymorphisms. In fact, not only are there racial and ethnic differences with regard to mtDNA polymorphisms, but remarkable variation occurs within sample populations.[62,88–109] This variability may be extremely informative for forensic analysis, especially when investigating highly divergent regions, such as the noncoding D-loop region of mtDNA.[68,72] The extent of polymorphism of the mtDNA D-loop is currently the subject of intense investigation.

Of particular evolutionary interest is the study done by Brown,[91] in which mtDNA RFLP data was used in an effort to predict the evolution of mankind. Despite the observation of sufficient polymorphic variation to establish identity of the samples, there was less mtDNA variation in humans compared with other mammalian species. Brown et al[66] have shown that the rate of mtDNA base substitution per million years for other mammalian species is 0.5% to 1.0%, while in humans there is a sequence heterogeneity of only 0.18%. Brown[91] proposed that this small amount of observed heterogeneity was due to a severe population constriction that occurred in the recent geological past. It was postulated that the human population went through a bottleneck 180,000 to 350,000 years ago. Due to this bottleneck, mtDNA became somewhat homogeneous (monomorphic) within the small human population. The lack of recombination, the high rate of fixation of mutations, and the pattern of maternal inheritance (which permits lineage tracing without the obscuring effects of Mendelian segregation) have enabled investigators to predict the time of divergence of races from the ancestral human stock subsequent to the population bottleneck. Although there is no definitive data to determine which of the races is ancestral, early work[97] suggested an Asian origin, while later work[95] suggested an African origin. The latter conclusion is consistent with additional genetic data, as well as with archeological and linguistic data.[110]

Interestingly, some reports attributing polymorphisms to sequence deletions observed by RFLP analyses in polyacrylamide gels appear to be unsubstantiated. It appears that secondary structure changes in segments of mtDNA can cause these particular fragments to migrate at rates that are different than those predicted for their actual size. Horai et al,[111] Singh et al,[112] and Vigilant et al[113] have shown that, when subsequently sequenced, base insertions-deletions (40 to 60 bases) determined by RLFP analysis are nothing more than simple base substitutions. Conformational secondary structural differences, although reproducible from run to run, may make base substitution interpretations more difficult when the samples are analyzed in polyacrylamide gels.

However, this observation does not preclude the existence of small insertions or deletions. Using PCR and direct sequencing of the amplified product, Wrischnik et al[114] demonstrated a rapid approach for detecting a nine-base deletion variant in Eastern Asians. While investigating the same deletion variant, Higuchi et al[35] demonstrated a method of analyzing the PCR-amplified product on an agarose gel containing ethidium bromide. However, it appears that most mtDNA polymorphisms are simple base substitutions, and only a few can be attributed to small insertions or deletions; all are genetically inherited and homogeneous within an individual.

METHODOLOGY

The first part of this chapter provided information familiarizing the reader with the features of mtDNA. The remaining portion of the chapter will define the techniques the authors are exploiting to characterize the genetic variability of mtDNA derived from body fluid and tissue samples. Technology presently exists that readily permits the analysis of nucleotide sequences derived from mtDNA. For a new genetic typing technique to gain acceptance and use in forensic serology, it must be genetically informative, permit analysis of a large number of samples, be reproductible, and be properly validated in a forensic context. It appears that the amplification of selected mtDNA sequences by PCR in concert with dot blots, sizing gels, and/or direct sequencing may be a fruitful avenue for research and development of a typing technique.

Polymerase Chain Reaction (PCR)

Depending upon the cell type, the number of copies of mtDNA per cell can range from 50 to 100,000. Therefore, there is a significantly greater number of copies per cell of mtDNA compared with nuclear DNA. Even though the cellular copy number of mtDNA can be quite high, trace quantities of biological materials found at crime scenes may not provide sufficient amounts of mtDNA for RFLP analysis. Furthermore, when evidentiary samples are exposed to environmental adversities, the mtDNA may degrade to a level that is inadequate for RFLP analysis. A method by which short target sequences of mtDNA could be quantitatively amplified to provide an analytical level sufficient for analysis would be extremely useful in the characterization of specimens of limited DNA yield. PCR[30–34] is such a technique.

The PCR methodology is characterized by a three-step process: (1) target DNA is denatured by exposure to an elevated temperature (94°C), (2) short, single-stranded oligonucleotide primers of known DNA sequence are annealed to regions that flank the target DNA sequence, and (3) a DNA polymerase, utilizing the four nucleoside triphosphates, synthesizes a new strand of DNA whose sequence will be directed by the template strand to which the primer was attached (primer elongation). Each cycle of denaturation, priming, and elongation potentially doubles the quantity of target-site DNA. Repetitive cycles of the PCR reaction are performed until the desired quantity of DNA is generated.

It becomes obvious that for PCR to be applied to the amplification of mtDNA, the sequence of the target site, or at least of the flanking regions of the target site, must be known in advance. Otherwise, proper oligonucleotide primers cannot be synthesized. The mtDNA is suitable for PCR since the entire genome has been sequenced.[37] The papers by Wrischnik et al[114] and Higuchi et al[35] used the primers (20-Mers)

8316-5'	ATGCTAAGTTAGCTTTACAG	3' - 8297
8196-5'	ACAGTTTCATGCCCATCGTC	3' - 8215

to flank Region V. Region V lies between the genes for cytochrome oxidase II and tRNA[LYS], and contains the site for the nine base deletion East Asian variant. Our own work has focused on amplifying portions of the highly divergent, noncoding D-loop region. The following primer sequences (20-mers) are being used in our investigations:

FORWARD PRIMERS

121 140
GCAGTATCTGTCTTTGATTC

136 155
GATTCCTGCCTCATCCTATT

160 179
ATCGCACCTACGTTCAATAT

16,140 16,159
TACTTGACCACCTGTAGTAC

90 109
GCGAGACGCTGGAGCCGGAG

16,003 16,022
TCTAATTTAAACTATTCTCT

REVERSE PRIMERS

375 356
GTTTTTGTTTCTTGGGATTG

390 371
TCTGGTTAGGCTGGTGTTAG

16,350 16,331
TTGACTGTAATGTGCTATGT

340 321
GTGTTTAAGTGCTGTGGCCA

489 470
ATTGATGAGATTAGTAGTAT

16,416 16,397
TTCACGGAGGATGGTGGTCA

Although data are only preliminary, these primers have been used successfully to amplify the mtDNA region they flank. For example, Figure 5–2 shows the amplified product using some of these primers to define sequence of interest.

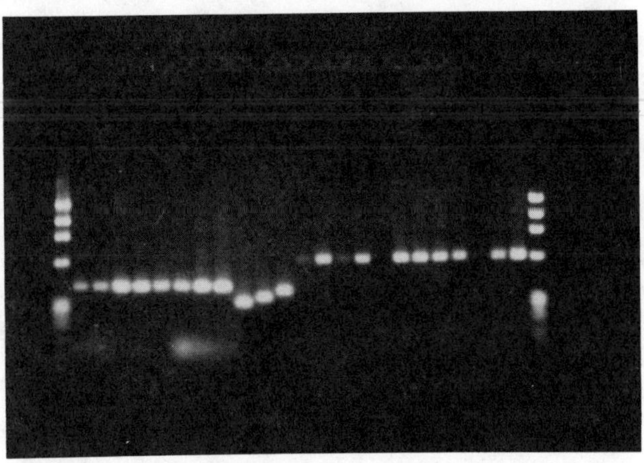

FIG 5–2.
PCR-amplified mtDNA fragments displayed in an agarose gel containing ethidium bromide.

Sequencing

After the PCR cycles have been completed, the amplified DNA can be analyzed by several methods to reveal genetic variation at defined sites. There are two basic sequencing methods: chemical cleavage (Maxam and Gilbert[115]) and chain termination (Sanger[116]). Since the method of Sanger is simpler and easier, and is the approach used in our research, only the Sanger method will be described.

The Sanger method of DNA sequencing is a conceptually simple approach for determining the order of bases on a particular DNA fragment of interest. To perform sequencing, certain reagents are required: the four deoxyribonucleoside triphosphates (dATP, dTTP, dCTP, and dGTP), purified single-stranded template DNA, an oligonucleotide primer, four dideoxyribonucleoside triphosphate analogs (ddATP, ddCTP, ddTTP, and ddGTP), and a DNA polymerase. Basically, an oligonucleotide primer is annealed to a highly purified, single-stranded DNA template. PCR can be the source of the template DNA; the approach could permit a large number of samples to be prepared easily, and would obviate in vivo cloning. The primer, which hybridizes adjacent to the target to be sequenced, is extended across the template sequence by the action of a DNA polymerase in the presence of the four deoxyribonucleoside triphosphates and one of the four dideoxyribonucleoside triphosphates. The dideoxyribonucleoside triphosphates compete with the normal deoxyribonucleoside triphosphates for inclusion in the growing DNA chain. The dideoxy analogs do not contain a 3' hydroxyl group necessary for phosphodiester bond formation. Hence, chain elongation is terminated when a dideoxyribonucleotide is added to the chain, and fragments of different lengths are generated corresponding to the specific sites where a particular dideoxyribonucleotide is inserted. The reaction is carried out in four separate tubes. Each tube contains one of the dideoxy analogs and all the necessary reagents. Thus, the fragments that are generated in a particular reaction tube will correspond to specific sites for one particular base. For example, if a reaction tube contains all four deoxyribonucleoside triphosphates and a dideoxy adenosine triphosphate (or ddATP), the fragment sizes would correspond to positions on the synthesized sequences where an adenine resides. The reaction mixtures are placed on a high resolution, denaturing polyacrylamide gel and subjected to electrophoresis in such a manner that fragments differing in length by only one nucleotide are resolved. As shown in Figure 5–3,A to C, the fragments from the four reaction tubes can be compared, read much like climbing a stepladder, and the DNA sequence of interest determined. Of course, the particular interest of the authors of this chapter is whether or not PCR-amplified mtDNA fragments can be sequenced directly. Although preliminary, our work (an example is shown in Fig 5–4) and that of others[35,114,117] demonstrate that direct sequencing of amplified mtDNA is feasible.

One of the deoxyribonucleoside triphosphates is radiolabelled so that the fractionated fragments on the polyacrylamide gel can be detected by autoradiography. Recently, an alternative detection method has been described, whereby the primer[118–120] or the terminator dideoxy analogs[121] have been tagged with fluorescent labels. The fluorescent labels can be stimulated by a laser and the subsequent emissions detected by an appropriate optics system. This approach permits automation of the sequence analysis portion of the assay, eliminates the need for radioactivity, and

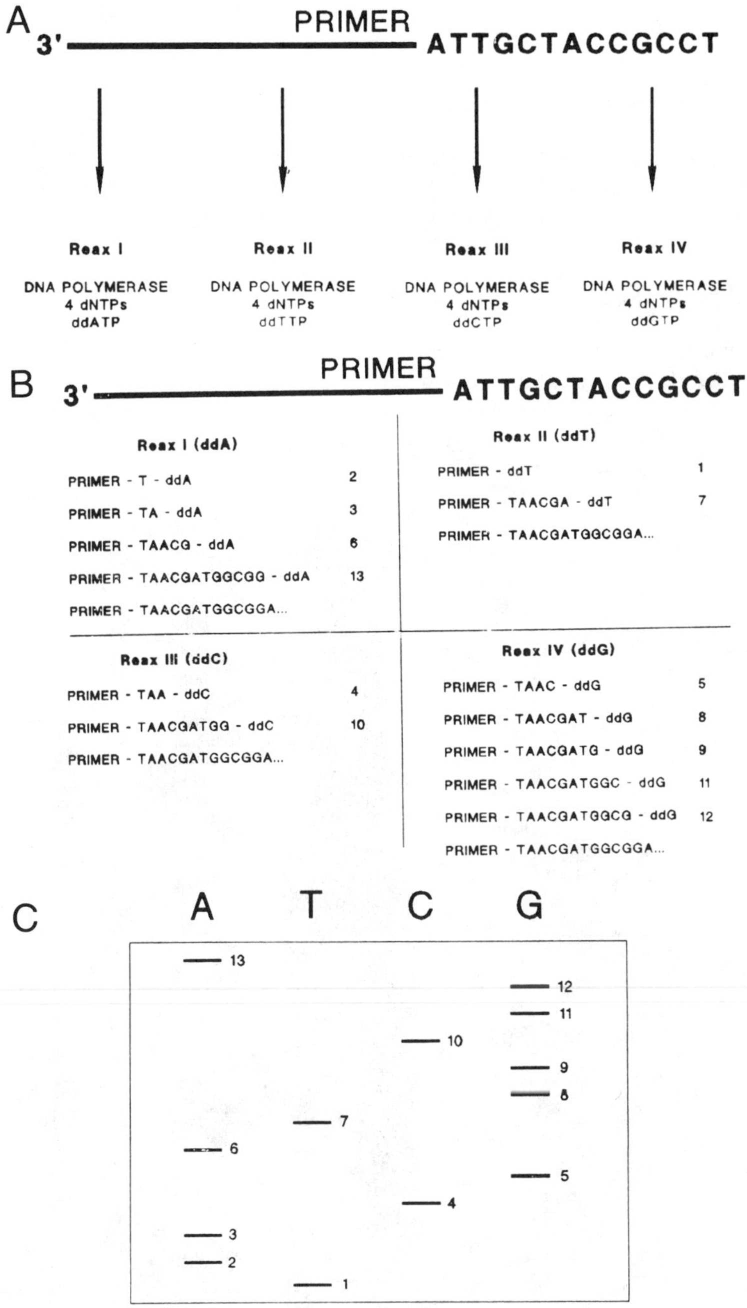

FIG 5–3.

A, an imaginary sequence displayed to demonstrate the chain termination reaction. The sequence, primer, and four deoxyribonucleoside triphosphates all are placed into four replicate tubes. Only one of the dideoxyribonucleoside triphosphates is placed into each tube. **B,** the fragments in each reaction tube generated by the chain termination reaction. The number to the right of each fragment is the number of nucleotides added on to the primer. **C,** pattern generated after polyacrylamide gel electrophoresis by the chain-terminated fragments. The numbers to the right of each band correspond to the number of nucleotides added onto the primer.

permits all four chain termination reactions to the run in one lane instead of four on the resolving gel. The authors presently are comparing the effectiveness of an automated DNA sequencer with manual sequencing approaches for typing mtDNA.

Alternative Typing Approaches

While DNA sequencing could provide significant typing information on PCR-amplified mtDNA fragments, alternative procedures may be easier to perform and still may provide a good deal of genetic information. The first reports of DNA analyses following PCR amplification were carried out by a dot blot procedure. In this pro-

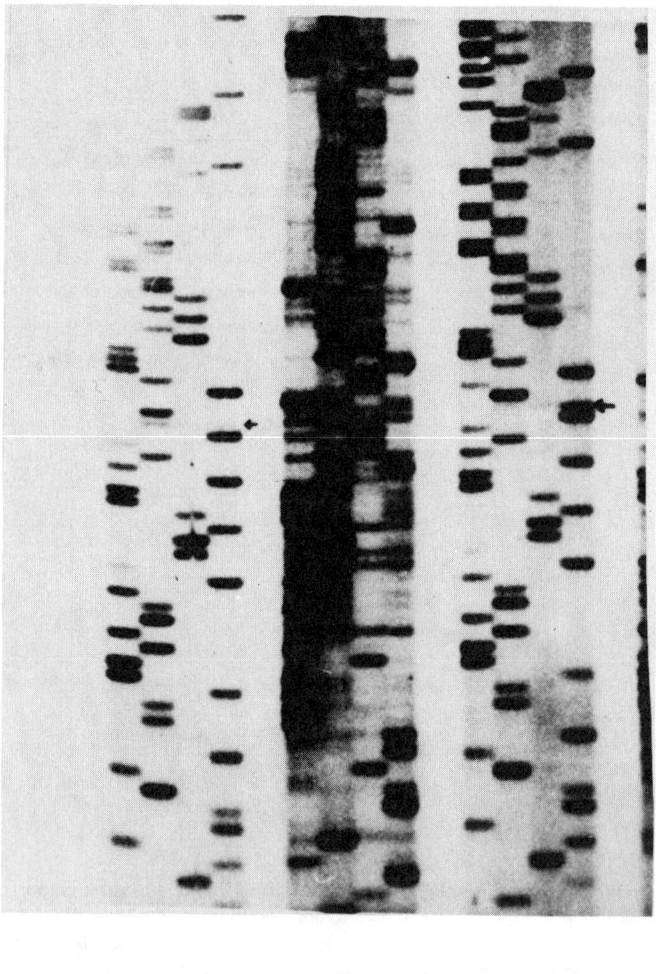

FIG 5–4.
An example of an mtDNA sequence generated from a PCR-amplified region.

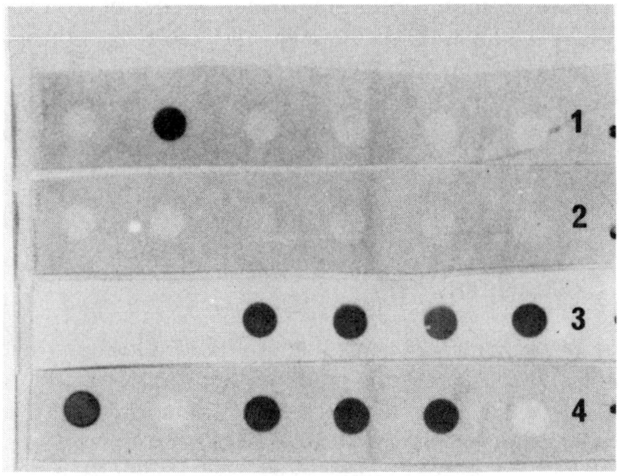

FIG 5–5.
A dot blot displaying HLA-DQ alpha phenotypes. From left to right the types are 4, 1, 3–4, 3–4, 3–4, and 3.

cedure, PCR-amplified material is bound to several membranes as a confined spot. After prehybridization, each membrane strip containing replicate DNA "dots" is challenged with allele-specific oligonucleotide (ASO) probes directed at a defined locus.[30–32] The ASO probes identify point mutation variations. Under appropriate hybridization conditions, the ASO probe and target DNA will associate only if there are no base pair mismatches. Thus, only the ASO with the exact complementary sequence to the immobilized DNA will hybridize and permit detection of the allele (Fig 5–5).

Recently, the Cetus Corporation[122] has reconfigured the above dot blot approach to simplify further the DNA typing test. In the new arrangement, the different ASO probes are bound to the membrane strip, and the amplified material is permitted to hybridize to the immobilized probes. Detection of the formed duplex is made possible by using biotinylated primers and an avidin-biotin complex assay. Thus, one strip can genetically characterize a sample for a defined locus. It is conceivable that such a scenario might be applicable to mtDNA analyses such that several polymorphisms could be identified simultaneously.

In the case where the amplified variants produce fragments of different lengths, a more simplified and rapid approach can be utilized. Higuchi et al[35] have demonstrated that amplified mtDNA products containing deletions can be typed by separation by electrophoresis in agarose gels in the presence of ethidium bromide. The nine base deletion of Region V was utilized. They amplified this region and produced two different size fragments, a 120 base pair fragment and a 111 base pair fragment (corresponding to the nine base pair deletion). After resolving these fragments by electrophoresis, the bands of different size could be observed under ultraviolet (UV) light. Thus, this simple approach combined PCR with fragment length polymorphisms (FLP). Although they are not utilizing mtDNA, R. White (personal communication) and others[123] (John Waye, RCMP, personal communication) have taken this technique a step further and are attempting presently to amplify several variable number tandem repeat loci and subsequently subject the fragments to electrophoresis for rapid typing. This approach would combine the increased sensitivity of the PCR technique with the informational content of RFLP typing. Allen and Budowle (unpublished data) have developed a high resolving, rehydratable polyacrylamide gel electrophoresis and subsequent silver staining technique to produce permanent copies of DNA electrophoretograms (Fig 5–6).

Validation Considerations

At the time of preparation of this manuscript (Fall, 1988), there has been little information provided to support the application of mtDNA typing for the characterization of evidentiary materials. However, it can be anticipated that the techniques developed to detect mtDNA polymorphisms will be subjected to a thorough legal scrutiny upon their introduction to the courts, and rightly so. It is the responsibility

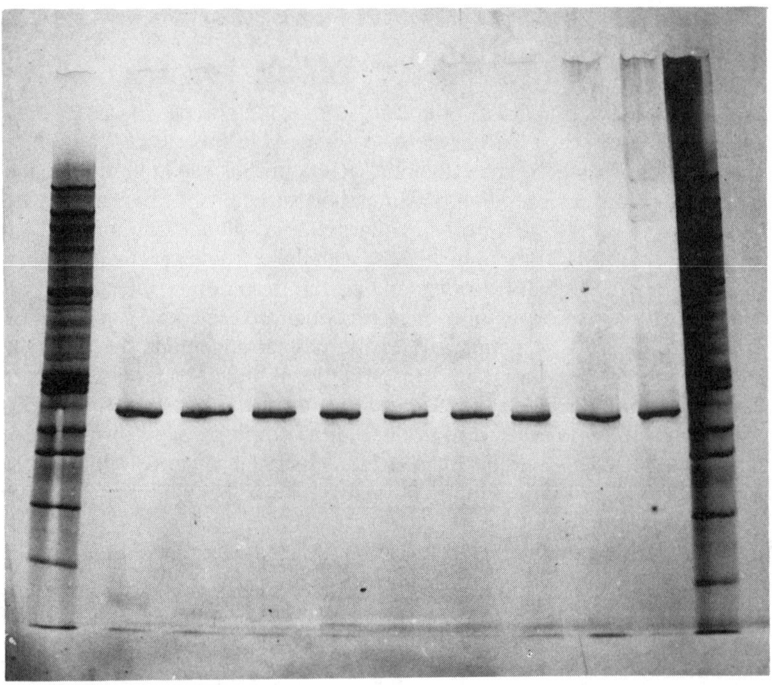

FIG 5–6.
A rehydratable polyacrylamide gel displaying a silver-stained, PCR-amplified product. The buffer system is tris-borate-sulfate. The single band in each lane is the 242 bp fragment of the HLA-DQ alpha locus.

of those engaged in research directed at the application of the mtDNA typing methods to forensic samples to ensure that these approaches have been comprehensively validated and can be applied legitimately to the types of specimens encountered in the forensic laboratory. The scientific validity of mtDNA typing methods per se is not likely to be the issue, for such methods are in widespread use by diverse groups of molecular biologists. The major focus in the validation process will be the reliability of results obtained from human tissue and fluid specimens that were removed from the body in an uncontrolled manner and could have been exposed to a myriad of environmental insults prior to collection. The validation criteria for mtDNA typing methods more than likely will follow the same path previously taken by the Forensic Science Research Unit of the FBI Laboratory for RFLP analyses. These steps are as follows:

1. Perfect the typing methods with fresh materials obtained and stored in a controlled manner.
2. Evaluate the reproducibility of the techniques using fresh specimens.
3. Establish population data.
4. Prepare dried stains using body fluids from donors of known genotypes and analyze the samples.
5. If required, modify the typing methods to ensure that the dried stains exhibit accurate, interpretable, and reproducible mtDNA profiles that agree qualitatively with the profiles obtained on liquid specimens.
6. Determine if the DNA profiles in dried stains change as a function of storage time.
7. Determine if DNA isolated from various tissues within an individual yields identical profiles.
8. Expose laboratory-prepared body fluid stains to a variety of adventitious substances to assess the impact of these substances on DNA profiles.
9. Examine DNA profiles derived from non-probative case-evidence stain materials as examples of stains that are likely to have been exposed to a wide variety of environmental insults. Special attention will be directed to a comparison of DNA profiles generated from victim's liquid blood versus victim's blood deposited on the substrata.
10. Determine if the methods detect mtDNA profiles in fluids and tissues from nonhuman sources.
11. For PCR-mediated techniques, establish protocols to minimize sample contamination within the laboratory during amplification and typing.

This approach should enable research scientists to establish the scientific validity of mtDNA typing methods as they are applied to the examination of evidentiary materials and should directly address the Frye standard[124] for the admissibility of evidence. The Frye standard should be satisfied if the methodology and validation test results are subjected to scrutiny by the scientific community and found to be generally accepted as reliable by a clear majority of this group. Publications in peer-reviewed journals and presentations at scientific conferences, workshops, and/or laboratory courses are excellent forums for the exchange of data, ideas, and opinions regarding the merit of DNA typing procedures. Such colloquia should put the relevant scientific community in a position to determine whether or not the data are worthy of acceptance.

Conclusion

Given the present body of knowledge regarding mtDNA, is development of PCR-mediated amplification methods followed by either sequencing, dot blots, or sizing gels for analyzing this genetic material in a forensic context a reasonable avenue to undertake? The available data do support such an endeavor. The mtDNA molecule is well-characterized. It has been sequenced completely and all gene assignments have been determined. The increased number of copies of mtDNA per cell compared with nuclear DNA provides greater quantities (on a per-copy basis) of DNA for analysis. Additionally, mtDNA exhibits a good deal of polymorphic nature between and within different racial and ethnic groups. The major concern, though, would be whether or not mtDNA is homogeneous within a tissue (or cell) and in all tissues within an individual. To date, mtDNA heterogeneity has not been observed in healthy individuals, even when mtDNA has been exposed to mutagenic agents.[86] There has been only one report of mtDNA heterogeneity related to a disease state. Holt et al[85] observed a 7,000-base pair deletion in 9 of 25 patients with mitochondrial myopathy. The mtDNA derived from the blood of these individuals did not present the 7,000-base pair deletion. However, muscle tissue did demonstrate the normal mtDNA type and the 7,000-base deletion type. First of all, this is the only reported disease state to display mtDNA heterogeneity. This type of phenomenon may also occur in other diseases, but encountering it would be extremely rare. Second, amplification by PCR could not have occurred if any portion of the target site or primer sites resided within the 7,000-base pair deletion. Thus, no result would be obtained for the deletion type. Third, after amplification of the desired target site, the length of the fragment can be determined by electrophoresis in agarose gels containing ethidium bromide. A fragment detected portraying a length different than expected should alert the analyst. Although microheterogeneity could exist, the presently available technologies could not detect it and, thus, it is not a serious concern for analysis. Although the individualization potential of mtDNA is unknown, investigating approaches to genetically characterize mtDNA that is derived from evidentiary biological materials should be a reasonable endeavor that should prove quite fruitful.

REFERENCES

1. Budowle B, Baechtel FS, Murch RS: Forensic applications of variable number tandem repeat DNA probes. Presented at the American Academy of Forensic Sciences, Philadelphia, Penn, February 1988.
2. Murch RS, Baechtel FS, Budowle B: Methods for recovery of DNA from liquid blood and bloodstains. Presented at the American Academy of Forensic Sciences, Philadelphia, Penn, February 1988.

3. Budowle B, Defenbaugh D, Brinkman J, et al: Enhancing sensitivity of detection of the restriction fragment length polymorphism methodology. Presented at the Electrophoresis Society of America, Charleston, SC, June 1988.
4. Baird M: Analysis of forensic materials using VNTR probes. Presented at the Meeting on DNA Technology in Forensic Sciences, FBI Academy, Quantico, Va, June 1988.
5. Cotton R: Analysis of forensic materials using multi- and single locus probes. Presented at the Meeting on DNA Technology in Forensic Sciences, FBI Academy, Quantico, Va, June 1988.
6. Parkin B: DNA research and development at the Metropolitan Police Laboratory. Presented at the Meeting on DNA Technology in Forensic Sciences, FBI Academy, Quantico, Va, June 1988.
7. Werrett DJ: DNA research update from the Home Office Forensic Science Service. Presented at the Meeting on DNA Technology in Forensic Sciences, FBI Academy, Quantico, Va, June 1988.
8. Budowle B: A simple RFLP technique for detection of small quantities of DNA. Presented at the Society for Forensic Haemogenetics, Liege, Belgium, September 1988.
9. Costantinides F, Russo V, Fattorini P, et al: Bloodstains identification: Case report. Presented at the Society for Forensic Haemogenetics, Liege, Belgium, September 1988.
10. Fiori A, Pascali V, d'Aloja E, et al: First experiences with individual DNA fingerprints from the 3'HVR hypervariable region probe. Presented at the Society for Forensic Haemogenetics, Liege, Belgium, September 1988.
11. Henke J, Henke L, Cleef S, et al: Forensic evaluation of oligonucleotide probes. Presented at the Society for Forensic Haemogenetics, Liege, Belgium, September 1988.
12. Prinz M, Berghaus G, Staak M: DNA extraction from bloodstains in respect to age and stained substrate. Presented at the Society for Forensic Haemogenetics, Liege, Belgium, September 1988.
13. Budowle B: Validation of DNA typing methods for application to forensic biological evidentiary materials. Presented at the Division of Chemistry and the Law, ACS, Los Angeles, Calif, September 1988.
14. Bowen JH, Hoar DI: RFLP analysis of single human hairs. Presented at the Canadian Society of Forensic Sciences, Toronto, Canada, October 1988.
15. Budowle B, Baechtel FS, Adams DE: Parameters for consideration in the design of RFLP methodology for forensic serology. Presented at the Society of Forensic Sciences, Toronto, Canada, October 1988.

16. Cheung LC, McNeil BK, Little D, et al: Application of DNA genetic typing to aircrash victim identification. Presented at the Canadian Society of Forensic Sciences, Toronto, Canada, October 1988.
17. Cotton R, Herrin G: DNA fingerprinting as a tool in criminal investigation. Presented at the Canadian Society of Forensic Sciences, Toronto, Canada, October 1988.
18. Keith T, Rose SD: DNA probes detecting highly polymorphic single loci: Use in parentage testing and forensic analysis. Presented at the Canadian Society of Forensic Sciences, Toronto, Canada, October 1988.
19. Shutler GG, Waye JS, Monteith N, et al: The merits of single locus as opposed to multilocus hybridization conditions for hypervariable RFLPs in forensic applications. Presented at the Canadian Society of Forensic Sciences, Toronto, Canada, October 1988.
20. Budowle B: DNA use in forensic pathology. Presented at the American Medical Association, San Diego, Calif, November 1988.
21. Gill P, Jeffreys AJ, Werrett DJ: *Nature* 1985; 318:577–579.
22. Jeffreys AJ, Brookfield JR, Semeonoff R: *Nature* 1985; 317:818–819.
23. Giusti A, Baird M, Pasquale S, et al: *J Forensic Sci* 1986; 31:409–417.
24. Kanter E, Baird M, Shaler R, et al: *J Forensic Sci* 1986; 31:403–408.
25. Gill P, Lygo JE, Fowler SJ, et al: *Electrophoresis* 1987; 8:38–44.
26. Gill P, Werrett DJ: *Forensic Sci Int* 1987; 35:145–148.
27. Werrett DJ: *Int Crim Pol Rev* 1987; Sept-Oct:21–25.
28. Budowle B, Deadman HA, Murch RS, et al: *Crime Laboratory Digest* 1988; 15:8–12.
29. Shutler GG: *R C M P Gazette* 1988; 50:22–27.
30. Saiki RK, Scharf S, Faloona F, et al: *Science* 1985; 230:1350–1354.
31. Erlich HA, Sheldon EL, Horn GT: *Biotechnology* 1986; 4:975–981.
32. Saiki RK, Bugawan TL, Horn GT, et al: *Nature* 1986; 324:163–166.
33. Li H, Gyllensten UB, Cui X, et al: *Nature* 1988; 335:414–417.
34. Oste C: *Biotechniques* 1988; 6:162–167.
35. Higuchi R, Von Beroldingen CH, Sensabaugh GF, et al: *Nature* 1988; 332:543–546.
36. Merril CR: *Proc Int Symp For App Electro*, FBI Academy, Quantico, Virginia, 1984; pp 3–13.
37. Anderson S, Bankier AT, Barrell BG, et al: *Nature* 1981; 290:457–465.
38. Clayton DA: *Cell* 1982; 28:693–705.
39. Clayton DA: *Ann Rev Biochem* 1984; 53:573–594.
40. Chomyn A, Mariottini P, Cleeter MW, et al: *Nature* 1985; 314:592–597.
41. Tzagoloff A, Myers AM: *Ann Rev Biochem* 1986; 55:249–285.
42. Attardi G, Chomyn A, Doolittle RF, et al: *Cold Spring Harbor Symp Quant Biol* 1986; 51:103–114.

43. Mariottini P, Chomyn A, Riley M, et al: *Proc Natl Acad Sci USA* 1986; 83:1563–1567.
44. Ojala D, Merkel C, Gelfand R, et al: *Cell* 1980; 22:393–403.
45. Ojala D, Montoya J, Attardi G: *Nature* 1981; 290:470–474.
46. Attardi G: *Int Rev Cytol* 1985; 93:93–145.
47. Grossman L, Watson R, Vinograd J: *Proc Natl Acad Sci USA* 1973; 70:3339–3343.
48. Arnberg A, VanBruggen EF, Ter Schegget J, et al: *Biochim Biophys Acta* 1971; 246:353–357.
49. Kasamatsu H, Robberson DL, Vinograd J: *Proc Natl Acad Sci USA* 1971; 68:2252–2257.
50. Crews S, Ojala D, Posakony J, et al: *Nature* 1979; 277:192–198.
51. Crews S, Attardi G: *Cell* 1980; 19:775–784.
52. Ojala D, Crews S, Montoya J, et al: *J Mol Biol* 1981; 150:303–314.
53. Tapper DP, Clayton DA: *J Biol Chem* 1981; 256:5109–5115.
54. Montoya J, Christianson T, Levens D, et al: *Proc Natl Acad Sci USA* 1982; 79:7195–7199.
55. Montoya J, Gaines G, Attardi G: *Cell* 1983; 34:151–159.
56. Cantatore P, Attardi G: *Nucleic Acids Res* 1980; 8:2605–2624.
57. Montoya J, Ojala D, Attardi G: *Nature* 1981; 290:465–470.
58. Barrell BG, Bankier AT, Drouin J: *Nature* 1979; 282:189–194.
59. Barrell BG, Anderson S, Bankier AT, et al: *Proc Natl Acad Sci USA* 1980; 77:3164–3166.
60. Fox TD: *Annu Rev Genet* 1987; 21:67–91.
61. Cann RL, Wilson AC: *Genetics* 1983; 104:699–711.
62. Cann RL, Brown WM, Wilson AC: *Genetics* 1984; 106:479–499.
63. Crick FH: *J Mol Biol* 1966; 19:548–555.
64. Wallace DC: *Hosp Pract* 1986; Oct:77–92.
65. Dawid IB: *Dev Biol* 1972; 39:139–151.
66. Brown WM, George M, Wilson AC: *Proc Natl Acad Sci USA* 1979; 76:1967–1971.
67. Brown WM, Prager EM, Wang A, et al: *J Mol Evol* 1982; 18:225–239.
68. Wilson AC, Cann RL, Carr SM, et al: *Biol J Linn Soc* 1985; 26:375–400.
69. Ferris SD, Brown WM, Davidson WS, et al: *Proc Natl Acad Sci USA* 1981; 78:6319–6323.
70. Ferris SD, Wilson AC, Brown WM: *Proc Natl Acad Sci USA* 1981; 78:2432–2436.
71. Aquardro CF, Greenberg BD: *Genetics* 1983; 103:287–312.
72. Greenberg BD, Newbold JE, Sugino A: *Gene* 1983; 21:33–49.
73. Aquardo CF, Kaplan N, Risko KJ; *Mol Biol Evol* 1984; 1:423–434.
74. Brown WM, in Nei M, Koehn R (eds): *Evolution of Genes and Proteins*. Sinauer, Mass, 1982, pp 62–88.

75. Giles RE, Blanc H, Cann HM, et al: *Proc Natl Acad Sci USA* 1980; 77:6715–6719.
76. Case JT, Wallace DC: *Somatic Cell Mol Genet* 1981; 7:103–108.
77. Wallace DC, Blanc H, Giles RE, et al: *Am J Hum Genet* 1980; 32:10A.
78. Hecht NB, Liem H, Kleen KC, et al: *Dev Biol* 1984; 102:452–461.
79. Dawid IB, Blacher AW: *Dev Biol* 1972; 29:152–161.
80. Potter SS, Newbold JE, Hutchison CA, et al: *Proc Natl Acad Sci USA* 1975; 72:4496–5500.
81. Monnat RJ, Loeb LA: *Proc Natl Acad Sci USA* 1985; 82:2895–2899.
82. Monnat RJ, Maxwell CL, Loeb LA: *Cancer Res* 1985; 45:1809–1814.
83. Monnat RJ, Reay DT: *Gene* 1986; 43:205–211.
84. White FA, Bunn CL: *Mechan Age Dev* 1985; 30:153–168.
85. Holt IJ, Harding AE, Morgan-Hughes JA: *Nature* 1988; 331:717–719.
86. Mita S, Monnat RJ, Loeb LA: *Cancer Res* 1988; 48:4578–4583.
87. Hayashi IJ, Tagashira Y, Yoshida MC: *Exp Cell Res* 1985; 160:387–395.
88. Benerecetti A, Scozarri R, Semino O, et al: *Ann Hum Genet* 1988; 52:39–56.
89. Bonne-Tamir B, Johnson MJ, Natali A, et al: *Am J Hum Genet* 1986; 38:341–351.
90. Brega A, Scozzari R, Maccioni L, et al: *Am J Hum Genet* 1986; 50:327–338.
91. Brown WM: *Proc Natl Acad Sci USA* 1980; 77:3605–3609.
92. Cann RL, Brown WM, Ferris SD, et al: *Am J Hum Genet* 1980; 32:140A.
93. Cann RL, Brown WM, Wilson AC: *Am J Phys Anthropol* 1981; 54:207–208.
94. Cann RL, Wilson AC: *Genetics* 1983; 104:699–711.
95. Cann RL, Stoneking M, Wilson AC: *Nature* 1987; 325:31–36.
96. Brega A, Gordella R, Semino O, et al: *Am J Hum Genet* 1986; 39:502–512.
97. Denaro M, Blanc H, Johnson MJ, et al: *Proc Natl Acad Sci USA* 1981; 78:5768–5772.
98. Harihara S, Hirai M, Omoto V: *Jpn J Hum Genet* 1986; 31:73–83.
99. Harihara S, Hirai M, Omoto K: *Jpn J Hum Genet* 1986; 31:176–177.
100. Harihara S, Hirai M, Saitou N, et al: *Jpn J Hum Genet* 1987; 32:193–194.
101. Harihara S, Saitou N, Hirai M, et al: *Am J Hum Genet* 1988; 43:134–143.
102. Griziotis G, Hawkins C, Mackinlay AG, et al: *Aust J Biol Sci* 1987; 40:171–180.
103. Horai S, Gojobori T, Matsunaga E: *Hum Genet* 1984; 68:324–332.
104. Horai S, Gojobori T, Matsunaga E: *Jpn J Hum Genet* 1985; 30:110–111.

105. Horai S, Matsunaga E: *Hum Genet* 1986; 72:105–117.
106. Horai S, Matsunaga E, Hirayama K, et al: *Jpn J Hum Genet* 1987; 32:142–143.
107. Johnson MJ, Wallace DC, Ferris SD, et al: *J Mol Evol* 1983; 19:255–271.
108. Scozarri R, Torroni A, Semino O, et al: *Am J Hum Genet* 1988; 43:534–544.
109. Wallace DC, Garrison K, Knowler WC: *Am J Phys Anthropol* 1985; 68:149–155.
110. Cavalli-Sforza LL, Piazza A, Menozzi P, et al: *Proc Natl Acad Sci USA* 1988; 85:6002–6006.
111. Horai S, Inoue T, Matsunaga E: *Hum Genet* 1987; 75:73–74.
112. Singh G, Neckelmann N, Wallace DC: *Nature* 1987; 329:270–272.
113. Vigilant L, Stoneking M, Wilson AC: *Nucleic Acids Res* 1988; 16:5945–5955.
114. Wrischnik LA, Higuchi RG, Stoneking M, et al: *Nucleic Acids Res* 1987; 15:529–542.
115. Maxam AM, Gilbert W: *Proc Natl Acad Sci USA* 1977; 74:560–564.
116. Sanger F, Nicklen S, Coulson AR: *Proc Natl Acad Sci USA* 1977; 74:5463–5468.
117. Paabo S, Gifford JA, Wilson AC: *Nucleic Acids Res* 1988; 16:9775–9787.
118. Smith LM, Fung S, Hunkapiller MW, et al: *Nucleic Acids Res* 1985; 13:2399–2412.
119. Smith LM, Sanders JZ, Kaiser RJ, et al: *Nature* 1986; 321:674–679.
120. Connell C, Fung S, Heiner C, et al: *Biotechniques* 1987; 5:342–348.
121. Prober JM, Trainor GL, Dam RJ, et al: *Science* 1987; 238:336–341.
122. Saiki RK, Erlich HA: *Am J Hum Genet* 1988; 43:A95.
123. Boerwinkle E, Chan L: *Am J Hum Genet* 1988; 43:A138.
124. Frye v. United States, 1923, 54 U. S. App. D. C. 46.

Chapter 6

Determination of the Sex of Origin of Blood and Bloodstains Using Recombinant DNA Techniques

Michal Witt, M.D., Ph.D.
Robert P. Erickson, M.D.

The precise determination of the sex of fetuses, individuals, or blood spots using molecular biology technology is a matter of interest to many laboratories. To this end, several rapid and accurate methods of "sexing" human DNA have been developed. These methods are extremely useful in clinical practice as an accessory for the prenatal diagnosis of sex-linked disorders, such as Duchenne's muscular dystrophy, hemophilia, or Lesch-Nyhan syndrome, in which fetal sex should be determined first, using amniotic cells or chorionic villi samples, because further testing is usually unnecessary if the fetus is female. These techniques can be used also in following host versus graft cells in patients with bone marrow transplants from the opposite sex,[1] or in searching for XO/XY mosaicism in patients with Turner's syndrome. Some of the methods may be of use in detecting structural aberrations of Y chromosomes.[2] Another major application of these methods may be the "sexing" of DNA for forensic purposes, if incompletely degraded DNA is available. Since, genetically speaking, the difference between males and females resolves itself into the presence or the absence of a Y chromosome, respectively, all of these methods focus on the detection of Y-specific chromosomal sequences.

In the classical model,[3] the human Y chromosome can be divided into two major regions of approximately equal size: a heterochromatic region on the long arm (Yql→qter) and a euchromatic region containing the short arm, the centromere, and part of the long arm (Ypter→qll). The Y chromosome constitutes about 2% of the total length of the haploid genome and consists of approximately $(4\text{-}6) \times 10^7$ base pairs (bp).[4] The heterochromatin of the Y chromosome contains at least two major repeated DNA families of sequences which are relatively male-specific. One of these, a 3.4 kb fragment found after Hae III digestion,[5] was used as a molecular probe to develop the first simple screening test for prenatal sex diagnosis at the DNA level.[6]

The procedure, reported by Lau et al, involved spinning down cells from 0.2 ml of amniotic fluid, heating the cell pellet with an alkaline solution in order to extract the DNA, spotting the DNA on a nitrocellulose filter, and hybridizing with the pY3.4 probe labelled with ^{32}P (dot hybridization). The pY3.4 probe hybridized 1,000 times more strongly to male than to female genomic DNA. The advantages of this method over tedious, 1 to 2 week long conventional chromosomal analyses were that a small amount of DNA was sufficient for the analysis (a 25 μl sample of amniotic fluid was the lower limit of this method), and complete DNA purification was not needed. In analogous experiments, an ability to sex 0.5 μg samples of genomic DNA or sets of chorionic villi samples was also shown.[7] The pY3.4 probe was useful not only for Southern blot or dot blot hybridizations, but also for in situ hybridization, whether it was labelled with radioactive or nonradioactive markers.[8–10] However, the use of a probe specific to the heterochromatic region of the Y chromosome may be of limited use because of the inability to detect Y sequences in individuals lacking this region of the Y chromosome. Deletions of Y heterochromatin occur occasionally even in normal, fertile males.[11] Conversely, this region of the Y chromosome may be present as a translocation in 1 out of 3,000 apparently normal females.[12] Thus, the probes to the heterochromatic region of the Y chromosome long arm have an increased chance for an incorrect diagnosis of sex. The use of a single-copy probe which mapped to the Y short arm was also reported, but the authors were unable to use this probe in a rapid and simple test.[13] The recent availability of probes specific for the sex-determining region of the human Y (ZEY) chromosome may allow one to finally overcome these difficulties in the future.[14,15]

Alphoid (alpha) satellite DNA is much more stable and, actually, is the only repetitive DNA family likely to exhibit the properties of significant chromosome specificity.[16] The fundamental repeated unit of this family in the human genome is a monomer of approximately 171 bp in length. The structure and localization of alphoid satellite DNA on chromosomes has been intensively studied[17,18] and the results indicated that, unlike dispersed repeat families, these sequences have different molecular organizations on each human chromosome. Alphoid satellite sequences on the Y chromosome have a higher repeat organization detected with restriction enzymes such as *Eco* RI[19]: a 5.5 kilobase pair (kb) *Eco* RI fragment was found to be characteristic of these Y alphoid repeats.[18] Dosage experiments demonstrated that there are about 100 to 500 copies of this fragment on the Y chromosome. Studies utilizing DNA from human-mouse hybrids containing only portions of the Y chromosome, and in situ hybridizations to chromosome spreads demonstrated a Y centromeric localization of the 5.5 kb *Eco* RI fragment which had been cloned from a Y library.[18,19] Some cross hybridization to autosomes 13, 14, and 15 was also seen. However, these chromosomes lacked detectable copies of the 5.5 kb *Eco* RI fragment. It was shown also that the Y chromosomal alphoid repeat was not closely related to the X chromosomal alphoid repeat.[18]

Cosmid Y97, containing sequences from the human alphoid centromeric repeat family, was originally isolated from a partial human Y chromosomal library.[18] This cosmid was used as a molecular probe to detect the 5.5 kb *Eco* RI fragment characteristic for the alphoid centromeric repeat in the human Y chromosome. The development of conditions for the reliable use of Y97 to detect small amounts of Y-derived

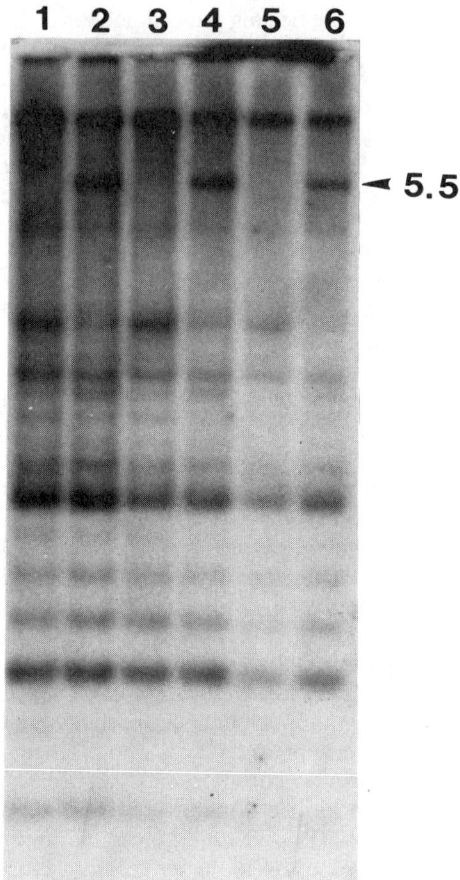

FIG 6–1.
Hybridization of *Eco* RI restricted female and male DNA with Y97. *Lane 1,* 40 ng of female DNA; *lane 2,* 40 ng of male DNA; *lane 3,* 20 ng of female DNA; *lane 4,* 20 ng of male DNA; *lane 5,* 10 ng of female DNA; *lane 6,* 10 ng of male DNA. Y97 was nick-translated to 5 × 10^8 cpm/μg; hybridization was performed as in reference 20. Position of 5.5 kb band shown on the right.

chromosomal material and for rapid sexing of human DNA was reported by Stalvey and Erickson.[20] When Y97 was hybridized to *Eco* RI-restricted female and male DNA, only lanes containing male DNA were positive for the 5.5 kb *Eco* RI fragment. The male-female difference in hybridization was unequivocal, even with amounts of total DNA as low as 10 ng per lane, indicating sufficient sensitivity to detect Y-derived sequences in very small samples of genomic DNA (Fig 6–1).

The ability to detect Y-specific sequences in the presence of female DNA, a situation which can occur in some clinical cases, was tested by hybridization of Y97 with different mixtures of *Eco* RI-restricted male and female DNA. When female and male DNA was mixed in varying proportions, the 5.5 kb *Eco* RI fragment was detected even when male DNA constituted as little as 5% of the mixture. Such a sensitivity allows the use of Y97 to detect Y-specific material even in low percentage mixtures, as in studying Turner's syndrome mosaicism or reconstitution in bone marrow recipients, or in sexing amniotic fluid cells.[2,20]

A rapid and simple sex diagnosis procedure for blotted, unrestricted male and female DNA (dots of 5 μg of DNA) was also developed using Y97. When hybridization was carried out at 42°C in 50% formamide, and filters were washed to different stringencies, unrestricted male DNA was not distinguishable from unrestricted female DNA. However, when hybridization stringency was increased, Y97 could be used to differentiate between male and female DNA in slot blots. The most striking difference occurred when hybridization was carried out at 52°C in 50% formamide and 1.0 M NaCl (Fig 6–2). Although hybridization of Y97 to female unrestricted DNA also occurred in these conditions, the slots containing male DNA gave markedly more intense signals than did those containing female DNA. The mean intensity of signal for male DNA, quantitated by scanning laser densitometer and compared to control hybridization for accurate estimation of total DNA, was 14-fold greater than that for female DNA. In the extreme case of the lowest male DNA ratio compared to the highest female DNA ratio, a six-fold difference of intensity still separated the sexes.

Completely new approaches to many problems in forensic science have become available as a result of new methods that have been developed in molecular biology labs. One of these, DNA fingerprinting, seems to be the most specific tool ever developed for the identification of individuals.[21] The classical forensic tests that can be conducted on the biological evidence usually found at crime scenes (including semen, blood, and hair) can identify a suspect with only about 90% to 95% certainty. DNA fingerprinting, using either Jeffreys' probes, which recognize minisatellite regions, or probes specific for variable number tandem repeats (VNTRs), potentially allows an unquestionable identification of one particular person from the whole world population. Because of its obvious advantages, it is expected that in several years this method will become routine in many crime laboratories.[22]

A second new forensic tool, the polymerase chain reaction (PCR), is, conceptually, a very simple method for amplifying nucleic acid sequences. It already has revolutionized molecular biology, especially human genetics, and can be very useful in different aspects of forensic science, including the sexing of DNA samples, blood stains, etc.[23, 24] PCR mimics the DNA replication process that occurs in all dividing cells. As in replication, the number of DNA molecules generated by PCR doubles after each cycle. The sites flanking the sequence to be amplified must have been sequenced so that a pair of synthetic oligonucleotides, the extension primers, can anneal to these sites. The sequence of interest does not have to be present initially in a pure form—it can be a very minute fraction of multicomponent mixture, e.g., whole or part of a single-copy gene present in human genomic DNA. The reaction results in a double-stranded DNA molecule (dsDNA) with termini corresponding to the 5'-ends of the oligomers used as primers.

The PCR method is based on the repetition of a three-step cycle in which all steps are conducted in succession under strictly controlled temperature conditions (Fig 6–3). In the first step (denaturation), the double-stranded genomic DNA template is denatured by incubation at high temperature (usually 92° to 94°C). This results in two dissociated DNA strands which remain free in solution at this temperature. In the second step (annealing), the temperature is lowered to various levels (e.g., 25°C, 37°C, 55°C) allowing primers to anneal to homologous sequences on both free strands of genomic DNA (the sequences flanking the fragment to be amplified). The primers should not be complementary to each other, not even in part. Usually primers of a length of 20 to 25 nucleotides are used. Because the primers are present in a large excess over the DNA template, the efficiency of formation of the primer-template complex prevails over reassociation of the two DNA strands.

In the third and final step (amplification, elongation), the reaction mixture is placed at a temperature optimal for the DNA polymerase used. A temperature of 37°C

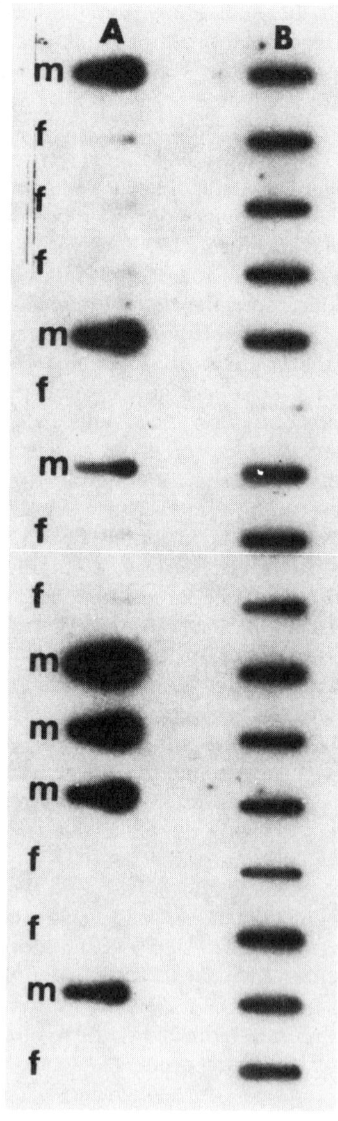

FIG 6–2.
Hybridization of unrestricted human DNA with Y97 and BLUR11 (human Alu-repeat sequence probe, which is found in both male and female DNA in equal abundance) in a representative slot blot. In *column A,* 5 μg samples of unrestricted human DNA were hybridized with Y97; samples in *column B* are the same samples as in *column A,* except that filters were stripped and rehybridized with pBLUR11. Hybridization conditions are described in reference 20; m - male, f - female. (From Stalvey JRD, Erickson RP: *Hum Genet* 1987; 76:240–243. Used by permission.)

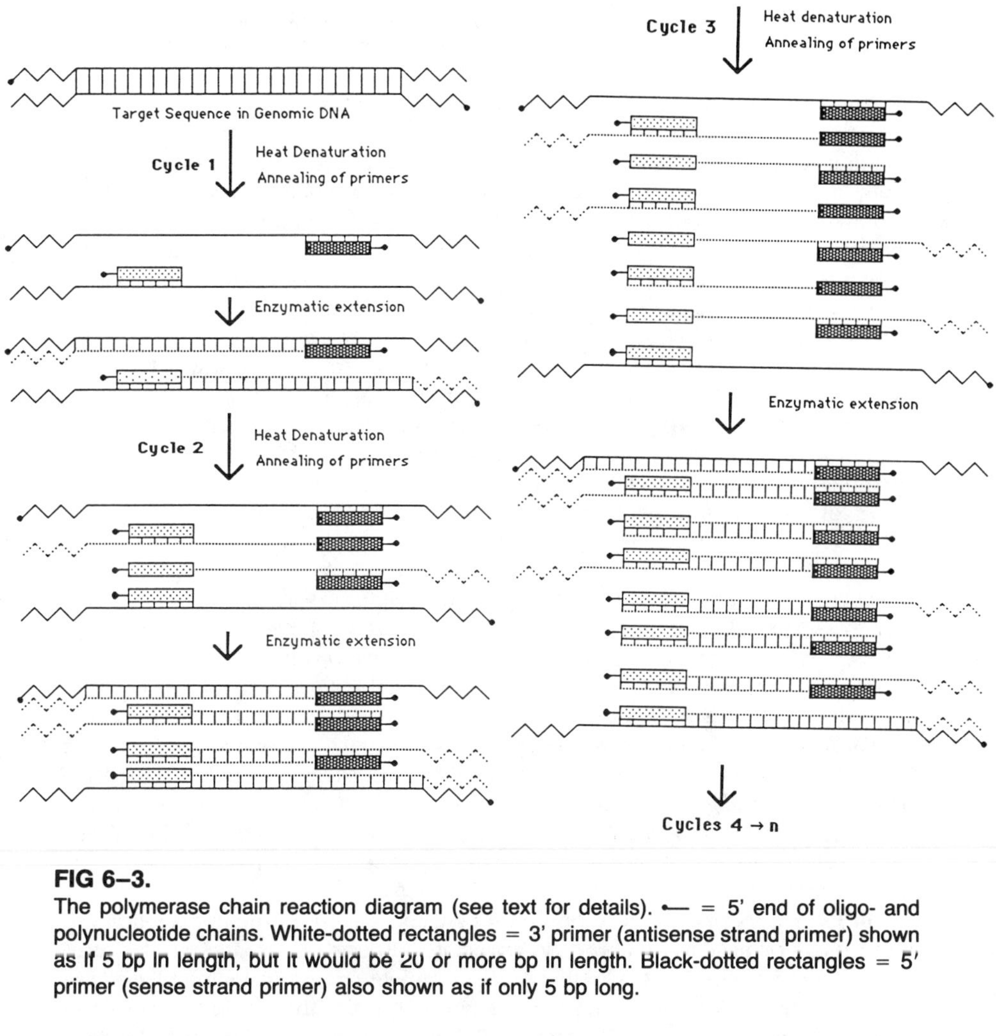

FIG 6–3.

The polymerase chain reaction diagram (see text for details). •— = 5' end of oligo- and polynucleotide chains. White-dotted rectangles = 3' primer (antisense strand primer) shown as if 5 bp in length, but it would be 20 or more bp in length. Black-dotted rectangles = 5' primer (sense strand primer) also shown as if only 5 bp long.

is optimal for the Klenow fragment of polymerase I isolated from *Escherichia coli*, while a temperature of 72°C is optimal for the *Taq* polymerase, enzyme isolated from the bacterium *Thermus aquaticus*, which lives in hot springs. The reaction mixture, along with the enzyme, contains all four deoxyribonucleoside triphosphates. The extension of the primer-template complex occurs in the 5'→3' direction, and primers themselves become "built-in" fragments of reaction products. The reaction proceeds with a speed of about 60 to 120 nucleotides per second. The primers hybridize to opposite strands of the target sequence and are oriented so that DNA synthesis by the polymerase proceeds across the region between the primers, effectively doubling the amount of that DNA segment. Moreover, since the extension products are also complementary to the primers and capable of binding to them, each successive cycle doubles the amount of DNA synthesized in the previous cycle. Twenty to 30 repetitions of the whole three-step cycle results in the exponential accumulation of the specific target fragment (see Fig 6–3).

The advantage of using *Taq* polymerase rather than Klenow fragment is due to its thermostability. At first, thermolabile Klenow fragment had to be replenished after each denaturation step. The introduction of thermostable *Taq* polymerase[25] to PCR greatly simplified the whole procedure, since the addition of fresh enzyme after each denaturation step was no longer required.[26] This modification, therefore, makes the whole procedure amenable to automation through the use of a thermal cycler.[27] Employing *Taq* polymerase instead of Klenow fragment also enhances the specificity of the reaction. The high reaction temperature in the former case causes dissociation of poorly matched primer-template hybrids so that only highly complementary substrate remains as the reaction mixture approaches the temperature at which catalysis occurs.[26] Thus, the higher annealing temperatures (e.g., 55°C) favor the subsequent synthesis of a specific product only, instead of the spectrum of products that is formed when this step is performed at lower temperatures (e.g., 25°C, 37°C). Similarly, the amount of nonspecific products of PCR also can increase as the extension time becomes longer or if the amount of enzyme is higher[26] (Table 6–1).

In general, the products of polymerase chain reaction multiply to amounts approximately equal to 2^n, where n is the number of cycles. Single-copy genomic sequences can be amplified by a factor of about 10,000,000 with high specificity. DNA segments up to 2 kb long can be amplified and visualized by detection with radioactive probes,[28] while fragments of at least 1 kb can be visualized in ultraviolet (UV) light directly in an agarose gel containing ethidium bromide (Witt and Erickson, unpublished data, April 1988). Because of its enormous sensitivity and specificity, the PCR amplification method already has been applied not only to cloning[29] and sequencing,[28, 30] but also to the diagnosis of several genetic disorders, such as β-thalassemia,[31] sickle cell anemia,[32, 33] phenylketonuria,[34] and hemophilia A[35]; to the detection of infectious disease pathogens like HIV-1[36] and HPV[37]; and to the identification of neoplastic cells bearing chromosomal aberrations.[38] The method has also been used successfully for HLA typing.[32]

In forensic science, PCR technology opens the way to a variety of applications, in that it can be used to identify or to exonerate suspects in rape and murder cases. The biological evidence found at the scene of violent crimes, including bloodstains, semen, and hair, is often of such poor quantity and quality that it cannot be analyzed by other forensic techniques. Because the PCR method works with partially degraded DNA, as well as with intact DNA, sequences of interest can be amplified and then compared with the suspect's DNA to obtain identification. A very elegant study was performed using single human hairs as a source of DNA for HLA typing by hybridization with allele-specific oligonucleotide probes following enzymatic amplification.[39] Direct sequencing of the amplified fragment also was performed. The recovery of DNA from each freshly plucked hair was about 200 ng and from each single shed hair was about 10 ng, amounting to about 1,000 copies of a single-copy HLA gene.

The use of the polymerase chain reaction as a tool for the determination of sex on DNA was reported by Kogan et al.[35] Because the authors were interested in the prenatal diagnosis of hemophilia A, an exact determination of fetal sex was of im-

TABLE 6–1.

Comparison of Different Conditions of the Polymerase Chain Reaction With Y Chromosome–Specific Alphoid Repeat Primers on the Template of Male DNA*

Conditions	Results
1. Reaction buffer according to Kogan et al,[35] 2 U of taq polymerase per sample, annealing at 37°C, 30 cycles.	+ + + Slight unspecific product
2. As in 1., except 4–6 U of taq polymerase per sample.	+ + + Growing amount of unspecific products
3. As in 1., except annealing at 55°C.	+/− Very poor yield of the reaction
4. As in 1., except annealing at 55°C and 6 U of taq polymerase per sample.	+ +
5. Reaction buffer according to Cetus Corp, 2 U of taq polymerase per sample, annealing at 37°C, 30 cycles.	+ +
6. As in 5., except 6 U of taq polymerase per sample.	+ Growing amount of unspecific products
7. As in 5., except annealing at 55°C.	+ + +
8. As in 5., except 6 U of taq polymerase per sample.	+ + Significant amount of unspecific products
9. As in 5., except annealing at 72°C.	−
10. As in 5., except 25 cycles.	+ +
11. As in 5., except 20 cycles.	+
12. As in 5., except 10 cycles.	−

*The scale used for evaluation of the specific product of PCR: + + + = distinct specific product, very bright band; + + = distinct specific product, bright band; + = distinct specific product, faint band; − = no specific product.

portance to them. The 23 nucleotide–long primers they used were designed to match the Y-specific 3.4 kb repeat sequence in the heterochromatic fragment of human Y chromosome[40] and to amplify a 154 bp sequence. The amplification of this fragment enabled them to distinguish between male and female DNA even when fetal DNA extracted from chorionic villi was used as a template. They also showed that DNA extraction prior to amplification is unnecessary by successfully amplifying the Y-specific fragment directly from villi of male fetuses. For this purpose, the villous sample was spun down, resuspended in alkaline solution containing nonionic detergent, and boiled to release DNA. Aliquots of the resulting solution were used to direct the PCR amplification reaction. As a control, amplification of a fragment of the Alu family was used. For unknown reasons, Kogan et al used 63°C as a temperature of the extension step, which is much below the optimum for *Taq* polymerase activity. The results of the sex diagnosis performed were confirmed by dot blot analysis of portions of amplified samples according to Lau et al.[6] However, our reservations concerning the use of a heterochromatic fragment of the Y chromosome as a molecular target for sex recognition (previously discussed in this chapter) can be applied also to the method described by Kogan et al.

For our PCR sexing of DNA, two sets of primers (called Y1,Y2 and Y3,Y4) flanking different 170 bp–long fragments of alphoid repeats of human Y chromosome were used. Their sequences were[19]:

Y1 - ATGATAGAAACGGAAATATG
Y2 - AGTAGAATGCAAAGGGCTCC
Y3 - ACGGTGGGAAAGGAAATATC
Y4 - ATAAGACCCAAAAGGCTCCA

For amplification of a 130 bp–long, X-specific fragment which we used as a positive control, primers called X1,X2 were used. Their sequences were[41]:

X1 - AATCTGCAAATGGAGATTTG
X2 - GTTCAGCTCTGTGAGTGAAA

The protocol recommended by Cetus Corporation was used, utilizing annealing at 55°C for 1 min, 2.5 U of *Taq* polymerase per 100 μl reaction mixture, and 1 μg of genomic DNA as a template. Genomic DNA was isolated according to the method of Kunkel et al,[42] with some modifications. Products of PCR were analyzed either by 12% polyacrylamide gel electrophoresis or by 4% agarose gel electrophoresis (a composite gel of 3% NuSieve and 1% regular low EEO agaroses).[43] In our experience, agarose gel provides separation of DNA fragments almost as well as does polyacrylamide gel, and it is much easier to handle.

When male or female DNA was used for PCR, the male template gave both fragments, that is, the 170 bp Y-specific fragment (using both Y1,Y2 and Y3,Y4 primers) and the 130 bp X-specific fragment were synthesized (Fig 6–4,A). With female DNA, only the X-specific 130 bp fragment was synthesized (Fig 6–4,B). The intensity of the Y-specific band synthesized with Y3,Y4 primers was usually lower than the one obtained with Y1,Y2 primers. The intensity of the 130 bp X-specific band synthesized on male DNA usually was higher than that of each of the Y-specific bands. This can be explained by the availability of target sequences within genomic DNA—alphoid blocs on the Y chromosome are repeated only about 100 times,[19] whereas alphoid blocs on the X chromosome are present in about 5,000 copies.[41]

An attempt was made to synthesize both fragments in one tube containing male DNA. Using a high temperature of annealing (55°C) to enhance the specificity of the reaction, the synthesis of both fragments was impossible, even when ratios of Y- and X-specific primers were changed in favor of the Y (1:1–100:1). In all cases only the 130 bp band was obtained (data not shown). Again, this is best explained by the relative availability of both template sequences and the competition for enzyme molecules. When annealing was performed at 37°C, synthesis of both 170 bp and 130 bp fragments in one tube was possible, but these mild conditions also permitted the synthesis of numerous unspecific products of higher molecular weight (Fig 6–5).

Blood spotted on filter paper may serve as a laboratory model of biological evidence such as bloodstains found at a crime scene. We attempted to use such a model for sexing DNA, assuming that this approach may be useful in the future for forensic science and also for clinical diagnosis. The application of dried blood spots and automated filter paper blotters already has improved, simplified, and quickened newborn screening procedures for several genetic diseases.[44] The use of PCR, with blood spots as a source of DNA, for population screening to detect carriers of phenylketonuria has been suggested in the literature.[34]

A DNA microextraction procedure from dried blood spots has been described.[45] The authors rehydrated the white blood cells in the dried specimen, separated these cells from the red cell hemolysate by centrifugation, lysed the cells with SDS, digested them with Proteinase K, and then performed phenol/ether extraction of DNA. This

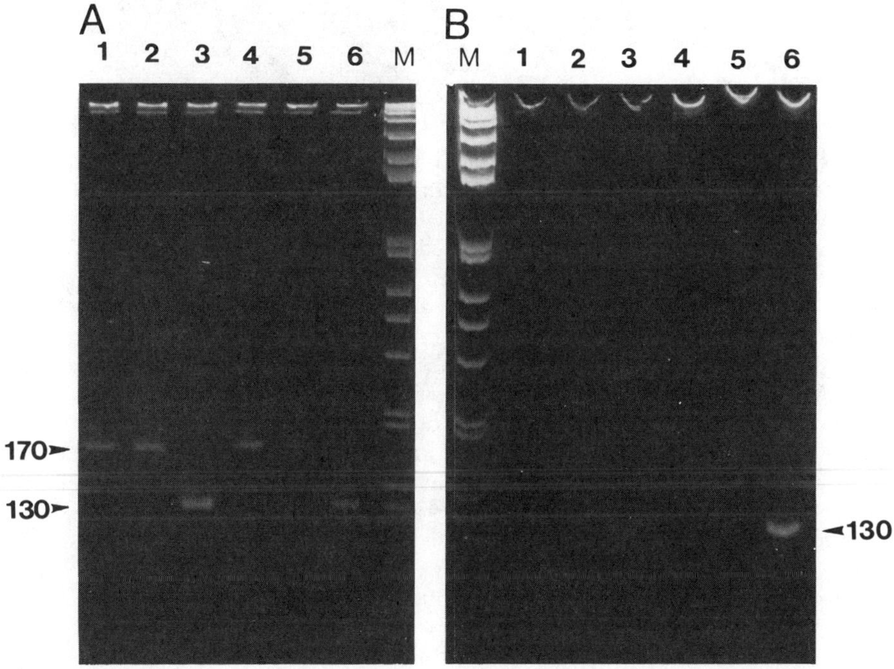

FIG 6–4.
Sexing of DNA using the polymerase chain reaction. **A,** 1 μg of male DNA from two different individuals (1-3 and 4-6, respectively) used as a template; *lanes 1 and 4,* primers Y1,Y2; *lanes 2 and 5,* primers Y3,Y4; *lanes 3 and 6,* primers X1,X2. Positions of 170 bp and 130 bp bands shown on the left. **B,** 1 μg of female DNA from two different individuals (1-3 and 4-6, respectively) used as a template; contents of lanes and primers as in **A.** Position of 130 bp band shown on the right. *M* = size markers (from the bottom: 142 bp, 154 bp, 200 bp, 298 bp, etc.). Temperature profile of the reaction: 1 minute at 94°C, 1 minute at 55°C, 3 minutes at 72°C, 30 cycles. Electrophoresis in 12% polyacrylamide gel in TBE buffer, stained with ethidium bromide.

FIG 6–5.
Products of the polymerase chain reaction on a template of male DNA. Temperature profile of the reaction: 1 minute at 94°C, 1 minute at 37°C, 3 minutes at 72°C, 30 cycles. *Lane 1,* primers Y1,Y2; *lane 2,* primers Y3,Y4; *lane 3,* primers X1,X2; *lane 4,* primers Y1,Y2, X1,X2. Electrophoresis and markers as in Figure 6–4. Positions of 170 bp and 130 bp bands shown on the right.

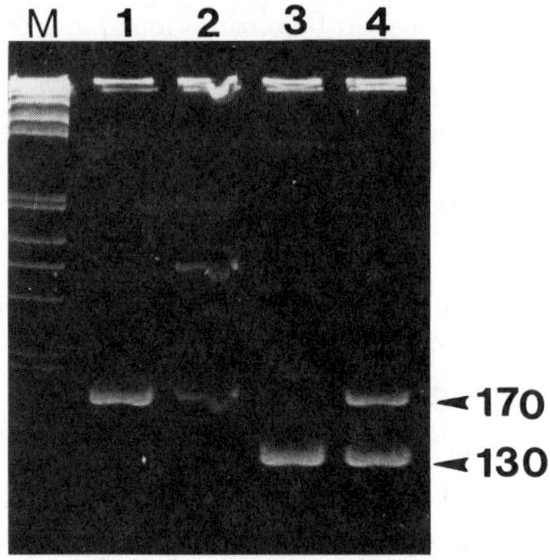

microextraction method from dried specimens seems to be superior to the one described previously.[21] The reproducible yield was 0.5 μg DNA from the dried equivalent of 50 μl whole blood (standard dried specimens, used for routine newborn screening). DNA in dried specimens stored at room temperature was shown to be stable on filter paper for over 4 months[45] and on cotton cloth for up to 4 years.[21] Similar methods of DNA microextraction can be applied also to hair roots, semen stains, and semen-contaminated vaginal swabs.[21] Such extracted DNA was quantitatively and qualitatively sufficient for Southern blotting[21, 45] and fingerprinting.[21]

In the procedure used in our study, dried specimens on Whatman 3MM filter paper were cut into pieces and rehydrated in 3 ml of 0.85% NaCl for 2 hours. Eluted cells were spun down in Eppendorf tubes and washed with 0.85% NaCl. The cellular pellet was resuspended in 50 μl of sterile water and boiled for 10 minutes in order to release DNA. The amount of DNA obtained in this way was below the sensitivity limit of a regular minigel (0.9% agarose containing 0.002% ethidium bromide). This DNA solution, however, was used successfully as a template for the polymerase chain reaction.

The conditions of the reaction in this case were the same as those for regular DNA preparations used as a template (i.e., denaturation at 94°C for 1 minute, annealing at 55°C for 1 minute, elongation at 74°C for 3 minutes). When DNA from dried specimens of male blood was used, the 170 bp fragment was effectively synthesized and was easily detectable under UV light in the agarose gel with ethidium bromide (Fig 6–6,A, lanes 1 and 2). However, using the same conditions of the reaction, the 170 bp fragment was also nonspecifically synthesized on female DNA template from dried spots. The intensity of this band in the gel was much lower when compared with the male dried spot DNA (see Fig 6–6,A, lanes 3 and 4). In order to enhance the specificity of the reaction, DNA solutions were treated with Proteinase K (100 μg per sample, temperature 42°C, overnight). This resulted in specific synthesis of the 170 bp Y-specific fragment only when DNA from male blood spots was used (Fig 6–

6,B, lanes 1 and 2). No products of PCR using Y-specific primers were detected on female DNA template (see Fig 6–6,B, lanes 3 and 4). Y-specific bands in Figure 6–6,A, lanes 3 and 4, and Figure 6–6,B, lane 2, are barely visible on the reproduced picture; they were much easier to notice directly in agarose gel. The intensity of the band of Y3,Y4 flanked fragment was lower than that of the band of Y1,Y2 flanked Y-chromosomal fragment. The synthesis of Y1,Y2 flanked fragment seems to be more specific than the synthesis of Y3,Y4 flanked fragment.

The reasons for the synthesis of the 170 bp fragment on female "dried spots" DNA are unclear; as digestion with Proteinase K suggests, this may be caused by some of the numerous proteins present in the whole blood. Probably some other changes in reaction conditions, such as a slight rise in stringency of annealing, may further enhance the specificity of the reaction.

In our work, we were able to amplify Y- and X-specific fragments on DNA from dried blood spots from an equivalent of as little as 10 μl of whole blood (not shown). Dried blood specimens of up to 8 years of age were used successfully and DNA released from these specimens was of sufficient quality for PCR.[46] However, when

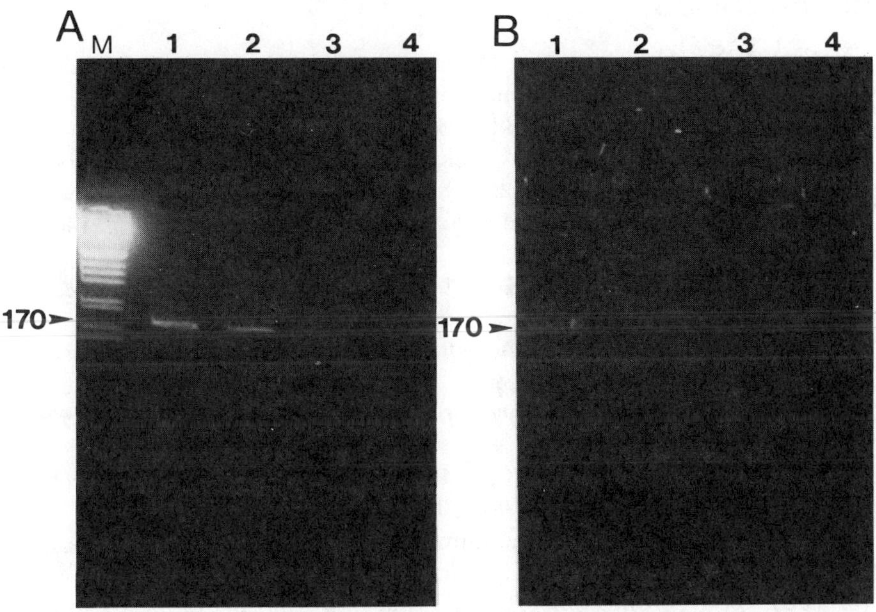

FIG 6–6.
Sexing by PCR of DNA from dried spots of 50 μl of whole blood. **A,** *lane 1,* male blood, primers Y1,Y2; *lane 2,* male blood, primers Y3,Y4; *lane 3,* female blood, primers Y1,Y2; *lane 4,* female blood, primers Y3,Y4. **B,** all blood samples digested with 100 μg of Proteinase K prior to the reaction; contents of lanes as in **A.** Electrophoresis in 4% composite agarose gel. Position of 170 bp band shown on the right.

older specimens were used, fainter bands of PCR products were obtained (data not shown).

The results presented in this review show that techniques of molecular biology can be used successfully for the sexing of purified DNA or impure, biological evidence. Hybridization techniques, as well as the polymerase chain reaction method, are not only up to date, but are also quick and reliable. There seems to be no doubt that molecular biology already has become a significant part of forensic science.

Acknowledgments

Critical reading of the manuscript by Linda Kalikin, the graphic work done by Brian Levy, and the excellent secretarial assistance of Ann Mogan are gratefully acknowledged. Michal Witt was the recipient of a Fulbright Research Award. Work performed in our laboratory was partially supported by NIH grant HD 20670 to Robert P. Erickson.

REFERENCES

1. Yam P, Petz LD, Ali S, et al: Development of a single probe for documentation of chimerism following bone marrow transplantation. *Am J Hum Genet* 1987; 41:867–881.
2. Stalvey JRD, Erickson RP, Dasouki M, et al: Clarification of chromosomal abnormalities associated with sexual ambiguity by studies with Y-chromosomal DNA sequences. *Cytogenet Cell Genet* 1988; 47:140–143.
3. Goodfellow P, Darling S, Wolfe J: The human Y chromosome. *J Med Genet* 1985; 22:329–344.
4. Paris Conference 1971: Standardization in human cytogenetics. *Birth Defects* 1972; 8:7.
5. Cooke H: Repeated sequences specific to human males. *Nature* 1976; 262:182–186.
6. Lau Y-F, Dozy AM, Huang JC, et al: A rapid screening test for antenatal sex determination. *Lancet* 1984; 1:14–16.
7. Lau Y-F: Organization of the human Y-specific Hae III 3.4 kb repeat sequence and their application in clinical diagnosis, in Sandberg AA (ed): *The Y chromosome, Part A: Basic characteristics of the Y chromosome*. New York, Alan R Liss, Inc, 1985, pp 177–192.
8. McDonough PG, Tho SP, Trill JJ, et al: Use of two different deoxyribonucleic acid probes to detect Y chromosome deoxyribonucleic acid in subjects with normal and altered Y chromosomes. *Am J Obstet Gynecol* 1986; 154:737–748.

9. Lau Y-F: Detection of Y-specific repeat sequences in normal and variant human chromosomes using in situ hybridization with biotinylated probes. *Cytogenet Cell Genet* 1985; 39:184–187.
10. Lau Y-F, Schonberg S: A male-specific DNA probe detects heterochromatin sequences in a familial Yq-chromosome. *Am J Hum Genet* 1984; 36:1394–1396.
11. McKay RDG, Bobrow M, Cooke HJ: The identification of a repeated DNA sequence involved in the karyotypic polymorphism of the human Y chromosome. *Cytogenet Cell Genet* 1987; 21:19–32.
12. Cooke HJ, Noel B: Confirmation of Y/autosome translocations using recombinant DNA. *Hum Genet* 1979; 50:39–44.
13. De Martenville B, Blakemore KJ, Mahoney MJ, et al: DNA analysis of first-trimester chorionic villous biopsis: Test for maternal contamination. *Am J Hum Genet* 1984; 36:1357–1368.
14. Page DC, Mosher R, Simpson EM, et al: The sex-determining region of the human Y chromosome encodes a finger protein. *Cell* 1987; 51:1091–1104.
15. Page DC: Is ZfY the sex determining gene on the human Y chromosome? *Philos Trans R Soc Lond [Biol]* 1988; 322:155–157.
16. Willard HF, Waye JS: Hierarchical order in chromosome-specific human alpha satellite DNA. *Trends Genet* 1987; 3:192–198.
17. Tyler-Smith C, Brown WRA: Structure of the major block of alphoid satellite DNA on the human Y chromosome. *J Mol Biol* 1987; 195:457–470.
18. Wolfe J, Darling SM, Erickson RP, et al: Isolation and characterization of an alphoid centromeric repeat family from the human Y chromosome. *J Mol Biol* 1985; 182:477–485.
19. Willard HF: Molecular organization of repeated DNA sequences on the human Y chromosome, in Sandberg AA (ed): *The Y chromosome, Part A: Basic characteristics of the Y chromosome*. New York, Alan R Liss, Inc, 1985, pp 125–140.
20. Stalvey JRD, Erickson RP: An improved method for detecting Y chromosomal DNA. *Hum Genet* 1987; 76:240–243.
21. Gill P, Jeffreys AJ, Werrett DJ: Forensic application of DNA "fingerprints." *Nature* 1985; 318:577–579.
22. Marx JL: DNA fingerprinting takes the witness stand. *Science* 1988; 240:1616–1618.
23. Mullis KB, Faloona FA: Specific synthesis of DNA in vitro via a polymerase catalyzed chain reaction. *Methods Enzymol* 1987; 155:335–350.
24. Saiki RK, Scharf S, Faloona F, et al: Enzymatic amplification of β-globin genomic sequence and restriction site analysis for diagnosis of sickle cell anemia. *Science* 1985; 230:1350–1354.

25. Chien A, Edgar DB, Trela JM: Deoxyribonucleic acid polymerase from the extreme thermophile *Thermus aquaticus. J Bacteriol* 1976; 127:1550–1557.
26. Saiki RK, Gelfand DH, Stoffel S, et al: Primer directed enzymatic amplification of DNA with thermostable DNA polymerase. *Science* 1988; 239:487–491.
27. Oste C: Polymerase chain reaction. *Biotechniques* 1988; 6:162–167.
28. Wrischnik LA, Higuchi RG, Stoneking M, et al: Length mutations in human mitochondrial DNA: Direct sequencing of enzymatically amplified DNA. *Nucleic Acids Res* 1987; 15:529–542.
29. Scharf SJ, Horn GT, Erlich HA: Direct cloning and sequence analysis of enzymatically amplified genomic sequences. *Science* 1986; 233:1076–1078.
30. Engelke DR, Hoener PA, Collins FS: Direct sequencing of enzymatically amplified human genomic DNA. *Proc Natl Acad Sci USA* 1988; 85:544–548.
31. Wong C, Dowling CE, Saiki RK, et al: Characterization of β-thalassaemia mutations using direct genomic sequencing of amplified single copy DNA. *Nature* 1987; 330:384–386.
32. Saiki RK, Bugawan TL, Horn GT, et al: Analysis of enzymatically amplified β-globin and HLA-DQα DNA with allele-specific oligonucleotide probes. *Nature* 1986; 324:163–166.
33. Chehab FF, Doherty M, Cai S, et al: Detection of sickle cell anemia and thalassaemias. *Nature* 1987; 329:293–294.
34. DiLella AG, Huang W-M, Woo SLC: Screening for phenylketonuria mutations by DNA amplification with the polymerase chain reaction. *Lancet* 1988; 1:497–499.
35. Kogan SC, Doherty M, Gitschier J: An improved method for prenatal diagnosis of genetic diseases by analysis of amplified DNA sequences. *N Engl J Med* 1987; 317:985–990.
36. Ou C-Y, Kwok S, Mitchell SW, et al: DNA amplification for direct detection of HIV-1 in DNA of peripheral blood mononuclear cells. *Science* 1988; 239:295–297.
37. Shibata D, Martin WJ, Arnheim N: Detection of human papilloma virus in paraffin-embedded tissue using the polymerase chain reaction. *J Exp Med* 1988; 167:225–230.
38. Lee M-S, Chang K-S, Cabanillas F, et al: Detection of minimal residual cells carrying the t(14;18) by DNA sequence amplification. *Science* 1987; 237:175–178.
39. Higuchi R, von Beroldingen CH, Sensabaugh GF, et al: DNA typing from single hairs. *Nature* 1988; 332:543–546.

40. Nakahori Y, Mitani K, Yamada M, et al: A human Y-chromosome specific repeated DNA family (DYZ1) consists of a tandem array of pentanucleotides. *Nucleic Acids Res* 1986; 14:7569–7580.
41. Waye JS, Willard HF: Chromosome-specific alpha satellite DNA: Nucleotide sequence of the 2.0 kilobasepair repeat from the human X chromosome. *Nucleic Acids Res* 1985; 13:2731–2743.
42. Kunkel LM, Smith KD, Boyer SH, et al: Analysis of human Y chromosome-specific reiterated DNA in chromosome variants. *Proc Natl Acad Sci USA* 1977; 74:1245–1249.
43. Maniatis T, Fritsch EF, Sambrook J (eds): *Molecular Cloning: A laboratory manual.* New York, Cold Spring Harbor Laboratory, 1983.
44. Guthrie R: Organization of regional newborn screening laboratory, in Bickel H, Guthrie R, Hammersen G (eds): *Neonatal Screening for Inborn Errors of Metabolism.* New York, Springer-Verlag, 1980, pp 259–270.
45. McCabe ERB, Huang S-Z, Seltzer WK, et al: DNA microextraction from dried blood spots on filter paper blotters: Potential application to newborn screening. *Hum Genet* 1987; 75:213–216.
46. Witt M, Erickson RP: A rapid method for detection of Y-chromosomal DNA from dried blood specimens by the polymerase chain reaction. *Hum Genet* 1989; 82:271–274.

Chapter 7

Labelling and Detection of Nucleic Acid Probes

Terry A. Landers, Ph.D.

The development of "molecular probes" has been a powerful innovation with applications in many areas of the biological sciences. Probes are molecules that are capable of finding and reporting on the presence of specific targets which are other molecules and macromolecular structures. These targets may be in solution, fixed to a filter, in a gel, or on a microscope slide. Probes are able to "report" their presence because they carry some distinguishable feature, or label, that allows the user to determine where the target was found and/or how much target was found by the probe. The development of probes has been made possible by the development of techniques for labelling macromolecules without significantly impairing their natural function. Antibodies, with radioisotopes or enzymes attached, are the most widely used molecular probes, capable of reporting qualitative and quantitative information on a spectrum of targets ranging from small hormone and drug metabolites to complex viral and cellular antigens. Compared to antibody probes, nucleic acid probes have a narrow range of target types (only other nucleic acids), but within that range they can be designed to recognize an almost infinite number of different nucleic acid sequences.

In this chapter, a number of methods of labelling or modifying nucleic acids to make them detectable as reporters will be reviewed, discussing the general mechanisms of labelling and detection used. Detailed protocols for the use of many of these techniques are given in several excellent molecular biology laboratory handbooks,[1–3] and reagent "kits" for many of these techniques are available from various commercial suppliers.

The most fundamental requirement of a nucleic acid probe is that it contain the complement of the target sequence that is to be detected. Molecules containing the necessary sequences can be derived from natural sources by recombinant DNA cloning techniques, by purification from enriched tissue sources, or by chemical synthesis of short nucleic acid molecules (oligonucleotides) of known sequence. A corollary requirement is that a probe must not contain significant amounts of sequences, such as a cloning vector, that might detect unintended targets.

The specificity of a nucleic acid probe depends on the ability of the probe to form a double-helical structure with the target through formation of Watson-Crick base pairs during the process of hybridization. In this process, single-stranded nucleic acids randomly "test" other nucleic acid molecules they encounter by forming a few base pairs. If the sequences are closely related and the initial pairs formed are properly oriented, the adjoining bases will then pair very rapidly to form a stable hybrid. Initial pairs that do not lead to full hybrid formation dissociate readily.

The specificity with which a probe recognizes its target is not necessarily absolute. Given the level of natural variation, probes normally are used under conditions which allow a low level of mismatch or error in probe-target hybrids so a positive signal will be seen even when a few bases cannot form proper base pairs. This "stringency" of match required for hybrid formation (and positive signal) can be adjusted according to the amount of variability known to occur in the target being sought. For some types of detection using oligonucleotide probes, absolutely perfect matches may be required. Stringency of hybridization also may be adjusted for the size of the probe and the type of label used, because some labels affect the pairing ability of the base to which they are attached.

To be useful as a nucleic acid probe, a nucleic acid molecule must be modified in some way so as to be detectable in the presence of a large excess of non-target nucleic acid. An average-size human gene may constitute less than one part per million of cellular DNA, and many of the targets of forensic interest are even smaller. To compound the detection problem, the total amount of DNA recovered from a sample is often on the order of 0.1 to 10.0 μg, the amount of DNA contained in a few thousand cells. Thus, the actual target may amount to no more than a fraction of a picogram (10^{-12} g), which requires methods of detection of picogram or sub-picogram quantities of the probe. The most reliable means for detecting the smallest amounts of target require the use of radioisotopes, most commonly ^{32}P. Non-isotopic methods are available also for the detection of more abundant targets.

METHODS OF LABELLING NUCLEIC ACIDS

Labels can be introduced into a nucleic acid molecule by enzymatic, nonenzymatic, or a combination of enzymatic and non-enzymatic methods. The enzymatic methods generally are the most widely used because they can generate either DNA or RNA probes in a wide range of sizes, the reactions are easily controlled, and the products are well defined. Some labels are attached to the sugar, others to the nitrogenous base of nucleotides. The term "labelled base" often is used as a synonym for "labelled nucleotide" without meaning that the label is necessarily in the base portion of a nucleotide. The terms "base" and "nucleotide" may be used interchangeably in discussions of nucleic acid lengths.

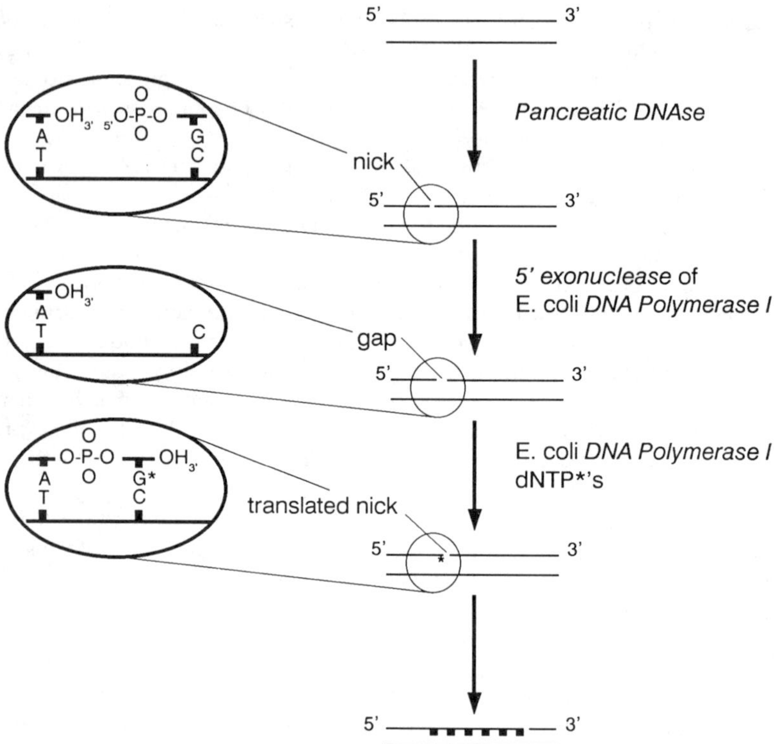

FIG 7–1.
Nick translation. Labelled nucleotides are incorporated into double-stranded DNA by the combined action of pancreatic DNAse I, and the 5' exonuclease and polymerase activities of *E. coli* DNA polymerase I.

Enzymatic Labelling Methods

Nick Translation.—Nick translation[4] (Fig 7–1) has been widely used to label double-stranded DNA. This technique is based on the properties of DNA polymerase I (Pol I) from *Escherichia coli*. As with all known DNA polymerases, this enzyme requires a single-stranded DNA as a *template* to direct the synthesis of new DNA strands, and a *primer*, with a 3'-OH group, hybridized to the 3'-end of the template to which the newly synthesized DNA will be attached. The new DNA is synthesized from deoxyribonucleoside triphosphates (dNTPs) precursors. DNA synthesis proceeds by attaching the deoxyribonucleoside *mono*phosphate portion of a dNTP to the 3'-end of the primer and releasing pyrophosphate. The new chain grows in a "5' to 3'" direction, with each new nucleotide being chosen according to the Watson-Crick base pairing rules to be the complement of the opposing base in the template.

In addition to its DNA polymerase activity, Pol I also has two exonuclease activities, one capable of removing nucleotides from the 3' end of double-stranded DNA, and the other of removing them from the 5' end. The 3'-exonuclease serves in vivo as a "proof reading" activity, removing incorrectly incorporated nucleotides from newly synthesized DNA. The 5'-exonuclease functions in vivo to remove damaged bases during one type of repair process. It is this repair capability that is used for "nick translation."

To perform a nick translation labelling reaction, the double-stranded DNA to be labeled is mixed with a small amount of pancreatic DNAse I, *E. coli* DNA polymerase I, and a mixture of dNTPs, at least one of which is labelled. Pancreatic DNAse I introduces nicks into the probe DNA by cleaving the phosphate-sugar backbone of either strand of the molecule at random. These nicks are recognized by Pol I as sites for repair. Pol I binds to a nick, and its 5'-exonuclease activity removes the nucleotide on the 5' side, leaving a one-nucleotide gap. The polymerase activity then repairs the gap, incorporating a new nucleotide from the pool of labeled dNTPs and attaching it to the 3' side of the nick. This process "translates" the nick one step in the 3' direction, because the 3'-OH of the newly incorporated nucleotide is not linked to the 5' end of the following nucleotide. There is still a nick. This process is repeated until the nick is translated to the end of the template, it meets another nick on the opposite strand, or the Pol I spontaneously releases itself from the nick.

Since DNAse I nicks both strands of DNA at random, labelled nucleotides are distributed evenly over both strands of all DNA in the reaction mixture. However, the labelled DNA is no longer in the form of continuous, full-length double strands due to the introduction of the nicks. When the starting DNA is relatively large, the introduction of nicks does not affect the utility of the probe, but this method is not useful for labelling DNAs less than ≈500 bases long as it leaves many fragments too small to hybridize efficiently.

Random Oligonucleotide Primers.—Another method for labelling probes uses a mixture of short oligonucleotides (average length 6 bases) of random sequence to prime DNA synthesis on single-stranded DNA molecules[5,6] (Fig 7–2). DNA synthesis is carried out by a modified form of *E. coli* DNA polymerase I. Pol I must be modified by enzymatic or genetic methods to remove the 5'-exonuclease activity which would otherwise degrade the oligonucleotide primers before they could be used. This modified form is referred to variously as "Klenow," "Klenow fragment," "DNA Polymerase I Large Fragment," or "Pol IK."

For oligonucleotide priming, the template DNA must be single stranded. Double-stranded DNAs can be denatured into the two complementary single strands either by heating to >95°C and then cooling quickly, or by raising the pH to >11.5 and then neutralizing quickly. Once the template is single stranded, the oligonucleotide primers, Klenow fragment, and labelled dNTPs are added. The short, random-sequence primers have a high probability of hybridizing to many places on the template DNA. When a Klenow fragment finds a hybridized primer, the polymerase activity then begins to elongate from the primer along the template. The newly synthesized DNA is attached to the primer and includes label from the pool of labelled dNTPs. If the Klenow fragment encounters another primer while elongating, the second primer is displaced so elongation can continue. Extension stops when the enzyme encounters the end of the template or another extended double-stranded stretch, or the enzyme spontaneously terminates. This technique works well for DNA molecules of almost any size, including those too small to label by nick translation. Since this procedure results in a net synthesis of new DNA (potentially one new strand for each template strand), rather than replacement of DNA as with nick translation, incorporation of label is usually more efficient. This procedure also benefits from not being dependent on the sometimes temperamental pancreatic DNAse.

A variant of this method uses a specific, rather than random, primer to direct synthesis from only a specified region of one strand of a DNA template. This specific primer reaction is basically the same as that used for DNA sequencing by the dideoxy method of Sanger.[7] The specific primers are generally synthetic oligonucleotides 12 to 20 bases long. With a carefully chosen primer, little or no probe complementary to any contaminating DNA, such as residual cloning vector, will be synthesized. This can be a problem with probes labelled by nick translation, or with random primers, because these methods label all DNAs in a solution, including residual cloning vector fragments. Labelled vector DNA may detect related sequences in samples containing contaminating bacterial DNA, giving false bands or high backgrounds.

T4 DNA Polymerase Replacement Synthesis.—T4 DNA polymerase is the DNA replication enzyme produced by bacteriophage T4 after infection of *E. coli*.

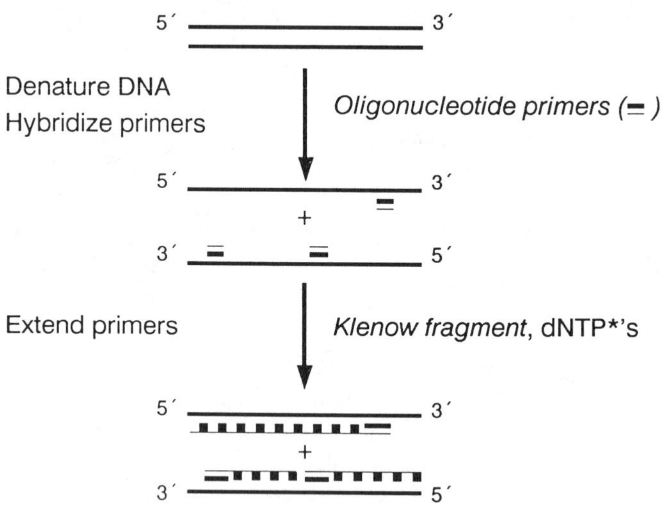

FIG 7–2.
Random oligonucleotide primers. Oligonucleotides hybridize to single-stranded DNAs to provide primers for the synthesis of labelled DNA by the Klenow fragment of *E. coli* DNA polymerase I.

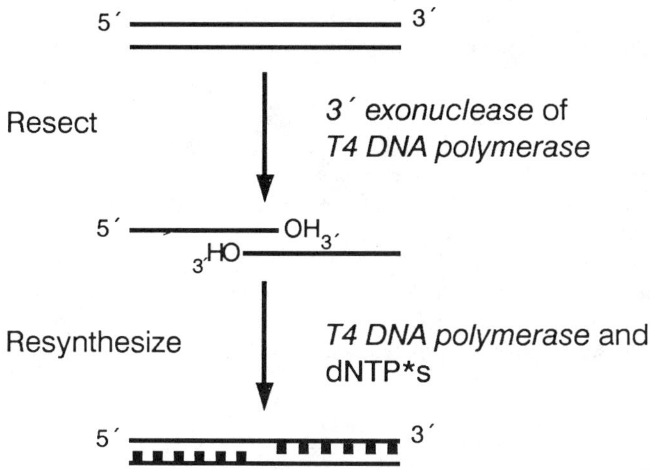

FIG 7–3.
T4 DNA polymerase replacement synthesis. The 3' exonuclease activity of bacteriophage T4 DNA polymerase removes nucleotides from the 3' end of DNA molecules in the absence of dNTPs. Upon the addition of labelled deoxynucleoside triphosphates, the polymerase synthesizes a labelled replacement of the DNA previously removed.

Enzymatically, it is similar to the Klenow fragment in that it has both DNA polymerase and 3'-exonuclease activities, but lacks a 5'-exonuclease activity. The principal difference between the two is the rate at which the 3' exonuclease acts. In the absence of dNTPs to polymerize, T4 DNA polymerase has a much more active 3' exonuclease activity. It will remove bases rapidly from the 3' ends of all DNA molecules in a solution, shortening all molecules simultaneously at approximately the same rate. It is this capability that has led to its use in "replacement labelling" procedures.[8,9]

In practice (Fig 7–3), T4 DNA polymerase is added to the double-stranded probe DNA in the absence of dNTPs for a specified length of time to allow the 3' exonuclease to resect (remove nucleotides from) the 3' ends of the molecules. The resection process exposes stretches of single-stranded DNA, which later will serve as templates, and shortened strands with free 3' ends, which later will serve as primers. Since resection proceeds from both ends of a molecule, care must be taken that it does not reach the middle of the molecule, or the primer strands will be too short to hybridize to the template strands.

After resection, labelled dNTPs are added to the reaction and the synthesis of new, labelled DNA begins on the resected molecules. Although the 3' exonuclease is still active, the polymerase is capable of adding nucleotides faster than they are removed by the exonuclease. Given sufficient dNTPs, the product is mostly full-length, double-stranded DNA. However, each individual strand is labelled only in its 3' half, and a region in the center of the molecule is not labelled. This asymmetry of labelling does not affect the utility of such probes for most uses. The efficiency of labelling is similar to that obtained by nick translation. With careful control of resection times, this method can be used on double-stranded DNAs ranging in length from 100 base pairs to >20,000 base pairs.

Polynucleotide Kinase.—Both single- and double-stranded polynucleotides can be labelled specifically at their 5' ends with ^{32}P by T4 polynucleotide kinase. This enzyme, isolated from bacteriophage T4-infected *E. coli*, is capable of either replacing or exchanging a monophosphate group at the 5' end of oligo- and polynucleotides[1] (Fig 7–4).

For labelling by polynucleotide kinase, the template must have either a hydroxyl group or a monophosphate at the 5' end. Labelling is most efficient for hydroxyl-terminated molecules. 5'-Monophosphate ends occur naturally, but normally are generated by cleavage of DNAs with restriction endonucleases and other exo- and en-

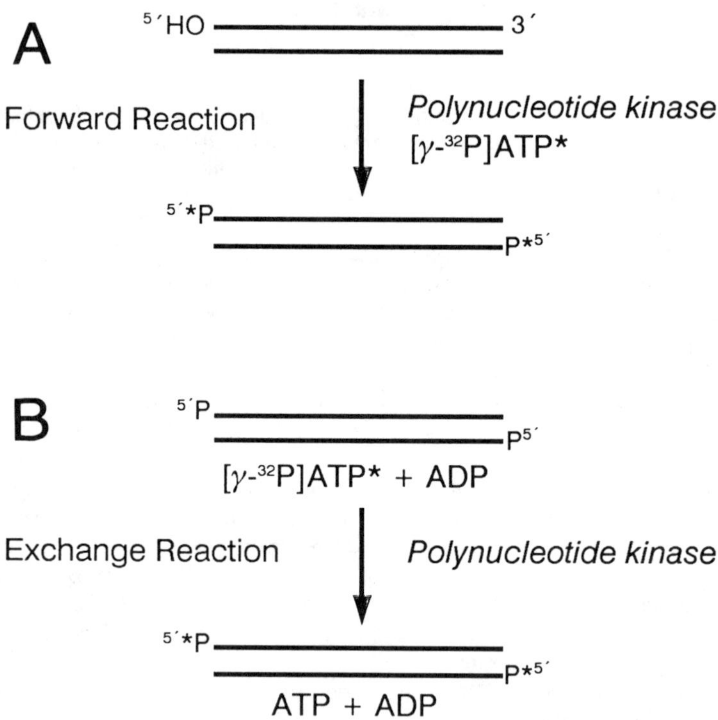

FIG 7–4.
Polynucleotide kinase. A, the forward reaction catalyzed by bacteriophage T4 polynucleotide kinase transfers the radioactive terminal phosphate residue from [γ-^{32}P]ATP to the 5'-hydroxyl group of a polynucleotide. B, under different reaction conditions, polynucleotide kinase catalyzes an exchange of phosphate groups between [γ-^{32}P]ATP and 5'-phosphate groups on polynucleotides. This reaction also requires ADP.

donucleases, such as pancreatic DNAse I. 5'-Hydroxyl ends are commonly found on synthetic oligonucleotides. Monophosphates may be removed from the 5'-termini of any DNA or RNA molecule by use of a phosphatase such as *E. coli* alkaline phosphatase or calf intestine alkaline phosphatase.

The only type of label used with polynucleotide kinase is [γ-^{32}P]ATP [the phosphorus in the γ (outermost) phosphate of the triphosphate is radioactive]. In the "forward reaction" (see Fig 7–4,A), polynucleotide kinase transfers the γ phosphate from ATP to the 5'-hydroxyl group of the polynucleotide, producing a phosphorylated polynucleotide and ADP. Under appropriate conditions, the enzyme also is capable of catalyzing the reverse reaction, transferring a 5'-monophosphate group from a polynucleotide to ADP to produce ATP and a 5'-OH polynucleotide. By selecting conditions where both the foward and reverse reactions can proceed, and by providing both ADP and [γ-^{32}P]ATP, an "exchange" reaction occurs with phosphorylated polynucleotides, producing labelled polynucleotides and unlabelled ATP (see Fig 7–4,B). The forward reaction is used frequently with high specific activity [γ-^{32}P]ATP to produce high specific activity oligonucleotide probes, but it is not an effective way to label large polynucleotides to high specific activity. The exchange reaction is used commonly to label electrophoresis standards where high specific activity is not necessary.

A characteristic of polynucleotides labelled by kinase is that when a mixture of molecules is labelled, all molecules receive approximately the same amount of label, regardless of size, since only 5' ends are labelled. This is in contrast to the previously described techniques in which molecules carry an amount of label proportional to their length. This feature of kinase labelling can be used to advantage when the number, rather than the mass, of molecules of different sizes must be determined.

Terminal Transferase.—Calf thymus terminal deoxyribonucleotidyl transferase (TdT) is a primer-dependent, template-independent polymerase. Like all known nucleic acid polymerases, it elongates by adding nucleotides to the 3' end of a primer, but in this case, without the direction of a template. The nucleotides must be supplied as dNTPs[10,11] (Fig 7–5). If it is provided with a labelled mixture of dNTPs, TdT will synthesize a "tail" of random sequence and random length on accessible 3' termini. If only a single type of dNTP is provided, the tails will be homopolymers of that nucleotide.

The primer for TdT may be either single- or double-stranded DNA. The efficiency of a primer depends on the structure of the 3' end of the molecule. If the 3' end is single-stranded or "blunt" (base paired exactly), as when cleaved with restriction endonucleases *Pst* I or *Hae* III, respectively, nucleotides are added readily. Different buffer conditions are required if the 3' end is "recessed" (there are unpaired bases at the 5' end of the opposite strand) such as is produced by *Eco* RI or *Hind* III.

The length of the tail can be controlled to some extent by the choice of time and reaction conditions. Tail lengths can be restricted to exactly one nucleotide by providing a deoxyribonucleotide analog lacking a 3'-hydroxyl group. Such analogs include the 2'- and 3'-dideoxynucleoside triphosphates used for DNA sequencing and 3'-dATP (cordycepin). Molecules with labelled, single-nucleotide 3' tails are similar to those labelled using the polynucleotide kinase procedure, in that only one label is attached per molecule. TdT also offers the possibility of attaching a single residue of a variety of types of modified nucleotides.

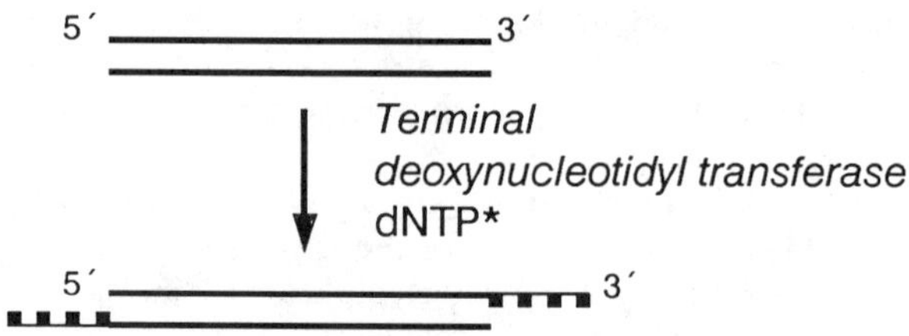

FIG 7–5.
Terminal transferase. Labelled nucleotides are attached to the 3' ends of DNA molecules by terminal deoxynucleotidyl transferase from calf thymus.

Bacteriophage RNA Polymerases.—The bacteriophages SP6, T7, and T3 each produce a phage-specific RNA polymerase upon infection of its host. Each phage RNA polymerase specifically recognizes only its own promoter sequences as the points at which to begin transcription, the synthesis of messenger RNAs. Normally found only in phage DNA at the beginning of genes, promoters indicate the strand of DNA that is to be synthesized and the point at which synthesis of an RNA copy of that strand of the phage DNA is to begin.

Phage RNA polymerases can be used in vitro to transcribe selected regions of DNA molecules by constructing appropriate recombinant DNA molecules. The probe sequence is inserted at a multiple cloning site downstream from the phage promoter in a specially designed vector.[12, 13] In some vectors, the multiple cloning site is between two opposing different phage promoters to allow either strand of the intervening DNA to be transcribed by selection of the appropriate RNA polymerase.

The cloned DNA is isolated from bacteria as a circular molecule. For in vitro work, the template is usually linearized by cleaving the probe DNA at the far end of the probe segment with a restriction endonuclease. On linear molecules, the RNA polymerase "runs off" the end and cannot continue on to transcribe vector sequences. With an adequate supply of NTPs, the phage RNA polymerases will transcribe a single template molecule many times, yielding a 5- to 20-fold net synthesis of probe transcript over input template (Fig 7–6).

With only minor changes, RNA probes can replace DNA probes in most procedures. RNA probes do require more care in handling at certain stages, because they are sensitive to degradation by the ribonucleases which are ubiquitous contaminants commonly found on fingertips. This is a particular problem during probe synthesis. However, this sensitivity can be used to advantage after hybridization to a blot, because the RNA in a DNA-RNA hybrid is protected from common ribonucleases. Thus, treating an RNA-probed blot with ribonuclease reduces backgrounds caused by unhybridized probes. RNA probes have an additional advantage over most DNA probes in that they are naturally single stranded. The absence of a complementary strand eliminates the self-hybridization that competes with target hybridization when double-stranded probes are used. If the template is properly prepared, the RNA transcripts contain virtually no vector-derived sequences, which reduces background from bacterial contamination of samples.

Radioactive labels are efficiently incorporated by the phage RNA polymerases. However, the enzymes seem to discriminate against incorporation of certain non-radioactively labelled nucleotide analogs,[13] and ways of circumventing such problems will be discussed below.

Non-Enzymatic Labelling Methods

A variety of non-enzymatic methods for labelling DNA and RNA have been developed. All involve attaching a recognizable substituent to an existing unlabelled nucleic acid, most frequently through covalent bonds to the nitrogenous bases of the nucleotides.

Photoactivated Compounds.—Light-generated free radicals are capable of rapidly forming new covalent bonds by insertion into many types of existing covalent bonds. This technique can be used for labelling nucleic acids (and proteins) with the vitamin/cofactor biotin by irradiating a mixture of the nucleic acid to be labelled and biotin linked to an arylazide ("photobiotin",[14] Fig 7–7). The modified benzene readily generates a nitrene radical when it is exposed to a common sunlamp. The photoactivated compound then inserts itself into other molecules that it encounters in solution. The detection of photobiotinylated probes is generally slightly less sensitive than that of enzymatically biotinylated probes.

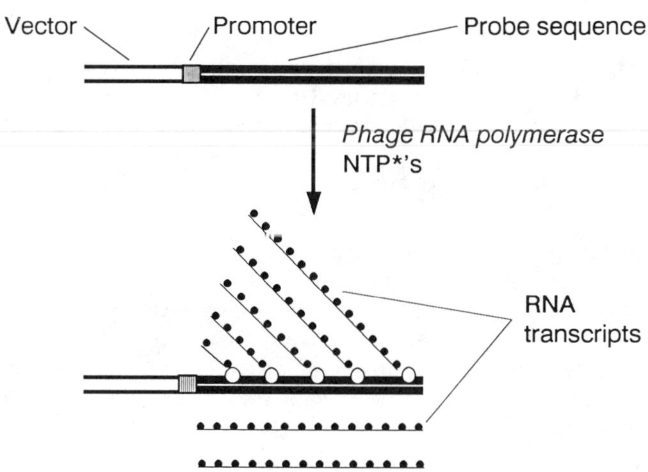

FIG 7–6.
RNA polymerases. Probe sequences cloned into special vectors can be transcribed into labelled RNA by bacteriophage RNA polymerases which initiate RNA synthesis at phage-specific promoter sequences.

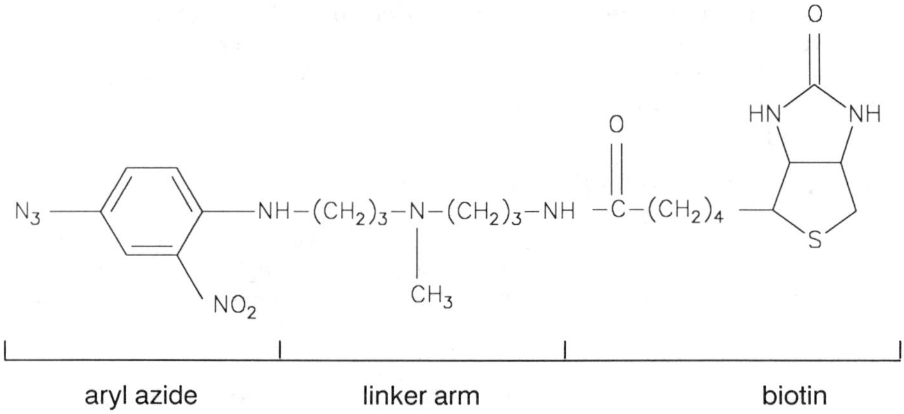

FIG 7–7.
Photobiotin. The photosensitive arylazide group of photobiotin is activated by exposure to light. The activated molecule then forms covalent bonds with nucleic acids in the solution to produce biotin-labelled probes.

Alkylating Compounds.—A wide variety of compounds are capable of alkylating the bases of DNA and RNA. Many of these chemicals are also carcinogens. N-acetoxy-N-acetyl-2-aminofluorene (AAF), which alkylates predominantly G residues and was originally studied as a carcinogen, has been used as a label for DNA detection.[15]

Iodination.—Direct oxidative iodination of nucleic acids to generate iodo-C (and iodo-U in RNA) residues has been used for a number of years as a way of introducing ^{125}I or ^{131}I into unlabelled molecules.[16] Iodo-C and iodo-U are also precursors for further chemical modications. The iodine linkage is not as stable as other modifications and exhibits a slow loss of label under some conditions.

Amino Substitution.—A two-step procedure for introducing amino-containing substituents to nucleic acids has been reported recently.[17] Bromine is introduced into T, G, or C residues under mild oxidative conditions. The bromine is then displaced by an amino group linked to a reporter group, such as dinitrophenol. Bisulfite catalyzes transamination between the amino group of cytidine and the substituted amines. This method has been used to attach amine-containing linker arms to CTP and dCTP for further modification.[18]

Glutaraldehyde Linking of Substituents.—Glutaraldehyde can be used to cross-link proteins, enzymes, and polyamines to nucleic acids in solution in a manner similar to that used for tissue fixation for microscopy.[19, 20] The degree of cross-linking must be controlled carefully to prevent inter-strand cross-links and the inhibition of hybridization efficiency.

Periodate Oxidation.—The 2',3'-cis hydroxyls at the 3' end of RNA molecules can be oxidized to a pair of aldehyde groups by periodate oxidation under mild conditions. The aldehydes are then targets for the addition of amino-containing compounds through a Schiff-base mechanism.

Chemical Synthesis.—The chemical synthesis of oligonucleotides permits the introduction of modified bases or their precursors at specified positions in the probe sequence. The modified oligonucleotide may be used directly as a probe[21] or as a primer.[22]

Enzymatic/Non-Enzymatic Labelling Methods

Some useful labelled nucleotide analogs are poorly or not significantly incorporated into nucleic acids by the appropriate DNA or RNA polymerases, probably due to the bulky or chemical characteristics of the label. Such labels can be incorporated by a two-step process, if a chemical precursor of the labelled nucleotide is acceptable to an RNA or DNA polymerase. As mentioned above, for example, phage RNA polymerases incorporate biotinylated nucleotides more slowly than normal nucleotides, reducing the size and yield of biotinylated RNAs. This problem can be circumvented by synthesizing the RNA with a precursor, such as allylamine-UTP (Fig 7–8,A), which is incorporated as efficiently as normal UTP.[13,23] The allylamine group provides a reactive primary amino function to which biotin can be attached chemically using ε-caproylamidobiotin N-hydroxysuccinimide ester (CAB-NHS ester, Fig 7–8,C).[23] Similarly, fluorescent DNA can be prepared by the incorporation of N^6-(6-aminohexyl)dATP (Fig 7–8,B) and subsequent reaction with fluorescein isothiocyanate (FITC) to attach fluorescein to the amino group. Proteins also have been linked to amino-substituted nucleic acids, by the use of bifunctional cross-linking reagents.[21]

LABELS AND DETECTION METHODS

Radioisotope Labels

Selection of Isotopes.—A number of radioisotopes can be introduced into nucleic acids as labels (Table 7–1) by either enzymatic or chemical means. The choice of isotope is determined by the source and type of nucleic acid to be labelled, the labelling procedures available, the desired method of detection, and the level of sensitivity needed.

^{32}P is the most frequently used isotope, because of its relatively high energy β particle (electron) emission and, more importantly, because of its high specific activity [disintegrations per minute (dpm) per mole or per microgram] and the fact that phosphorus is a normal constituent of all nucleic acids.

^{35}S is also a high specific-activity isotope, but it has a less energetic β emission,

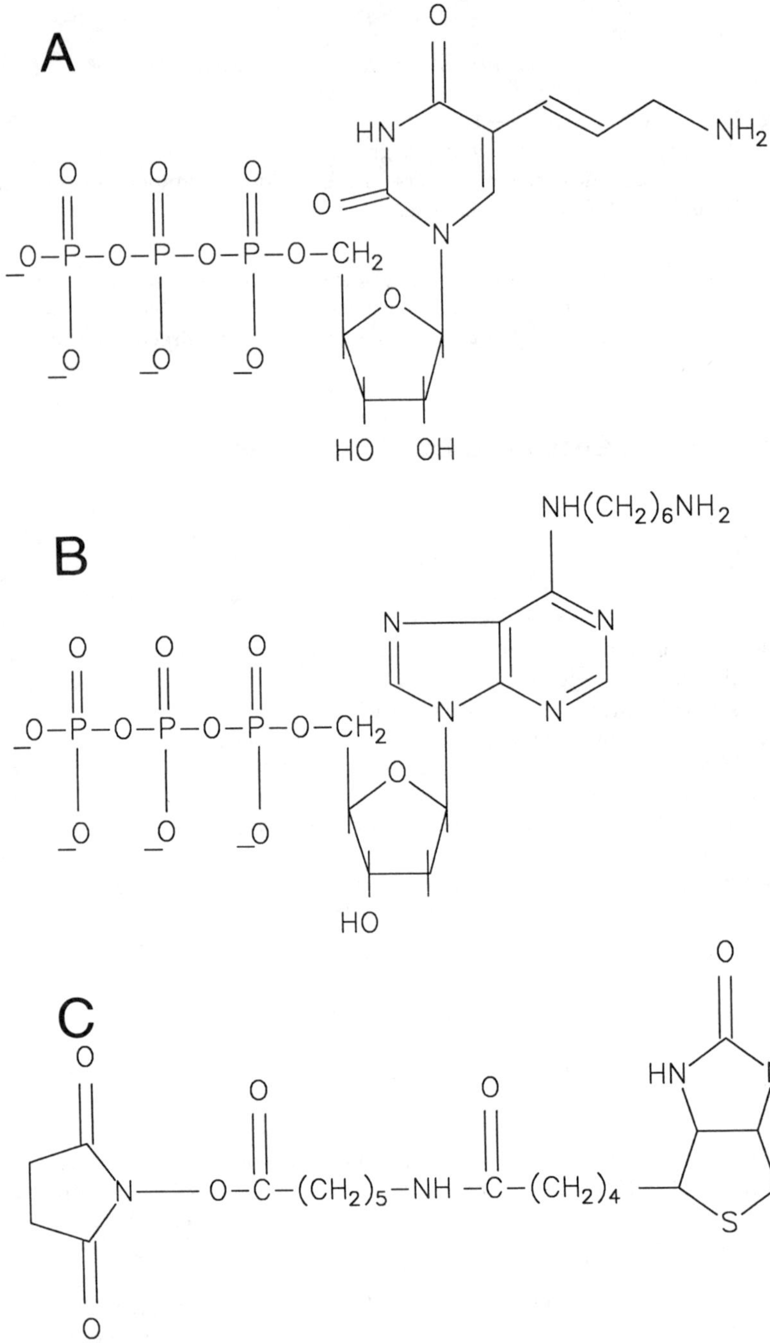

FIG 7–8.

Amine-containing nucleotides. **A,** allylamine-UTP is readily incorporated into RNA by phage RNA polymerases. **B,** N^6(6-aminohexyl)dATP is a DNA precursor which can be modified by attachment of fluorescein or biotin. **C,** ϵ-caproylamidobiotin N-hydroxysuccinimide ester (CAB-NHS ester) reacts with primary amines such as those above to attach biotin labels to nucleic acids.

TABLE 7–1.
Radioisotope Label Characteristics

Isotope	Relative Energy	Half-Life	Method of Incorporation
^{32}P	High	14 days	Enzymatic
^{35}S	Moderate	89 days	Enzymatic
^{125}I	Moderate	60 days	Enzymatic or chemical
^{3}H	Low	12 years	Enzymatic

making common methods of detection less sensitive. In addition, when it is incorporated into nucleotides as an oxygen analog, it is not accepted by some enzymes.

^{125}I has a specific activity between that of ^{35}S and ^{32}P. It emits γ radiation (photons) of moderate energy. Iodine can be introduced directly into nucleic acids by chemical means (see above) or by coupling to a nucleoside triphosphate followed by enzymatic incorporation of the modified nucleotide.

Tritium (^{3}H) has a relatively low specific activity and a very low energy β emission. Due to the abundance of hydrogen in nucleic acids, many tritium atoms can, in theory, be introduced to give a high specific activity per mole of nucleotide, but the difficulty of detecting the low energy emissions efficiently and conveniently has limited the use of ^{3}H in molecular biology applications.

Detection of Radioisotopes

Autoradiography.—The detection of radioactive compounds by their ability to expose photographic film has a long history. The development of specialized films and improved exposure techniques has made autoradiography a very sensitive method. It is currently the most sensitive method available for detection of moderate or strong β emitters on solid substrates such as filters and gels when spatial relationships must be determined.

For "direct autoradiography," a dry filter or gel is simply pressed against a sheet of film for a period of time, after which the film is developed to reveal areas exposed by the radioactive emissions. The sensitivity of detection depends on the type of isotope, the type of film, and the length of time of the exposure. When detecting ^{32}P (Fig 7–9,A) sensitivity can be enhanced by using a "fast" film with photographic emulsion on both surfaces. The electron emitted by ^{32}P is energetic enough to travel completely through a sheet of x-ray film and expose silver grains on both surfaces. Further sensitivity is obtained by the use of an x-ray intensifying screen in a "sandwich" format. These screens contain compounds which fluoresce or scintillate when struck by x-rays, γ-rays or high energy β particles. The light emitted further exposes the autoradiographic film around the point at which the decay event occurred. The use of double-emulsion films and intensifying screens increases sensitivity by two- to five-fold, at the expense of resolution. Bands on gels will be substantially broader when enhancing techniques are used, but for most applications the loss of resolution is not a serious problem. Efficient autoradiographic detection of ^{125}I *requires* the use of intensifying screens, because the γ-rays frequently pass through the film without exposing a silver grain.

^{35}S also can be detected by direct autoradiography, but with substantially less sensitivity than ^{32}P. The β particle emitted by ^{35}S is not energetic enough to penetrate the plastic base of the film and so can expose only the layer of photographic emulsion that is facing the filter (Fig 7–9,B). Thus, for ^{35}S, double-sided films and intensifying screens are of little value. Both ^{32}P and ^{35}S detection are enhanced by exposure of films at very low (−70°C) temperatures. The low temperature stabilizes partially exposed silver grains. At maximal sensitivity, bands containing less than 0.1 dpm of ^{32}P can be detected with an exposure of a few days.

Fluorography.—The sensitivity of detection of weaker β emitters, such as ^{35}S and ^{3}H, can be increased by the use of fluorographic techniques.[24,25] If a gel or filter is soaked in a radio-sensitive scintillant compound, radioactive emissions generate a flash of light that can be detected on x-ray or photographic film. Fluorography improves the film detection of ^{35}S approximately 10-fold and of ^{3}H 10- to 50-fold for filters. Like intensifying screens, fluorographic detection reduces the resolution of closely spaced bands.

Scintillation Counting.—The reliable detection of low levels of radioisotopes by scintillation counting (liquid scintillation spectrometry) requires the accumulation of a statistically significant number of detected emissions above a well-determined background. These conditions generally can be met with liquid-phase and dot blot-type nucleic acid hybridization assays, but are difficult to achieve when analyzing Southern blot filters. Since filters must be cut into pieces for such counting, the resolution of bands is significantly reduced unless pieces are very small.

Geiger-Mueller Counting.—The detection of ionizing radiation, such as β particles, by the Geiger-Mueller (GM) method is not as sensitive as autoradiography or liquid scintillation spectrometry, but with recent improvements it may become a valuable technique for some applications. Commercial instruments are capable of

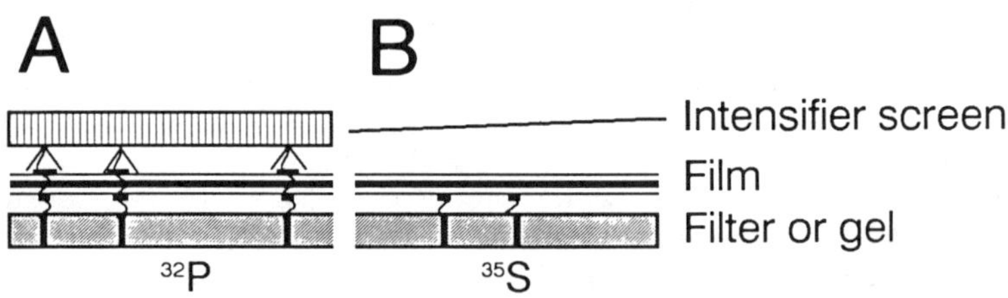

FIG 7–9.
Autoradiography. **A,** detection of ^{32}P is enhanced by the use of double emulsion x-ray films and an intensifying screen that emits light when hit by a radioactive decay particle. **B,** ^{35}S emissions are not energetic enough to penetrate the plastic base of x-ray film, so it only exposes the closest layer of photographic emulsion.

scanning filters and accumulating "x,y" plots of radioactivity with data being stored and analyzed by an associated computer. With appropriate data collection times and analysis, the sensitivity of this method (but not the resolution) is beginning to approach that of autoradiography.

Non-Radioactive Labels

Fluorescent Labels.—Nucleic acids can be modified to fluoresce either by the incorporation of fluorescent nucleotides during enzymatic or chemical synthesis, or by post-synthesis modification such as that described above. The addition of large, usually hydrophobic fluorescent groups may have a significant effect on the hybridization behavior of the probe. Detection of such probes on filters is often difficult, since many of the common filter materials are fluorescent themselves. In addition, colored impurities in some samples may cause variable degrees of fluorescence quenching, particularly in dot blot assays. Fluorescent polynucleotides or conjugates can be detected efficiently when the nucleic acid is in solution, under in situ hybridization conditions where cells and DNA are fixed to a microscope slide, or undergoing electrophoresis, as in automated DNA sequencing.[26, 27]

Enzyme-Linked Probes.—Enzymes such as alkaline phosphatase and horseradish peroxidase can be linked to nucleic acids as reporters, as is done for antibody-based ELISAs. In a two-step method, a strongly basic protein or polyamine is attached to DNA with glutaraldehyde, then the reporter enzyme is conjugated to the protein-DNA complex.[19] Synthetic oligonucleotides which incorporate a primary amine have been cross-linked to alkaline phosphatase with bifunctional cross-linking reagents.[21] The reporter enzymes used for this technique must be stable to the treatment that is encountered in hybridization reactions, including the use of detergents such as sodium dodecylsulfate and high temperatures of 40 to 70°C. The attachment of enzymes to probes can have a significant effect on the hybridization kinetics and optima of the system. Having the reported enzyme directly attached to the probe significantly reduces the processing time for blot development after hybridization.

Haptens and Cofactors.—A wide variety of haptens and cofactors (including biotin, N-acetoxy-N-acetyl-2-aminofluorene, dinitrophenol, fluorescein, digoxigenin, glucose, and sulfonate residues) have been attached to DNA or RNA as distinguishing targets for secondary detection systems. The principal means of detecting these substituents is with antibodies raised against the hapten. Antibodies bound to the hapten-DNA (or -RNA) are detected using conventional immunodetection methods (Fig 7–10). Direct immunodetection procedures use anti-hapten (primary) antibodies conjugated to a reporter, such as an enzyme or fluorophor. Indirect immunodetection procedures use a "sandwich" method: the unmodified primary antibody is allowed to bind to the hapten-DNA, then the bound primary antibody is detected by a secondary (anti-primary) antibody to which reporter groups are attached.

If biotin is used to label a nucleic acid, the initial binding step commonly uses

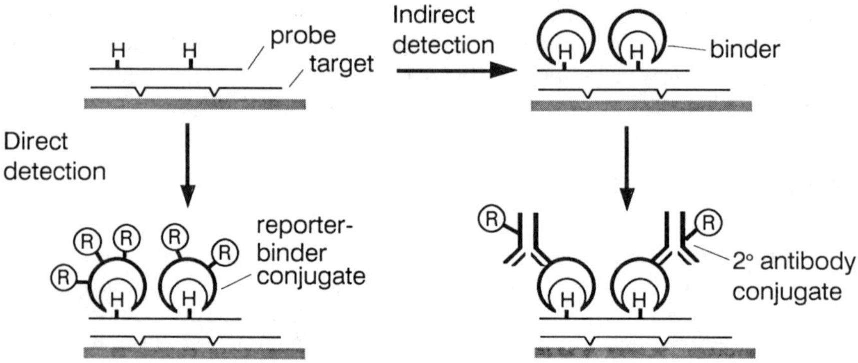

FIG 7–10.
Non-radioactive detection of hapten or biotin-labelled probes. For direct detection of hapten-labelled DNA, antibodies to the hapten (or streptavidin if the label is biotin) are conjugated to a reporter molecule, such as alkaline phosphatase or fluorescein. This antibody-reporter conjugate is then allowed to bind to the labelled probe hybridized to the target. Indirect detection uses secondary antibodies conjugated to a reporter to detect the binding of the anti-hapten antibody to a labelled probe.

avidin or streptavidin to detect the labelled probe.[28] These proteins are capable of binding four molecules of biotin and have affinities for biotin $>10^6$-fold higher than those found in most antibody-hapten binding systems. Reporter groups can be conjugated directly to streptavidin, analogous to direct immunodetection, or the protein can be detected by its ability to bind biotinylated reporter molecules in an indirect method.

Non-Radioactive Reporters.—For most blot applications, enzymes are the preferred reporters, whether they are linked directly or indirectly to a probe. Calf intestine alkaline phosphatase and horseradish peroxidase conjugated to secondary antibodies and streptavidin are commercially available. They have well-characterized soluble and insoluble chromogenic substrates. When applied to Southern blots, the colored products of the reaction must be insoluble in order to deposit color only at the sites where the reporter enzyme is bound to the filter through the hybridized probe. The chromogenic substrates used are the same as those used for immunocytochemical assays and western blots. Alkaline phosphatase detection is normally 2 to 5 times as sensitive as horseradish peroxidase.

A non-colorimetric method of detecting horseradish peroxidase is based on chemiluminescence.[29] The breakdown of hydrogen peroxide by the enzyme results in the release of light from luminol in the presence of an enhancer such as *p*-hydroxycinnamic acid. The emitted light can be detected by a luminometer for dot blots, or by the exposure of high-speed Polaroid film for Southern or dot blots.

Colloidal gold conjugates of antibodies or strepavidin can be used as a non-enzymatic chromogenic detection system. The gold particles make a reddish-brown deposit on a filter which can be intensified by further treatment to deposit black silver grains on the gold.[30] The sensitivity is similar to that of enzymatic DNA hybrid detection methods.

Conclusions

Comparison of ^{32}P and Non-Radioactive Detection.—Although a great deal of effort has been and continues to be invested in developing sensitive non-radioactive detection methods for nucleic acids, ^{32}P autoradiography is currently the method of choice for the detection of hybridization in samples where the amount of DNA is limiting. Commercially available non-radioactive systems yield a signal similar to that of a 4- to 18-hour autoradiograph.[31] This is satisfactory for laboratory-drawn specimens, but film exposures can be extended reliably to greater than 100 hours to yield the 5- to 20-fold improvement in sensitivity needed for typical forensic material.

Part of the reason for the greater sensitivity of radioactivity is the linear relationship between the amount of radioisotope that is incorporated and the signal on the film. The amount of isotope that is incorporated can be increased by increasing the specific activity of the labelled nucleotide, or by using more than one labelled nucleotide. Experiments with biotin have revealed that the sensitivity of detection reaches a plateau beyond approximately 4 biotinylated residues per 100 bases, presumably due to steric interference between adjoining streptavidin molecules.[32] Another difficulty with most non-radioactive detection systems is control of non-specific background, because the blocking of non-specific binding by reporter proteins to blotting membranes is generally less complete than the blocking of the binding of unhybridized nucleic acid probes. Further improvements in non-radioactive detection will come primarily in the reporter portion of this system with additional enhancements from changes in membrane blocking techniques.

This chapter has discussed only a fraction of the wide variety of labels, labelling methods, and detection methods available for use with nucleic acid probes. Experience has shown that no single system is appropriate for all applications or laboratory situations. This is an area that is still changing rapidly, even after many years of research. The challenge of practical, routine applications in forensic and medical laboratories is spurring even more activity to simplify, stabilize, and improve the sensitivity of nucleic acid probe labelling and detection methodology.

Acknowledgments

I would like to thank R. Blakesley and J. Harding for their critical reading of the manuscript, and D. Simms for the preparation of the chemical structure figures.

REFERENCES

1. Maniatis T, Fritsch EF, Sambrook J: *Molecular Cloning: A Laboratory Manual*. Cold Spring Harbor, New York, Cold Spring Harbor Laboratory, 1982.
2. Ausubel FM, Brent R, Kingston RE, et al: *Current Protocols in Molecular Biology*. New York, Greene Publishing/Wiley-Interscience, 1987.
3. Berger SL, Kimmel AR (eds): *Guide to Molecular Cloning Techniques: Methods in Enzymology*, vol 152. San Diego, Calif, Academic Press/Harcourt Brace Jovanovich, 1987.
4. Rigby PWJ, Dieckmann M, Rhodes C, et al: Labeling deoxyribonucleic acid to high specific activity in vitro by nick translation with DNA polymerase I. *J Mol Biol* 1977; 113:237–251.
5. Feinberg AP, Vogelstein B: A technique for radiolabeling DNA restriction endonuclease fragments to high specific activity. *Anal Biochem* 1983; 132:6–13.
6. Feinberg AP, Vogelstein B: Addendum to "A technique for radiolabeling DNA restriction endonuclease fragments to high specific activity." *Anal Biochem* 1984; 137:266–267.
7. Sanger F, Nicklen S, Coulsen AR: DNA sequencing with chain-terminating inhibitors. *Proc Natl Acad Sci USA* 1977; 74:5463–5467.
8. O'Farrell P: Replacement synthesis method of labeling DNA fragments. *Focus* 1981; 3(3):1–3.
9. Deen KC, Landers TA, Berninger M: Use of T4 DNA polymerase replacement synthesis for specific labeling of plasmid-cloned inserts. *Anal Biochem* 1983; 135:456–465.
10. Roychoudhury R, Wu R: Terminal transferase-catalyzed addition of nucleotides to the 3' termini of DNA, in Grossman L, Moldave K (eds): *Methods in Enzymology*, vol 65, part I. New York, Academic Press, 1980, pp 43–62.
11. Kumar A, Tchen P, Roullet F, et al: Nonradioactive labeling of synthetic oligonucleotide probes with terminal deoxynucleotidyl transferase. *Anal Biochem* 1988; 169:376–382.
12. Green M, Maniatis T, Melton D: Human β-globin pre-mRNA synthesized in vitro is accurately spliced in Xenopus oocyte nuclei. *Cell* 1983; 32:681–694.
13. McCracken S: Preparation of RNA transcripts using SP6 RNA polymerase. *Focus* 1985; 7(2):5–8.
14. Forster AC, McInnis JL, Skingle DC, et al: Non-radioactive hybridization probes prepared by the chemical labelling of DNA and RNA with a novel reagent, photobiotin. *Nucleic Acids Res* 1985; 13:745–761.

15. Tchen P, Fuchs RP, Sage E, et al: Chemically modified nucleic acids as immunodetectable probes in hybridization experiments. *Proc Natl Acad Sci USA* 1984; 81:3466–3470.
16. Piatyszek MA, Jarmolowski A, Augustyniak J: Iodo-Gen-mediated radioiodination of nucleic acids. *Anal Biochem* 1988; 172:356–359.
17. Keller GH, Cumming CU, Huang D-P, et al: A chemical method for introducing haptens onto DNA probes. *Anal Biochem* 1988; 170:441–450.
18. Gillam IC, Tener GM: N^4-(6-aminohexyl)cytidine and -deoxycytidine nucleotides can be used to label DNA. *Anal Biochem* 1986; 157:199–207.
19. Renz M, Kurz C: A colorimetric method for DNA hybridization. *Nucleic Acids Res* 1984; 12:3435–3444.
20. Al-Hakim AH, Hull R: Studies towards the development of chemically synthesized non-radioactive biotinylated nucleic acid hybridization probes. *Nucleic Acids Res* 1986; 24:9965–9976.
21. Jablonski E, Moomaw EW, Tullis RH, et al: Preparation of oligodeoxynucleotide-alkaline phosphatase conjugates and their use as hybridization probes. *Nucleic Acids Res* 1986; 14:6115–6128.
22. Smith LM, Fung S, Hunkapiller MW, et al: The synthesis of oligonucleotides containing an aliphatic amino group at the 5' terminus: Synthesis of fluorescent DNA primers for use in DNA sequence analysis. *Nucleic Acids Res* 1985; 13:2399–2412.
23. Anonymous: Preparation and use of biotinylated RNA probes. *Focus* 1987; 9(4):10.
24. Bonner WM, Laskey RA: A film detection method for tritium-labelled proteins and nucleic acids in polyacrylamide gels. *Eur J Biochem* 1974; 46:83–88.
25. Roberts PL: Comparison of fluorographic methods for detecting radioactivity in polyacrylamide gels or on nitrocellulose filters. *Anal Biochem* 1985; 147:521–524.
26. Connell C, Fung S, Heiner C, et al: Automated DNA sequence analysis. *BioTechniques* 1987; 5:342–348.
27. Prober JM, Trainor GL, Dam RJ, et al: A system for rapid DNA sequencing with fluorescent chain-terminating dideoxynucleotides. *Science* 1987; 238:336–341.
28. Leary JJ, Brigati DJ, Ward DC: Rapid and sensitive colorimetric method for visualizing biotin-labelled DNA probes hybridized to DNA or RNA immobilized on nitrocellulose: Bio-blots. *Proc Natl Acad Sci USA* 1983; 80:4045–4049.

29. Matthews JA, Bakti A, Hynds C, et al: Enhanced chemiluminescent method for the detection of DNA dot-hybridization assays. *Anal Biochem* 1985; 151:205–209.
30. Tomlinson S, Lyga A, Huguenel E, et al: Detection of biotinylated nucleic acid hybrids by antibody-coated gold colloid. *Anal Biochem* 1988; 171:217–222.
31. Donovan RM, Bush CE, Peterson WR, et al: Comparison of non-radioactive DNA hybridization probes to detect human immunodeficiency virus nucleic acid. *Molec Cellular Probes* 1987; 1:359–366.
32. Gebeyehu G, Rao PY, SooChan P, et al: Novel biotinylated nucleotide analogs for labeling and colorimetric detection of DNA. *Nucleic Acids Res* 1987; 15:4513–4534.

Chapter 8

The Ag-System, a Genetic Polymorphism of Human Low Density Lipoprotein, and Its Application in Forensic Serology

Professor Doctor René Bütler

INTRODUCTION

Genetic polymorphisms occur in a large majority of the proteins of human blood and it can be speculated that genetically controlled variants exist for all known serum proteins, and may be revealed by the application of appropriate methods. The methods used for detection of these polymorphisms thus far have been based on differences in the antigenic structure (e.g., for the Gm-system), or the electrophoretic mobility (e.g., for the Hp-system) of the variants. Accordingly, immunological as well as various electrophoretic methods are used for this purpose.

It is not surprising that genetic polymorphisms have been observed also within the family of human (and animal) lipoproteins. The lipoproteins represent one of the most complex groups of the human serum proteins. The classification is based mainly on their behavior in the ultracentrifugal sedimentation analysis. According to their densities, a distinction is made between very low density lipoproteins (chylo- or lipomicrons, VLDL), low density lipoproteins (LDL), and high density lipoproteins (HDL). The low density lipoproteins are heterogeneous, with densities ranging from 1.063 to 1.006 g/ml. This corresponds to a flotation constant of Sf 0–20, a molecular weight of 2.3–2.5 $\times$ 10^6 daltons, and a particle diameter (calculated as a spheroid) of 200–240 Å. LDLs are more or less identical to the serum protein class which, based on its electrophoretic properties, was designated as β-lipoprotein. They contain between 75% and 80% lipids (triglycerides, phosphatides, esterified and non-esterified cholesterol, and free fatty acids in varying proportions); nevertheless, their chemical properties are determined primarily by the protein moiety (apolipoprotein). Furthermore, they contain considerable amounts of carbohydrate, such as 3.2% hexose, which may be of importance with respect to their antigenic structure. The presence of hundreds of different molecular entities within the group of the LDLs can be assumed from the number of subfractions with defined physico-chemical properties that they contain.

Various studies reported in the literature demonstrate the existence of genetic lipoprotein polymorphisms. However, not all of these can be mentioned within the scope of this article. The three most important and most thoroughly investigated systems are the Ag, the Lp, and the apo E groups. In 1961, Allison and Blumberg[1] demonstrated an isoprecipitin in the serum of a multiply transfused patient (C. de B.) which reacted with 57.1% of sera from white Americans. Family studies showed that the antigen, designated Ag(a), was inherited in an autosomal dominant fashion. Later, the serum protein carrying the Ag(a) epitope was identified as LDL.

In 1963, Berg[2] produced a precipitating immune serum by immunizing rabbits with purified LDL preparations from individual donor sera, which, in an immunodiffusion test, enabled the detection of an apparently group-specific antigen called Lp(a), present in about 35% of the tested individual sera. Family studies demonstrated the genetic control of this antigen. Further investigations showed that the dominant gene Lp^a probably does not code for a qualitative characteristic; it is more likely that this gene is one of various alleles responsible for the regulation of the synthesis of the "Lp(a) protein" (later shown to be the pre-β1 lipoprotein which is closely related to LDL). The regulator genes for the higher concentrations of "Lp(a) protein" are dominant over the genes for the lower concentrations. The apo E groups were discovered by Utermann[3] in 1977 both by isoelectric focusing in polyacrylamide gel of the isolated apo E prepared from purified serum VLDL, and by two-dimensional polyacrylamide gel electrophoresis. Apoprotein E is a major protein component of VLDL. Family studies revealed the existence of three codominant alleles at the apo E locus. Due to the fact that the Lp groups do not represent a genuine serum group system and that the methods for detection of the apo E groups are very complex and cumbersome, only the Ag-system has been seriously considered as to its application in forensic serology. The various aspects of this system will be discussed in detail below.

COMPOSITION OF THE Ag-SYSTEM

Since the publication of Allison and Blumberg,[1] a number of additional isoprecipitin-containing human sera, defining other LDL epitopes, have been discovered. In 1974, the ten Ag-factors depicted in Table 8–1 were known and no additional Ag-specificity has been observed since that date.

Two periods can be distinguished in the discovery of the Ag-system. Between 1961 and 1966, the detection of Ag-antigens was based exclusively on immunodiffusion techniques using human sera with precipitating antibodies. In 1966, we described a passive hemagglutination assay for studying Ag-antibodies which would also allow the detection of non-precipitating Ag-antibodies.[4] The first example of such an antibody was discovered by us in 1967.[5] By means of this method, we then were able to detect a series of new Ag-specificities.

TABLE 8–1.
The Ten Antigens of the Ag-System

Accepted Notation	Other Notations	Year of Detection	Author(s)
Ag(x)	Ld(a)	1964	Hirschfeld and Blombäck[42]
Ag(a_1)	Ag(r)	1964	Hirschfeld et al[6]
Ag(z)		1964	Hirschfeld et al[6]
Ag(y)	Lp^{nuoro}	1966	Contu[43]; Okochi[32]
Ag(t)	Ag(b)	1966	Hirschfeld et al[44]
Ag(c)		1967	Bütler et al[5]
Ag(d)		1970	Bütler et al[45]
Ag(g)		1970	Bütler et al[46]
Ag(h)		1973	Bütler et al[47]
Ag(i)		1974	Bütler and Brunner[13]

In Table 8–1, the absence of the first observed Ag-factor, namely the Ag(a) factor of Allison and Blumberg, is immediately apparent. In a re-examination of the anti-Ag(a) serum (C. de B.) with the aid of absorption experiments, Hirschfeld et al[6] showed that this serum contained isoprecipitins against three different Ag-specificities, which they called Ag(a_1), Ag(x), and Ag(z). Thus, epitope Ag(a) can no longer be considered a genuine Ag-factor.

In addition to the Ag-antigens listed in Table 8–1, some other Ag-factors have been reported in the literature. Some of them, like Ag(r) and Ag(b), later were shown to be identical to factors already described. The detection of another factor, Ag(m), never has been confirmed. Finally, our factor, Ag(e), turned out to be unrelated to the Ag-system.[7–9]

GENETICS OF THE Ag-SYSTEM

Extended family and population studies conducted both by us and also by other authors have revealed the following factors[10, 11]:

1. All Ag-factors are inherited according to an autosomal dominant mode of transmission.

2. The genes coding for the Ag-antigens are all closely linked.

3. No genetic relationship or linkage could be observed between the Ag-factors and the Lp system on one hand, or between the Ag-groups and the blood group antigens ABO, M, N, P_1, rhesus(C,c), K, and Fy(a), as well as the serum groups Gm(1), Gm(5), Km(1), Hp, and Gc, on the other hand.[12]

4. If the Ag-factors of defined individuals are arranged in pairs of two antigens according to the four phenotypical combinations Ag(+ +), Ag(+ −), Ag(− +), and Ag(− −), one can observe that certain Ag(− −) combinations never occur [namely Ag(x− y−), Ag(a_1 − d−), Ag(c − g−), Ag(t − z−), and Ag(h − i−)], whereas practically all other phenotypical combinations do occur. This means that the Ag-antigens behave

as five pairs of antithetical factors as follows: Ag(x)/Ag(y), Ag(a_1)/Ag(d), Ag(c)/Ag(g), Ag(t)/Ag(z), and Ag(h)/Ag(i).

As an interpretation of the genetic data, we have proposed a chromosome model for the Ag-system that assumes the existence of five closely linked loci, each with two codominant alleles (Fig 8–1). The sequence of the five loci is, of course, entirely arbitrary. In addition, no recombination has been observed so far, based on our analysis of family material comprising some 40 families with about 130 children. Therefore, crossing over appears to be a very rare event, if it occurs at all. This fact would have allowed us to consider the Ag-chromosome under the aspect of multiple alleles on one gene locus (identical to the haplotypes we have observed up to the present). However, the model outlined above appeared simpler, and possessed the advantage of not needing revision should new phenotypes be encountered.

Regarding notation, we use the following procedure, which has been adopted by the majority of authors in this field:

- For single Ag-factors: Ag(x), Ag(y), etc. (as introduced originally by Allison and Blumberg, Hirschfeld, and others).
- For Ag-genes: Ag^x, Ag^y, etc.
- For partial Ag-phenotypes: Ag(x+y+), Ag(a_1+d−), etc.
- For complete Ag-phenotypes: Ag(x−y+a_1−d+c+g+t+z−h−i+), etc.
- For Ag-haplotypes: Ag^{ydgti}, etc.
- For Ag-genotypes: Ag^{ydgti}/Ag^{xdcti}, etc.

Table 8–2 shows the frequencies of the ten Ag-factors and their corresponding genes.[10,13] The Hardy-Weinberg equilibrium was analyzed for the five pairs of antithetical factors in this material. The observed figures were found to be in excellent

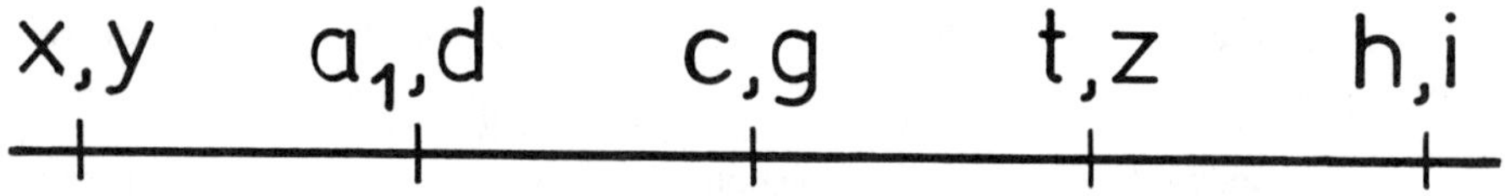

FIG 8–1.
Model for the "Ag-chromosome."

TABLE 8–2.
Frequencies of Single Ag-Factors and Their Corresponding Genes in the Swiss Population (n = 362)

Antithetical Factors (%)		Genes (Codominant Alleles)	
Ag(x)	Ag(y)	Ag^x	Ag^y
39.5	96.7	0.214	0.786
Ag(a_1)	Ag(d)	$Ag^{a}1$	Ag^d
72.1	75.7	0.482	0.518
Ag(c)	Ag(g)	Ag^c	Ag^g
51.4	90.3	0.305	0.695
Ag(t)	Ag(z)	Ag^t	Ag^z
95.9	37.8	0.790	0.210
Ag(h)	Ag(i)	Ag^h	Ag^i
16.9	98.3	0.093	0.907

agreement with the expected values, thus providing additional evidence for the co-dominant allelism of the five pairs of genes. The gene frequencies for Ag^x, Ag^y, $Ag^{a}1$, Ag^t, and Ag^z that have been obtained by other authors for various European populations (Germans, Italians, Swedes, Bulgarians), as well as for white Americans, do not differ significantly from the Swiss figures. On the other hand, we found some striking differences in the frequency of a number of Ag-factors in non-white populations that we studied (Indians, Chinese, Tibetans, Senegalese, South African Bantus, Australian aborigines)[10, 14] (Tables 8–3 and 8–4).

Based on our genetic model, the theoretical number of complete phenotypes for the Ag-factors is 243. We have observed a total of 51 Ag-phenotypes in the genetic material of our population that has been analyzed thus far. Forty-nine phenotypes and their corresponding frequencies in seven populations are represented in Table 8–3. Two additional phenotypes, namely Ag($x+y-a_1+d-c+g-t+z-h-i+$) (No. 123) and Ag($x+y-a_1-d+c+g-t+z-h-i+$) (No. 150), were encountered in an Indonesian population that is presently under study.[15] The phenotype numbers we have used are taken from an internal code system established for the total of the 243 possible combinations. The fact that 192 possible phenotypes have not yet been observed suggests that they must have a very low incidence, if they exist at all. Furthermore, some of the 53 phenotypes observed were found only in selected human populations. This situation is reflected also in the list of observed haplotypes (see Table 8–4).

According to the genetic model outlined above, the existence of a maximum of 32 haplotypes can be postulated. Fourteen haplotypes are required in order to interpret the 51 Ag-phenotypes. (The indicated haplotype frequencies were kindly calculated by Dr. G. Breguet of Geneva, Switzerland, with the aid of a computer program.) As for the phenotypes, the numbers assigned to the haplotypes are taken from an internal code system designed for the total number of possible haplotypes. The haplotype table shows, even more clearly than does the phenotype table, the striking differences in distribution for various populations and races. Some haplotypes may even be "race-specific"; haplotype Ag^{ydgzi} (No. 32) appears to be typical for black

TABLE 8–3.

Frequencies of Observed Complete Ag-Phenotypes in Seven Populations

Phenotype Number	Ag										Swiss		Indians		Chinese		Tibetans		Senegalese		Bantus		Australian Aborigines	
	x	y	a_1	d	c	g	t	z	h	i	n	%	n	%	n	%	n	%	n	%	n	%	n	%
1	+	+	+	+	+	+	+	+	+	+	1	0.3	0	—	0	—	0	—	0	—	0	—	0	—
3	+	+	+	+	+	+	+	+	−	+	3	0.8	0	—	1	2.3	2	2.3	0	—	0	—	0	—
4	+	+	+	+	+	+	+	−	+	+	12	3.3	0	—	0	—	0	—	0	—	0	—	13	16.5
6	+	+	+	+	+	+	+	−	−	+	27	7.4	7	10.0	3	7.0	6	7.0	0	—	0	—	17	21.5
15	+	+	+	+	+	−	+	−	−	+	0	—	0	—	0	—	1	1.2	0	—	0	—	0	—
21	+	+	+	+	−	+	+	+	−	+	3	0.8	1	1.4	0	—	0	—	4	4.0	2	2.1	0	—
22	+	+	+	+	−	+	+	−	+	+	2	0.6	0	—	0	—	0	—	0	—	0	—	1	1.3
24	+	+	+	+	−	+	+	−	−	+	32	8.8	11	15.7	1	2.3	2	2.3	7	7.0	2	2.1	2	2.5
30	+	+	+	−	+	+	+	+	−	+	1	0.3	0	—	0	—	1	1.2	0	—	0	—	0	—
33	+	+	+	−	+	+	+	−	−	+	1	0.3	0	—	0	—	2	2.3	0	—	0	—	0	—
48	+	+	+	−	−	+	+	+	−	+	35	9.6	4	5.7	1	2.3	8	9.3	1	1.0	0	—	0	—
51	+	+	+	−	−	+	+	−	−	+	10	2.7	3	4.3	5	11.6	3	3.5	0	—	0	—	2	2.5
54	+	+	+	−	−	+	−	+	−	+	0	—	0	—	0	—	1	1.2	0	—	0	—	0	—
58	+	+	−	+	+	+	+	−	+	+	0	—	0	—	0	—	0	—	2	2.0	0	—	0	—
60	+	+	−	+	+	+	+	−	−	+	1	0.3	0	—	1	2.3	2	2.3	1	1.0	1	1.1	0	—
69	+	+	−	+	+	−	+	−	−	+	1	0.3	1	1.4	0	—	0	—	0	—	0	—	1	1.3
75	+	+	−	+	−	+	+	+	−	+	0	—	0	—	0	—	0	—	3	3.0	1	1.1	0	—
78	+	+	−	+	−	+	+	−	−	+	2	0.6	5	7.2	0	—	0	—	7	7.0	5	5.3	0	—
87	+	−	+	+	+	+	+	−	−	+	0	—	1	1.4	6	14.0	4	4.6	0	—	0	—	0	—
96	+	−	+	+	+	−	+	−	−	+	0	—	0	—	0	—	1	1.2	0	—	0	—	0	—
105	+	−	+	+	−	+	+	−	−	+	2	0.6	1	1.4	5	11.6	5	5.8	0	—	0	—	0	—
114	+	−	+	−	+	+	+	−	−	+	0	—	1	1.4	0	—	12	13.9	0	—	0	—	0	—
129	+	−	+	−	−	+	+	+	−	+	1	0.3	0	—	0	—	0	—	0	—	0	—	0	—
132	+	−	+	−	−	+	+	−	−	+	9	2.5	14	20.0	18	41.9	25	29.1	0	—	0	—	29	36.7
159	+	−	−	+	−	+	+	−	−	+	0	—	0	—	0	—	0	—	1	1.0	0	—	0	—
163	−	+	+	+	+	+	+	+	+	+	10	2.7	0	—	0	—	0	—	0	—	0	—	0	—

165	−	+	+	+	+	+	+	+	−	+	25	6.9	2	2.9	0	—	0	—	0	—	0	—	1	1.3
166	−	+	+	+	+	+	+	−	+	+	9	2.5	0	—	0	—	0	—	0	—	0	—	0	—
167	−	+	+	+	+	+	+	−	+	−	1	0.3	1	1.4	0	—	0	—	0	—	0	—	0	—
168	−	+	+	+	+	+	+	−	−	+	10	2.7	1	1.4	1	2.3	0	—	2	2.0	1	1.1	3	3.8
174	−	+	+	+	+	−	+	+	−	+	2	0.6	0	—	0	—	0	—	0	—	0	—	0	—
183	−	+	+	+	−	+	+	+	−	+	26	7.2	3	4.3	0	—	3	3.5	11	11.0	3	3.2	0	—
186	−	+	+	+	−	+	+	−	−	+	8	2.2	0	—	0	—	1	1.2	4	4.0	6	6.4	1	1.3
189	−	+	+	+	−	+	−	+	−	+	0	—	0	—	0	—	0	—	1	1.0	0	—	0	—
192	−	+	+	−	+	+	+	+	−	+	1	0.3	1	1.4	0	—	0	—	0	—	0	—	0	—
198	−	+	+	−	+	+	−	+	−	+	1	0.3	0	—	0	—	0	—	0	—	0	—	0	—
208	−	+	+	−	−	+	+	+	+	+	1	0.3	0	—	0	—	0	—	0	—	0	—	0	—
210	−	+	+	−	−	+	+	−	−	+	13	3.6	0	—	0	—	2	2.3	0	—	0	—	0	—
213	−	+	+	−	−	+	+	−	−	+	1	0.3	0	—	1	2.3	0	—	0	—	0	—	0	—
216	−	+	+	−	−	+	−	−	−	+	14	3.8	1	1.4	0	—	4	4.6	2	2.0	0	—	0	—
219	−	+	−	+	+	+	+	−	−	+	0	—	0	—	0	—	0	—	0	—	2	2.1	0	—
220	−	+	−	+	+	+	+	−	+	+	11	3.0	2	2.9	0	—	0	—	4	4.0	2	2.1	0	—
222	−	+	−	+	+	+	+	−	−	+	37	10.2	8	11.5	0	—	0	—	6	6.0	4	4.2	0	—
229	−	+	−	+	+	−	+	−	+	+	9	2.5	0	—	0	—	0	—	0	—	0	—	5	6.3
230	−	+	−	+	+	−	+	−	+	−	5	1.4	0	—	0	—	0	—	0	—	0	—	0	—
231	−	+	−	+	+	−	+	−	−	+	18	5.0	0	—	0	—	1	1.2	0	—	0	—	4	5.1
237	−	+	−	+	−	+	+	+	−	+	0	—	0	—	0	—	0	—	8	8.0	18	19.2	0	—
238	−	+	−	+	−	+	+	−	+	+	0	—	0	—	0	—	0	—	2	2.0	0	—	0	—
240	−	+	−	+	−	+	+	−	−	+	17	4.7	2	2.9	0	—	0	—	34	34.0	47	50.0	0	—
49 phenotypes											362	100	70	100	43	100	86	100	100	100	94	100	79	100

TABLE 8–4.
Distribution of Ag-Haplotype Frequencies in Seven Populations

Haplotypes No.	Type	Swiss	Indians	Chinese	Tibetans	Senegalese	Bantus	Australian Aborigines
2	xa_1cti	.002	.010	.012	.108	—	—	—
6	xa_1gti	.191	.395	.638	.511	.040	.018	.597
8	xa_1gzi	.009	—	—	.007	—	—	—
10	xdcti	.003	.014	.085	.045	—	—	.007
14	xdgti	.010	.052	.063	.040	.095	.040	.019
20	ya_1cti	.008	—	—	—	—	—	—
21	ya_1gth	.005	—	—	—	—	—	—
22	ya_1gti	.075	.038	.115	.050	.037	.046	.033
24	ya_1gzi	.193	.093	.022	.145	.098	.011	.006
25	ydcth	.085	.021	—	—	.029	.011	.117
26	ydcti	.207	.133	.059	.051	.046	.043	.207
29	ydgth	.003	—	—	—	.011	—	.006
30	ydgti	.210	.243	.006	.045	.577	.704	—
32	ydgzi	—	—	—	—	.067	.128	—
14	Haplotypes	1	1	1	1	1	1	1

populations, whereas haplotype Ag^{xdcth} (No. 9) could be a marker for the Australian aborigines. Such observations are of considerable interest for population geneticists. In addition, the differences in the distribution of Ag-types in various populations have to be taken into consideration when this system is applied in forensic serology for the elucidation of cases of disputed paternity.

METHODS FOR THE DETECTION OF Ag-ANTIGENS

As already mentioned in the introduction, immunodiffusion methods were used initially for the detection of the Ag-factors. Later, passive hemagglutination/inhibition techniques were introduced, and these proved to be a very successful tool for this purpose. These two methods, briefly presented in this section, use mainly human immune sera containing antibodies to Ag-epitopes. Alternative sources of Ag-antibodies will be discussed later.

Double Immunodiffusion (DID) in Agar Gel

In our own experiments, we used plates coated with an agar gel layer with six circular wells filled with the sera to be typed arranged around a central well containing the anti-Ag serum. Precipitation lines indicating a positive reaction were read before and after staining with Sudan Black (for technical details see reference 16). As an example, Ag(x)-typing performed by this technique is shown in Figure 8–2.

Immunodiffusion provides satisfactory results as long as the anti-Ag serum contains a strongly precipitating and monospecific antibody. However, precipitating anti-Ag antibodies are not common, and for some Ag-specificities we have never encountered antibodies with this property. Monospecific human antisera likewise are not often at our disposal. Polyspecific sera with more than one anti-Ag antibody are unsuitable for typing; they will yield confusing reaction patterns which cannot be interpreted in most instances. We agree that the requirement of monospecificity is not an absolute one, since polyspecific antisera can be made monospecific by absorption with serum or LDL of an appropriate phenotype. In our experience, the mixture of antiserum and absorbing serum may lead to unspecific reactions, and it is sometimes difficult to find a proper ratio for the two components of the anti-Ag typing system. Nevertheless, one special application for the immunodiffusion techniques should be mentioned: it allows the investigation of two antisera for the immunologic identity or non-identity of the antibodies by placing the sera into two neighboring wells and allowing simultaneous immunodiffusion against various normal sera in a so-called comparative immunodiffusion assay. Such experiments were conducted in the early phase of the investigation of the Ag-system and were helpful in the characterization and definition of the first Ag-specificities.

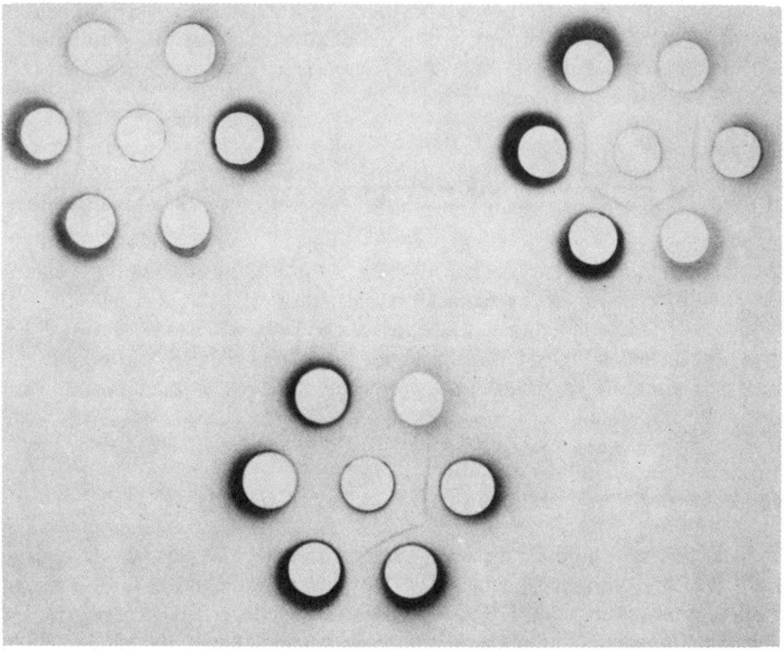

FIG 8–2.
Ag(x)-typing by double immunodiffusion (DID). Central well of rosettes contains precipitating anti-Ag(x); peripheral wells contain sera to be typed. Upper row, left rosette shows 2 Ag(x+) sera; right rosette shows 4 Ag(x+) sera; lower rosette shows 2 Ag(x+) sera.

The Passive Hemagglutination/Inhibition Assay (PHAIA)

In 1966 we showed that anti-Ag antibodies can be demonstrated by passive hemagglutination using red cells coated with LDL, and that Ag-factors can be detected by a corresponding hemagglutination/inhibition assay.[4] The principle of this assay, applied to Ag(x)-typing for example, is as follows. Purified Ag(x+) LDL obtained by ultracentrifugation is fixed to red cells by coupling with bisdiazotized benzidine. The cells are agglutinated by the addition of anti-Ag(x) serum. If Ag(x+) serum is simultaneously introduced into the system, the agglutination will be inhibited due to the reaction of the anti-Ag(x) antibody with the Ag(x+)-LDL contained in the serum. Inhibition thus indicates that the serum to be typed is Ag(x+). Correspondingly, the addition of Ag(x−) serum will not inhibit the agglutination reaction; agglutination is therefore expressing a negative typing result for the Ag(x)-factor (Fig 8–3) (for technical details see reference 16). The assay was evaluated exhaustively in 1971 by H. Boman, and the influence of the variation of the test conditions was studied in detail.[17]

The usefulness of the method was fully confirmed, and complete concordance was obtained in comparative studies of the passive hemagglutination/inhibition and immunodiffusion methods.[17, 18]

Since that time, we have modified and improved our technique, making two main changes (replacing bisdiazotized benzidine with chromium chloride for the fixation of LDL to the red cells, and using microtiter plates). Since our present procedure is the one which we would recommend for routine typings, we provide the details below.

The materials used are as follows:

1. Phosphate buffered saline (PBS), pH 7.4: 4.383 g Na_2HPO_4. 2 H_2O and 0.743 g KH_2PO_4 are dissolved in 3,000 ml of NaCl 0.15 M.
2. Diluent: Bovine serum albumin (30%) 1:60 in PBS, pH 7.4.
3. Chromium-III-chloride: Stock solution = 100 mg $CrCl_3$. 6 H_2O dissolved in 10 ml distilled water. Working solution = 1 volume of stock solution + 19 volumes of NaCl 9%.
4. LDL solution (prepared by ultracentrifugation): Serum is centrifuged at 3,000 rpm for 30 minutes (e.g., Spinco, rotor 30.2, 9 ml serum/10.5 ml tube). Chylomicrons (the white, fatty top layer) are quantitatively removed by suction. Samples of 5 ml of chylomicron-free serum are mixed with 4 ml NaCl solution (density = 1.11) and centrifuged at 30,000 rpm. for 16 hours (approximately 80,000 g). LDL floating on the surface layer can be quantitatively removed with a capillary pipette. The LDL preparation is dialyzed against saline for a period of 24 hours.

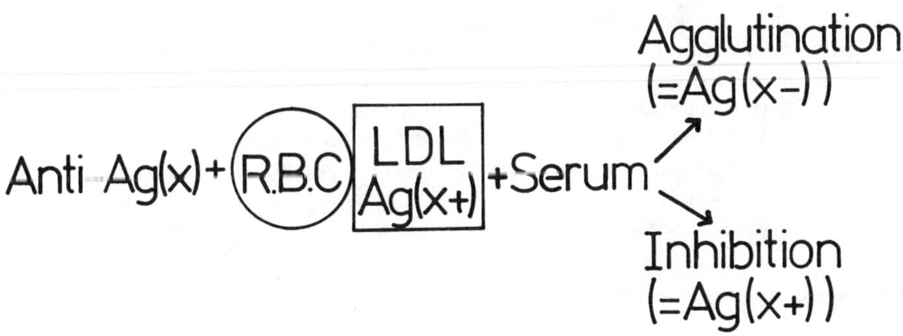

FIG 8–3.
Principle of Ag(x)-typing by passive hemagglutination/inhibition assay (PHAIA). *RBC* = red blood cell; *LDL* = purified low density lipoprotein; *Serum* = serum to be typed for Ag(x).

5. LDL determination: LDL concentration is measured photometrically at 280 nm (LDL diluted 1:100 in saline).

$$\frac{g\ \% = 1\% \cdot OD \cdot dilution}{17} \quad (OD\ 280\ nm\ of\ LDL\ 1\%,\ 1\ cm = 17)$$

6. Red cells: Human red cells, blood group 0, rhesus negative, washed 3 to 4 times with saline.

The method used is as follows:

1. Coating of the red cells with LDL: In a centrifuge tube 0.1 ml of LDL solution (4 mg/ml) and 0.1 ml of chromium-III-chloride working solution are mixed, then 0.05 ml of washed packed red cells are added and incubated for 5 minutes at room temperature under constant gentle mixing. The cells then are washed three times with 5 ml of saline and finally are suspended in 5 ml of diluent. The cell suspension is stable for up to 3 days when kept in the refrigerator.

2. Hemagglutination/inhibition assay (for Ag-typing in sera): Two dilutions (1:4 and 1:8 with diluent) of the sera to be tested are dispensed in microtiter (V) plates (0.025 ml each). 0.025 ml of antiserum (appropriately diluted with diluent according to the result of preliminary titrations) of the corresponding specificity is added, followed by 0.025 ml (1 drop with the microtiter dropper) of sensitized red cell suspension (LDL-coat corresponding to the same Ag-specificity). The plates are shaken and placed at 4°C. The first reading is made after 2 hours, and a second reading is made after 16 to 20 hours without disturbing the pattern of settled red cells.

3. Controls: Ag-antiserum plus sensitized red cells without a serum sample must show complete agglutination. Serum samples diluted 1:4 plus sensitized red cells shall not give agglutination.

As already mentioned above, the main advantage of the passive hemagglutination/inhibition assay is the fact that it can be applied easily using polyspecific Ag-antisera. The typing system is made monospecific by the choice of an appropriate Ag-phenotype for the LDL red cell coat. This must be positive for only one of the Ag-specificities, corresponding to the antibodies contained in the antiserum and negative for the other ones. Thus, a tetraspecific antiserum can be used for the typing of all four Ag-factors corresponding to the antibodies of this serum. Table 8–5 shows a few examples of polyspecific antisera that we are using for routine Ag-typing.

Enzyme Linked Immunosorbent Assay (ELISA)

Recently, an ELISA using monoclonal Ag-antibodies has been shown to be a new possibility for Ag-typing. This procedure will be discussed in section 8.

MOLECULAR BASIS OF THE Ag-EPITOPES

The attribution of the first detected "Ag-factor" [Ag(a)] to the LDL was demonstrated by immunoelectrophoresis, comparative immunodiffusion techniques, and

TABLE 8–5.
Some Ag-Typing Systems for Passive Hemagglutination/Inhibition Used in Our Laboratory

Antiserum			
Code	Ag-Antibodies, Anti-	Ag-Type of LDL Red Cell Coat	System Used for Typing Ag
Ger	y,d,c,	y+d−c−	y
		y−d+c−	d
ZZ	x,d,c,t	x−d−c−t+	t
		x−a_1−c+h−	c
Tur	x,a_1,c,h	x−a_1+c−h−	a_1
		x+a_1−c−h−	x
		x−a_1+g−	a_1
Gh	x,a_1,g	x−a_1−g+	g
		x+a_1−g−	x
		x+h−	x
P 504	x,h	x−h+	h

specific lipid staining.[19,20] Allison and Blumberg[1] showed that their factor Ag(a) was still demonstrable in sera after heating for 40 minutes at 56°C, after 7 days of storage at room temperature, and after 4 years of storage at −25°C. In 1973, we were able to demonstrate the presence of Ag-epitopes in VLDL, Lp(a) protein, and apolipoprotein B (apo B), in addition to LDL.[21] Since apolipoprotein B is the major apoprotein of LDL and also is present in VLDL and Lp(a) protein, the results of our study provided evidence that the Ag-epitopes are antigenic structures of the apolipoprotein B. The fact that we were not able to demonstrate all of the Ag-factors that were originally present in the LDL in the corresponding apo B protein suggested that some lipids may be necessary in order to guarantee a configuration of the apo B molecule(s), which enables the presentation of Ag-epitopes in a suitable manner for the immunologic reaction. Alternatively, a lack of sensitivity of the typing method may have been the reason for the phenomenon. Recent experiments have shown that the Ag-epitopes are not affected by treatment of the LDL with neuraminidase (a mixture of glycosidases), or with competing glycoproteins.[22] These results suggest that the Ag-epitopes are not on the carbohydrate structures of the apolipoprotein B. Therefore, one can assume that the Ag-system expresses variation of the amino acid sequence of the apo B polypeptides. Consequently, the Ag-system appears to be controlled genetically by the structural gene(s) of the apo B molecule(s).

A lot of work was necessary for biochemists to elucidate the structure of the LDL particles. Based upon the most recent of these investigations, a new model for the LDL particle has been proposed. The particle is claimed to be spherical, and to contain a liquid core of cholesteryl ester and triglyceride and a shell of phospholipid, cholesterol, and apo B protein, the latter consisting of one single polypeptide chain.[23,24] Since the apo B protein has been cloned and its entire amino acid sequence determined very recently,[25] it soon will become possible to assign the Ag-epitopes to defined amino acid variations in the polypeptide chain by sequencing individual apo B proteins of various phenotypes. Furthermore, the gene for apo B protein has just been located in the p24 region (near the tip of the short arm) of chromosome 2,[26] resolving the question of the chromosome assignment of the Ag-loci.

If it is true that the LDL-particle contains only one apo B molecule, then individuals who are not entirely homozygous for all five Ag-loci would possess two populations of LDL particles in their blood, one with the epitopes corresponding to one haplotype, and the other with those corresponding to the second haplotype. As an example, a person with the phenotype Ag($x+y+a_1+d-c-g+t+z-h-i+$), corresponding to the genotype $Ag^{xa}1^{gti}$ / $Ag^{ya}1^{gti}$ would exhibit the x, a_1, g, t, and i epitopes in one-half of his LDL-particles and the y, a_1, g, t, and i epitopes in the other. Future studies will reveal whether or not this assumption is correct. Furthermore, in our example, one would expect that the individual would possess a "single dose" of Ag(x)- and Ag(y)-epitopes, and a "double dose" of Ag(a_1)-, Ag(g)-, Ag(t)-, and Ag(i)-epitopes. In order to test this hypothesis, we conducted some experiments in 1977 and 1978.[11] The results showed a trend in the expected direction, but the method employed (titrations scores) apparently was not very suitable for the purpose, as it did not allow a convincing discrimination between single and double doses of Ag-epitopes.

HUMAN ALLOANTIBODIES AGAINST Ag-ANTIGENS

For a long time, the only source of antibodies to Ag-antigens, which represent the main reagent for Ag-typing, was human sera obtained from certain groups of patients. It soon became clear that formation of such antibodies was due to post-transfusion alloimmunization. However, many transfusions are required in order to induce immunization. Various studies, summarized in Table 8–6, show that homozygous thalassemics particularly are prone to produce such antibodies, whereas other multiply-transfused patients with comparable numbers of transfusions are at least ten times less susceptible to undergoing alloimmunization. The reason for this significant difference is still obscure. The studies also show that feto-maternal alloimmunization to Ag-epitopes does not seem to occur. The finding of Dürwald et al[27] that precipitating "anti-Ag(a)" may occur in the sera of pregnant women could never be confirmed. One must assume that Dürwald's precipitation reactions were not due to Ag-antibodies. Finally, "natural" Ag-antibodies have never been encountered in non-immunized individuals.

As can be seen in Table 8–7, 61 antibody-positive sera were observed among a total of 291 patients in two studies (thalassemics and hemophiliacs). Thirty-five of these sera (57%) were monospecific, 17 were bispecific (27%), 8 were trispecific (13%), and 1 was tetraspecific (2%). Some of the antibodies, such as anti-Ag(a_1), anti-Ag(d), anti-Ag(g), and anti-Ag(t), were not observed in monospecific sera. This illustrates the importance of the passive hemagglutination/inhibition assay, which allows the use of polyspecific antisera as monospecific reagents; there is no other way in which to type for the corresponding Ag-factors with human antisera.

TABLE 8–6.

Prevalence of Ag-Antibodies in Various Groups of Persons

Condition	Patients (n)	Transfusions (n)	Ag-Antibody (%)	Author
Thalassemics	47	5–200	29.8	Blumberg et al[48]
	80	5–250	12.5	Vierucci et al[33]
	60	10–200	33.8	Economidou et al[49]
	178	50–300	28.1	Bütler et al[50]
	139	10–200	25.2	Bütler et al[11]
	39	?	38.5	Boman et al[51]
Hemophiliacs	113	*	9.8	Mandalaki et al[52]
	108	*	2.8	Bütler[11]
Patients with various diseases	102	5–200	3.9	Blumberg et al[48]
	24	?	4.2	Hirschfeld et al[42]
	1,699	10–200	1.2	Bütler et al[11]
Multiparous women	380	†	0	Bütler et al[53]
	101	††	0	Boman et al[54]
Blood donors, healthy individuals	931	–	0	Bütler et al[11]
	70	–	0	Boman et al[54]

*Patients having received blood transfusions, clotting factors, and/or fresh frozen plasma.
†Women with four or more pregnancies.
††Women with three births or more.

TABLE 8–7.

Specificities and Frequencies of Ag-Antibodies Observed in Two Groups of Patients

Anti-Ag Specificities	Thalassemics N = 178[34]		Hemophiliacs N = 113[36]	
	n	%	*n*	%
anti-Ag(x)	19	10.7	7	6.2
anti-Ag(y)	0	0	1	0.9
anti-Ag(c)	1	0.6	0	0
anti-Ag(z)	4	2.3	0	0
anti-Ag(h)	3	1.7	0	0
anti-Ag(x,a_1)	12	6.7	0	0
anti-Ag(x,g)	1	0.6	0	0
anti-Ag(x,t)	0	0	1	0.9
anti-Ag(x,z)	0	0	1	0.9
anti-Ag(x,h)	1	0.6	0	0
anti-Ag(y,c)	1	0.6	0	0
anti-Ag(x,a_1,g)	4	2.3	1	0.9
anti-Ag(y,d,c)	1	0.6	0	0
anti-Ag(y,c,h)	1	0.6	0	0
anti-Ag(d,c,h)	1	0.6	0	0
anti-Ag(y,d,c,z)	1	0.6	0	0
Total	50	≈28%	11	≈10%

If one looks into the distribution of antibody specificities contained in Table 8–7, it becomes evident immediately that anti-Ag(x) is the most frequently occurring antibody. Among the 61 antibody-positive sera, a total of 97 Ag-antibodies were observed, specifically, 47 anti-Ag(x) (49% of the antibodies), 17 anti-Ag(a_1) (18%), 6 anti-Ag(c) (6%), 6 anti-Ag(g) (6%), 6 anti-Ag(z) (6%), 6 anti-Ag(h) (6%), 5 anti-Ag(y) (5%), 3 anti-Ag(d) (3%), and 1 anti-Ag(t) (1%). The frequency of the occurrence of an Ag-antibody as a result of post transfusion alloimmunization is dependent upon the frequency of the corresponding antigen's occurrence in the population. However, if we take the Ag(x)- and Ag(c)-factors, for example, there are around 60% of Ag(x−) individuals in the white population who are susceptible to form anti-Ag(x), as compared with roughly 50% of Ag(c−) individuals who are susceptible to form anti-Ag(c), although the frequency of the Ag(x) antibodies is about eight times higher than that of the Ag(c) antibodies. This means that there are striking differences in the immunogenicity of the various Ag-epitopes. There is no doubt that Ag(x) is the strongest immunogen, not only among thalassemic patients who have a high incidence of Ag-alloimmunization, but also among other multiply transfused patients (e.g., hemophiliacs) who have a lower incidence. Such variation of immunogenicity in post-transfusion alloimmunization is well known for other human blood antigens (e.g., for red cell antigens), even within one blood group system (rhesus blood group epitopes)!

RABBIT ANTISERA TO Ag-ANTIGENS

Because of the scarcity of human Ag-antibodies, we have tried to produce anti-Ag by immunizing rabbits with purified LDL. In experiments conducted from 1977 to 1980, we were able to raise heteroantibodies against a few Ag-factors.[11] The LDLs were prepared from plasma of entirely homozygous persons with not more than five Ag-antigens (the minimum number of possible Ag-factors in an individual), in order to minimize the number of possible antibodies in the antiserum. The LDLs were purified as for the red cell coat material used for the passive hemagglutination assay. Solutions containing 10 mg LDL per ml in saline were mixed with equal amounts of complete Freund adjuvant. Each animal received an inoculum of 5 mg LDL (divided into two equal portions and injected i.m. into the buttocks) for the initial immunization as well as for the booster injections, which were administered at intervals of 2 to 3 weeks. Blood samples were drawn from the ear vein 5 weeks after the initial injection as well as immediately before the booster injections, which were repeated up to three times. Larger bleedings (15–20 ml blood) were done when the properties of the antisera looked most promising. For use in passive hemagglutination, the sera were preabsorbed 3 to 5 times with equal volumes of packed human red cells (group 0), in order to remove the heteroagglutinins, until no more agglutination with human red cells could be observed. Occasionally, sera were also tested in immunodiffusion assays for precipitating anti-LDL antibodies. Antibodies of this type were observed in all instances. Several series of animals were immunized according to this scheme in the 3-year period indicated above.

TABLE 8–8.
Rabbit Antisera to Ag-Antigens Produced in Our Laboratory

Code of Antiserum	The Five Ag-Factors Present in the Inoculum	Partial Ag-Phenotype of the Absorbing Serum	Relevant Ag-Factors of LDL-Coat in PHAIA	Observed Ag-Antibody
124	y,a_1,g,z,i	$y+a_1+g-z+i+$	$g+$	anti-Ag(g)
125	y,a_1,g,z,i	$y+a_1-g+z-i+$	a_1+ $z-$	anti-Ag(a_1)
126	y,d,c,t,i	$y+d+c+t+i-$	$i+$	anti-Ag(i)
129	x,a_1,g,t,i	$x-a_1+g+t+i+$	$x+$	anti-Ag(x)

The rabbits all formed strongly reacting antibodies to LDL which agglutinated LDL coated red cells irrespective of their Ag-phenotype. This outcome was as we expected. We were aware of the fact that the rabbits would form primarily antibodies against common antigenic determinants of LDL. In order to investigate whether Ag-specific antibodies were present besides the antibodies with a broad specificity for LDL, we conducted comprehensive absorption experiments by mixing the rabbit antisera with various amounts of normal sera containing appropriate Ag-phenotypes. In the most successful series of experiments, comprising eight animals, four sera were found to contain Ag-antibodies in the passive hemagglutination assay (Table 8–8). The specificities were confirmed in inhibition tests. However, only one antiserum (number 129) proved to be a reliable reagent for Ag-typing. This serum was used in parallel to human antisera for Ag(x)-typing in routine paternity testing and no contradictory results were observed. In summary, while we were able to produce rabbit Ag-antisera, it is important to note that only a small proportion of the sera obtained from immunized animals gave suitable antisera, and the absorbtion conditions required for the preparation of monospecific reagents were extremely difficult to establish.

MONOCLONAL ANTIBODIES TO Ag-ANTIGENS

Several groups of researchers, including our own, have prepared monoclonal antibodies to human LDL produced by mouse/mouse hybridoma cells in recent years. Schumaker and co-workers recorded binding profiles to individual LDLs obtained with a battery of such monoclonal antibodies.[22] They could distinguish three categories of binding profiles, representing three phenotypes, which were shown to be genetically controlled. In further studies, one of the monoclonal antibodies of this set turned out to have anti-Ag(c) specificity.[28,29] It could be shown that this monoclonal antibody distinguishes between strong reactors, intermediate reactors, and weak reactors in binding assays (using the ELISA technique), corresponding to a "double dose," a "single dose," and a "zero dose" of the Ag(c) antigen, and thus reflecting the phenotypes Ag(c+g−), Ag(c+g+), and Ag(c−g+), respectively. Determinations of the Ag(c,g) phenotypes were performed simultaneously with the passive hemagglutination/inhibition assay that was executed on 50 individuals, and gave completely concordant results. The outcome of these recent studies now confirms our previous assumption (which we were unable to prove properly using human antisera and the passive hemagglutination inhibition assay) that it should be possible to recognize single and double doses of Ag epitopes in heterozygous and homozygous individuals, respectively (see section 5).

In our own experiments, we have been able to produce monoclonal antibodies which detect the epitopes Ag(c) and Ag(d). However, with our present test system, we have not yet succeeded in discriminating between the homozygous and heterozygous carriers of these two epitopes.[30]

In conclusion, based upon the preparations available at present, typing of three out of the ten Ag-factors [Ag(c), Ag(g), Ag(d)] by means of monoclonal antibodies is now possible. Therefore, we have good reason to assume that test systems which use monoclonal antibodies will be promising reagents for Ag-typing in the future.

BIOLOGICAL SIGNIFICANCE OF THE Ag-SYSTEM

It is well documented that Ag-epitopes can induce post-transfusion alloimmunization, as already described in section 6. From the distribution of the Ag-factors in the population, one can easily conclude that immunologically incompatible transfusions related to the Ag-system occur very frequently. The question then arises whether Ag-sensitized patients undergo adverse reactions as a consequence of such incompatible transfusions. Several authors have reported mild transfusion reactions which were attributed to Ag-incompatibility. However, other possible causes of these reactions were not properly excluded in practically all cases.[19, 31–33] It also has been suggested that Ag-antibodies may lead to a less than average patient survival time.[34] However, this also could be explained by the fact that the degree of patients' Ag-alloimmunization depends upon the number of transfusions they receive. Therefore, the patients who require the highest number of transfusions already constitute the most severe cases with the worst prognoses. In summary, it has not been established that Ag-incompatible transfusions lead to reactions in sensitized patients. This could be due to the fact that, according to a study conducted by our group, Ag and anti-Ag immune complexes do not seem to activate the complement system.[35]

The most interesting biomedical aspect of the Ag-system is its possible role in lipid metabolism. The lipoproteins are responsible for the transport of the exogenous dietary fat and the endogenous synthesized lipids. LDL, in particular, supplies the tissues with cholesterol, which is an important structural component of the cell membrane and a raw material for the synthesis of steroid hormones and bile acids. LDL is fixed to the cells by specific receptors with a high affinity, and subsequently is taken up by the cell, and its components metabolized by the enzymatic battery of the liposomes. An elevated level of plasma LDL will lead to an increased uptake of this lipoprotein by the cell, inhibiting endogenous cholesterol synthesis. However, if the uptake of LDL by the cell is disturbed, disrupting the metabolization mechanisms, the LDL may accumulate in the intercellular space and form cholesterol deposits. If this takes place around the endothelial cells of the arterial wall, one major prerequisite for atherogenesis is fulfilled. It is well known that an elevated LDL level is an important risk factor for atherosclerosis, whereas an elevated VLDL level is slightly less dangerous, and the chylomicrons (which are too large to penetrate the arterial wall) are practically harmless. HDL, on the other hand, can be considered a protective factor, due to its capacity to transport cholesterol from tissue cells to the liver, where it is catabolized and excreted. The uptake of LDL by the cell may be impaired by a receptor deficiency. Such a condition leads to hypercholesterinemia and atherogenesis. However, the uptake mechanism could be disturbed also by an abnormality of the receptor combining site on the LDL particle. Since this combining site is located on the surface of the LDL particle as part of the apo B structure, a connection may exist between such an abnormality and the Ag-epitopes. Therefore, this possible relationship between the Ag-phenotypes and atherosclerosis or cardiovascular disease has been the subject of much investigation. Early clinical studies, conducted from 1965 to 1967 on patients with coronary artery disease and patients with diabetes, did not reveal any definite correlation with the Ag-system.[19,36] However, based upon combined data from 10 different populations, Berg et al found a significantly higher level of serum cholesterol and triglycerides present in Ag(x−) individuals compared with Ag(x+) individuals.[37] Unfortunately, no studies were undertaken by other groups in order to confirm or disprove these important findings. In addition, large-scale clinical studies were always hampered by the scarcity of anti-Ag sera. Recently, a new effort, facilitated by the availability of monoclonal antibodies, has been made simultaneously by a number of research groups, and several clinical studies are presently underway in collaboration with our laboratory.

Another aspect of LDL thus far entirely unexplored is its possible role in immunomodulation. It has been suggested that lipoproteins may be important in regulating immune response. LDL, in particular, appears to inhibit DNA synthesis in the initially activated lymphocytes and to suppress cell division and lymphocyte proliferation.[38] It remains to be elucidated whether these immunoregulative functions of the LDL depend upon the Ag-phenotype. Such a correlation could be of considerable interest for the understanding of immunological pathomechanisms.

APPLICATION OF THE Ag-SYSTEM IN PATERNITY ANALYSIS

Considering the complexity and distribution of the numerous Ag-factors in the population, one would expect that the Ag-system would be extremely informative for the investigation of disputed paternity. However, as stated repeatedly, only a small part of the system can be used in routine paternity testing, due to the restricted availability of antisera. In fact, only the factors Ag(x) and, to a certain extent, Ag(y) have been used for this purpose, recalling that anti-Ag(x) is the most frequently occurring antibody and that anti-Ag(y) also is not uncommon. Typing for both Ag(x) and Ag(y) factors in paternity cases allows the application of the first rule of exclusion (factor present in the child and absent in the mother and the alleged father) as well as of the second rule of exclusion (opposite homozygosity between the child and the alleged father). We have been typing for the Ag(x,y) factors since 1969 as one of the 26 hemogenetic systems used by our institute in paternity investigations.

In regard to all other hemogenetic systems used in forensic serology, two requirements must be fulfilled to justify their application: the assertion of the dominant mode of inheritance, and the reliability of the method of typing.

Basic information about the genetics of the Ag-system has been given in section 3. A major publication prepared by J. Hirschfeld in 1967 was devoted to this subject.[39] At that time, it already had been shown that no Ag(x−y−) sample could be observed among 1,570 unrelated individuals belonging to five different populations. The author then presented a review of published family studies on Ag(x), comprising 906 families with a total of 2,463 children. This material included 294 "critical families" with 815 children. Three apparent exceptions to the dominant mode of inheritance were found within these critical families, representing a reliability ratio of 99.6%. This degree of reliability would not be fully acceptable according to our present quality requirements. However, it must be borne in mind that the typings were done in an early phase of Ag-investigations and used the immunodiffusion method exclusively. It is obvious to us (and also is the opinion of Hirschfeld) that the exceptions were not due to abnormalities in the mode of inheritance but to imperfect typing methodology. This situation has changed completely since the passive hemagglutination/inhibition assay has turned out to be much more reliable than the immunodiffusion technique. We will come back to the question of methodological reliability below. Regarding the mode of inheritance, we never have observed an Ag(x−y−) type in the past 17 years. Furthermore, we have studied 1,631 mother/child pairs taken from our cases of disputed paternity (Table 8–9). Among the 1,071 "critical pairs," no exception from the codominant mode of inheritance of the alleles Ag^x and Ag^y was observed. Thus, we can conclude that the first requirement mentioned above is fulfilled.

It is a bit more difficult to demonstrate the reliability of the typing methods by means of figures. Our standard procedure consists of duplicate typing, using two different hemagglutination/inhibition typing systems (two different antisera and/or two different LDL coats for the red cells). Disagreement between the two results is very rare. In those exceptional cases where it does occur, we repeat the testing, which almost invariably leads to unequivocal results. In extremely rare situations, no clear-cut result can be obtained due to unspecific agglutination of the control red cells by the serum of the propositus. In these cases, we are unable to apply the Ag-system.

TABLE 8–9.

Ag(x,y)-Groups of 1,631 Mother-Child Pairs (Cases of Disputed Paternity)

Children/Mothers	N Ag(x+y−)	N Ag(x+y+)	N Ag(x−y+)	N
Ag(x+y−)	24	61	0	85*
Ag(x+y+)	71	274	215	560
Ag(x−y+)	0	206	780	986*
Total				1,631
*Total "critical" mother/child pairs				1,071

TABLE 8–10.
Ag(x,y) Exclusions in 1,623 Cases of Disputed Paternity

Number of Exclusions	Number of Other Hemogenetic Systems With an Additional Exclusion
3	0 (exclusively Ag-exclusion)
11	1 additional exclusion
25	2 additional exclusions
18	3 additional exclusions
11	4 additional exclusions
13	5 additional exclusions
3	6 additional exclusions
2	7 additional exclusions
1	8 additional exclusions
87	Total Number of Exclusions With Ag(x,y)

The Ag-epitopes are fairly stable; serum samples can be kept at 4°C for up to 1 week without deterioration of the antigenic structure. However, it is recommended that the sample be examined for turbidity in order to make sure that no gross bacterial contamination has occurred. Such a contamination could lead to a degradation of the LDL and its Ag-structures. Reliable typings are still possible in frozen sera (kept at −20°C) after more than 1 year. The possibility of determining the Ag-groups in dried blood stains has not yet been investigated. It was shown by us, as well as by other authors, that the Ag-determinants of LDL are synthesized by the newborn within a few hours after birth, and that a passive transfer of LDL from the mother to her offspring does not take place.[39–41] Based on these facts, one can exclude misinterpretation of Ag-typing results in infants and children. In summary, our second requirement for the application of this hemogenetic system in forensic serology (the methodological reliability), can be regarded as fulfilled beyond any doubt.

The "exclusion power" of the Ag(x,y) pair of antithetical factors is remarkable. On the basis of our Swiss gene frequencies, we have calculated an average maximal chance of exclusion for falsely alleged fathers of 14.0%. This figure is in close agreement with the one reported by Hirschfeld, who found it to be 14.2% for the Swedish population.[39] The value is also very similar to that of the A1,A2,B,O-blood group system (14.7% in the Swiss population). We have depicted in Table 8–10 the Ag(x,y) exclusions in the 1,623 cases of disputed paternity already mentioned. As can be seen, a total of 87 Ag(x,y) exclusions resulted in this material, whereas 3 exclusions were obtained exclusively with this system. From this material one can calculate an overall practical (or realistic) chance of exclusion of 5.4%.

In conclusion, the Ag(x,y) factors proved to be a useful tool in paternity testing. The usefulness of the Ag-system could be drastically improved if typings could be extended to the remaining Ag-factors. This may become possible in the future when monoclonal Ag-antibodies of the other specificities become available in sufficient quantities.

REFERENCES

1. Allison AC, Blumberg BS: An isoprecipitation reaction distinguishing human serum protein types. *Lancet* 1961; I:634.
2. Berg K: A new serum type system in man—the Lp system. *Acta Pathol Microbiol Scand* 1963; 59:369.
3. Utermann O, Hess M, Steinmetz A: Polymorphism of apolipoprotein E and occurrence of dysbetalipoproteinaemia in man. *Nature* 1977; 269:604.
4. Bütler R, Brunner E: A new sensitive method for studying the polymorphisms of the human low density lipoproteins. *Vox Sang* 1966; 11:738.
5. Bütler R, Brunner E, Politis E, et al: A non-precipitating anti-Ag antibody. *Vox Sang* 1967; 13:508.
6. Hirschfeld J, Blumberg BS, Allison AC: Relationship of human anti-lipoprotein allotypic sera. *Nature* 1964; 202:706.
7. Bütler R, Brunner E: A second example of a non-precipitating anti-Ag antibody. *Vox Sang* 1968; 14:230.
8. Bütler R, Brunner E: On the genetics of the low density lipoprotein factors Ag(c) and Ag(e). *Hum Hered* 1969; 19:174.
9. Bütler R, Brunner E: A new interpretation of the serum factor 'Ag(e)'. *Vox Sang* 1970; 18:370.
10. Bütler R, Brunner E, Morganti G: Contribution to the inheritance of the Ag Groups - A population genetic study. *Vox Sang* 1974; 26:485.
11. Bütler R, Bütler-Brunner E, Scherz R, et al: The Ag-system of low density lipoprotein - an up-dating, in Peeters H (ed): *Protides in the Biological Fluids, 25th Colloquium 1977*. Oxford, Pergamon Press, 1978, pp 255–261.
12. Morganti G, Beolchini PE, Vierucci A, et al: Contribution to the genetics of the serum β-lipoproteins in man -III. Lack of association and linkage between the Ag(x,y,a_1) factors and some blood and serum protein antigens. *Humangenetik* 1968; 6:275.
13. Bütler R, Brunner E: Ag(i): Detection of an antithetical factor to Ag(h). *Vox Sang* 1974; 27:550.
14. Hitzeroth HW, Bütler R, Bütler-Brunner E: A population genetic study on the Ag polymorphism in South African Indians and Negroids. *Hum Hered* 1980; 30:94.
15. Breguet G, et al, in preparation.
16. Bütler R, Brunner E, Vierucci A, et al: Comparative studies on anti-Ag sera in immunodiffusion and passive hemagglutination methods. *Vox Sang* 1967; 13:327.

17. Boman H: Studies on inherited antigenic variation of human serum β-lipoprotein by passive hemagglutination. I. Methodological studies. *Int J Protein Research II* 1970; 209.
18. Boman H, Solaas MH: Studies on inherited antigenic variation of human serum β-lipoprotein by passive hemagglutination. II. Comparison of the passive hemagglutination inhibition and immunodiffusion methods. *Int J Protein Research* 1971; III:175.
19. Allison AC, Blumberg BS: Serum lipoprotein allotypes in man, in Steinberg HG, Bearn HG (ed): *Progress in Medical Genetics*, vol IV. New York, Grune and Stratton, 1965, p 176.
20. Blumberg BS, Dray S, Robinson JC: Antigen polymorphism of a low density lipoprotein. *Nature* 1962; 194:656.
21. Ehnholm C, Bütler R, Brunner E: The occurrence of Ag determinants in different lipoproteins. *Vox Sang* 1973; 25:281.
22. Schumaker VN, Robinson MT, Curtiss LK, et al: Anti-apoprotein B monoclonal antibodies detect human low density lipoprotein polymorphisms. *J Biol Chem* 1984; 259:623.
23. Jacobs JC, Schumaker VN, LeBoef RC, et al: A new model for low density lipoproteins. In preparation.
24. Milne RW, Marcel YL: Monoclonal antibodies against human low density lipoprotein. Stoichiometric binding studies using Fab fragments. *FEBS Lett* 1982; 146:97.
25. Knott TJ, Pease RJ, Powell LN, et al: Complete protein sequence and identification of structural domains. *Nature* 1986; 323:734.
26. Knott TJ, Rall SC, Innerarity TL, et al: Human apolipoprotein B: Structure of carboxyl-terminal domains, sites of gene expression and chromosomal localization. *Science* 1985; 230:37.
27. Dürwald W, Leopold D, Krämer RH: The formation of precipitating antibodies after multiple pregnancies. *Vox Sang* 1965; 10:94.
28. Tikkanen MJ, Ehnholm Ch, Bütler R, et al: Monoclonal antibody detects Ag polymorphism of apolipoprotein B. *FEBS Lett* 1986; 202:54.
29. Robinson MT, Schumaker VN, Bütler R, et al: Ag(c): Recognition by a monoclonal antibody. *Arteriosclerosis* 1986; 6:341.
30. Schlapfer P, Nydegger T, Bütler-Brunner E, et al: Two monoclonal antibodies that discriminate between allelic variants of human low density lipoprotein. *Hybridoma* 1987; 6:575.
31. Blumberg BS, Bernanke D, Allison AC: A human lipoprotein polymorphism. *J Clin Invest* 1962; 41:1936.
32. Okochi K: Serum lipoprotein allotypes Ag(x) and Ag(y) in Japanese. *Vox Sang* 1967; 13:319.
33. Vierucci A, Morganti G, Varone D, et al: New anti-beta-lipoprotein antisera in transfused children. *Vox Sang* 1966; 11:427.

34. Blumberg BS, personal communication, 1973.
35. Bütler R, Brunner E: Inability of Ag/anti-Ag complexes to fix complement and its significance. *Vox Sang* 1969; 17:462.
36. Berg K, Aarseth S, Lundevall J, et al: Blood groups and genetic serum types in diabetes mellitus. *Diabetologia* 1967; 3:30.
37. Berg K, Harnes C, Dahlen G, et al: Genetic variation in serum low density lipoproteins and lipid levels in man. *Proc Natl Acad Sci USA* 1976; 73:937.
38. Cuthbert JA, Lipsky PE: Immunoregulation by low density lipoproteins in man, low density lipoprotein inhibits mitogen-stimulated human lymphocyte proliferation after initial activation. *J Lipid Res* 1983; 24:1512.
39. Hirschfeld J: Application of the Ag(x) antigen in medico-legal investigations. *Vox Sang* 1968; 14:95.
40. Morganti G, Beolchini PE, Vierucci A, et al: Contribution to the genetics of the serum β-lipoproteins in man: I. Frequency, transmission and penetrance of factors Ag(x) and Ag(y). *Humangenetik* 1967; 4:262.
41. Vierucci A, Dettori M, Morganti G, et al: Synthesis of β-lipoproteins (Ag groups) in the foetus and the newborn. *Vox Sang* 1968; 14:151.
42. Hirschfeld J, Blombäck M: A new anti-Ag serum (L.L.). *Nature* 1964; 201:1337.
43. Contu L: Un nouvel antigène des béta-lipoprotéines humaines. *Nov Rev Fr Hematol* 1966; 6:671.
44. Hirschfeld J, Unger P, Ramgren O: A new anti-Ag serum, Serum B. N. *Nature* 1966; 212:206.
45. Bütler R, Brunner E, Scaloumbacas N, et al: Ag(d), a further factor of the Ag-system. *Vox Sang* 1970; 18:90.
46. Bütler R, Brunner E, Morganti G, et al: A new factor of the Ag-system: Ag(g). *Vox Sang* 1970; 18:85.
47. Bütler R, Brunner E, Morganti G, et al: Ag(h), an additional factor of the Ag-system. *Vox Sang* 1973; 24:267.
48. Blumberg BS, Workman PL, Hirschfeld J: Gammaglobulin, group specific and lipoprotein groups in U.S. white and negro population. *Nature* 1964; 202:561.
49. Economidou J, Constantoulakis H, Augustaki O, et al: Frequency of antibodies to various antigenic determinants in polytransfused patients with homozygous thalassaemia in Greece. *Vox Sang* 1971; 20:252.
50. Bütler R, Gerber H, Economidou J, et al: Immunization of thalassaemic patients against red cell, leucocyte antigens and against IgA and low density lipoprotein (abstract Tu-112). *19th Congress Intl Soc Haematol*, Budapest, 1982.

51. Boman H, Lanzkowsky P, Berg K: Studies on inherited antigenic variation of human serum β-lipoprotein by passive hemagglutination. VII. Isoantibodies in sera from children with thalassaemia. *Clin Genet* 1972; 3:207.
52. Mandalaki T, Bütler R, Bütler-Brunner E, et al: Alloimmunization in polytransfused haemophiliacs against low density lipoproteins (system Ag) and IgA (abstract No 185). *XVth World Federation of Hemophilia Congress*, Stockholm, 1983.
53. Bütler R, unpublished data.
54. Boman H, Klausen H: Studies on inherited antigenic variation of human serum β-lipoprotein by passive hemagglutination. VI. Screening for antibodies in sera from multiparous women and from normal individuals. *Clin Genet* 1972; 3:180.

Chapter 9

Forensic Applications of Immunoglobulin Allotypes (GM, AM and KM)

Moses S. Schanfield, Ph.D.

GENETICS AND BIOCHEMISTRY

Introduction

In the United States, the acquisition of new genetic markers for the individualization of blood and body fluids in forensic serology has progressed rapidly in recent years, including the introduction of electrophoretic procedures such as isoelectric focusing. However, until recently, the second oldest system for the individualization of blood stains (the use of genetic markers on antibodies, or allotypes), had not been widely used in North America. The first genetic marker to be found on human antibodies or, more accurately, on immunoglobulins, was identified in 1956 and called "Gm a."[1] By 1961, the application of this genetic marker to the individualization of blood stains was being reported[2] and, by 1963, both Ducos and colleagues[3] and Kobiela[4] were reporting that "Gm" was the only reliable marker for the individualization of blood stains other than the ABO blood groups. In Europe, it became routine to use Gm allotypes and then Km allotypes in the individualization of blood stains and body fluids. Until recently, though, the lack of a regular supply of commercially available reagents precluded the widespread use of these markers in the United States and Canada. Now that the availability of reagents for these very useful genetic markers has increased, allotyping has spread to North America.

In 1956, Grubb was studying individuals with hypogammaglobulinemia (low levels of immunoglobulins) using an agglutination inhibition test, which included an indicator red blood cell (RBC) consisting of RBC coated with immunoglobulins of the class IgG and antihuman IgG. He found that the serum of one patient agglutinated the IgG-coated indicator RBC, but not the uncoated RBC, and that the agglutination was inhibited by some sera and not by others.[1,5] The marker was called "Gm a," the

Gm standing for gammaglobulin. In 1959, a second marker was reported; it was called "Gm x" and was found only in some Gm a–positive individuals.[6] The same year a third marker was reported and was called "Gm b," because it appeared to be allelic to Gm a.[7] Based on these three test systems, the Swedish population could be divided into five phenotypes: GM a; Gm a,x; Gm a,b; GM a,x,b; and Gm b. In 1961, another system was found by researchers in France[8] and was called InV for the original antibody donor, "*In*hibitor *V*irmentois"; however, it is now called KM. This system is genetically independent of Gm, but is found also on gammaglobulin-coated indicator red blood cells. The genetic markers found on gammaglobulin were subsequently called allotypes. The term "allotype" had been coined originally by Oudin[9] to indicate polymorphic markers in rabbit serum proteins that are detected serologically.

The immunoglobulin allotypes now are known to be composed of five linked loci and one unlinked locus. The five linked loci consist of the genes for heavy chains of the immunoglobulins G1, G2, G3, A2, and E, and the unlinked locus is that of the Kappa (K) light chain. A total of 24 immunoglobulin allotypes have been defined thus far. Allotypes on G1, G2, G3, A2, and K light chains are defined routinely by agglutination inhibition testing, while the marker on the E heavy chain has thus far been detected only by radioimmunoassay.

Nomenclature

The nomenclature of the immunoglobulin allotypes is tied directly to our knowledge of the structure and concentration of immunoglobulins. Human immunoglobulins consist of a two-chain structure. Each molecule is made up of two identical heavy chains and two identical light chains. Thus, even though an individual may be heterozygous, a given antibody molecule will carry only one of two alleles at a locus. Immunoglobulins are divided into five major subdivisions, with "Ig" standing for immunoglobulin: IgG, IgA, IgM, IgD, and IgE in order of descending concentration. Further, IgG and IgA are divided into subclasses based on differences in heavy chains and ordered by concentration into IgG1, IgG2, IgG3, IgG4, IgA1, and IgA2. Light chains are divided into Kappa and Lambda types based on amino acid substitutions in the light chains. The Lambda light chain genes do not have allotypes. Thus, blood and body fluids consist of mixtures of immunoglobulins, each possessing two identical heavy chains and two identical light chains (approximately 60% to 70% with K chains and 30% to 40% with L chains). With two exceptions, each allotype occurs only on a single heavy or light chain type.

In 1974, a World Health Organization (WHO) meeting was held to review the nomenclature and verify the definition of all allotypes known at that time.[10] A series of recommendations were proposed regarding nomenclature for allotypes, phenotypes, and genotypes, and those previously defined allotypes which were no longer testable because of a lack of reagent were identified. In 1979, the "International System for Human Gene Nomenclature (1979)" was approved and disseminated by the Human Gene Mapping Workshop.[11] In order to be consistent with the 1979 guidelines, the 1974 WHO recommendations for human immunoglobulin allotypes have been modified to conform to the recommendations on genetic marker nomenclature made at a recent meeting of the Human Gene Mapping Workshop (Subcommittee on Nomenclature, September 4–5, 1986, Ann Arbor, Michigan). The primary change made was the capitalization of all letters in genetic marker designations. Thus, Gm, Am, and Km became GM, AM, and KM. Further, all alphabetic designations of alleles or markers were capitalized, such that G1m a became G1M A. Alleles, which are italicized, were presented as the gene symbol and an asterisk with no spaces. Thus, the G1M A allele was designated *G1M*A*, and serological results were presented as G1M A. The other changes will be presented in the relevant sections of this chapter.

In contrast to the HLA system, in which an individual can have only one serologically-defined antigen in an allele, in the genetic marker system, each individual must have two alleles at each locus and most alleles consist of more than one allotype. This is similar to the Rh system, in which each allele consists of multiple serologically-defined specificities (D, C, c, CW, E, e, EW, etc.). Initially, all of the allotypes were given alphabetic or alphabetic plus numeric (alphameric) designations. However, the use of numbers only was recommended at a WHO meeting in 1966.[12] Unfortunately, that meeting did not set criteria for the assignment of specificities, and as new antisera were found they were assigned new numbers. However, many of the antisera that were given different numbers had the same specificities, including G1M 3 and 4, 5 and 12, and 13 and 25. The 1974 meeting reversed the position of the 1966 meeting, but allowed the previous numbers and alphameric assignments to be retained. Further, antisera were exchanged, the specificities available at that time were all verified, and the nomenclature was corrected. Finally, guidelines were established for the identification of new specificities.

Only the alphameric designations will be used in this chapter unless the numeric designation is the only accepted nomenclature. This is done for several reasons. First, in most cases this maintains continuity with the historical designations of the allotypes. Second and most important, it indicates the relationship between allotypes that are inherited together in alleles and are serologically related to each other. For example, different laboratories use different G3M B reagents, either B0, B1, B3, or B5. It is easy to see that all of these are related to each other and are inherited in whites as part of "B" allele. It is much more difficult to see immediately that the same numerically designated specificities are related to each other; G3M 11, 5, 10, and 13. Also, it is not possible to talk about a "B" allele in this nomenclature, because the numbers refer to only a single specificity. Finally, much of the early forensic literature uses the alphameric notation system and refers to G3M B, without identifying any subspecificities. To aid the reader, Table 9–1 contains the 1974 recommendations for allotype designation and the changes consistent with the 1979 recommendations, as well as all of the previous designations found in the literature.

Immunoglobulin Allotypes

KM Kappa Allotypes.—Approximately 60% to 70% of all immunoglobulins carry Kappa (K) light chains. Therefore, the genetic markers on the Kappa light chains (KM) are present in amounts that are approximately equal to those of the allotypes on IgG1 (G1M). In some body fluids (such as saliva), they are present in much higher

TABLE 9–1.
Currently Testable Immunoglobulin Allotypes

Location	Alphameric	Numeric	Previous Designations	
IgG1	G1M A	G1M 1	Gm, G1m a,	Gm, G1m 1,
	F	3	bw, b2, f	3, 4
	X	2	x	2
	Z	17	z	17
IgG1/3	G1/3M G5	28	G3 m g5	G3m 28
IgG2	G2M N	23	Gm, G2m n	Gm, G2m 23
IgG3	G3M B0	11	Gm G3m b^{β}, b0	Gm G3m 11
	B1	5	b, b1, b^{γ}	5, 12
	B3	13	b3, Bet	13, 25
	B4	14	b4	14
	B5	10	b^{α}, b5	10
	C3	6	Gm-like, c, c3	6
	C5	24	Gm-like, c, c5	24
	G	21	g	21
	S	15	s	15
	T	16	t	16
	U	26	Pa, u	26
	V	27	Ray, v	27
IgA2	A2M 1	1	Am, A2m 1 Am_2	1
	2	2	2	2
Kappa chain	KM 1	1	InV, Inv, Km 1 = lower case L	Inv 1
	2	2	a	2
	3	3	b	3

concentrations (see below). There are three KM allotypes, designated 1,[13] 2,[8] and 3.[14] KM 2 is of little use forensically because no source of antisera is available. Further, it has a relationship with KM 1 that is similar to the relationship between G1M X and G1M A. There are three alleles: *KM*1,2, KM*1,* and *KM*3*. However, the *KM*1* allele occurs only in whites, and at barely polymorphic levels.[13] The allotype KM 1 is polymorphic in almost all populations, with a frequency almost always less than that of KM 3. The frequency of KM 1 is lower in U.S. white populations (approximately 16%) than in U.S. black populations (approximately 56%). The gene and phenotype frequencies in several U.S. populations are presented in Tables 9–2 and 9–3 and in Appendix 9–1.

G1M IgG1 Allotypes.—Immunoglobulin subclasses are numbered according to their concentration in human serum, with IgG1 having the highest concentration. In terms of forensics, IgG1 is detected normally in blood stains or semen, if KM markers have been detected. There are five allotypes at the G1 locus (A, F, G5, X, and Z) which are inherited in 5 alleles that have a worldwide distribution and in a single allele found only in the Ainu people of Japan. Without exception, all of the alleles contain either G1M F or G1M Z, because of the location and nature of the amino acid substitutions that created these two allotypes (Fig 9–1). As a suggested form of shorthand notation, the allotypes present in each allele and the populations in which the allele primarily is found are presented in Table 9–4.

G1M A was the first GM factor to be discovered.[15] The phenotype frequency of G1M A is approximately 51% in the U.S. white population and exceeds 99% in the U.S. black population (see Table 9–2). In most non-white populations the frequency is either close to or exactly 100%.

G1M F was discovered independently by several groups.[15,16] G1M F and G1M A appeared to be allelic markers in whites, but were not found to be so in Asiatic and Oceanic populations. However, in forensic applications, if G1M A is absent, then G1M F should be present or the stain is not interpretable. The reverse is also true. G1M F is found in 91% of the U.S. white population, but in only 19% of the U.S. black population (see Table 9–2), and rarely, if at all, in the African black population. Its presence in the U.S. black population is almost certainly a result of white admixture.

G1/3M G5 was described originally by two groups of researchers as a new allotype on IgG3.[17–19] However, from the author's first experience with the antisera detecting this specificity, it was obvious that the sera from U.S. and African blacks behaved differently than sera from all other races. A study by van Loghem et al[20] of an unusual black sera confirmed that G5 can occur on IgG1 in blacks. The occurrence of G1/3M G5 without G3M G normally has been reported only in blacks. However, it recently

TABLE 9–2.

Immunoglobulin Allotype Frequencies in Different U.S. Populations*

Allotype	Whites	Blacks	Hispanics
KM 1	.157	.564	.477
KM 3	.993	.884	.923
G1M A	.512	.992	.866
G1M F	.909	.193	.574
G1M G5 (G3M G−)	.001	.355	.015
G1M X	.184	.032	.128
G2M N	.671	.119	.409
G3M B0	.914	.997	.687
G3M C3	.001	.360	.012
G3M C5	<.001	.307	.012
G3M G	.491	.110	.763
G3M S	.008	.114	.028
G3M T	.007	ND‡	.024
A2M 1	.999	.561	1.000 (.988)†
A2M 2	.040	.884	.207

*The allotype frequencies presented in this table are compiled from the data used to produce Appendices 9–1–9–4.

†The expected phenotype frequency for A2M 1 in U.S. Hispanics is 0.988. However, only about 100 have been tested for A2M 1 and 2 and thus far no A2M 1− individuals have been identified.

‡ND = not detected.

TABLE 9–3.

IGH Haplotypes* and KM 1 Frequencies in Several U.S. Populations

Haplotype†	White (4,483)	Black (2,358)	Mexican-American (250)
F N B 1	0.421	0.053	0.234
F N′ B 1	0.271	0.042	0.117
A N′ G 1	0.185	0.030	0.445
A N′ G 2	0.006	0.013	0.026
X N′ G 1	0.089	0.010	0.067
A N′ B 1	0.008	0.140	0.038
A N′ B 2	0.002	0.287	0.043
G5 N′ B 2	††	0.162	0.009
A N′ C5 1	>0.001	0.039	0.006§
A N′ C5 2	>0.001	0.106	
A N′ C3 1	>0.001	0.013	ND¶
A N′ S 1	>0.001	0.012	ND
G5 N′ S 2	>0.001	0.045	ND
A N′ T 2	0.003	ND	0.012
KM 1	0.082 (>10,000) (64)	0.340	0.277

*IGH indicates immunoglobulin heavy chain region. Haplotype frequencies are based on the data presented in Appendices 1–4, with the exception of the KM 1 frequency for whites, which is taken from reference 64. The numbers in parentheses indicate the number of samples tested.

†Shorthand notation for alleles from Tables 9–2 and 9–4 used. N′ = tested for G2M N and found to be negative.

††Only 1,024 samples were tested for both G1/3M G5 and G3M G. One sample was found to be G-G5 positive, indicating an approximate frequency of 0.0005.

§A2M allotypes not determined in the G3M C3,5 positive samples; A2M status unknown.

¶ND = haplotype not detected in the samples tested.

has been reported to occur in admixed Tunisians, where it is also located on IgG1.[21] In a recent study, approximately 35% of U.S. blacks typed as G1/3M G5 positive and G3M G negative (see Table 9–2), while approximately 44% of black Africans from the Congo were G1/3M G5 positive and G3M G negative (Schanfield MS, Spedini G, in preparation). Thus far, the author's laboratory has tested over 1,000 U.S. whites with both G1/3M G5 and G3M G and has found only one G1/3M G5 positive/G3M G negative individual. Therefore, the occurrence of G1/3M G5 without G3M G appears to be limited to African blacks and derived populations and, forensically, can be presumed to indicate a black donor of blood or body fluids. G1/3M G5 has been detected also in semen stains in the absence of IgG3 markers, which supports the presence of G1/3M G5 on IgG1 in the U.S. black population.[22]

As previously stated, G1M X was the second allotype to be reported, and it subdivides G1M A–positive individuals.[6] It is associated almost always with G1M Z and G1M A. Rarely, whites (less than 0.1%) (Appendix 9–2) have been found to possess G1M X without G1M A or Z. Studies of individuals from one of these families indicate that the G1M X occurs on G1M F–bearing IgG1 proteins.[23] G1M X occurs in approximately 18% of whites but is rare in blacks (approximately 3%) (see Table 9–2). Most of the G1M X present in the U.S. black population is due to white admixture, but rare phenotypes do occur (Appendix 9–3).

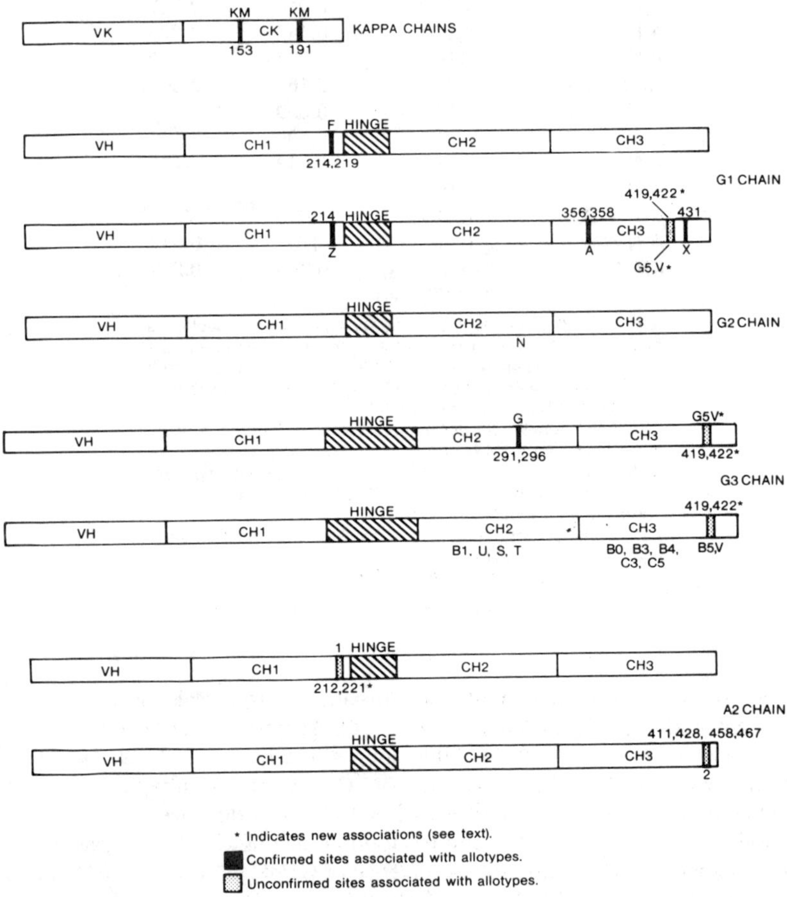

FIG 9–1.

Diagrammatic localization of immunoglobulin allotypes to specific chains, domains, and amino acid sequences. The number opposite the allotypes indicates the number of the amino acid substitution associated with a specific allotype, or the location of substitutions associated with specific alllotypes, such as KM.

TABLE 9–4.
G1M Alleles, Allotypes, Location and Population Distributions

Distribution of G1M Allotypes on IgG1						Population Distribution*
Allele	CH1			CH3		
F	F	NZ†	NA	—	—	Whites
A	—	Z	A	—	—	All populations
G5	—	Z	A	G5	—	Black Africans
X	—	Z	A	—	X	All except black Africans
AF	F	NZ	A	—	—	Southeast Asians, Oceanians
X'	—	Z	—	—	X	Ainu of Japan

*Populations with polymorphic frequencies (>0.01).
†NZ and NA are "isoallotypes." Isoallotypes are serologically-defined markers that behave as allotypes on one subclass, but occur on all members of at least one other subclass. Thus, if whole serum is typed, all sera will be positive for the isoallotype. They reflect the evolution of allotypes from common amino acid sequences shared by the heavy chains.

Litwin and Kunkel described G1M Z,[24] which they produced by immunizing rabbits with Fab fragments of G1M A proteins in an attempt to find the allelic allotype for G1M F. Forensically, G1M Z is of limited use in U.S. casework because of its close relationship to G1M A. Virtually all G1M A–positive samples will be G1M Z–positive also. G1M Z is useful only in identifying blood from Orientals, Southeast Asians, and Pacific Islanders, who are G1M A+, F+, and Z−, respectively. Out of 2,000 paternity cases we found G1M Z useful only twice.[25]

G2M IgG2 Allotypes.—G2M N was described first by Kunkel, Yount and Litwin[26] who detected this marker using a precipitating antiserum produced in a monkey immunized with IgG2 proteins and carrying no detectable Gm allotypes. A human example of anti-G2M N has not been described yet. Even though the normal method of producing G2M N ACRBC is not possible because IgG2 Rh antibodies are not found (see below), agglutination inhibition using chemically produced G2M N protein-coated ACRBC is still the preferred method for typing. Rabbits readily produce hemagglutinating anti-G2M N. G2M N increases the number of polymorphic white phenotypes from five to seven. Approximately 67% of the U.S. white population and 12% of the U.S. black population are G2M N–positive (see Table 9–2) (Schanfeld MS, in preparation). No other allotypes on the IgG2 have been described yet, making a negative result for G2M N useful only if IgG3 allotypes have been detected.

G3M IgG3 Allotypes.—The number of different IgG3 G3M allotypes alone is greater than the total number of GM allotypes known for all of the other IgG subclasses. However, the total number of possible IgG3 alleles is restricted, because multiple markers are present simultaneously on the same polypeptide chain, and the evolution of these markers has not allowed them to be randomly associated. Table 9–5 presents a suggested shorthand notation for the published IgG3 alleles.

The first example of anti-G3M B was reported by Harboe[7] to be antithetical to G1M A in Swedes. However, studies on black and other non-white population indicated that *GM*AB* alleles existed in these populations.[27] This was explained when the different subclasses of IgG were delineated and it was determined that G3M B was located on IgG3, while G1M A was located on IgG1.[28,29] In the 1960s more studies were conducted on non-white populations and it became obvious that not all G3M B agglutinators were detecting the same specificities.[30–33] A total of five different specificities have been identified: G3M B0, B1, B3, B4, B5. The original B2 was found to be the same as F[34,35] and to be located on IgG1. The name G1M F was chosen so that it would not be confused with the IgG3 G3M allotypes.[10] With rare exceptions, all G3M B alleles are positive for G3M B0 and may or may not have other G3M B specificities. Most examples of anti-G3M B found are mixtures of different G3M B specificities. In general, any serum or material which is G3M B0–positive is referred to as G3M B–positive. In white populations, as a rule, all of the G3M B specificities co-occur. In black and other non-white populations, one or more of these may be absent when G3M B0 is present, because of the presence of other G3M allotypes (see Table 9–5). From a forensic point of view, G3M B0 is the only G3M B allotype that must be tested since it behaves as if allelic to G3M G. G3M B0 is common in all U.S. populations and is a useful marker for confirming negative test results for G1M markers. Approximately 91% of the U.S. white population and 99% of the U.S. black population are G3M B0–positive (see Table 9–2). The frequency is much lower in Mexican-Americans (see Table 9–2) and American Indian populations.

The factor originally described as "Gm-like"[36] and later as "Gm c"[37,38] was subsequently divided into G3M C3 and G3M C5.[33] In addition, there appear to be two G3M C3 specificities based on the original antibody donors which were initially designated by van Loghem[33,39] as G3M C3V and G3M C3Br. In order to remain consistent with the HLA notation, the splits of G3M C3 probably should be referred to as G3M C3.1 and G3M C3.2. Recently, G3M C3 was found to occur on IgG2 in a rare white haplotype.[20] In many early publications it is not clear whether the G3M C reagent

TABLE 9–5.
IgG3 Alleles, Allotypes, Locations and Population Distributions

	Distribution of G3M Allotypes on IgG3 Fc*								Population Distribution
Allele	CH2			CH3					
G	G	NB1††	U	—	G5	V	—	NBO	All except black Africans†
B	NG	B1	U	B4	B5	V	B3	B0	All populations
C5	NG	B1	U	—	—	C5	C3	B0	Black Africans
C3	NG	B1	U	B4	B5	V	C3	B0	Black Africans
S	NG	—	S	—	B5	V	B3	B0	Black Africans
T	NG	—	T(S)	—	B5	V	B3	B0	Orientals, Amerindians

*The order presented reflects serological relationships and not necessarily precise locations, based on amino acid substitutions.
†There is evidence that the allele "G" occurs polymorphically in East Africans and Bushmen, two populations that did not contribute significantly to the U.S. black gene pool.
††Isoallotypes. See Table 9–4 for a description of isoallotypes.

was G3M C3, G3M C5, or a mixture of both, leading to the variations in frequencies seen in some of the early reports. The frequency of G3M C is approximately 36% in the U.S. black population and about 0.1% in the U.S. white population (Table 9–2). G3M C has been detected in Mexican-Americans (approximately 1%) (see Appendix 9–4) and other admixed populations. From a forensic point of view, the detection of G3M C (normally as G3M C3,C5 or G3M C3) in a stain or body fluid almost certainly indicates that the donor is black. G3M V was described originally by Schanfield and Fudenberg.[40] It behaves as the allele to G3M C5. It has been observed recently that in Africans, G3M V can occur also on IgG1 with G1/3M G5, indicating that the two determinants G1/3M G5 and G3M V probably are very similar in structure.[20] Since almost all blacks that have G1/3M G5 on IgG1 also have G3M V on IgG3, there is little point in designating the marker G1/3M V. The marker is of little use forensically because of the low frequency of G3M C5 homozygous individuals that would be G3M V–negative.

G3M G was first described by Natvig[41] using antisera found in G3M G–negative patients with rheumatoid arthritis; however, the reagents behaved like SNaggs rather than Raggs (see below). In fact, Steinberg and Wilson[42] may have identified G3M G first, since they reported a specificity called "Gm aw" which was analogous to "Gm bw" in that it occurred in G1M A–positive whites but not in blacks. However, no further studies were reported for the antisera. Though the original antisera were found in humans, human examples are uncommon. However, the reagent is easily produced in laboratory animals. G3M G was found to behave as the allele of G3M B in family and population studies. Forensically, G3M G occurs more commonly in U.S. whites (approximately 49%) than in U.S. blacks (approximately 11%) (see Table 9–2). In addition to increasing the individualization of blood and body fluids, another major forensic importance of G3M G is in the confirmation of G3M B–negative test results. Since virtually all G3M B–negative individuals are G3M G–positive, then a G3M B–negative result should be confirmed by the presence of G3M G. If the sample is both G3M B– and G-negative, then either the stain or material is too weak or the test system is too insensitive and false-negatives are being detected. In whites, and in all other populations except blacks, when G3M G is present, G1/3M G5 is genetically present also in almost every case. However, there appears to be variation in the ability of some agglutinators to detect G3M G5, such that when G3M G5 is on IgG3, the levels are too low to give good inhibition. Other examples do not seem to make this distinction.

G3M S and G3M T were reported by Martensson et al.[43] The occurrence of G3M S without T in casework is indicative of a black origin of the material, since G3M S only occurs polymorphically in the absence of G3M T in black populations (see Table 9–5). Approximately 11% of the U.S. black population is B3M S–positive and T–negative, while only approximately 0.8% of the U.S. white population is G3M S–positive and T–negative (see Table 9–2). In contrast, G3M S with G3M T is only polymorphic in Orientals, American Indians, Eskimos, and Mexican-Americans. In the U.S., the highest frequencies occur in the Apache and Navajo Indians of the southwest (approximately 45%). It also occurs in Eskimos (approximately 27%) and Japanese (approximately 45%), and low frequencies exist for other American Indians (approximately 4%) and for Mexican-Americans (approximately 2%) (unpublished data).[44]

TABLE 9–6.
Discriminating Power of Immunoglobulin Allotypes in White, Black, and Mexican-American Populations*

Systems	White	Black	Mexican-American
GM	0.674	0.893	0.811
KM	0.267	0.595	0.560
GM, KM	0.761	0.957	0.917
GM, KM, ABO†	0.910	0.984	0.965

*Based on phenotype frequencies found in Appendices 1–4.
†ABO phenotype frequencies based on gene frequencies found in reference 64.

The phenotype is rare in U.S. whites (approximately 0.7%) and has not been detected at all in U.S. blacks. Anti-G3M U was originally produced in a baboon by van Loghem and Grobbelaar,[45] who found it to be the serological allele of G3M S and S,T. A human example of anti-G3M U was reported[46] and other examples have been found. This antigen is restricted to humans and represents a link in the evolutionary dissociation of IgG3 alleles.[45] The marker is of little forensic interest because very few individuals are homozygous for G3M S or S,T.

A2M IgA2 Allotypes.—Thus far, serologically defined allotypes have been found only on the IgA2 subclass of IgA. Using an agglutination assay consisting of ACRBC chemically coated with IgA1 and IgA2 proteins, Vyas and Fudenberg[47] looked for antibodies to IgA in patients with non-hemolytic (anaphylactoid or urticarial) transfusion reactions. They found a serum which reacted with an IgA2-coated RBC and detected an allotype which they called "Am(1)" (now designated A2M 1). Shortly afterward, Kunkel et al[48] described a genetic marker on IgA2 which was detected by precipitation, and later was shown to be identical to A2M 1. A second allotype of IgA2 was discovered by van Loghem et al[49] which was designated A2M 2. These two allotypes behave as alleles, with there being only rare IgA-deficient individuals who are negative for both markers. A2M 2 is uncommon in U.S. whites (approximately 4%) but common in U.S. blacks (approximately 88%) (see Table 9–2). Thus, it can serve as an additional indicator of the non-white origin of blood or body fluids.[50] The IgA2 levels in blood are comparable to IgG3 allotypes (Table 9–6). IgA levels are much higher than IgG levels in saliva, making the IgA2 allotypes potentially useful in the individualization of saliva stains. The allotypes A2M 1 and 2 have been detected in saliva,[47] in semen and vaginal secretions,[22] and in blood stains.[50, 51]

EM IgE Allotypes.—IgE is found in extremely low levels in most normal serum, and the normal method of quantitating it requires a radioimmunoassay. The only allotype on IgE (EM 1) was detected using a monoclonal antibody in a radioimmunoassay.[52] Em(1) is common in all populations. Thus far, some blacks, Orientals, and Pacific Islanders have been found to be EM 1–negative. However, it does not appear that EM 1 will be useful forensically.

Linkage Disequilibrium

As seen above, the immunoglobulin heavy chain region (IGH) consists of a series of closely linked loci. Allotypes occur on the IgG1, IgG2, IgG3, IgE, and IgA2 loci. The loci are linked very closely, and the author is not aware of any verified crossovers observed within families, although recombinant genes are present in the population. Each individual inherits one IGH region from each parent, and each region carries allotypic markers for each locus having allotypes. These groups of allotypes inherited together are called haplotypes. The concept is similar to that of the groups of Rh antigens that are inherited together. The distribution of allotypes by loci is not random. This lack of random association of allotypes on different subclasses is referred to as "linkage disequilibrium." The IGH structural genes show marked linkage disequilibrium, while the HLA system expresses it at a much lower level.

The 1979 Gene Mapping Conference[11] recommended that IGH region loci be listed in their linkage order, something which was not known in 1974. The linkage sequence is now known to be G3, G1, G2, E, and A2 for the allotype-bearing heavy chains.[53–55] Thus, the presentation of allotypes for both phenotypes and haplotypes should be in linkage order, instead of subclass order. However, since the linkage order is not consistent with either the historical presentation or the concentration in serum, the traditional order is recommended. Within each locus the allotypes should be in normal ascending order, i.e., A,F,X,Z. Thus, a GM-AM phenotype would be listed as IGH A,F,X N B0,G 1,2; the same phenotype as a genotype would be *IGH*F N B0 1 / *A,X N′ G 2*; and, as individual alleles, it would be *IGH*F N B0 1* and *IGH*A,XN′ G 2*. "N′" is used to indicate the G2M N has been tested and found to be negative, when G3M allotypes have been detected.

Chromosomal Localization.—The IGH region is located on the distal segment of the long arm of Chromosome 14 at bands 32, making the address for the IGH region 14Q32.[56–58] The KM allotypes are located on the short arm of Chromosome 2,[59] and the lambda light chains are located on Chromosome 22 (IGL).[60]

Population Genetics

Each population can be characterized by the presence of unique haplotypes, or by differences in the frequencies of the haplotypes that are present. From an anthropological point of view, the IGH haplotypes are one of the most robust tools in the classification and study of human populations.[61] Table 9–3 presents the polymorphic haplotypes found in U.S. whites, blacks, and Mexican-Americans. There is a large volume of literature regarding the distribution of GM and KM allotypes worldwide. A small review can be found in Schanfield,[61, 62] while more extensive reviews can be found in Schanfield[44] and Steinberg and Cook.[63] To assist the forensic serologist, Appendix 9–1 illustrates the KM phenotype distribution for U.S. whites, blacks, and Mexican-Americans; Appendix 9–2 illustrates the distribution of GM phenotypes in U.S. whites; Appendix 9–3 illustrates the distribution of GM phenotypes in U.S. blacks; and Appendix 9–4 illustrates the distribution of GM phenotypes in Mexican-Americans.

Paternity Testing

Although the polymorphism found in the IGH allotypes is not as extensive as that of the HLA system, complete IGH typing, especially in the U.S. black population, is the second most informative system.[25] GM and KM typing have been used extensively since the 1960s in the investigation of cases of disputed paternity, because they fulfill the criteria of a useful system in these cases (see reference 25 for a detailed review). In brief, these criteria are as follows: (1) the mode of inheritance is well established, and (2) the testing techniques are reproducible. The fact that the trait is not fully developed at birth, and therefore cannot be used in newborn infants has not proved to be a problem in practice.

Discriminating Power of Immunoglobulin Allotypes

The discriminating power of a genetic system, or the probability of being able to discriminate between two samples using one or more genetic systems, is expressed by the following equation[65]:

$$DP = 1 - P$$

P is the probability that two random samples will be identical, and it is calculated by the following equation:

$$P = p1^2 + p2^2 + p3^2 \ldots \ldots \ldots + pn^2$$

In this equation, p1, p2, p3, and ... pn are the different phenotypes. In order to combine the discriminating power of different genetic systems the following equation is used:

$$DPTotal = 1 - PA*PB*PC* \ldots ..*PN$$

As a frame of reference, the discriminating power for the ABO system in U.S. whites is 0.622, and for PGM1 with subtyping it is 0.747 (calculated from reference 64). The discriminating power for immunoglobulin allotypes in three U.S. populations are presented in Table 9–6, along with the combined discriminating power of immunoglobulin allotypes and the ABO blood group. The lowest value observed for GM and KM is for whites (0.761), the highest value is for blacks (0.957), and Mexican-Americans fall inbetween. Though the data are not presented, the discriminating powers for GM and KM in most other populations will fall between those observed for whites and blacks. The addition of the ABO blood groups brings the value to 91% in whites, and to approximately 98% for blacks. Thus, immunoglobulin allotypes potentially are very useful in the individualization of blood or other stains, either used alone or in conjunction with only a single system. Using additional specificities, such as G2MN and A2M 1 and 2, will increase the discriminating power, while using smaller numbers of reagents will decrease the number of phenotypes and thus decrease the discriminating power (for more details, see the section on maximizing allotype information).

Biochemistry and Serology

Antigens.—Immunoglobulins and, therefore, immunoglobulin allotypes are found in all body organs and in most body fluids in varying concentrations (see below for details). The highest concentration of immunoglobulins is found in the serum and serous extravascular fluid that bathes organs, while the lowest concentration is found in sweat and urine (see Table 9–6).

Immunoglobulins are glycoproteins composed of two identical light polypeptide chains and two identical heavy polypeptide chains (see Fig 9–1). The light polypeptide chains have a molecular weight of 25,000 daltons and consist of two domains. There are two types of light chains: the Kappa light chains, which carry the KM allotypes; and the Lambda light chains, which have no allotypes. The first domain (VK or VL) has a variable sequence associated with antibody specificity, and contributes to the antibody combining site. It is important to note that the antibody combining site, or recognition site of an antibody molecule, is similar to the catalytic site of an enzyme. The second domain of the Kappa chains (CK) contains the amino acid substitutions associated with the KM 1, 2, and 3 allotypes.[66] The KM allotypes are assembled allotypes which are expressed only when the molecule is intact and in a specific three-dimensional structure. Dissociation of the heavy and light chains leads to a reduction in reactivity with some test systems,[67] while enzymatic cleavage of the light chains leads to a loss of KM activity.[68]

The heavy chains have molecular weights ranging from 51 to 72,000 daltons, and are divided into four or five domains. With the exception of the E heavy chain, the allotype-bearing heavy chains have only four domains. The first domain (Fig 9–2) is the variable region (VH), which is associated with antibody recognition. There are no confirmed allotypes on the VH region. The purported variable region allotype VH(1), was reported to be unlinked to the IGH markers.[69] Since the IGH markers are known to be linked to the VH region,[70] the status of VH(1) as an IGHV marker is in question. The second domain is the first of the constant region domains, and is referred to as the CH1 domain. Three allotypes have been localized to the CH1 domain (see Figs 9–1 and 9–2): G1M F,[34,71] G1M Z,[25] and the A2M 1 allotype.[72] The VH domain and the CH1 domain, together with VL and CL, form the Fab fragment. The Fab portion is the antibody-binding portion of the molecule. Fab or F(ab')2 fragments can be prepared by cleaving intact molecules with either papain (Fab) or pepsin (F[ab']2). The third domain, which is the second constant region domain, is called the CH2

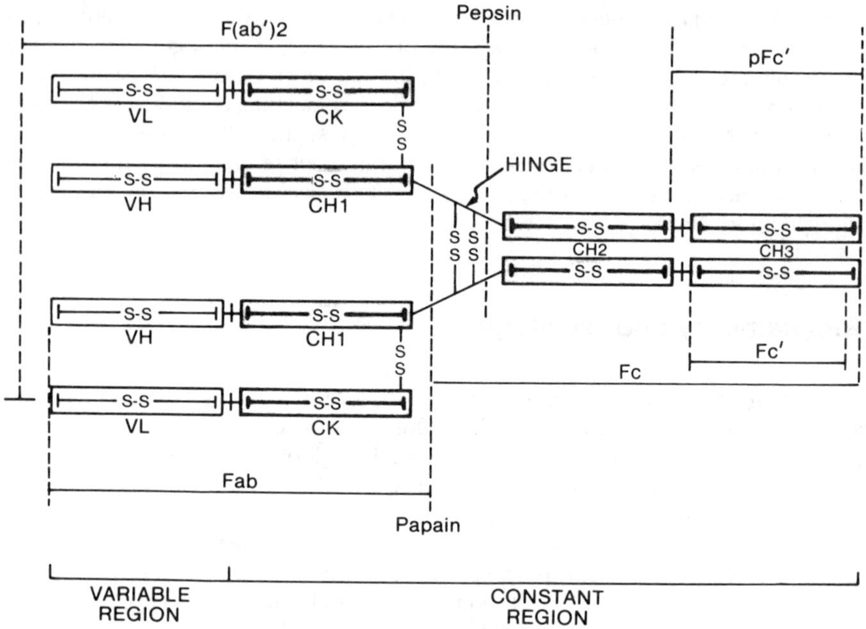

FIG 9–2.
Diagram of IgG molecule indicating chain types, domains, and cleavage sites for proteolytic enzymes.

domain (see Fig 9–2). The allotypes G2M N, G3M B1, G, S, T, and U have been associated with this domain (see Fig 9–1).[73] The fourth domain, which is the third constant region, is referred to as the CH3 domain (see Fig 9–2). This domain is associated with the largest number of allotypes (see Fig 9–1). G1M A and X, G3M B0, B3, B4, B5, C3, C5, G5, V, and A2M 2 are associated with the CH3 domain, since they are present on the pFc' fragments (see Fig 9–2), but not on the Fc fragments.[66] Amino acid substitutions have been confirmed for G1M A and X, and suggested for G3M B5, G5, V, and A2M 2.[66] The G1M A and X allotypes appear to be assembled antigens in that they require the presence of an intact disulfide bond on the CH3 domain since they are detectable on the pFc' fragment but not on Fc' or cFc' fragments.[74,75] The G1M F[34,76] and G1M Z[67] allotypes are also assembled antigens, since they require the presence of heavy and light chains, as well as an intact heavy chain for expression. No studies using dissociated heavy chains have been performed on the other IGG1, 2, or 3 allotypes, and nothing is known about the localization of the EM 1 marker.[51]

Agglutinators.—The agglutinators that were used originally for GM typing came from patients with rheumatoid arthritis and became known as *R*heumatoid *agg*lutinators, or Raggs. These reagents usually contained a mixture of antibodies against the patient's own allotypes and immunoglobulins. The fact that these antibodies were mixtures of antibodies against native and foreign antigens may explain why Raggs often showed prozone effects, sometimes making it impossible to differentiate phenotypes at different dilutions, i.e., G1M A–positive versus G1M A–negative.

The observation of Ropartz and Lenoir[77] that antibodies to GM antigens may be found in the sera of healthy blood donors, though not in as high a frequency, was a major breakthrough. They called them SNaggs (*S*erum *N*ormal *agg*lutinators). The quality of these antisera was much superior to the Ragg antisera originally used, since they have no prozone effect and their titers are usually lower. Human antibodies to GM and KM antigens are generally of the IgM class. All agglutinators currently in routine use are SNagg-type antibodies from either human or animal sources.

There appear to be only two common sources for the stimulation of allotype-specific agglutinators. The most common is the immunization of the fetus or newborn by genetically incompatible maternal IgG.[42, 78, 79] Virtually all immunoglobulin present in the fetus is maternal in origin, such that at birth the serum of the fetus reflects the GM/KM type of the mother and not of the fetus.[80] As maternal IgG disappears, it is replaced by infant immunoglobulins, and by sometime around 3 months of age infant antibodies have entirely replaced maternal IgG. Examination of the G1M A–negative infants of G1M A–positive mothers at 1 year of age reveals about 95% of them to have anti-G1M A present.[78] Thus, the formation of antibodies to incompatible maternal factors seems to be the rule in newborns. However, without further stimulation these antibodies usually disappear between the ages of 5 and 10 years,[79] such that between 1% and 2% of adults have GM- or KM-specific agglutinators, the majority of which are anti-G1M A[79] (Schanfield MS, unpublished observation). Agglutinators to other GM or KM specificities are much less common, but will vary in frequency depending upon the race of the donors (Schanfield MS, unpublished observation). For example, anti-G1M F is uncommon in whites because over 90% of the population is G1M F–positive. However, it is much more common in blacks and Japanese because of their much lower frequency of G1M F. Also, anti-G1M A is not found in Japanese and is rare in blacks because of the universal or near-universal frequency of G1M A (Schanfield MS, unpublished observation).

The second source of immunization is via the transfusion of blood products containing plasma, or the injection of gamma globulin preparations. The rate of immunization and the specificities produced appear to depend on the genetic type of the individual and the amount of material immunized. For example, in a study of transfused thalassemics, 45.8% of GM F B0 individuals (n = 264) made anti-G1M A, anti-G1M A + X(A), or anti-G1M A plus G3M G, while only 8% of GM A, F B0, G individuals (n = 66) made either anti-G1m X or anti-G3M T.[81] In contrast, a white child receiving one gamma globulin shot produced an example of anti-G3M C3 (Schanfield MS, unpublished observation). There is also one report of a mother being immunized by a genetically incompatible fetus[82]; however, this appears to be an extremely rare event.

Unlike the antibodies to the GM or KM markers, which are usually IGM and are not usually associated with clinical transfusion reactions, the antibodies to IGA and A2M are usually IGG and have been associated with severe non-hemolytic transfusion reactions.[83] The original A2M 1 donor was found because of a near-fatal non-hemolytic transfusion reaction.[47] The origin of IGA and A2M antibodies is less clear, since many children of IGA-deficient mothers with anti-IGA share these characteristics[83, 84] (Schanfield and Schoeppner, unpublished observations, 1981).

A second source of GM and KM agglutinators is the immunization of laboratory animals. Historically, many allotypes were defined originally by heteroimmune polyclonal antisera, some of which were found later in humans and some of which have been made only in laboratory animals. The original examples of G1M Z, G2M N, and G3M U were made in laboratory animals, as were G1M A, X, and F, G3M B, C, G, and T, and KM 3. To date, laboratory animals are still the only source of G2M N; the other specificities all have human examples reported. Animals used thus far include rabbits,[25, 85, 86] primates,[26, 87, 88] and goats.[89] Recently, several monoclonal antisera with GM specificity have been produced in some test procedures. Of these, only G1M F[90] and G3M G[91] have been shown to be specific in the agglutination-inhibition test, although some have been shown to be specific in enzyme-linked immunosorbent assays (ELISA) only under special conditions.[90, 92] It is possible that some of these may become useful in forensic applications in the future.

In general, commercially available agglutinators are monospecific, at least when they are used in a specific typing system (see below). However, when agglutinators are found they can contain multiple antibodies. This usually occurs when there are multiple stimulating antigens, or when the stimulating change is complex, such as with G3M B. Some of the antibodies observed are anti-G1M G, anti-G3M T plus anti-G1M A, and anti-G1M F plus G3M B0 + B3 (Schanfield MS, unpublished observations). It is very common to find multiple antibodies to G3M B, such as anti-G3M B0 + B1 + B4, and anti-G3M B3 + B5, and anti-G3M B0 + B4 (Schanfield MS, unpublished observations). Thus, uncommon agglutinators should be well tested against large panels of known sera before they are used in routine work. Many of the original examples of anti-G3M B were not identified as different because the white *G3M*B* allele contains all of the G3M B specificities. It is only the use of a large number of non-white sera that allows for the definition of these different specificities. In general, the commercially available reagents have been well characterized, but under certain circumstances even these may give atypical inhibition patterns, especially G3M B reagents (Schanfield, personal observation).

Coating Antigens.—The selection of coating antigens is as important as the selection of agglutinators. In reality, the coating antigens came first, since the agglutinators would not have been found if the coating antigens had not possessed the genetic markers. The easiest method of producing allotype-coated indicator red blood cells is to use non-agglutinating antibodies to red blood cell antigens, and the ones most commonly used are antibodies to Rh D or CD antigens. Antibodies to Rh blood groups can be of either the IGG1 or the IGG3 subclass, and therefore potentially can carry any of the G1M, G3M, or KM allotypes. The ideal coating antibodies will only coat a single subclass and a single allele; however, this may not be possible for some of the rarer specificities. This is discussed further in the methods section. For the IGG2 and IGA2 allotypes there are no blood group antibodies available to coat indicator red blood cells. For these, purified antibodies from patients with multiple myeloma, a form of B-cell leukemia which produces large amounts of a single protein, are coated onto red blood cells using a chemical coupling agent such as chromic chloride.[93]

AGGLUTINATION INHIBITION TEST

Introduction

Immunoglobulins and their allotypes are present in blood and body fluids as proteins in solution and inside plasma cells in the spleen, bone marrow, and lymph nodes. The antigenic determinants of immunoglobulins can be recognized by chemical and immunological methods. Chemical methods such as amino acid sequence analysis and sensitivity to enzymatic splitting, can be applied only to certain special cases. There are direct and indirect immunological methods. The direct demonstration of allotypes by precipitation,[26,48] ELISA,[92,94] or RIA[95] have been described only occasionally for man.[25,47] The immunological method most commonly used for detecting GM, AM, and KM allotypes is an indirect one, namely inhibition of a test agglutination system. Estimating the degree of inhibition by testing progressive dilutions of test samples can provide insight into the concentration of various antigenic determinants.

The agglutination inhibition method is based on the inhibition of agglutination of indicator allotype-coated red blood cells (hereafter referred to as ACRBC). The agglutinator (i.e., the antibody against the allotypic determinant) will be neutralized if the allotype is present in the sample tested, thus inhibiting the agglutination of the indicator ACRBC. If the allotype is not present, the agglutinator will not be neutralized and the ACRBC will be agglutinated.

The agglutination inhibition test can be represented schematically as follows:

1. Diluted serum, extract, or other unknown to be tested.
2. Add the appropriately diluted agglutinator (mix).
3. Add the appropriate indicator ACRBC and mix.
4. Incubate 30 to 120 minutes at room temperature (22 to 24°C) or in the refrigerator (2 to 6°C).
5. Centrifuge or settle.
6. Read by the appropriate method.
7. Result: no agglutination (inhibition) = factor present; agglutination (no inhibition) = factor absent.

Controls must include:

1. Agglutinator control: ACRBC + agglutinator must show sufficiently strong agglutination.
2. Inhibitor control: ACRBC + agglutinator + known inhibitor for allotype tested must show inhibition.
3. Sample control: ACRBC + diluted serum or extract tested must not show agglutination. Of note, this generally is not tested on forensic samples.

Selection of Red Blood Cells and Coating Antigen

Human red cells of blood group O are chosen to avoid unwanted agglutination by anti-A or B blood group antibodies. In practice, the coating antigens generally will be incomplete Rh(D) antibodies; therefore, red cells with strong Rh(D) antigen must be selected. R1R1 or R1r RBCs give the best results; although they have more Rh antigen available, R2R2 RBCs do not work as well in the method described. This is discussed below. Further, there appears to be a variation in the ability to take up anti-D among different donors with the same Rh phenotype. Males and females work equally well or poorly. The only consistent observation is that RBCs from Oriental O R1R1 individuals consistently tend to work better and show less variation that RBCs from white donors (Schanfield MS, unpublished observation, 1973).

Coating of Indicator Red Blood Cells (ACRBC)

Only R1R1 or R1r red blood cells collected in anticoagulant or in preparations of cell suspensions in preservative should be used. RBCs collected in yellow-topped (ACD) vacuum blood collection tubes can be used for 2 to 3 weeks after collection. RBCs collected in anticoagulant should be used as a 25% suspension, although it is possible to use volumes of washed packed RBCs. Usually 2 to 4 parts of undiluted anti-Rh coating antigen are added per part of packed RBC equivalent. Thus, the volume can be scaled up or down depending on the volume of ACRBC needed. Further, coating for G1M F and Z and KM 1 and 3 works better with a higher serum to cell ratio (3:4). The sera and cells are usually placed in 10 × 75 or 12 × 75 glass test tubes and mixed. The mixture is incubated at 37°C for 30 to 60 minutes. Maximum uptake of antibody occurs by 50 to 60 minutes. RBC coated for 60 minutes may be used for up to 3 to 4 days when suspended in 0.1 M of pH 7.3 phosphate buffered saline (PBS) with 1% bovine serum albumin (BSA) or Alsevers solution. If ACRBCs are going to be used only on the day coated, a 30-minute incubation is usually sufficient. The ACRBCs are washed three times with normal saline to remove the allotypes present in the liquid. A stock suspension of ACRBCs is prepared by completely decanting the saline after the last wash and adding 1% BSA PBS or Alsevers solution to the ACRBCs in the test tube. Enough suspension medium (1% BSA PBS or Alsevers solution) should be added to prepare a 2% cell suspension. For testing in V-bottom microplates, a suspension of ACRBCs is prepared by diluting the 2% ACRBC suspension 1:10. For example, 200 microliters (0.2 ml) of 2% suspension are added to 2.0 ml of normal saline or PBS in a 10 × 75 or 12 × 75 test tube. When the 0.2% to 15% suspensions are made in 0.85% saline they will begin hemolyzing within 24 hours. However, if they are made in pH 7.3 PBS with or without 1% BSA, they will last much longer (Schanfield MS, unpublished observation).

Optimization of Allotyping Systems

An immunoglobulin allotyping test system consists of two components: RBCs coated with the allotype to be tested, and the agglutinators. In general, it is desirable to have the maximum amount of allotype on the RBCs. Antigens closer to the surface of the RBCs will require more antigenic sites on the RBCs to produce agglutination equivalent to that of the antigens away from the RBC membrane. The exact reason for this is not known, but it is a safe assumption that it is harder for an agglutinator to get close to the surface through the "thick woods" of coating antigens than it is for one to bind to the tops of the trees (see Fig 9–1). In practice, if the coating anti-Rh antibody has a titer of 500 or greater, and the majority of that antibody is a single allotype, then a coating ratio of 2 to 4 parts of serum to 1 part of packed RBC equivalent should saturate all of the Rh D sites on the RBCs. Some individuals mistakenly think that they can optimize sensitivity by doing a checkerboard titration of both the coating antigen and the agglutinators. However, with rare exception, there are few Rh antibodies that are so potent that they must be diluted to get good inhibition. These are usually IgG3 coating antigens. The effect of diluting the coating antigen is to require higher concentrations of agglutinator to obtain equivalent reactivity. The sensitivity of the assay (the amount of antigen required for inhibition) usually is determined by the endpoint of the titration, and dilution of the coating antigen lowers the endpoint. In some cases, dilution of the coating antigen yields an endpoint so low that the system is not useful.

Agglutinators are optimized by titration against their appropriate ACRBCs in the presence of a known positive sera diluted as it would be in a test system, and against an agglutinator control (the author normally uses the agglutinator diluent 1% BSA in saline). If plasma or serum is going to be typed, the dilution of the plasma or serum normally used for testing (1/20, for example) would be a good inhibitor control. However, if blood stains and dilute body fluids are going to be tested, a more dilute control would be appropriate (1/100 to 1/200). In the classic doubling dilution titration, the positive reaction before the last reactive dilution is considered to be two agglutinating units. In one study performed using the method described below with purified immunoglobulins of different subclasses and allotypes, the average amount of allotype-specific protein needed for inhibition of the test system used ranged from 2 μg/ml to less than 1 μg/ml (1 μg/ml was the lowest level tested) (Schanfield MS, unpublished data, 1977).

When an agglutinator is titrated in the presence of inhibitor and agglutinator control, the difference in subclass concentration becomes apparent. There is approximately eight times as much IgG1 as IgG3. Therefore, it is rare for the condition of antibody excess to exist for antibodies to IgG1 determinants. For instance, an anti-G1M A antisera with a titer of 2,000 will be inhibited by 1/20 dilution of G1M A–positive serum even when the anti-G1M A is at a dilution of 1/10. On the other hand, a potent anti-G3M reagent must be diluted to get inhibition (Schanfield MS, unpublished observations). The difference in the number of dilutions between the dilution at which inhibition first occurs (when using a standardly-diluted control) and the dilution which marks the endpoint of the titration can be considered to be a "the window of inhibition," a term which reflects the very broad range of inhibition that should be seen. Empirically, it has been observed that the use of R2R2 RBCs produces a very narrow window when testing for IgG3 allotypic determinants. This can lead to the occurrence of false-negative reactions, probably due to a lack of sensitivity. Of note, whenever RBCs from a different donor or new lots of reagents are used, or when new reagents are obtained, the agglutinator must be titrated with and without inhibitor. Further, in forensic testing, if weak stains such as seminal fluid are to be tested, the typing systems should be standardized against weak inhibitors. The author currently uses material diluted approximately 1/100 to 1/200 as a sensitivity control for forensic work.

In general, if the same RBC donor and the same volume of coating antigen are used, established dilutions of agglutinators can be used over prolonged periods of time. If reagents have not been used for a prolonged period of time, titration should be performed, using the previous dilution as a starting point.

There are several possible ways in which to check the sensitivity of a test system. One of these is by using purified myeloma proteins of different genetic types. However, these normally are not available outside of specialized immunology laboratories. Another way is by the titration of the serum of known phenotypes. Using a Technicon AutoAnalyzer™, Litwin and Balaban[96] quantitated the amount of G1M A and F and G3M B and G in homozygous and heterozygous sera. They determined that homozygous G1M A sera have 5,302 ± 1,220 μg/ml of G1M A–specific protein, while heterozygous G1M A sera have 2,990 ± 950 μg/ml. Homozygous G1M F sera contained 6,700 ± 1,560 μg/ml of G1M F, and heterozygous G1M F sera contained 3,520 ± 1,140 μg/ml of G1M F. For G3M G, homozygotes had 520 ± 240 μg/ml, while heterozygotes had 270 ± 120 μg/ml. Homozygous G3M B sera had 1,250 ± 650 μg/ml of G3M B compared to 660 ± 500 μg/ml of G3M B in heterozygotes. Thus, for an IgG1 allotype such as G1M A, serum from a heterozygous individual should inhibit a test system with a sensitivity of 1 μg/ml to a dilution of between 1,000 and 5,000. A similar test system for G3M B should be inhibited by heterozygous sera to a dilution between 50 and 1,600. Therefore, the endpoints of titration of known sera should provide some indication of sensitivity.

Given the concentrations of IgG that are found in serum and assuming a sensitivity of 1 μg/ml, it should be possible to dilute serum at least 1/100 and detect almost all allotypes. If the concentration of IgG1 in seminal fluid is 90 μg/ml (see Table 9–6), then detection should not be a problem; however, significant dilution may make the detection of IgG3 markers difficult, assuming that the subclass distribution in semen is the same as that in serum. Further, if the test system is sensitive at 1 μg/ml, then IgG1 allotypes may be detectable in saliva with an IgG concentration of 8 μg/ml (see Table 9–6), but IgG3 allotypes are not likely to be detectable. In general, these numbers appear to agree with the experience of the author's laboratory. However, it appears that many of the forensic applications reviewed below are significantly less sensitive, detecting serum dilutions of G1M A only to a dilution of 16 to 32.

V-Bottom Microplate Inhibition Test

The method described for V-bottom microplates is a modification[97] of one used in forensic testing that is described in detail elsewhere.[51] Ten microliters of agglutinator control, inhibitor control, and the serum or material to be tested are added across the rows of a labelled V-bottom microplate (antisera down the columns; agglutinator control, inhibitor control, and samples to be tested across the rows). Ten microliters of diluted agglutinators are added down the columns, followed by 10 microliters of appropriate indicator ACRBCs diluted to a 0.15% to 0.2% concentration. The material is mixed in the plates by gently tapping the sides of the microplate and making sure that all reactants are in the bottom of the well. Incubation is done at room temperature (22 to 25°C) for 30 to 120 minutes. If room temperature exceeds 28°C, the trays are incubated in a refrigerator (2° to 6°C). After incubation, the microplates are centrifuged using a microplate carrier at 1,000 RCF (approximately 2,000 RPM in most laboratory centrifuges) for 15 to 30 seconds. After centrifugation, the V-bottom microplate is placed on a reader at 60° to the horizontal. Results are interpretable in 10 to 15 minutes. Inhibition is indicated by streaming of the cells from the central button, while agglutination appears as a discreet button in the middle of the well (Fig 9–3).

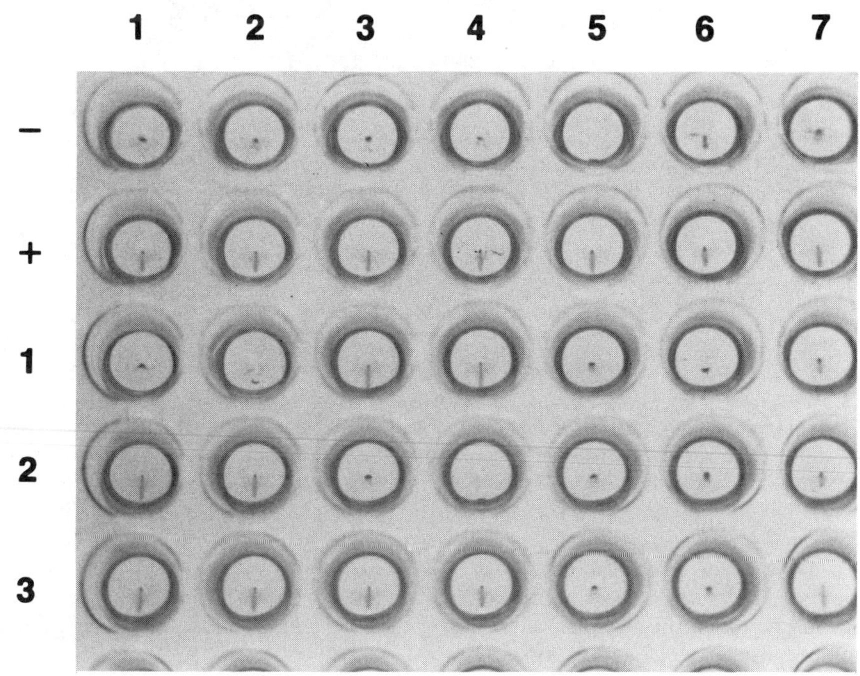

FIG 9–3.
Photograph of a section of a V-bottom microplate allotyping of blood stains. The rows are as follows: − is the agglutinator control; + is the inhibitor control; and **1, 2,** and **3** are different stains. The columns are as follows: **1** and **2** are G1M F; **3** and **4** are G1M A; **5** and **6** are G1M X; and **7** is G3M G. The phenotypes of the samples are as follows: **1** is G1M A+,F−,X−G3M G−; **2** is G1M A−,F+,X− G3M G−; and **3** is G1M A+,F+,X− G3M G+.G3M G+. (See section in text regarding nomenclature for the correct presentation of phenotypes; these phenotypes are for illustrative purposes. Figure 9–4 uses the correct phenotype presentation.)

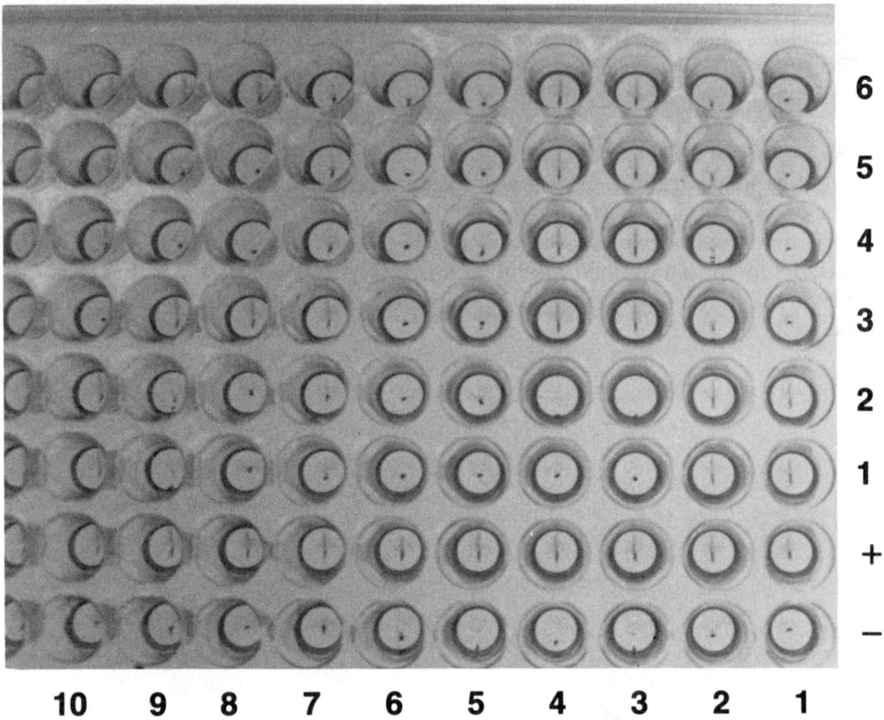

FIG 9–4.
Photograph of a RIFed microplate, showing the streaming patterns and agglutinates as well as some of the variations. The rows and columns are the same as those in Figure 9–3, with the addition of columns 8 (G1/3M G5), 9 (G1/3M G5), and 10 (G3M B0). The phenotypes in order from 1 to 6 are GM F B0, GM A G, GM A B0, GM A B0, and GM A, G5 B0.

With forensic samples (stains and body fluids), it has been noted that the newly-formed buttons often may not be completely interpretable after initial streaming. The interpretability can be improved by RIFing the microplate (RIFing has been coined to indicate that the microplate has been rotated 180°, such that the ACRBCs stream in the opposite direction) (Fig 9–4) and re-reading the streaming pattern in the opposite direction. Weak stains appear to be more readily detected after RIFing, and irregular agglutinates tend to firm into a more distinct button.

Controls.—The agglutinator control consists of either diluted serum that is negative for the allotype tested, saline, or the diluent used for agglutinators (the author uses 1% BSA-saline containing 0.1% sodium azide) in place of the negative serum. This should always show agglutination. Using the agglutinator diluent instead of serum that is negative for the factor also provides a control to show that the diluent has not become contaminated. Lack of agglutination in this control indicates that either the agglutinator has been diluted too much, the wrong ACRBC was added, or the diluent has become contaminated.

The inhibitor control consists of diluted serum that is positive for the allotype tested in place of the unknown serum. This should always show inhibition. This control should be diluted the same as the samples being tested. The inhibitor control also serves as a control to show that the ACRBCs are not agglutinating by themselves. Agglutination in this control indicates that either the agglutinator has not been diluted sufficiently to be at the appropriate level of sensitivity or that the ACRBCs are agglutinating by themselves.

The sample control consists of the material being tested and the ACRBC suspension. A control must be set up for each different ACRBC used. The agglutination of any ACRBCs invalidates the results of the typing for the allotype(s) using those ACRBCs, these should never show agglutination. Agglutination may be due to antibodies against RBCs or, more commonly, to antibodies to IgG. The agglutinating capacity of the unknown serum usually can be removed, either by heating the diluted serum at 65% to 70°C for 10 to 20 minutes, or by adsorption with the appropriate ACRBC. The serum is then retyped. This control normally is not run on forensic samples.

There are additional controls which usually are run when testing plasma or serum, but which are relevant to forensic samples. The most important one is used when running extracted stains, and can be called a "stain" control. This control consists of testing for specificities presumed not to be present. This controls for false-positives caused by improperly centrifuged extracts. A clean pattern of inhibition and agglutination indicates that the sample has been centrifuged properly. If the case material tested does not have positives and negatives for all of the specificities being tested, it may be desirable to have extracts available from known stains to serve as agglutination and inhibition controls for actual stains, rather than plasma, which may not react the same as stains.

INTERPRETATION OF TEST RESULTS

The following results are valid only if the controls reacted as described above. No agglutination (indicated by a smooth vertical stream in the V-bottom microplate) indicates that the allotype tested is present in the unknown being tested (see Fig 9–3). Agglutination (indicated by a round button in the middle of the V-bottom microplate) indicates that the allotype tested is not present in the unknown being tested, or is present below the level of detection of the test system (see Fig 9–3).

Sources of Error

Samples Tested.—Specimens that have been aged, repeatedly frozen and thawed, and bacterially contaminated may give weaker reactions than those observed with fresh serum. This is true especially for the IgG3 allotypes. In reality, few things short of boiling will destroy all allotypic activity (see section on forensics below).

The inadequate removal of contaminants can cause either false-positive or false-negative results. If the material being tested has not been centrifuged adequately, it is possible that non-sticky particulates will physically obstruct the agglutination of the ACRBCs, leading to all test wells appearing as positive. When this occurs, the buttons are usually larger than normal and all buttons start streaming very rapidly. The best control for this is to make sure that at least some tests are always negative. A clean pattern of positive and negative results across the row will indicate that contamination is not a problem. If sticky material is picked up inadvertently from the bottom of the test sample, this can lead to false-negative results by making the ACRBCs stick together. This normally occurs only in the first well or wells pipetted, and the buttons usually have identifiable debris in them and a rather distinct appearance.

Test Procedure.—An improper incubation time or temperature may be problematic. However, unless the incubation is very short, this normally is not a cause of test failure. Since human agglutinators do not react when room temperature exceeds 28°C (85°F), it is not recommended that allotyping be performed if the room temperature is elevated. Agglutinators react best in the cold, as do A, B, H, and Lewis antibodies[98] (Schanfield MS, unpublished observations). Microplates are routinely incubated in the refrigerator in our laboratory to eliminate variation in room temperature as a problem. In other laboratories the room temperature may be adequate for testing. If the ACRBCs did not take up sufficient antibody, this would be indicated by streaming in the agglutinator control.

Immunoglobulin allotyping is relatively foolproof. However, if the established procedure is not followed, and especially if the incubation time is markedly shortened (i.e., from 2 hours to 30 minutes), it is possible that agglutination will not occur in some test systems. This will be detected by a failure of the agglutinator control.

Bacterial contamination of agglutinator or control sera could cause false reactions. This usually is characterized by grainy splattering of the ACRBCs over the bottom of the well in V-bottom microplates (Schanfield MS, unpublished observation). All wells containing the contaminated reagent should show the same pattern. Test tube procedure seems to be relatively insensitive to this problem, and heat inactivation of serum at 56°C followed by microcentrifugation normally will eliminate it.

In theory, overcentrifugation could cause the cell button to stick to the bottom of the test tube, requiring excessive agitation in order to resuspend the button, and causing a false-negative reaction. In V-bottom microplates this will lead to increased time before the plates are interpretable. However, there is a procedure in which the microplates are centrifuged for 5 minutes and remain interpretable.[99] Thus, this is not likely to be the cause of false-negative results.

Undercentrifugation leads to insufficient force, causing the cell button to form weakly and leading to false-positive reactions. In V-bottom microplates, the button will be very poorly formed, which may lead to false-negative interpretations. However, this should be detected as a failure of the agglutinator control.

IMMUNOGLOBULIN ALLOTYPING OF DRIED BLOOD STAINS AND BODY FLUIDS

Introduction

Unlike some enzymes, immunoglobulins are ubiquitous in the human body. They are found in the same concentration in the intravascular space, the extravascular space, and the bone marrow. Reduced levels of IgG and IgA are found in semen, vaginal secretions, bile, saliva, and sweat. The concentrations of IgG and IgA present in various body fluids are presented in Table 9–7.

The immunoglobulin allotypes readily divided European populations into five phenotypes by 1959–1960 (see above). By 1961, forensic scientists started publishing the results of studies on the use of GM markers in the individualization of stains. Outside of the ABO blood groups, the consensus was that GM, and later KM, were the stablest markers available for the study of blood[3,4] (reviewed in detail below).

Serum or Plasma Preparation

No special preparation is needed for the testing of serum or plasma, and either can be tested equally well. Samples should be diluted before testing. Sera and plasma have been typed successfully over a wide range of dilutions, but the normal dilution used is between 1/10 and 1/30. Diluted sera or plasma should be heat-inactivated by placing the samples in a 65° to 70°C water bath for 15 to 20 minutes. Undiluted serum or plasma should not be heat inactivated as it will gel. Heat inactivation will remove most anti-immunoglobulins that can cause problems in the sample control, it will kill bacteria and viruses, and it will remove clotting factors from plasma. Further, the water level of the water bath should be the same as or higher than the fluid level in

TABLE 9–7.

Distribution of Immunoglobulin Classes and Subclasses in Different Body Fluids*

Fluid	IGG μg/ml	IGG1 %	IGG2 %	IGG3 %	IGA μg/ml	IGA2 %
Blood†	5,495	71.5	19.4	8.4	802	16
Semen	100				30	NT‡
Vaginal secretions	140				210	NT
Bile	166				99	26
Saliva	8				65	40
Sweat	7				—	NT

*Data in this table is based on references 100–104.
†Blood is assumed to be 50% serum, based on Blake and Sensabaugh.[103]
‡NT = not tested.

the samples to ensure that the samples are heat-inactivated. After heat inactivation the samples must be centrifuged to remove any debris or insoluble material. For heat-inactivated diluted serum or plasma, a clinical centrifuge set on high speed for 2 to 3 minutes is adequate.[51]

In general, immunoglobulin allotypes are extremely stable. Both serum stored over 20 years at −20°C and serum dried in the bottom of test tubes has been typed successfully, as has liquid serum, plasma, and occasionally hemolyzed blood specimens that have been stored for months in the refrigerator (Schanfield MS, unpublished observations).

Putrification does not appear to significantly affect testing. For example, sera arrived at the Detroit airport from Taiwan in July, 1970 and stayed on a loading dock there for 3 weeks. When it was finally received, it was obvious that the specimens were contaminated. After the addition of sodium azide and incubation at 37°C for 30 minutes (sodium azide will not kill all bacteria), the specimens were heated at 56°C for 30 minutes in order to kill anything the azide had missed. After centrifugation had removed a large amount of cellular debris, the samples tested as clean as fresh serum (Schanfield MS, unpublished, 1970).

Stain Extraction Procedures

Blood Stains.—The extraction of blood stains assumes that there is a large amount of immunoglobulin in blood. Using 100 μl stains (approximately 50 μls of serum), it was determined that one saturated square centimeter of cotton cloth should be extractable in up to 300 microliters of extraction fluid and yield approximately a 1/20 dilution of serum. If the stain is smaller, the cloth is thin, or the stain is limited to the surface of the material, or if only a few tests are going to be performed, less extraction fluid can be used. Extracts have been prepared with 1% to 3% BSA-saline (pH 7.4), 1% BSA 0.1 M PBS (pH 7.3) (hereafter referred to as BSA-PBS), and 0.1 M PBS (pH 7.3) (hereafter referred to as PBS). In the author's experience, the latter two are the best, since the phosphate buffer may have detergent characteristics. The PBS without BSA is the better medium if the extract is going to be concentrated. The advantage of the PBS is that the saline is hypertonic, leading to crenation and less lysis of the RBCs in the extraction procedure, and yielding cleaner extracts. Extraction normally is done at room temperature. If prolonged extractions are to be performed, 0.1% sodium azide will limit contamination of extracts stored at room temperature for prolonged periods of time. Preserved non-dessicated stains extract rapidly, whichever method is used. Using 1% BSA-saline, BSA-PBS, or PBS, and working with stains up to 2 years old (this is the oldest stain tested and not necessarily the oldest stain testable), that have been stored frozen or refrigerated, extraction occurs rapidly and is relatively complete in 10 to 30 minutes, as determined by the color of the extract and the material. In contrast, old stains that are stored at room temperature, unprotected from dessication, may take days to extract. Dried blood crusts 33 years old were extracted for 3 days in saline and successfully typed.[105] Stains stored unprotected at room temperature for 10 months took 3 to 6 days to extract. Color started appearing after several days; however, the samples were not tested until they had been extracted for 6 days. If the material can be made soluble or rehydrated, it probably can be tested. Hemolyzed specimens, cadaver blood, and other similar materials all can be tested, usually successfully, if the outlined procedures are followed.

Extraction from stains on cloth normally is performed in 1.5 ml polypropylene microcentrifuge tubes, with polyethylene tops (SOFTOP Extraction System, Allo-Type Genetic Testing, Inc.) that can be perforated easily to relieve pressure during heating and to remove liquid from the stains. After the extraction is completed, the extracts are heated in a 65° to 70°C waterbath for 15 to 20 minutes to denature non-immunoglobulin material and minimize the agglutination of ACRBCs by specimens. The extracted cloth is placed in the top of the microcentrifuge tube, and the tube is centrifuged at 13–15,000 rpm for 5 minutes in order to pellet insoluble material and extract fluid from the cloth simultaneously. After centrifugation, samples are tested as above. Contaminated specimens, autopsy blood, and badly hemolyzed specimens are diluted 1/20 to 1/40 in PBS and treated as an extract, with heating and centrifugation in a microcentrifuge. Two-year–old autopsy blood has been tested successfully by this method.[51] Note that due to the high hematocrit of cord blood, fetal blood should not be diluted more than 1/10.

Semen or Saliva Stains.—In contrast to the large amount of immunoglobulin that is present in blood, there is much less present in semen, vaginal secretions, and saliva (see Table 9–6). Thus, even a strong stain of any of these substances should be extracted in no more than 100 μl of PBS, and, if possible, more than 1 square centimeter of material should be used. Shaler[106] extracted one square centimeter and concentrated it down to one drop (approximately 50 μl), which is more concentrated than the procedure described. If there is reasonable P30 or acid phosphatase present, the material should be typable. If there is any question and additional stain is available, double extraction should be performed with a second fresh 1 centimeter square of stain. If a large stain is available, it is possible to extract in a larger volume of PBS and concentrate back to 100 μl with an Amicon, B–15 Minicon™ concentrator. Stains from sexual assault cases stored frozen for up to 3 years have been tested successfully using this method of extraction.[22] For saliva or other body fluid stains, 3 to 6 square centimeters should be extracted and concentrated back to 100 to 200 μl. After extraction and, if necessary, concentration, these extracts are treated exactly the same as blood stain extracts, with the following exceptions. If the samples are to be concentrated, the cloth or paper should be removed before concentration. Removal of excess liquid from the substrate can also be done with a microcentrifuge. Heating should be done before centrifugation at 10,000 to 15,000 RPM. However, if P30, acid phosphatase, or enzyme electrophoresis are to be performed on the extract, these tests should be performed before heat treatment, since heat is detrimental to most proteins and enzymes.

Importance of Centrifugation of Specimens.—Testing for immunoglobulin allotypes on V-bottom microplates is very susceptible to any particulate that will centrifuge out. This can cause the ACRBCs to stick together and produce a false-negative reaction. Extracts from cloth, seminal aspirates, and old blood specimens all contain fibers, cell debris, and other particulates that can stick together and create problems. Very few problems have been encountered with extracts that have been centrifuged in a microcentrifuge at 10,000 to 15,000 RPM (13,000 RCF) for 5 minutes. Pipetting then is done carefully to avoid removing any material from the bottom of the microcentrifuge tube.

Immunoglobulin Allotypes in Blood Stains

The first report on the testing of blood stains for immunoglobulin allotypes was that of Planques, Ruffie, and Ducos in 1961.[2] They investigated known stain crusts made on glass, metal, and stone; stains made on cloth, plaster, paper, earth, and other permeable substrates; and a series of unknown stains up to 10 years old. Using both SNagg and Ragg antisera, they investigated the allotypes G1M A, G1M X, and G3M B in varying amounts of material. They found that 15 mg of antigen-positive stain would inhibit their test system, while 250 mg of antigen-negative stain would not inhibit. They found that large amounts of stain would inhibit within 2 hours, but very weak stains could take up to 24 hours to inhibit their test system. The SNagg reagents worked better than the Ragg reagents. Their test system incubated 0.5 cm^2 of stained cloth or 20 mg of stain crust with 250 μls of anti-GM having a titer of 16–32. After the adsorption, the reaction was centrifuged and the supernatent antibody doubling dilution titered and then tested against the appropriate ACRBC. A sample was considered to be positive if it reduced the titer of the antibody by three or four dilutions, and negative if there was no decrease in titer. They were completely accurate in the testing of G1M A (26 positive and 26 negative) and G1M X (17 positive and 17 negative), but had two false-negative results among 13 sera that were positive for G3M B. This could have been due to either the sensitivity of their test method or the fact that the antiserum was a Ragg. They further reported the detection of G1M A in stains up to 10 years old and of G3M B in stains up to 7 years old.

The same year, Funfhausen and Sagan[107] briefly reported that they had successfully typed stains from wood, paper, and other surfaces. The details of their research were published later.[108,109] They studied G1M A and G1M X in blood stains made from five individuals on glass, porcelain, linoleum, plastic (PVC), newspaper, wrapping paper, cardboard, leather, fabric, planed and unplaned wood, and brick (wood and brick were tested only for G1M A). The appropriate results were detected in all cases, including those in which the material had been allowed to become moldy. They estimated that they could detect G1M A from blood stains at a concentration of 0.5 mg percent. Heating solutions of stains at 100° and 120°C had no effect, and the complete destruction of all material occurred at 150° to 200°C. They found ultraviolet radiation, ultrasound, and soap to have no effects.

In 1962, Ducos, Ruffie, and Varsi[110] published the results of more extensive tests that had been proposed previously in their original publication.[2,111] They tested a total of 12 anti-G1M A (SNagg), 7 anti-G1M A (Ragg), 3 anti-G1M X (SNagg), and 3 anti-G3M B (Ragg) adjusted to a titer of 16. They tested known stains up to 48 hours old and unknown stains up to 10 years old. Crusts were prepared by drying blood in petri dishes, and stains were prepared on boiled white cloth. A total of 290 known stains were tested for G1M A: 139 for G1M X and 116 for G3M B. They obtained results similar to those of their first report. Raggs did not inhibit as well as SNaggs for either G1M A and G3M B. For G1M A they found 14 potential false-negatives out of 83 genetic positives (17%) when stains were tested with Raggs versus no false-negatives out of 86 stains tested with SNaggs. For G3M B–positive stains tested with Raggs, 24% were potentially false-negatives (18/76). For the old, unidentified stains, they reported that SNagg reagents worked better than Ragg reagents. However, allowing both types of reagents up to 48 hours for adsorption enabled them to classify stains that were up to 10 years old.

In 1963, Nielsen and Henningsen[112] also published the results of their studies on stains from three known donors prepared on linen, nylon, cotton, and silk, and tested after room temperature storage, room temperature high-humidity storage, and storage at 37°C, for 2, 5, and 11 weeks. The anti-G1M A, anti-G1m X and anti-G3M B were all Raggs, with adjusted titers between 6 and 25. They tested either a 1-drop stain extracted in 4 drops of saline and incubated overnight at 4°C, or a 3-drop stain extracted in 12 drops of saline and incubated overnight at 4°C. Each extract was titrated by doubling dilution and tested against a fixed dilution of agglutinator in a test system consisting of one drop extract dilution, one drop agglutinator, and one drop ACRBC. Positive extracts inhibited to a dilution of 8 to 16 for G1M A, a dilution of 16 for G1M X, and a dilution of 4 to 6 for G3M B. The only deterioration of stains occurred in the ones that had been stored in high humidity. No allotypes were detectable after 5 weeks of storage.

Additional studies were reported by Gohler and Hunger[113] who studied blood stains from 48 individuals for G1M A, G1M X, G3M B, and KM 2. This was the first report of KM typing of stains. Prokop and Byrdy[114] reported on the testing of 667 unknown specimens up to 15 years old for G1M A and G1M X. The results indicated that the results matched the expected phenotype frequency for the study population. In 1966, Lenoir and Muller[115] studied stains from 10 known donors on linen, wool, nylon, cotton, and silk, in ambient and humid air, and up to 12 weeks old for G1M A, G1M X, and G3M B. Their results were similar to those of Nielsen and Henningsen.[112] Budyakov[116] reported the results of studies done on G1M A in Russia. The second report of testing KM markers in blood stains was from Merli and Ronchi[117] on KM 1, with results similar to those for G1M A.

Turowska,[118] in a study of 706 known stains over 5 years, noted a false-negative rate of 0.19%, pointing out that a negative result for G1M A or G1M X is probably a true negative. She is the first to report on the successful typing of hemolyzed blood that is 12 months old, indicating the stability of GM in this type of specimen.

The Ph.D. thesis done by Gortz[119] in 1969 was the first report of G1M F, G3M C, and some of the subdivisions of G3M B (specifically G3M B1, B3, and G3M B5), and the first report on typing blood stains from non-whites. He extended and confirmed the studies originally reported by Ducos, Ruffie, and Varsi,[110] including successfully typing stains up to 15 years old. The results of the thesis were subsequently published in a series of articles on allotypes in stains,[120,121] the value of GM typing for the determination of the racial origin of blood stains,[122] and the detection of KM 1 and KM 2 in blood stains.[123]

Abe and Nakajima[124] reported on the investigation of G1M A, G1M F, G1M X,

G3M B1, G3M G, G3M T, and KM 1 in three known stains from Japanese. They were the first to report on G3M G and G3M T in stains, and also the first to report on the elution of anti-G1M A and anti-G3M G from stains as small as 0.5 mg.

Studies performed since the ones cited thus far basically have confirmed or added to the results presented above. These include a study by Khalap, Pereira, and Rand[125] of G1M A, G1M X, and KM 1; a study by Hoste, Brocteur, and Andre[105] who demonstrated G1M A, G1M X, G3M B5, and KM 1 in blood stains 29 to 33 years of age; and a study by Freidrich and Oepen[126] who investigated the effects of heat, humidity, and ultraviolet radiation on G1M A, F and X, G3M B1, B5, and G, and KM 1. Khalap and Divall[127] studied G3M B1 and reported on the value of using it to confirm negative reactions for G1M A and G1M X. Schmitter[128] investigated the effect of protein concentration on the detection of G1M A, F and X, G3M B5, and KM 1. von Mittmeyer[129] extended the work of Schmitter, using the IgG concentration in stains tested for G1M A, F and X, G3M B5, and KM 1 to determine that false-negatives could occur below a concentration of 500 μg/ml. Tahir[130] was the first to report on the detection of G3M B0 in stains. Gaensslen et al[131] evaluated GM and KM sera in the testing of blood stains, and reported on various aspects of the procedures, including their success in typing aged stains.

Broctuer and Moureau[132] were the first to report on the use of G1M A, G1M X, and G3M B in an actual case involving the identification of blood stains found in an automobile. This was followed by Ducos et al,[133] who reported on the use of G1M A, G1M X, and G3M B in the testing of blood stains from a sexual assault case. Blanc et al[134] reported on the non-specific inhibition of G1M A by insecticide on substrate, although attempts to verify this have not been successful.[135] Blanc, Gortz, and Ducos[123] were the first to report the results of KM typing evidence. Tahir and Brown[136] reported on the testing of a blood stain for G1M A and X.

Over the last 16 years there has been a large number of publications on the typing of GM and KM markers in blood stains (see above) and one mention of the typing of old hemolyzed liquid blood. In addition to the markers listed above, G1M Z, G1/3M G5, G2M N, G3M C3, C5, and S, A2M 1 and 2, and KM 3 all have been detected in prepared blood stains or in actual casework.[51] It is evident also that dried blood stains normally are extremely stable; in fact, with the possible exception of the ABH antigens, they may be the most stable genetic markers in dried stains. They appear to be more stable than ABH in hemolyzed post-mortem or old blood specimens, since allotypes can be determined long after ABH activity is gone. Two-year–old post-mortem blood has been typed with no apparent difficulties.[51] On several occasions, fresh blood samples have been typed and retested 3 to 6 months later after significant hemolysis has occurred; they have yielded identical results.[51] Being stored dry, even unprotected, at room temperature does not appear to destroy the allotypes. A series of prepared stains stored both frozen and unprotected can still be typed after 10 months. The unprotected stains, however, take 3 to 6 days to extract in order to type them, while the freezer-stored stains extract in less than one-half hour.[51] The only thing that appears to lead to significant loss of GM and KM allotypes in stains is storage in high humidity[112,115,126] for several weeks.

The occurrence of allotypes in the stain substrate is a topic not dealt with directly in any of the publications. In general, immunoglobulin allotypes are limited to man and some of his closer relatives. The phenotypes observed in non-human primates are not the same as those observed in man,[137] making man and his non-human primate relatives readily differentiable. Except for humans and other primates, there is no other known source of immunoglobulin allotypes. With rare exceptions, substrate has not posed a problem. Khalap, Pereira, and Rand[125] reported a problem with false-positive results when directly testing stains on wool or wool blends. However, if the material is extracted and tested or dried onto cotton threads there are no false-positive results. Newall[135] has not been able to repeat the false-positive results obtained for G1M A, and reportedly caused by the presence of orthochlorophenol or parachlorophenol. All of the data available indicate that false-positive results are unlikely to be caused by substrate; however, sample preparation must be meticulous to avoid particulates that can cause non-specific stearic interference. Two controls that must be included in the forensic testing of stain extracts are a substrate control (unstained material, cloth, dirt, etc.) and at least one allotype that is expected to be negative (agglutinated). A clean pattern of positive and negative reactions serves to indicate that false-positive reactions due to particulate interference have not occurred. When they do occur, they will affect all of the test systems used.

Immunoglobulin Allotypes in Semen Stains

The number of genetic markers detectable in semen is limited; therefore, any additional markers that help to individualize semen or vaginal secretions are extremely useful forensically. Immunoglobulins are present in semen at about one-fiftieth of the level at which they are present in serum,[101, 103] and a similar level has been reported for vaginal secretions.[100] Thus, although the levels are significantly lower than those of blood, it should be possible to detect allotypes in semen, semen stains, and mixtures. Klose and Schraven[138] reported the results of testing semen from 40 individuals for G1M A. Nineteen were G1M A–positive. They detected G1M A in 68% of the semen and got false-negative results in 32% of the semen. No false-positive results were observed. They attributed the false-negative results to the secretor status of the individuals (non-secretors gave false negatives), though they retracted this in an unpublished note to Nielsen and Henningsen.[112] As part of a study of G1M A in tissues and body fluids, Kramer[139] studied sperm from 30 G1M A–positive and 20 G1M A–negative individuals. He could detect G1M A in 17% of the G1M A–positive individuals, 83% false-negative results, and no false-positive results. Kramer could detect G1M A only after the material had been centrifuged extensively. Nielsen and Henningsen[140] did not detect G1M A, X or G3M B in any of the 23 samples of semen that they tested. It should be noted that Nielsen and Henningsen[140] state that they used the same method to test the semen as they use in their laboratory to test serum. Therefore, on their article on testing blood stains,[112] they were using a rather insensitive system. Davie and Kipps[141] were the first to report on the testing of semen for KM 1. They typed 31 matched serum and semen samples and found 11 of them to be KM 1–positive. In general, they found complete concordance among all samples, as long as the samples were frozen, thawed, and centrifuged before testing. However, even with this preparation, one sample caused non-specific aggregation of ACRBCs. Unfortunately, they had limited success typing stains and concluded that a more sensitive technique was needed. Jorch and Oepen[142] studied 7 semen samples for G1M A, F and X, G3M B1, and G, and 15 semen samples for KM 1, extending the number of allotypes detected. However, in order to obtain good results they used very large stains (approximately 4 cm^2). These researchers used serum, whole semen samples (n = 23), and seminal plasmas (n = 15), and found G1M A and X in only 31 semen stains. For the whole semen and seminal plasma the results were 100% concordant with the serum type; 3 of the 27 whole semen samples could not be typed because of weak reactions in the test system; and there were no false-negative or false-positive results obtained. In typing 31 semen stains they had 2 false-negative (3.2%) and 1 false-positive (1.6%) result. Schwerd and Fehrer's data[143] indicated that there was no correlation between secretor status and the detection of allotypes. The most recent discussion of testing semen stains is by Shaler,[106] who gives his method of typing semen stains for G1M A, F, and X, and G3M B1, and discusses interpretation of the results.

Correct interpretation of the results of testing for immunoglobulin allotypes in sexual assault cases is contingent upon our knowledge of the presence of these allotypes in contaminating body fluids such as vaginal secretions, saliva, and possibly sweat. Of these fluids, vaginal secretions are by far the most important. Schwerd and Stock[144] have published the only report of testing matched serum and vaginal secretions. They tested 43 sets of serum and vaginal secretions for G1M A and X, and KM 1. One sample was false-positive for both G1M A and X (5.6%), 3 were false-negatives for G1M A (15.8%), and 1 was false-negative for G1M X (16.7%). There was 1 false-negative result (14.3%) and no false-positive results for KM 1. The overall accuracy was 93.9% for the 115 tests that were interpretable. The authors concluded that G1M A, G1M X, and KM 1 are detectable in vaginal secretions.

Immunoglobulin Allotypes in Sexual Assault Cases.—Data from 17 sexual assault cases were analyzed by the author[22] (details to be presented elsewhere). A total of 28 pieces of evidence were tested for G1M, G3M, and KM allotypes. Additionally, some of the evidence was tested for G2M and A2M allotypes. With the exception of 1 liquid aspirate, all of the samples tested were extracts, either submitted in this form or prepared by the author. The evidence was divided such that approximately two-thirds of the extracts were derived from drainage sites (panties, panty liners, sheets, clothing or carpeting) and one-third were derived from swabs (vaginal or introital).

Immunoglobulin allotypes were detected in 89% of the samples tested. Three samples gave no inhibition at all and one gave very poor inhibition. Two of the non-reactive samples were extracts prepared from a blanket that had been stored unprotected for 3 years at room temperature, and had been extracted for only a short period of time. The third non-reactive sample was an extract prepared from a vaginal swab taken from a decreased victim after what appeared to be a second sexual assault (allotypes were detected in two pieces of drainage site evidence). The fourth sample was only the second extract that had ever been prepared from a semen stain and the method had not been standardized. In 77% of the samples (17/22) with detectable allotypes, one or more victim allotypes were detected, indicating that vaginal immunoglobulins contribute to the allotypes detected. In 42% of the samples with detectable allotypes, the results of the allotyping were informative as to the phenotype of the semen donor. In an additional 15% of the samples, the allotyping results were informative when other information was known (e.g., that the husband could not have had sex with the victim), indicating that a total of 58% of the evidence could have provided information on the semen donor. Broken down by evidence type, 69% of the drainage site evidence was informative, while only 37% of the typeable swabs were informative; however, due to the small sample size, the difference is not statistically significant.

As expected, the detection of allotypes correlated with the normal levels of immunoglobulins. Among stains with detectable allotypes, G1M and KM were detected in 96% of the tests (23/24 and 24/25, respectively); G3M N was detected in 70.2% (8/17) when the percentage was corrected for the proportion of G2M N–positives in the population; and G3M allotypes were detected in 52% (13/25). The A2M allotypes were detected 75% of the time, but only four samples were tested. Allotypes of either vaginal or seminal origin which were detected in this study and had not been reported previously were G1M Z, G1/3M G5, G2M N, G3M B0, and S, A2M 1 and 2, and KM 3. These results suggest that immunoglobulin allotypes can be detected in semen stains or in mixed vaginal-seminal stains from sexual assault cases. Furthermore, the allotype data that are generated are informative in a significant proportion of cases.

Immunoglobulin Allotypes in Other Body Fluids and Organs

Immunoglobulin Allotypes in Other Body Fluids.—Saliva and sweat appear to be the next candidates for forensic study. The levels of IgG are very low in saliva (8 μg/ml) and in sweat (7 μg/ml); the levels of IgA are higher in saliva (65 μg/ml) than in sweat (undetectable)[101] (see Table 9–6). Thus, GM allotypes are poor candidates for detection in saliva or sweat, but the A2M markers and KM may be detectable in saliva. Thus far, the published literature supports these expectations. Kramer[139] tested saliva from ten G1M A–positive and five G1M A–negative individuals and could not differentiate the two sets of samples. Davie and Kipps[141] reported that they successfully typed 115 saliva specimens for KM 1 from individuals of known KM type, after freezing and thawing the saliva; however, 10 additional specimens could not be tested because they non-specifically aggregated the ACRBCs. Jorch and Oepen[142] reported that they could detect KM 1 in saliva but not in sweat. They reported further that stamp glue non-specifically affects testing for KM 1. However, Newall[135] has not been able to confirm that observation. The only observation that the author can make on the detection of allotypes in saliva is that A2M 1 and 2 were successfully detected in cigarette butts submitted as evidence.[50] Also, in the testing of saliva from a single GM F B0 KM 1+,3NT individual, G1M F and KM 1 were detected, while G3M B0 was not (Schanfield MS, unpublished observation). Jorch and Oepen[142] reported that G1M A, F, and X, G3M B1 and G, and KM 1 could be detected in nasal secretions after extracting 2 to 10 cm² pieces of paper handkerchiefs.

Kramer[139] reported that G1M A could not be detected in the urine of healthy individuals, but could be detected in patients with kidney disease. Given the low levels of immunoglobulin in urine, it is possible that if it is concentrated enough it may be typeable. Kramer[139] reported also that pleural exudate from G1M A–positive individuals was not typeable, and neither were tears, milk, or serous liquid from blisters. Given the levels of immunoglobulin present in some of these body fluids, certainly A2M and KM should be detectable, if not G1M allotypes. In contrast, Turowska and Trela[145,146] tested matched serum and inner ear fluid samples and accurately detected G1M A in 51 of 152 samples tested; G1M X in 19 of 133 samples (with one false-negative); and KM 1 in 18 of 133 samples (with one false-negative). Finally, using matched blood and hyaluronidase-treated vitreous humor, Dimo-simonin, Brandt-Casadevall, and Gujer[147] demonstrated the successful detection of G1M A, F, and X, G3M B5 and G, and KM 1 in 121 samples. In two cases, G1M F and G3M B5 were not determinable because of positive sample controls and, in 3 cases, there were false-negatives for G3M G. The false-negative results all occurred in Le (a − b −) individuals. However, the authors found no relationship between secretor status and the detection of allotypes.

The detection of immunoglobulin allotypes in body fluids other than blood will depend largely on the concentration of immunoglobulins in the fluid under investigation. Fluids such as semen, vaginal secretions, cerebral spinal fluid, amniotic fluid, and aqueous humor all appear to be superfiltered serum with immunoglobulin levels about one-fiftieth those of serum. Depending on the concentration of these fluids, many or all allotypes may be detected in them. In contrast, actively secreted fluids such as saliva, tears, and gastrointestinal juices (feces) tend to have very low levels of IgG and relatively high levels of IgA. In these latter fluids, A2M and KM markers will be the most readily detected, with less chance of detecting G1M allotypes.

Immunoglobulin Allotypes in Organs.—Kramer[139] reported that G1M A could be detected in basically all vascularized organs (whole skin, muscle, vessels, bone, liver, spleen, kidney, or brain), but not in avascular tissues (hair, epidermis, cornea, or cartilage). Oepen[148] reported on the testing of muscle extracts for G1M A and X, and KM 1. Unwashed material had a lower non-determination rate than did washed material. The most extensive study of the detection of immunoglobulin allotypes in organs is that of Tausch et al[149] who studied G1M A, F, and X, G3M B5, and KM 1 in tissue fluid from myocardium, kidney, spleen, liver, and blood obtained at autopsy from 12 individuals, over a period of up to 10 weeks. The best results were obtained using 1/20 dilutions of tissue fluid. These researchers found that all of the allotypes tested could be detected up to 8 weeks after death; however, only G1M A and X could be demonstrated past that time. Henke and Wirtz[150] studied G1M A, F, and X, G3M B5 and G, and KM 1 in stomach extracts. In samples from 55 fresh cadavers, one false-negative for G1M A and two false-negatives for G3M G were observed, and one false-negative and one false-positive were reported for KM 1. In ten decayed cadavers, they found four false-negatives for G3M B5, one of which also had a false-negative for G3M G. The author's experience with tissue fluid is limited to muscle extracts. In one case, a saline extract of muscle from a torso found in San Francisco Bay was sent to us for testing. The phenotype IGH A N′ B0,1,3,5,C3,5 1,2 KM 3 was found (Schanfield MS, unpublished data). Another case involved a frozen piece of intercostal muscle from a deceased infant that had been exposed for approximately 10 days during the winter; most of the body had been eaten by animals. The liquid collected after the muscle had thawed was typed as GM F B0 KM 3, which was consistent with the suspect who had pleaded guilty to child abandonment (Peterson M, Schanfield MS, unpublished data).

Henke and Bauer[151] and Henke, Bauer, and Schweitzer[152] reported that G1M A, F, and X, G3M B1, B5, and G, and KM 1 are reliably detectable in tooth pulp from teeth that are harvested from cadavers, putrified cadavers, and skeletonized cadavers.

In general, it is safe to assume that vascular organs are going to be readily typeable for immunoglobulin allotypes, since they have concentrations of immunoglobulins similar to those found in blood.

Reviews

There have been several reviews of immunoglobulin allotypes which include forensic applications. These include Prokop and Uhlenbruck,[153] Grubb,[154] Kipps,[100] and Gaensslen.[155]

Unique Forensic Applications

Child Abandonment Cases.—Immunoglobulin allotypes, or immunoglobulins in general, can provide unique information in certain situations. As stated previously, virtually all of the IgG present in the fetus or newborn infant is maternal in origin. Therefore, in cases of child abandonment, the allotypes in the infant provide physical evidence of maternity. For all practical purposes, they are "maternal blood stains left at the scene of the crime." In five cases of child abandonment in which a suspect was developed, the immunoglobulin allotypes of the child matched those of the alleged mother (Schanfield et al, in preparation). The data for these cases are summarized in Table 9–8.

The relative levels of IgG and IgA in the serum of umbilical cords, young children, and adults also can be used to differentiate adult blood from that of children or newborns. Though cord blood contains IgG of maternal origin, IgA and IgM are not actively transported across the placenta and, thus, are present in very low levels or are not detectable at all. Further, children do not reach adult levels of IgA until they are around 10 years of age.[102] For example, all of 45 cord bloods tested for GM, AM, and KM allotypes had detectable GM and KM allotypes but no detectable AM allotypes (Schanfield MS, Gotlieb K, unpublished data). Given this information, it is possible to differentiate blood stains of maternal origin from blood from newborns and children in cases of child abandonment. Since IgA appears to have survival properties similar to those of IgG in stains, the ratio of IgG to IgA can be used to differentiate adult blood from child and newborn blood. An IgG:IgA ratio of about 6 is characteristic of adults.[102] As the ratio gets higher, it becomes more likely that the stain originated from a child.[102] If adult levels of IgG are detected and IgA is not detected, the blood is from either a child or an infant. The ratio of IgG to IgA also can be used to help

TABLE 9–8.
Data From Five Cases of Child Abandonment

ID	Race	Child IGH	Child KM	Alleged Mother IGH	Alleged Mother KM	Likelihood*	Probability of Maternity†
83–050701	White	F B0,1,3,4,5	3	F B0,1,3,4,5	3	40.9%	71.0%
85–032701	White	F N B0,1,3,4,5	3	F N B0,1,3,4,5 1	3	31.0%	76.35%
IADCI	White	F B0	3	F B0	3	40.9%	71.0%
86–081302	MexAmer	A N′ B0,G,G5,S,T	1,3	A N′ B0,G,G5,S,T 1	1,3	1.0%	99.0%
86–081901	White	A,F§	1,3	A,F N B0,G,G5 1	1,3	4.2%	95.9%

*Likelihood: The chance that child and alleged mother would match by chance.
†Probability of Maternity: Bayesian probability that the alleged mother is the true mother of the child. Calculated P(Mat) = Pr*Mother/*Pr Mother + Pr*Notmother. Pr = prior probability = 0.5.
‡A2M tested but not detected.
§Results of immunoglobulin allotyping of skeletal remains of child. Only G1M and KM were detected.

identify amniotic fluid versus other types of serous fluid. The total level of IgG in amniotic fluid is low (about the same as in semen or vaginal secretions), and there is little or no IgA (in contrast to semen or vaginal secretions which appear to have the normal IgG:IgA ratio) (Schanfield MS, in preparation).

Confirmation of Negative Results.—One of the unique features of immunoglobulin allotype testing is the possibility of confirming the lack of an allotype by the presence of another allotype. With the exception of G2M N, which has no allele, all allotype loci have multiple alleles, which can lead to the interpretation of negative findings by means of exclusion. For example, if a sample is G1M A– and G1M X–negative, it must be G1M F–positive in order to be interpretable. Similarly, if a sample is G3M B0–negative, it should be G3M G–positive. The same is true for A2M 1 and KM 1. For the system to be maximally utilized, confirmation should always be within the same subclass or chain type. The European system of testing for G1M A, X and G3M B, has a problem in that a weak stain could type as G1M A−, X−, G3M B−, and in fact be G1M A−, F+, X−. This is especially true when typing body fluid stains in which it is more likely to pick up G1M and KM allotypes than G3M. For example, in the study of sexual assault evidence cited above,[22] G1M and KM allotypes were detected approximately 96% of the time, while G3M allotypes were detected only 56% of the time. Therefore, when choosing the allotypes to be tested in a given case, it is important to choose reagents that will confirm negative findings in addition to maximizing information (see below for a discussion).

The occurrence of allotypes on different subclasses with different concentrations provides a second level of confirmation of negative results. In 1969, Turowska[118] indicated that she felt that negative reactions for G1M A and X indicated true negative reactions, even though they were not confirmed by the presence of G1M F or G3M B. However, the detection of G3M allotypes with one-eighth the concentration adds additional support to this belief. The possibility exists that a slight variation in sensitivity might cause a G1M A, F individual to test as G1M F in a weak stain; however, if the stain types as GM F B0, it is almost certain that G1M A and X are not present. The detection of G3M and A2M also can confirm negative reactions for G2M N, which does not have an allele. It should be noted though, that the detection of any allotype in lower concentration can confirm the absence of higher concentration. Based on the work of Turowska,[118] the absence of a lower concentration allotype does not negate the interpretation of the absence of higher concentration allotypes which have been confirmed by the presence of those of similar concentration.

Maximizing Information From Immunoglobulin Allotypes

One of the questions being raised by individuals who are starting to do allotyping regards the number of markers that are needed. To a large extent the number of markers needed depends on the population being tested. If all of the samples being tested come from white individuals, the European battery of G1M A, X and G3M B is quite suitable. On the other hand, if the population is mixed, a great deal of information can be gathered by testing for additional markers. To demonstrate this, the data from

TABLE 9–9.

Effects of Different Sets of Allotyping Reagents on the Detection of Racially Specific Phenotypes

Population	White			Black		
Allotypes Tested	G1M A,X G3M B0	A,F,X B0,G	A,F,G5,X B0,C3,G	A,X B0	A,F,X B0,G	A,F,G5,X B0,C3,G
Polymorphic Phenotypes	5	6	6	2(1)	4(2)	10(2)
White	3	5	5	(1)	(2)	(2)
Frequency	.570	.965	.965	.009	.017	.017
Black	—	—	—	—	1	8
Frequency	—	—	—	—	.706	.818
Probably Black	—	—	—	—	1	1
Frequency	—	—	—	—	.068	.056
Ambiguous	2	1	1	2	2	1
Frequency	.430	.021	.016	.982	.197	.091
DP*	.653	.674	.674	.082	.467	.853
Misclassification†	1.5%	1.8%	1.8%	—	.7%	.3%

*DP calculated as described above for all of the observed phenotypes.

†White misclassification is the percent of individuals classified as white that would actually be black, based on the frequency of white phenotypes in blacks divided by the frequency of white phenotypes in whites. Black misclassification is the percent of individuals classified as black that would actually be white, based on the frequency of black phenotypes in whites, divided by the frequency of black phenotypes in blacks. Ambiguous = phenotypes not white, black, or probably black. Black = phenotypes occurring at least 20 times as frequently in blacks as in whites. Frequency = the total frequency of all phenotypes in this category. Parentheses = phenotypes with a frequency of 0.008–0.009. Polymorphic Phenotypes = phenotypes with a frequency of 0.01 or greater. Probably Black = phenotypes occurring 10–19 times as frequently in blacks as in whites. White = phenotypes occuring at least 20 times as frequently in whites as in blacks.

Appendices 9–2 and 9–3 were tabulated assuming that three different sets of reagents were used. The first is the "European" set of G1M A, and X and G3M B0; the second is the "white" allotypes G1M A, F, and X and G3M B0 and G; and the third set is the "white" set plus the two most common black specificites, G1/3M G5 and G3M C3. The results of the analysis using these three sets is presented in Table 9–9. A phenotype was designated as racially specific if it occurred 20 times as often (95% likelihood of assignment) in whites or blacks versus the reciprocal population, and as probably racially specific if it occurred 10 to 19 times as often (greater than 90% likelihood of assignment). The "white" and "black" phenotypes are listed for convenience in Table 9–10.

When testing white individuals, it is apparent that the addition of more reagents does not significantly increase the DP or the number of phenotypes. The addition of the white reagents increases the number of "white" phenotypes from 3 to 4 and includes approximately 96% of the white population. No advantage is gained by the addition of "black" allotypes, with the exception that the black misclassification rate drops slightly. The black misclassification rate is the percentage of time that stains would be identified as black when they are actually white individuals with black phenotypes. It is the frequency of black phenotypes in the white population (from Appendix 9–2) divided by the frequency of black phenotypes in the black population (from Appendix 9–3). Due to the occurrence of white admixture in the U.S. black population, white genes occur in the black population more often than black genes occur in the white population. Thus, the white misclassification rate is higher than the black misclassification rate. However, the error is still relatively small, such that 98% of the time the donor of a stain with a white phenotype actually will be white.

In contrast to the above, the identification of black phenotypes improves dramatically as reagents are added. The increase in information generated for GM allotypes is indicated by the five-fold increase in the VDP that occurs after the addition

TABLE 9–10.
White and Black Phenotypes Detected With Different Reagent Sets

Phenotype	White			Black		
Reagents						
G1M	A,X	A,F,X	A,F,G5,X	A,X	A,F,X	A,F,G5,X
G3M	B0	B0,G	B0,C3,G	B0	B0,G	B0,C3,G
Phenotype	A	AG	A G		A B0,G	A B0,G
Frequency	.042	.041	.041		.068	.056
Phenotype	A,X	A,X G	A,X G		A B0	A B0,C3,G
Frequency	.042	.042	.042		.706	.015
Phenotype	B0	A,F B0,G	A,F B0,G			A,X B0,G
Frequency	.486	.261	.261			.019
Phenotype		A,F,X B0,G	A,F,X B0,G			A,F B0,C3
Frequency		.137	.137			.031
Phenotype		F B0	F B0			A,F,G5 B0
Frequency		.485	.485			.047
Phenotype						A B0
Frequency						0.202
Phenotype						A,G5 B0
Frequency						.200
Phenotype						A B0,C3
Frequency						.200
Phenotype						A,G5 B0,C3
Frequency						.104

of "white" allotype reagents to the "European" set, and an additional near-doubling of the VDP that occurs after the addition of the "black" allotype reagents. The addition of the additional markers used in Appendix 9–3 only increases the black VDP from 0.853 to 0.893. The misclassification rate for blacks is much lower than that for whites because of the low frequency of black genes in white individuals. Therefore, the assignment of a stain or semen donor as black because of the presence of a black phenotype will be correct over 99% of the time.

The choice of allotypes to be tested depends on several factors. One consideration is the ability to confirm negative reactions, as described above. Thus, even though the addition of KM 3 may not yield a significant increase in the VDP in whites, it allows for the confirmation of a KM 1–negative phenotype as KM 3–positive. In general, the logic for the choice of reagents has been outlined by Blanc, Gortz, and Ducos.[122] The author uses the following guidelines. If standards from the victim and suspect are available, then they are both completely phenotyped. If differences are detected, the case evidence is tested for the informative allotypes, for at least one expected negative reaction, and for allotypes which will allow for the confirmation of negative results. When the sample volume is limited, the author tests for G1M and KM markers first, followed in order by G2M, G3M, and A2M allotypes. If there is only a victim standard, and evidence or suspected material, as many markers as possible are tested, following the same guidelines as above. Even if only G1M and KM allotypes are detected, using G1M A, F, G5 and X with KM 1 and 3 will still result in a DP of 0.751 for whites and a DP of 0.888 for blacks. However, the detection of any number of allotypes can provide some information.

Conclusions

For a genetic system to be useful forensically it should have good discriminative power among individuals. The genetic markers should be present in blood and body fluids and stable in dried stains. It also is desirable for the system to have a simple, reliable test procedure. Based on these criteria, immunoglobulin allotypes are good candidates for forensic genetic markers. The published record indicates a wide acceptance of these markers in the forensic communities of Japan, Canada, Russia, Poland, Germany, Denmark, Belgium, France, Italy, and England. Though there is some variation in the results obtained by different investigators, it is probable that most of the false-negative results are due to variations in the sensitivity of test systems (especially in those studies reported in the early literature), and that most causes of false-positive results probably are due to problems in sample preparation. The current availability of immunoglobulin allotyping reagents in the United States and Canada should allow forensic scientists in these countries to join their colleagues in Europe and Asia in the application of these extremely useful markers to forensic casework. Of all the literature presented above, there appears to be no better summary of the use of immunoglobulin allotypes than that made by Ducos, Varsi, and Marty in 1963[3] in which they state, "in medico-legal practice, where the identification has usually to be done on minimal traces of blood, the demonstration of antigens of the Gm and ABO systems will supply the most certain and valuable bases for the identification of blood-stains."

APPENDICES

APPENDIX 9–1.

Distribution of KM Phenotypes in U.S. Whites, Blacks, and Mexican-Americans*

	Whites	Blacks	Mexican-Americans
Number Tested	>10,000	2,365	250
KM 3	0.8427	0.4361	0.523
1,3	0.1506	0.4485	0.400
1	0.0067	0.1153	0.077

*The data from U.S. whites are taken from reference 64, while the data for American blacks and Mexican-Americans are the same data set as used in Appendices 9–3 and 9–4.

APPENDIX 9–2.

Distribution of GM Phenotypes in U.S. Whites*

Phenotype Observed	IGG1 A,F,G5,X IGG2 NT IGG3 NT/ND IGA2 NT	Phenotype Observed	IGG1 A,F,G5,X IGG2 NT IGG3 B0,C3,C5,G,G5,S,T IGA2 NT
F	0.4867	F B0	0.4849
A,F	0.2819	A,F B0,G,G5*	0.2605
A,F,X	0.1385	A,F,X B0,G,G5*	0.1372
A	0.0464	A,X G,G5*	0.0419
A,X	0.0448	A G,G5*	0.0406
F,X	0.0007	A,F B0	0.0154
A,F,G5	0.0009	A,F B0,S,T	0.0045
A,G5	0.0003	A B0,G,G5*	0.0047
		F B0,G,G5*	0.0018
		A,F G,G5*	0.0016
		A B0*,G,G5*,S,T	0.0009
		A,F,X B0	0.0009
		F,X B0	0.0007
		A,F B0,C3,C5	0.0004
		A,F B0,S	0.0004
		A B0*,C3,C5,G,G5*	0.0002
		A,F,X B0,C5,G,G5*,S	0.0002
		A,F,X B0,C3,C5,G,G5*	0.0002
		A,X B0*,C3,C5,G,G5*	0.0002
		A,F B0,C3,G,G5*,S,T	0.0002
		A,F,X B0,S	0.0002
		A,F,X G,G5*	0.0002

Data is based on testing 4,483 U.S. whites for G1M, A,F,X, and G3M B0,C3,C5,G,S and T. Some samples were tested for G1M Z, A2M 1 and 2 and G1/3M G5. One white was found to be A,F,G5 B0 out of 1,024 tested for both G1/3M G5 and G3M G5, indicating an approximate phenotype frequency of 0.001. In the same series, 17 A,F B0 individuals were G1/3M G5− of a frequency of 0.0166. Thus, in U.S. whites, A,F B0 appears to be about 17 times as common as A,F,G5 B0. Indicating that G1/3M G+, G3m G− is rare in whites. G5 indicates that G5 may not inhibit or inhibit poorly when on IGG3, with some reagents. B0* indicates that sometimes when G3M G+ and S+, S,T+ or C3,C5+ samples will type as B0− or only weakly inhibit.

APPENDIX 9–3.

Distribution of GM Phenotypes in U.S. Blacks*

Phenotype Observed	IGG1 A,F,G5,X IGG2 NT IGG3 NT/ND IGA2 NT	Phenotype Observed	IGG1 A,F,G5,X IGG2 NT IGG3 B0,C3,C5,G,G5,S,T IGA2 NT
A	0.4019	A B0	0.1903
A,G5	0.3039	A,G5 B0	0.1429
A,F	0.1222	A B0*,C3,C5	0.1674 (*0.0106)
A,G5*	0.0727	A,G5 B0*,C3,C5	0.0672 (*0.0030)
CA,F,G5	0.0505		
A,X,G5*	0.0259	A,G5 B0*,S	0.0567 (*0.0017)
A,F,G5*,X	0.0030	A B0*,S	0.0110 (*not detected)
F	0.0085	A B0,C3	0.0284
A,F,G5*	0.0089	A,G5 B0,C3	0.0131
A,X	0.0021	A,F B0	0.0882
A,F,X	0.0008	A,F,G5 B0	0.0360
		A B0*,C3,C5,S	0.0034
		A,G5 B0*,C3,C5,S	0.0191
		A,F B0,C3,C5	0.0271
		A,F,G5 B0,C3,C5	0.0025
		A B0,G,G5*	0.0500
		A,X B0,G,G5*	0.0187
		A B0*,C3,C5,G,G5*	0.0114
		A,G5 B0,C3,S	0.0038
		A,F B0,C3	0.0038
		A,F,G5 B0,C3	0.0008
		A,F B0,S	0.0030
		A,F,G5 B0,S	0.0110
		A B0,C3,G,G5*	0.0030
		A B0,G,G5*,S	0.0055
		A,X B0*,C3,C5,G,G5*	0.0051
		A,X B0,C3,G,G5*	0.0004
		A,X B0*,G,G5*,S	0.0004
		F B0	0.0085
		A,F B0,G,G5*	0.0089
		A,F,X B0,G,G5*	0.0030
		A G,G5*	0.0021
		A,X G,G5*	0.0013
		A,F,X B0	0.0008
		A,X B0,C3,C5	0.0013
		A,X B0	0.0008
		A,G5,X B0	0.0008
		A B0,C3,C5,G,G5*,S	0.0008

Data is based on testing 2,358 U.S. blacks for G1M A,F, and X, G1/3M G5, G3M B0,C3,C5,G,S, and T, and A2M 1 and 2. Some samples were tested for G1M Z. G5 indicates that G5 may not inhibit or may inhibit poorly when on IGG3, when G3M G with some reagents. B0* will sometimes type as B0− or only weakly inhibit B0 when G3M G+ and S+, or C3,C5+ are present, or the samples are C3,C5, or S homozygous. The numbers in parentheses indicate the phenotype frequency of the G3m B0* phenotype.

APPENDIX 9–4.

Distribution of GM Phenotypes in U.S. Mexican-Americans*

Phenotype Observed	IGG1 A,F,G5,X IGG2 NT IGG3 NT/ND IGA2 NT	Phenotype Observed	IGG1 A,F,G5,X IGG2 NT IGG3 B0,C3,C5,G,G5,S,T IGA2 NT
A	0.020	A G,G5*	0.229
A,F	0.069	A,X G,G5*	0.084
A,G5*	0.317	A,F B0,G,G5*	0.321
A,G5*,X	0.088	A B0,G,G5*	0.064
A,F,G5*	0.332	A B0*,G,G5*,S,T	0.012
A,F,G5*,X	0.040	A B0*,C3,C5,G,G5*	0.008
F	0.133	A,F,X B0,G,G5*	0.040
		F B0	0.129
		A,F B0	0.055
		A,F,G5 B0	0.009
		A,F B0,C3,C5	0.004
		A B0	0.014
		A,G5 B0	0.010
		A,F B0,S,T	0.012
		A,X B0,G,G5*	0.004
		F B0,C5,S	0.004

Data is based on testing 249 US Mexican Americans for G1M A,F, and X, G3M B0,C3,C5,G,S, and T. Some samples were tested for G1/3M G5, G2M N, and A2M 1 and 2. G5 indicates that G5 may not inhibit or may inhibit poorly when on IGG3, with G3M G with some reagents. B0* will sometimes type as B0− or only weakly inhibit B0 when G3M G+ and S,T+, or C3,C5+ are present or the samples are C3,C5 or S homozygous.

Note: Due to the small sample size, some of the possible GM phenotypes were not observed. Given the sample size, it would be safe to use 0.01 as a frequency estimate for any new phenotypes.

Acknowledgments

I would like to extend my gratitude to the many individuals who contributed to the preparation of this chapter. First and foremost are the staff of the Interlibrary Loan Section, Health Sciences Library, Emory University, who obtained many of the publications cited in this chapter. The second are the forensic scientists that have submitted the samples and case evidence for testing which has allowed the development of some insight into the testing of forensic samples. I would like to thank Drs. R. Gaensslen and H. Lee who forced me to take the time to pull all of this information together. Finally, I would like to thank my wife Nancy, who spent many hours on the word processor editing and making corrections on this manuscript.

REFERENCES

1. Grubb R: Agglutination of erythrocytes coated with 'incomplete' anti-Rh by certain rheumatoid arthritic sera and some other sera. The existence of human serum groups. *Acta Pathol Microbiol Scand* 1956; 39:195–197.

2. Planques J, Ruffie J, Ducos J: Le systems Gm en medecine legale. *Toulouse Med* 1961; 62:685–699.
3. Ducos J, Varsi M, Marty Y: Our experience regarding the identification of blood stains, in *Forensic Immunology, Medicine, Pathology and Toxicology*. International Congress Serial No. 80, Amsterdam, Excerpt Med Found, 1963.
4. Kobiela J: Investigation of blood stains in practice, in *Forensic Immunology, Medicine, Pathology and Toxicology*. International Congress Serial No. 80, Amsterdam, Excerpt Med Found, 1963; 52–53.
5. Grubb R, Laurell AB: Hereditary serological human serum groups. *Acta Pathol Microbiol Scand* 1956; 39:390–398.
6. Harboe M, Lundevall J: A new type in the Gm-system. *Acta Pathol Microbiol Scand* 1959; 45:357–370.
7. Harboe M: A new haemagglutinating substance in the Gm system, anti-Gm(b). *Acta Pathol Microbiol Scand* 1959; 47:191–198.
8. Ropartz C, Lenoir J, Rivat L: A new inheritable property of human sera: The Inv factor. *Nature* 1961; 189:586.
9. Oudin J: L' 'allotype' de certains antigenes proteidiques du serum. *C R Acad Sci* 1956; 242:2606–2608.
10. WHO Meeting on Nomenclature of Human Immunoglobulin Allotypic Markers (Rouen, France, July 1974): Review of the notation for the allotypic and related markers of human immunoglobulins. *J Immunogenet* 1976; 3:357–362.
11. Shows TB, Alper CA, Bootsma D, et al: International system for human gene nomenclature (1979). *Cytogenet Cell Genet* 1979; 25:96–116.
12. World Health Organization: Notation for genetic factors of human immunoglobulin. *Bull WHO* 1965; 33:721–724.
13. Ropartz C, Rivat L, Rousseau P-Y: Deux nouveaux facteurs dans les systemes hereditaire de gamma-globulin: Le Gm (e) and l' Inv (1), in *Proc IXth Congress of the ISBT. Mexico. Bibliotheca Haematol.*
14. Steinberg AG, Wilson J, Lanset S: A new human gamma globulin factor determined by an allele at the Inv locus. *Vox Sang* 1963; 8:51–57.
15. Steinberg AG, Wilson AJ: Studies on hereditary gamma-globulin factors: Evidence that Gm(b) in whites and negroes is not the same and that Gm-like is determined by an allele at the Gm locus. *Am J Hum Genet* 1963; 15:96–105.
16. Gold ER, Martensson L, Ropartz C, et al: Gm(f)—a determinant of human γ-globulin. *Vox Sang* 1965; 10:299–302.
17. Blanc M, Dugoujon J, Ruffie J: Hematology: A new genetic mark of human IgG3 usually associated with the Gm(21) factor found in the

Caucasian and Mongolian population. *Weekly Report From the Academie des Sciences* 1976; 283:1461.
18. van Loghem E, Blanc M, de Lange G: Human IgG3 allotypes, with special reference to a new allotype related to G3m(g) (G3m21). *J Immunogenet* 1977; 4:371–383.
19. Rivat L, Rivat C, Cook CE, et al: Gm(28) un nouvel allotype du system Gm present sur les IgG3: Interet particulier se son etude dan les populations negroides. *Ann Inst Pasteur Immunol* 1978; 129:33–45.
20. van Loghem E, de Lange G, van Leeuwen AM, et al: Human IgG allotypes co-occurring in more than one IgG subclass. *Vox Sang* 1982; 43:301–309.
21. LeFranc M-P, Helal A-N, de Lange G, et al: Gene conversion in human immunoglobulin γ locus shown by unusual location of IgG allotypes. *FEBS Lett* 1986; 196:95–102.
22. Schanfield MS, Blake E: Usefulness of immunoglobulin allotypes in sexual assault evidence (abstract). Presented at the California Association of Criminalists/Northwest Association of Criminologists Meeting, May 15, 1987.
23. Natvig JB, Michaelsen TE, Nielsen JC: IgG1 protein and corresponding IgG1 gene with the genetic Gm markers f, non a, and x. *Scand J Immunol* 1974; 3:127–131.
24. Litwin SD, Kunkel HG: A γ-globulin genetic factor related to Gm(a) but localized to a different portion of the same heavy chains. *Nature* 1966; 210:866.
25. Schanfield MS: Application of immunoglobulin heavy chain (GM, AM) and light chain (KM) allotypes in cases of disputed paternity. *Exper Clin Immunogenet* 1989; 6:112–122.
26. Kunkel HG, Yount WJ, Litwin SD: Genetically determined antigen of the ne subgroup of gamma-globulin: Detection by precipitin analysis. *Science* 1966; 154:1041–1043.
27. Steinberg AG, Stauffer R, Boyer SH: Evidence for a Gm^{ab} allele in the Gm system of American Negroes. *Nature* 1960; 188:169–170.
28. Martensson L, Kunkel HG: Distribution among the γ-globulin molecules of different genetically determined antigenic specificities of the Gm system. *J Exp Med* 1965; 122:799–811.
29. Terry WD, Fahey JL, Steinberg AG: Gm and Inv factors in subclasses of human IgG. *J Exp Med* 1965; 122:1087–1102.
30. Steinberg AG, Goldblum R: A genetic study of the antigens associated with the Gm(b) factor of human gamma-globulin. *Am J Hum Genet* 1965; 17:133–147.
31. Ropartz C, Rivat L, Rousseau P-Y: Le Gm (b) et ses problemes. *Vox Sang* 1963; 8:717–723.

32. Ruffie J, Ducos J, Varsi M: Sur les variations du pouvoir inhibiteur du facteur Gm (b) suivant le phenotype serologique Gm des sujets. *C R Acad Sci* 1964; 258:357–360.
33. van Loghem E, Martensson L: Genetic (Gm) determinants of the γ_{2c}(Vi) subclass of human IgG immunoglobulins. *Vox Sang* 1967; 13:369–392.
34. Steinberg AG, Polmar SH: The relation of the S and F fragments and the H and L chains of gamma globulin to Gm groups. *Vox Sang* 1965; 10:369–370.
35. Steinberg AG: Comparison of Gm(f) with Gm(b^2) [Gm(b^w)] and a discussion of their genetics. *Am J Hum Genet* 1965; 17:311–319.
36. Steinberg AG, Giles BD, Stauffer R: A Gm-like factor present in negroes and rare or absent in whites. Its relation to Gm*a* and Gm*x*. *Am J Hum Genet* 1961; 12:44–51.
37. Steinberg AG, Stauffer R, Dunford J: Studies on hereditary gammaglobulin factors: Detection of the factor Gm-like in a white family. *Vox Sang* 1963; 8:51–57.
38. van Loghem E, Steinberg AG: A second example of a white family in which Gm(c) occurs, and a further analysis of the first example. *Vox Sang* 1966; 11:38–44.
39. van Loghem E, Shuster J, Fudenberg HH: Gm factors in non-human primates. *Vox Sang* 1968; 14:81–94.
40. Schanfield MS, Fudenberg HH: Gm-(Ray), a new allotypic marker on human IgG_3. *Vox Sang* 1974; 26:133–140.
41. Natvig JB: Gm(g)—a 'new' gammaglobulin factor. *Nature* 1966; 211:318–319.
42. Steinberg AG, Wilson JA: Hereditary globulin factors and immune tolerance in man. *Science* 1963; 140:303–304.
43. Martensson L, van Loghem E, Matsumoto H, et al: Gm(s) and Gm(t): Genetic determinants of human γ-globulin. *Vox Sang* 1966; 11:393–418.
44. Schanfield MS: Immunoglobulin haplotypes: Tlaxcaltecans and other populations, in Crawford M (ed): *The Tlaxcaltecans:* Prehistory, Demography, Morphology and Genetics. Lawrence UK Press, 1975, pp 150–154.
45. van Loghem E, Grobbelaar BG: A new genetic marker of human IgG3 immunoglobulins. Evolutionary dissociation of Gm allotypes. *Vox Sang* 1971; 21:405–410.
46. Steinberg AG: A human antibody to Gm (26): An antigen usually present on the γ-3 chain of IgG when Gm (15) is absent. *Vox Sang* 1977; 33:266–269.
47. Vyas GN, Fudenberg HH: Am(1), the first genetic marker of human immunoglobulin A. *Proc Natl Acad Sci USA* 1969; 64:1211–1216.

48. Kunkel HG, Smith WK, Joslin FG, Natvig JB, Litwin SD: A genetic marker of the γA2 subgroup of γA immunoglobulins. *Nature* 1969; 223:1247–1248.
49. van Loghem E, Wang AC, Shuster J: A new genetic marker of human immunoglobulins determined by an allele at the a2 locus. *Vox Sang* 1973; 24:481–488.
50. Schanfield MS: Forensic applications of human immunoglobulin A (IgA) allotypes (abstract). Presented at the American Academy of Forensic Science, San Diego, Calif, February 1987.
51. Schanfield MS: *Laboratory Manual for Human Immunoglobulin Allotyping.* Atlanta, Allotype Genetic Testing, 1987, pp 8, 1–13.
52. van Logham E, Aalberse RC, Matsumoto H: A genetic marker of human IgE heavy chains, Em(1). *Vox Sang* 1984; 46:195.
53. Schanfield MS: The immunoglobulin heavy chain linkage sequence is probably G3, G1, G2, (G4), A2. *Am J Hum Genet* 1977; 29:94a.
54. Ellison J, Hood L: Linkage and sequence hemology of two human immunoglobulin heavy chain constant region genes. *Proc Natl Acad Sci USA* 1982; 79:1984–1988.
55. Migone N, Feder J, Cann H, et al: Multiple DNA fragments polymorphisms associated with immunoglobulin μ chain switch-like regions in man. *Proc Natl Acad Sci USA* 1984; 80:467–471.
56. Croce CM, Shander M, Martinis J, et al: Chromosomal location of the genes for human immunoglobulin heavy chains. *Proc Natl Acad Sci USA* 1979; 76:3416–3419.
57. Hobart MJ, Rabbits TH, Goodfellow PN, et al: Immunoglobulin heavy chain genes in humans are located on chromosome 14. *Ann Hum Genet* 1981; 45:331–335.
58. Cox DW, Markovic VD, Teshima IE: Genes for immunoglobulin heavy chains and for a_1-antitrypsin are localized to specific regions of chromosome 14q. *Nature* 1982; 297.428 430.
59. McBride OW, Hieter PA, Holis GF, et al: Chromosomal location of human kappa and lambda immunoglobulin light chain constant region genes. *J Exp Med* 1982; 155:1480–1490.
60. Erikson J, Martinis J, Croce CM: Assignment of the genes for human L chains to chromosome 22. *Nature* 1981; 294:173–175.
61. Schanfield MS: The anthropological usefulness of highly polymorphic systems: HLA and immunoglobulin allotypes, in Crawford M, Mielke J (eds): *Current Developments in Anthropological Genetics.* New York, Plenum Press, 1980, pp 65–85.
62. Johnson WE, Kohn PH, Steinberg AG: Population genetics of the human allotypes Gm, Inv and A2m. *Clin Immunol Immunopathol* 1977; 7:97–113.

63. Steinberg AG, Cook CE: *The Distribution of the Human Immunoglobulin Allotypes*. Oxford, Oxford Medical Publications, 1981.
64. Dykes DD: The use of frequency tables in parentage testing, in Silver H (ed): *Probability of Inclusion in Paternity Testing: A Technical Workshop*. Arlington, American Association of Blood Banks, 1982, pp 15–44.
65. Jones DA: Blood samples: Probability of discrimination. *J Forensic Sci Soc* 1972; 12:355–359.
66. Schanfield MS, van Loghem E: Human immunoglobulin allotypes, in Weir DM, Herzenberg LA, Blackwell C, et al (eds): *Handbook of Experimental Immunology. Vol. 3: Genetics and Molecular Immunology*. Oxford, Blackwell Scientific, 1986, pp 1–18.
67. Litwin SD, Kunkel HG: The relationship between the Inv(1) and (2) genetic antigens of Kappa human light chains. *J Immunol* 1967; 99:603–609.
68. Solomon A, McLaughlin CL, Steinberg AG: Bence-Jones proteins and light chains of immunoglobulins. III. Inv antigenicity: A genetic expression with serologic dependency on the intact kappa light chain molecule. *Immunochemistry* 1970; 7:709.
69. Pandey JP, Tuny E, Mathur S, et al: Linkage relationship between variable and constant region allotypic determinants of human immunoglobulin heavy chains. *Nature* 1980; 286:406–407.
70. Johnson MJ, Natalli AM, Cann HM, et al: Polymorphisms of a human variable heavy chain gene show linkage with constant heavy chain genes. *Proc Natl Acad Sci USA* 1984; 81:7840–7844.
71. Kronvall G: Gm(f) activity of human gamma globulin fragments. *Vox Sang* 1965; 10:303–313.
72. Tsuzukida Y, Wang CC, Putman FW: Structure of the A2m(1) allotype of human IgA-a recombinant molecule. *Proc Natl Acad Sci USA* 1979; 76:1104–1108.
73. Natvig JB, Turner MW: Localization of Gm markers to different molecular regions of the Fc fragment. *Clin Exp Immunol* 1971; 8:685–700.
74. Turner MW, Martensson L, Natvig JB, et al: Genetic (Gm) antigens associated with subfragments from the Fc fragment of human immunoglobulin G. *Nature* 1969; 221:1166.
75. Turner MW, Komvopoulos A, Bennich H, et al: Antigenic and immunological characteristics of Tryptic and Chymotryptic subfragments of the Cγ3 homology region of human immunoglobulin G. *Scand J Immunol* 1972; 1:53–62.
76. Polmar SH, Steinberg AG: The effect of the interaction of heavy and light chains of IgG on the Gm and Inv antigens. *Biochem Genet* 1967; 1:117–130.

77. Ropartz C, Lenoir J: Les antiglobulines humaines presentes dans les serum du sujects normaux. II Frequence et characteristique serologiques. *Rev Hemat* 1960; 15:40–51.
78. Speiser P: Über Antikorperbildung von Sauglingen and Kleinkindern gegen mutterliches γ2-Globulin. Ein bisher bekanntes dem Erythroblastose-mechanismus kontrares Phänomen mit anscheinend immunogenetish obligaten Charakter. *Wien Med Wochenschr* 1963; 113:966–971.
79. Wilson JA, Steinberg AG: Antibodies to gamma globulin in the serum of children and adults. *Transfusion* 1965; 5:516–524.
80. Schanfield MS: Antibody mediated perinatal disease, in Wenk R (ed): *Clinics in Laboratory Medicine: Symposium on Perinatal Diagnosis.* New York, Saunders, 1981, pp 239–263.
81. Schanfield MS, Scalise G, Economidou I, et al: International Symposium on Viral Hepatitis, Milan, December 1974: Immunogenetic factors in thalassemia and hepatitis B infection, a multicentre study. *Biol Stand* 1975; 30:257–269.
82. Fudenberg HH, Fudenberg BR: Antibody to hereditary human gamma globulin (Gm) factor resulting from maternal-fetal incompatibility. *Science* 1964; 145:170.
83. Vyas GN, Perkins HA, Fudenberg HH: Anaphylactoid transfusion reactions associated with anti-IgA. *Lancet* 1968; 2:312–313.
84. van Loghem E: Familial occurrence to isolated IgA deficiency associated with antibodies to IgA. Evidence against a structural gene defect. *Eur J Immunol* 1974; 4:57.
85. Litwin SD, Kunkel HG: Genetic factors of human gammaglobulin detected by rabbit antisera. *Transfusion* 1966; 6:140–145.
86. Tamaki Y, Shibata K, Ito S, et al: Preparation of anti-Gm sera by immunization of rabbits with protein A-fractionated normal IgG proteins from Japanese. *Jpn J Legal Med* 1979; 33:696–698.
87. Hess M, Butler R: Anti-Gm specificities in sera of Rhesus monkeys immunized with human gammaglobulin. *Vox Sang* 1962; 7:93–95.
88. Alepa FP, Steinberg AG: The production of anti-Gm reagents by Rhesus monkeys immunized with pooled human gamma globulin. *Vox Sang* 1964; 9:333–339.
89. Kolokolova GP: Determination of Gm(1) antigen in bloodstains with goat immune sera (Russian). *Sud Med Ekspert* 1980; 23:36–7.
90. Bird P, Lowe J, Jefferis R, et al: Monoclonal antibodies to an immunoglobulin allotype marker G1m (f). *Vox Sang* 1984; 47:366–372.
91. Tamaki Y, Takahashi N, Kishida T, et al: Production and characterization of monoclonal anti-G3m(g) antibody. *Jpn J Legal Med* 1984; 38:152–154.

92. Kishda T, Tamaki Y: Gm typing by enzyme linked immunosorbent assay (ELISA). *Z Rechtsmed* 1984; 93:23–27.
93. Schanfield MS, Fudenberg HH: The anthropological usefulness of the IgA allotypic markers, in Watts EB, Johnston FE, Lasker GW (eds): *Biosocial Interrelationships in Population Adaptation*. Hague, Mouton, 1975, pp 105–114.
94. Newall P: An enzyme linked immunosorbent (ELISA) for the identification of Km(3) in dried blood stains. *Can Soc Forensic Sci J* 1984; 17:99–107.
95. Salier JP, Sarvas H, Reisner HM, et al: Quantitative studies of Gm allotypes-III. Some effects of IgG aggregation in radioimmunoassays using human IgM and rabbit IgG anti-Gm antibodies. *Mol Immunol* 1979; 16:217–224.
96. Litwin SD, Balaban S: A quantitative method for determining human γG allotype antigens (Gm). II Differences in Gm gene expression for γG1 and γG3 H chains in sera. *J Immunol* 1972; 108:991–999.
97. Schanfield MS, Polesky H, Sebring B: Gm and Inv testing, in Polesky HF (ed): *Peternity Testing*. Chicago, ASCP-EMS, 1975, pp 45–54.
98. von Funfhausen G, Prokop O, Runge E: Untersuchungen uber die Temperaturamplitude von Anti-Gm-Seren. *Z Immunit Forsch* 1961; 122:158–163.
99. Baechtel FS: Secreted blood group substances: Distributions in semen and stabilities in dried semen stains. *J Forensic Sci* 1985; 30:1119–1129.
100. Kipps A: Gm and Km typing in forensic science - A methods monograph. *J Forensic Sci Soc* 1979; 19:27–47.
101. Lentner C (ed): *Geigy Scientific Tables 1. Units of Measurement, Body Fluids, Composition of the Body, Nutrition,* 8th ed. West Caldwell, Ciba-Geigy, 1981.
102. Lentner C (ed): *Geigy Scientific Tables 3. Physical Chemistry, Composition of Blood, Hematology, Somatometric Data,* 8th ed. West Caldwell, Ciba-Geigy, 1984.
103. Blake ET, Sensabough G: Genetic markers in human semen. II: Quantitation of polymorphic proteins. *J Forensic Sci* 1978; 23:717–729.
104. Mestecky J, Russell MW: IgA Subclasses. *Monogr Allergy* 1986; 19:277–301.
105. Hoste B, Brocteur J, Andre A: Indefinite storage of dried Gm and Km (Inv) antigens: (Examination of bloodstains 33 years old). *Forensic Sci* 1978; 11:109–113.
106. Shaler RC: Interpretation of Gm testing results: Two case histories. *J Forensic Sci* 1982; 27:231–235.

107. Funfhausen G, Sagan Z: Uber die Moglichkeit des Nachweises der Gruppeneigenschaft Gm in Blutspuren. *Dtsch Gesundheitswes* 1961; 16:2468–2469.
108. Funfhausen G, Sagan Z, Schramm H: Uber den Nachweis von Gm in Blutspuren. *Dtsch Z Gericht Med* 1962; 53:18–27.
109. Sagan Z, Funfhausen G: Gm group characteristics in blood stains. *Arch Immunol Therap Exp* 1965; 13:149–156.
110. Ducos J, Ruffie J, Varsi M: Mise en evidence des antigens Gm^a, Gm^b, Gm^x, dans les taches de sang sec. *Vox Sang* 1962; 7:722–731.
111. Ducos J, Ruffie J, Varsi M: Interet de la determination des antigenes Gma, Gmb, Gmx pour identifier les taches de sang. *Transfusion* 1963; 6:63–67.
112. Nielsen J, Henningsen K: Experimental studies on the determination of the Gm groups of blood stains. *J Med Sci Law* 1963; 3:49–58.
113. Gohler W, Hunger H: Der Nachweis von Gm- und InV-Eigenschaften in Blutspuren. *Z Aertzl Fortbild* 1964; 58:794–5.
114. Prokop O, Byrdy M: Das Verhalten der Gm(a)- und Gm(x)-Gruppenproteine in jahrelang aufbewahrten, getrockneten Blutproben, in Vamosi M (ed): *Aktuelle Fragen der Gerichtlichen Medizin*. Halle, Martin Luther University, 1965, pp 61–62.
115. Lenoir L, Muller PH: Determination des groupes Gm sur taches de sange. *Annales Med Legal* 1966; 46:191–193.
116. Budyakov OS: Possibility of using serum γ-globulin Gm factors in medico-legal expert examination (Russian). *Sud Med Ekspert* 1967; 10:41–45.
117. Merli S, Ronchi GV: La determinazione su macchie di sangue del sistema Inv. Indagini preliminari sull'Inv(1). *Zacchia* 1967; 42:249–255.
118. Turowska B: Grupowo swoiste uklady bialkowe i enzymatyczne w plamach krwi ludzkiej. *Folia Med CracoV* 1969; 11:411–445.
119. Gortz R: *La Recherche des Antigenes Gm Dans les Taches de Sang Pour Leur Identification Biologique et Medico-Legale,* Paris, Heermann, 1969.
120. Gortz R, Blanc M, de Boissezon JF, et al: Les cause d'erreur au cours de l'identification des facteurs Gm dans les taches de sang sec. *Arch Belg* 1970; 28:465–472.
121. Blanc M, Gortz R: Identification of a new factor Gm "Bet" in blood stains. Application in forensic Medicine. *Vox Sang* 1971; 20:263–266.
122. Blanc M, Gortz R, Ducos J: The value of Gm typing for determining the racial origin of blood stains. *J Forensic Sci* 1971; 16:176–182.
123. Blanc M, Gortz R, Ducos J: Identification d'une tache de sang minime grace a la mise en evidence des facteurs Inv (1) et Inv (2) au cours d'une expertise medico-legale. *C R Soc Biol* 1973; 167:777–780.

124. Abe T, Nakajima H: Gm and Inv allotypes of the Japanese and Gm and Inv typing in dried blood stains. *Act Crim Japon* 1974; 40:56–64.
125. Khalap S, Pereira M, Rand S: Gm and Inv grouping of bloodstains. *Med Sci Law* 1976; 16:40–43.
126. Freidrich W, Oepen I: Zum Nachweis der Gm- und Inv-Merkmale an Blut- und Sekretspuren. *Arch Kriminol* 1978; 161:41–46.
127. Khalap S, Divall GB: Gm(5) grouping of dried bloodstains. *Med Sci Law* 1979; 19:86–88.
128. Schmitter H: Die Nachweisbarkeit der Serumgruppenmerkmale Gm (1, 2, 4, 10) und InV (1) in Blutspuren in Abhangigkeit von der Proteinkonzentration in Spurenextrakt. *Arch Kriminol* 1980; 165:35–39.
129. von Mittmeyer H-J: Untersuchungen zur Feststellung von Transformationen im Gm- und Inv-System. *Beitr Gerichtl Med* 1983; 41:191–197.
130. Tahir MA: Gm(11) grouping of dried bloodstains. *J Forensic Sci* 1984; 29:1178–1182.
131. Gaensslen RE, Lee H, Pagliaro EM, et al: Evaluation of antisera for blood stain grouping II. Ss, Kell, Duffy, Kidd and Gm/Km. *J Forensic Sci* 1985; 30:655–676.
132. Broctuer J, Moureau P: Un cas d'application pratique des groupes plasmatiques Gm a l'identification de taches de sang. *Ann Med Leg* 1964; 44:315–321.
133. Ducos J, Madrange R, Varsi M, et al: Identification de taches de sang minimes par la mise en evidence des antigenes Gm^a et Gm^x. *Ann Med Leg* 1965; 45:141–144.
134. Glanc M, Gortz R, Ducos J, et al: Pouvoir inhibiteur d'un support de tache sur le serum anti-Gm(1) au cours d'une expertise medico-legale. *Med Leg* 1971; 4:15–18.
135. Newall P: Forensic applications of human immunoglobulin allotypes, in Schanfield MS (ed): *Human Immunoglobulin Allotypes*. Boca Raton, CRC Press, submitted for publication.
136. Tahir MA, Brown ML: Blood grouping in a sexual assault case: Criteria and methodology for genetic marker analysis. *J Forensic Sci* 1984; 29:660–662.
137. Dugoujon JM: Gm, Km and Am polymorphisms in non-human primates, in Schanfield MS (ed): *Human Immunoglobulin Allotypes*. Boca Raton, CRC Press, submitted for publication.
138. Klose I, Schraven J: Die Eigenschaft Gm^a in menschlichen Sperma und ihre Beziehung zur ABO-Ausscheidereigenschaft. *Dtsch Z Gerichtl Med* 1962; 52:610–614.
139. Kramer K: Untersuchungen uber das Vorkommen von Gm^a-Substanz in menschlichen Geweben und extravasalen Korperflussigkeiten. *Dtsch Z Gerichtl Med* 1963; 53:131–141.

140. Nielsen JC, Henningsen K: Note on the possibility of demonstrating the Gm-factors in semen. *Med Sci Law* 1963; 3:272–274.
141. Davie MJ, Kipps A: Km(1) [Inv(1)] typing of saliva and semen. *Vox Sang* 1976; 31:363–367.
142. Jorch G, Oepen I: Nachweis der Faktoren Gm (1,2,4,5,21) und InV(1) in menschlichen Sekreten: Speichel, Schweis, Nasensekret un Sperma. *Z Rechtsmed* 1977; 79:1–6.
143. Schwerd W, Fehrer HD: Nachweis von Gammaglobulin- und Inv-Merkmalen im Sperma und Speichel sowie von Haptoglobin im Sperma. *Z Rechtsmed* 1979; 83:185–190.
144. Schwerd W, Stock D: Nachweis von Gammaglobulin- und Inv-Merkmalen im Vaginalsekret. *Z Rechtsmed* 1983; 89:237–242.
145. Turowska B, Trela F: Gm(1) Factor in human inner ear fluid. *Forensic Sci* 1975; 6:89–90.
146. Turowska B, Trela F: Gm(2) and Inv(1) Factors in human inner ear fluid. *Forensic Sci* 1977; 9:43–44.
147. Dimo-simonin N, Brandt-Casadevall C, Gujer H-R: Gm(1,2,4,10,21) and Km(1) factors in vitreous humor. *Forensic Sci Int* 1986; 30:23–27.
148. Oepen I: AB-, Rh-, Gm-, InV- und PGM-Bestimmung an Haut, Muskulatur, Milz und Niere zur Identifizierung von Leichenteilen. *Beitr Gerichtl Med* 1973; 31:300–306.
149. Tausch D, Platt B, Gramer L, et al: The feasibility of demonstration of GM- and InV-Systems in decaying organs. *Z Rechtsmed* 1977; 79:245–256.
150. Henke J, Wirtz JH: Gm- und Km-Allotypenbestimmung aus frischen und verfaulten, wasbrigen Magenextrakten. *Z Rechtsmed* 1984; 93:187–191.
151. Henke J, Bauer L: Uber den Nachweis von Gm- und Km-Allotypen in der menschlichen Zahnpulpa. *Z Rechtsmed* 1980; 85:149–152.
152. Henke J, Bauer L, Schweitzer H: Gm-, Km- und ESD-Bestimmungen and der Zahnpulpa menschlicher Leichen. *Z Rechtsmed* 1982; 88:271–276.
153. Prokop O, Uhlenbruck G: *Human Blood and Serum Groups,* 2nd ed. New York, Wiley Interscience, 1969, pp 598–652.
154. Grubb R: *Molecular Biology, Biochemistry and Biophysics 9. The Genetic Markers of Human Immunoglobulins*. Berlin, Springer Verlag, 1970.
155. Gaensslen RE: *Sourcebook in Forensic Serology, Immunology and Biochemistry*. Washington, US Government Printing Office, 1983.

Chapter 10

The HLA System in Paternity Testing

Professor Doctor Wolfgang R. Mayr
Mia Kirnbauer

THE HLA SYSTEM

Historical Survey

The first HLA antigen (human leukocyte antigen, locus A) was described by Dausset in 1958.[1] This antigen, which is called "Mac" and is identical to HLA-A2, has been defined by antibodies found in the sera of polytransfused patients. Although Dausset claimed at the time of his discovery that such antigens might be of importance for organ transplantation, the next HLA factors were not described until 1963 when van Rood and van Leeuwen[2] discovered the antigens 4a and 4b (now HLA-Bw4 and HLA-Bw6). Since that time, knowledge of the HLA system has increased quickly, largely as a result of a remarkable international cooperation involving international histocompatibility workshops. As of December, 1986, nine such workshops had been organized. The first one took place in Durham, North Carolina, USA (1964); the second in Leiden, The Netherlands (1965); the third in Torino, Italy (1967); the fourth in Los Angeles, California, USA (1970); the fifth in Evian, France (1972); the sixth in Aarhus, Denmark (1975); the seventh in Oxford, England (1977); the eighth in Los Angeles, California, USA (1980); and the ninth in Munich, West Germany and Vienna, Austria (1984). In these workshops, several laboratories from all over the world tested various aspects of the HLA system with a common cell panel or a common serum set. The results of this work have been published in several volumes.[3–10] The enormous progress that has been made in the standardization of the definition of HLA gene products, and in the recognition of the biological and clinical significance of the HLA system issued from these international workshops.

The development of the HLA system has been facilitated also by the introduction of a highly reproducible and simple technique for the definition of the HLA antigens:

the microlymphocytotoxicity assay.[11] This test is now performed using the standard technique of the National Institute of Health (NIH).[12] First, living lymphocytes (around 2,000 cells in 1 μl medium) are incubated with specific antisera (1 μl), then rabbit serum (5 μl) is added as a complement source. If the cells carry the antigen corresponding to the antibodies in the specific serum, the complement is activated by the antigen-antibody complexes on the cell surface, and the activated complement causes damage of the cell membrane and death of the lymphocytes. If the cells do not possess the antigen, they remain alive. In order to discriminate between living and dead cells, stains such as eosin or trypan blue are added to impart color to the dead cells. Alternatively, fluorescence techniques can be used. These involve adding either fluorescein diacetate or carboxy-fluorescein diacetate to mark the living cells, or ethidium bromide or propidium iodide to color the nuclei of the dead lymphocytes.

The human sera used for the detection of HLA antigens are usually immune sera; naturally-occurring antisera with HLA specificity are extremely rare. The immunization of the sera is caused by pregnancy, blood transfusions, and/or organ transplantations. Monoclonal antibodies which are mainly produced by xenogeneic immunizations (usually by the immunization of mice with human lymphocytes and fusion of the murine immune spleen cells with murine myeloma cells) are available also for some specificities.[13,14] According to a recommendation by the World Health Organization's (WHO) committee on HLA nomenclature,[15] the following rules apply to the designation of HLA factors:

1. HLA designates the system.
2. A, B, C, etc. designate the locus or the region.
3. 1, 2, 3, etc. correspond to the specificit within one locus.
4. A "w" designates a provisional specificity which is not yet very well defined. The "w" is dropped when the specificity is confirmed; for the HLA-C factors Cw1 to Cw6, the "w" is kept although they can be considered well defined in order to avoid possible confusions with complement proteins.[16]
5. If HLA factors can be split, the supertypic (broader) specificity can be added in parentheses to the subtypic (narrower) one, e.g., A23(9) or A25(10).
6. Phenotypes are designated HLA-A1,3; B7,8; Cw7; DR2,3; etc.
7. Genotypes are designated HLA-A1, B8, Cw7, DR3/A3, B7, Cw7, DR2, etc.

Genetics

The HLA system encompasses approximately one-thousandth of the human genome.[17] It represents the major histocompatibility complex (MHC) of man and contains several closely-linked loci.[18] The chromosomal localization of the HLA system is on the short arm of chromosome 6 between the bands 6p21.31distal (HLA-D region) and 6p21.33distal (HLA-ABC region). On the short arm of chromosome 6, there are two other polymorphic loci linked with the MHC: GLO (glyoxalase I) and F13A (subunit A of the coagulation factor XIII). The third locus of phosphoglucomutase, PGM3, which also is linked with HLA, is situated on the long arm of chromosome 6 (on band 6q12). The genetic structure of this part of chromosome 6 and the distances in

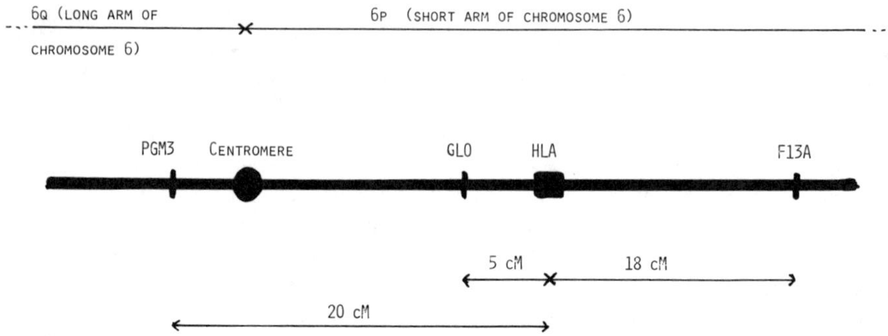

FIG 10–1.
Sequence of the polymorphic loci on chromosome 6.

centimorgans (cM) (1 cM corresponds to a crossing-over frequency of 1% and contains approximately 1 million bases of a DNA strand [1,000 kilobases]) are shown in Figure 10–1.

Within the HLA system, several loci can be distinguished according to the biochemistry and function of their gene products:

1. The HLA-ABC (class I) loci code for glycosylated polypeptides with a molecular weight of approximately 44,000 daltons. By using molecular genetics, it can be shown that the HLA complex contains around 30 such loci; several of them, however, seem to be pseudogenes which are not expressed. HLA-A, HLA-B, and HLA-C, and others are class I loci which define alloantigens and possibly differentiation antigens on T-lymphocytes. The size of the class I loci corresponds to approximately 10 kilobases (kb).
2. The HLA-D region (class II) loci code for α chains (glycosylated polypeptides of 34,000 daltons) and β chains (glycosylated polypeptides of 29,000 daltons). Each of these class II loci encompasses approximately 10 kb.
3. At least four loci define proteins of the complement system (sometimes called class III gene products): C2, C4A, C4B, and Bf (Bf = factor B of properdin = C3-proactivator). The loci C4A and/or C4B can be duplicated, and the sizes of the four loci are 18 kb, 22 kb, 16 kb, and 6 kb, respectively.
4. The structural gene for the 21-hydroxylase. A lack of this enzyme causes one form of congenital adrenal hyperplasia. There are two 21-hydroxylase loci in the HLA system: 21-OHB and 21-OHA (an inactive pseudogene). Both loci are 4 to 6 kb each.

The most probable sequence of these loci within the MHC is shown in Figure 10–2, although the order of the loci coding for the complement proteins which are located close to HLA-B (between HLA-D and HLA-B) is not absolutely certain. The distance between C2 and Bf is less than 1 kb; the distances from Bf to C4A and from C4A to C4B are also rather short (30 and 10 kb, respectively). Between C4A and 21-OHA as well as between C4B and 21-OHB, there are approximately 2 to 3 kb.[19–21] The erythrocyte alloantigens Ch^{a}[22] and Rg^{a}[23] are determinants on C4B and C4A molecules which are not produced by the red cells, but are adsorbed onto the erythrocyte surface.[24]

The alleles of each locus of the HLA system which are situated on one chromosome are usually transmitted en bloc. The combination of all these alleles carried by one chromosome is called a haplotype.

HLA-ABC

The HLA-ABC (class I) loci define polypeptides which are post-translationally glycosylated. β2-microglobulin, a non-polymorphic polypeptide coded for by chromosome 15 (locus located between bands 15q21 and 15q22), is bound to this molecule in a non-covalent form. The heterodimer of the HLA-ABC gene product and β2-microglobulin carries the serologically-defined class I antigenic epitopes; the presence of β2-microglobulin is necessary for the existence of these sites.

The class I gene product consists of an extracellular part (278 amino acids with the NH2-terminal end of the molecule), a transmembrane part (28 hydrophobic amino acids), and an intracellular part (32 amino acids with the COOH end of the molecule). The extracellular part is comprised of three domains: α1, α2, and α3 (with 90, 92, and 96 amino acids, respectively). The antigenic determinants are carried by the α1 and α2 domains. A comparison of these two domains coded for by different alleles reveals that there are several similar sequences, but also some hypervariable regions (amino acids 9–12, 40–45, 62–83, 94–97, 105–116, 137–163, and 173–194). The third domain, α3, situated close to the membrane, is rather constant, and shows similarities to IgG domains, especially to CH3.

The genomic structure of the class I genes corresponds very well to the biochemistry of the gene products, in that the three extracellular domains and the transmembrane region are coded for by four different exons and the intracellular part corresponds to three further exons. The complete amino acid sequence of several class I gene products is already known.[25–27]

The HLA-ABC gene products are present with quantitative differences on all nucleated cells of the organism. It can be demonstrated with absorption tests that the highest antigen concentration is found on spleen cells, followed by lung and liver

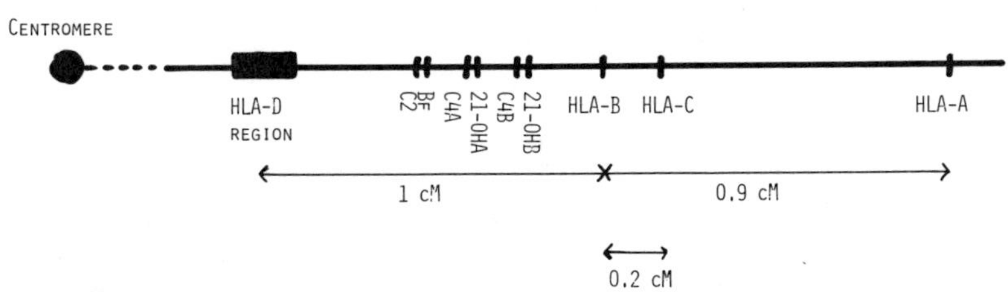

FIG 10–2.
Sequence of the loci within the HLA system.

TABLE 10–1.
Officially Recognized HLA-ABC Factors

HLA-A	HLA-B	HLA-C
A1	B5 {B51, Bw52}	Cw1
A2	B7	Cw2
A3	B8	Cw3
A9 {A23, A24}	B12 {B44, B45}	Cw4
A10 {A25, A26, Aw34, Aw66}	B13	Cw5
A11	B14 {Bw64, Bw65}	Cw6
A28 {Aw68, Aw69}	B15 {Bw62, Bw63}	Cw7
A29, A30, A31, A32, Aw33 } Aw19	B16 {B38, B39}	Cw8
Aw36	B17 {Bw57, Bw58}	
Aw43	B18	
	B21 {B49, Bw50}	
	Bw22 {Bw54, Bw55, Bw56}	
	B27	
	B35	
	B37	
	B40 {Bw60, Bw61}	
	Bw41	
	Bw42	
	Bw46	
	Bw47	
	Bw48	
	Bw53	
	Bw59	
	Bw67	
	Bw70 {Bw71, Bw72}	
	Bw73	
	Bw4	
	Bw6	

cells. Fatty tissue is not able to absorb the activity of HLA-ABC antibodies at all.[28] Reticulocytes,[29] as well as some erythrocytes,[30] carry class I antigens. The antigens of the Bennett-Goodspeed system[31] are HLA-ABC factors which can be demonstrated on red blood cells (Bg^a = HLA-B7, Bg^b = HLA-B17, Bg^c = HLA-A28).[32,33]

The loci HLA-A, -B, and -C show a remarkable multiple allelism. The specificities which are recognized officially for the moment by the WHO nomenclature committee[16] are listed in Table 10–1. From this table, it can be seen that several specificities defined by sera with broad reactivity (supertypic factors) can be split into antigens defined by sera with narrower specificity (subtypic factors). This phenomenon is due to the fact that the HLA-ABC molecules carry several antigenic determinants; for example, in addition to the A9 epitope, the gene product of A9 possesses an antigenic site specific for A23 or A24. For the formal genetics of HLA, it is possible to replace the allele governing the supertypic factor with the alleles defining the subtypic specificities.

Population and family studies demonstrate that not all alloantigens of the loci HLA-A, -B, and -C can be recognized serologically. The alleles corresponding to the unknown factors are called AX, BX, and CX. The frequencies of the officially recognized HLA-A, -B, and -C alleles in whites, Orientals, and blacks[34] are given in Table 10–2. There are many differences between the allele frequencies in the three main races, and this is very important for the anthropological investigations which can be performed easily using HLA data.[7,35]

A strong linkage disequilibrium can be seen between various HLA-ABC alleles, meaning that some haplotypes are found more frequently than expected and others more infrequently.

Many cross-reactions can be observed between the gene products of one locus.[36] These cross-reactions are either classical in that they are due to similarities in the surface structure of several gene products, or are due to the fact that identical epitopes are carried by more than one gene product. The most frequent cross-reactions for HLA-A, HLA-B, and HLA-C, respectively, are A1xAw36, A2xA28, A3xA11, A10xAw19, and A10xAw34xAw66; B5xB35xBw53, B7xB27xB40xBw22xBw42xBw73, B8xB14, B8xBw59, B12xB21, and B13xB40xBw47; and Cw4xCw6 and Cw5xCw8. The determinants Bw4 and Bw6 are epitopes which are present on many HLA-B gene products: HLA-Bw4 is carried by the gene products of B5, B13, B17, B27, B37, B38, B44, Bw47, B49, Bw53, Bw59, and Bw63, and Bw6 is present on the molecules defined by B7, B8, B14, B18, Bw22, B35, B39, B40, Bw41, Bw42, B45, Bw46, Bw48, Bw50, Bw62, Bw67, Bw70, and Bw73.[16] The cross-reactivity of human alloantisera between gene products of different loci is rare; known examples are A9xBw4, A11xBw6, and A2xB17. Such an inter-locus cross-reactivity can be found more frequently in monoclonal antibodies.[14]

Based on the alleles listed in Table 10–1 and on one X allele in HLA-A, -B, and -C, respectively, the number of possible HLA phenotypes is 191 for HLA-A, 704 for HLA-B, and 37 for HLA-C. The total number of HLA-ABC phenotypes reaches 4,975,168. The number of possible genotypes is higher than 23 million. However, these figures are obviously too small, as the X alleles are heterogeneous and as several alleles can be further subdivided by serological, cellular, or biochemical techniques (e.g., A2, A9, Aw19, B7, B8, B15, B16, B27, B44, and Cw3).

It is possible to demonstrate polymorphic and monomorphic class I antigens on subpopulations of T-lymphocytes. Several systems are involved in the genetic regulation of these factors. The loci which code for the heavier chain of these antigens are probably situated near HLA-A.[37–39]

The HLA-D Region

The alloantigens governed by the HLA-D region (class II antigens) are heterodimers of two polypeptides which are glycosylated post-translationally in a different

TABLE 10–2.
HLA-ABC Allele Frequencies in the Three Main Racial Groups (Values × 10^3)

		Whites	Orientals	Blacks
HLA-A	A1	142	10	81
	A2	289	281	175
	A3	132	15	67
	A11	63	117	19
	A23	14	1	80
	A24	103	314	48
	A25	24	0	0
	A26	32	72	45
	A28	47	21	99
	A29	29	4	49
	A30	35	23	110
	A31	29	52	16
	A32	39	4	23
	Aw33	14	60	39
	Aw34	1	3	51
	Aw36	1	1	32
	Aw43	0	0	13
	Aw66	2	5	3
	AX	4	17	50
HLA-B	B7	115	47	121
	B8	96	2	55
	B13	29	38	16
	B18	55	3	42
	B27	34	16	19
	B35	105	102	71
	B37	16	6	13
	B38	25	7	16
	B39	20	4	0
	Bw41	9	1	23
	Bw42	2	5	58
	B44	123	60	77
	B45	4	1	23
	Bw46	1	36	0
	Bw47	2	4	0
	Bw48	0	16	0
	B49	18	3	23
	Bw50	11	3	6
	B51	62	78	19
	Bw52	20	73	6
	Bw53	5	3	67
	Bw54	1	67	0
	Bw55	16	21	0
	Bw56	11	15	3

	Bw57	29	7	29
	Bw58	18	19	107
	Bw59	0	12	0
	Bw60	38	65	23
	Bw61	21	117	15
	Bw62	61	96	26
	Bw63	7	0	19
	Bw64	11	0	13
	Bw65	26	2	16
	Bw67	0	1	0
	Bw71	1	4	8
	Bw72	3	5	71
	Bw73	1	2	0
	BX	4	59	15
HLA-C	Cw1	33	163	10
	Cw2	41	10	119
	Cw3	126	273	83
	Cw4	116	53	140
	Cw5	69	6	30
	Cw6	86	38	129
	Cw7	243	121	241
	Cw8	37	3	35
	CX	249	333	213

way. The α chain has a molecular weight of 33,000 daltons and possesses two carbohydrates, and the β chain has a molecular weight of 29,000 daltons and possesses only one carbohydrate. Both chains are non-covalently linked and show a similar structure: an extracellular part with two domains (85–95 and 107 amino acids, respectively), a transmembrane region (23 hydrophobic amino acids), and an intracellular part (8–15 amino acids). The alloantigenic epitopes are situated on the outer domain of the extracellular part. The second domain being close to the membrane shows almost no variability and is similar to the α3 domain of the class I heavy chains and to the CH3 domain of IgG1. The genomic structure corresponds well with the biochemistry in that the two extracellular domains are coded for by two exons.[40–46]

The HLA-D region can be subdivided into at least three subregions: HLA-DR, HLA-DQ, and HLA-DP. The sizes of the three subregions are approximately 205 kb, 100 kb, and 90 kb, respectively. Within these three subregions there are several loci governing the α and β chains; the most probable structure is shown in Figure 10–3.

The HLA-DR alloantigens are situated on molecules consisting of the gene products of the DRα and the DR1β locus. No polymorphism can be found on the DRα chain. Therefore, the polymorphic alloantigens must reside on the DR1β chain. Hypervariable regions can be observed on amino acid positions 9–13, 25–33, and 70–78. The HLA-DR alloantigens are not present on all cells of the organism. They can

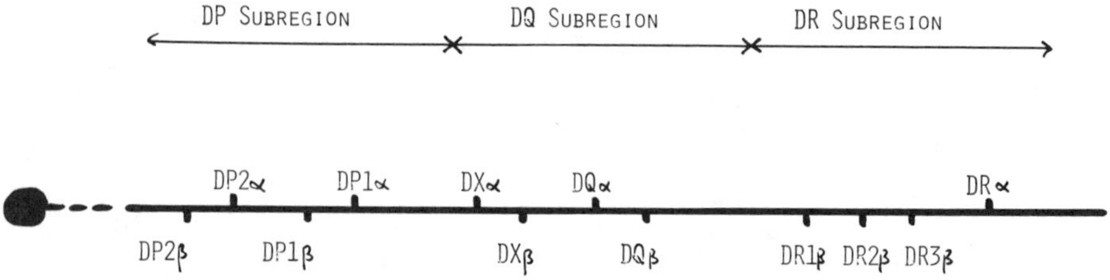

FIG 10–3.
Loci of the HLA-D region.

be detected on B-lymphocytes, activated T-cells, monocytes, macrophages, and some endothelial and epithelial cells.[47] In the HLA-DR system, there is also a remarkable multiple allelism with the factors listed in Table 10–3.[16] HLA-DR5 can be split in DRw11 and DRw12, and DRw6 can be split into DRw13 and DRw14. For the moment, not all DR gene products are detectable; the gene coding for the "unknown" specificities is called DRX. The HLA-DR allele frequencies in the three main racial groups are given in Table 10–4.[34]

The factors which were named MT2 and MT3 previously are now designated DRw52 and DRw53. They are probably alloantigens on molecules built up by the gene products of DRα and DR2β; however, they might be present on other DR molecules. Due to a very strong linkage disequilibrium, DRw52 includes DR3, DR5, DRw6, and DRw8, and DRw53 includes DR4, DR7, and DRw9. DR3β is probably a pseudogene without function. The following cross-reactions can be found between the HLA-DR gene products: DR1xDRw10, DR2xDRw6, DR3xDRw6, DR4xDR7xDRw9, DR5xDRw8.

With the DR specificities listed in Table 10–3 and one X allele, the number of DR phenotypes can be computed to be 79. This value is also an underestimation, however, as factors such as DR2 and DR4 can be split into subtypic specificities. Considering the officially recognized HLA-A, -B, -C, and -DR specificities, the total

TABLE 10–3.
Officially Recognized HLA-DR Factors

DR1	
DR2	
DR3	
DR4	
DR5	DRw11
	DRw12
DRw6	DRw13
	DRw14
DR7	
DRw8	
DRw9	
DRw10	
DRw52	
DRw53	

TABLE 10–4.
HLA-DR Allele Frequencies in the Three Main Racial Groups (Values × 10^3)

HLA-DR	Whites	Orientals	Blacks
DR1	95	50	51
DR2	158	151	151
DR3	120	18	149
DR4	127	218	76
DR7	120	29	132
DRw8	30	73	8
DRw9	8	115	15
DRw10	8	5	23
DRw11	123	40	165
DRw12	20	72	34
DRw13	54	29	38
DRw14	58	68	107
DRX	79	132	51

number of phenotypes amounts to 393,038,272, and the number of possible genotypes is approximately 4 x 10^9. The HLA system, therefore, shows a polymorphism which is not reached by any of the other known human markers.

A linkage disequilibrium exists between the HLA-DR and -A, -B, and -C alleles. The most significant positive linkage disequilibria in the three main racial groups are shown in Table 10–5.[36, 48, 49] This linkage disequilibrium also may include other loci of the MHC, such as C2, C4A, C4B, or Bf.[50]

In the HLA-DQ subregion, there are four loci: DQα, DQβ, DXα, and DXβ. The DQ alloantigens (previously designated MB, DC, or DS) consist of a DQα and a DQβ chain. They are present on B-lymphocytes, on subpopulations of monocytes, and on endothelial cells.[47] The α and β chains of the DQ genes are polymorphic, the α chains having hypervariable regions at amino acid positions 45–56; and the β chains at 26–30, 46–57, 66–77, and 84–90. It is not yet clear whether the serologically-defined alloantigenic epitopes are situated on the α or β chain. Thus far, three factors are known: DQw1, DQw2, and DQw3.[16] These have allele frequencies of 0.32, 0.18, and 0.23, respectively, in whites.[34] DQw3 can be split into two subtypic factors by anti-TA10 sera. The polymorphism of the DQ gene products is further increased by the possibility of trans-complementation, i.e., the production of molecules built up by the DQα chain of one haplotype and the DQβ chain of the other one.[51]

The DX loci (DXα and DXβ) are also polymorphic and probably represent intact genes rather than pseudogenes; for the moment, however, the gene products of these two loci are not known. A strong linkage disequilibrium exists between DR1β and the locus defining the DQ polymorphism. DQw1 is associated with DR1, DR2, and DRw6; DQw2 is associated with DR3 and DR7, and DQw3 is associated with DR4 and DR5. No linkage disequilibrium can be found between DQ and DX; as the physical distance on the chromosome between DQα and DXβ is rather small, a recombination hot spot must exist between these two loci.

The HLA-DP subregion also contains four loci. The HLA-DP specificities (previ-

TABLE 10–5.
Significant Positive Linkage Disequilibria in HLA-A, B, C, DR

1. Whites
1.1. Two-locus haplotypes

A/B	A/C	A/DR	B/C	B/DR	C/DR
A1,B8	Aw33,Cw8	A1,DR3	B35,Cw4	B8,DR3	Cw6,DR7
A30,B13	A1,Cw7	A29,DR7	Bw65,Cw8	B7,DR2	Cw7,DR3
A25,B18	A11,Cw4	A30,DR7	Bw62,Cw3	B13,DR7	Cw4,DR1
A3,B7	A30,Cw6	A3,DR2	B27,Cw2	Bw57,DR7	Cw7,DR2
A26,B38	A1,Cw6	A3,DR1	Bw64,Cw8	B35,DR1	Cw6,DRw10
Aw33,Bw65	A2,Cw5	Aw33,DR1	B44,Cw5	Bw65,DR1	Cw5,DR4
A29,B44	A32,Cw2	A23,DR7	Bw57,Cw6	Bw64,DR7	Cw8,DR1
A1,Bw57	A23,Cw4		B13,Cw6	B44,DR7	Cw8,DR7
A11,Bw52	A2,Cw3		B7,Cw7	B18,DRw11	
A11,B35	A3,Cw7		Bw60,Cw3	B44,DR4	
A11,Bw55	A3,Cw4		Bw56,Cw1	B51,DRw11	
Aw33,Bw58			B8,Cw7	Bw52,DR2	
A26,Bw41			B37,Cw6	B38,DRw14	
A23,B49			Bw61,Cw2	Bw61,DRw11	
A1,B37			B27,Cw1	Bw62,DR4	
A3,B35			Bw50,Cw6	Bw63,DRw13	
A28,Bw53			Bw55,Cw3	Bw50,DR7	
A31,B51			B49,Cw7	Bw47,DR7	
A2,Bw60			B45,Cw6		
A2,B44			B51,Cw1		
A2,Bw62			Bw53,Cw4		
A32,Bw61			B18,Cw5		
A23,B44			Bw47,Cw6		
A32,Bw64					
A3,Bw47					

1.2. Three-locus haplotypes

A/B/C	A/B/DR
A23,B44,Cw4	A1,B8,DR3
Aw33,Bw65,Cw8	A2,Bw52,DR2
A3,B35,Cw4	A29,B44,DR7
A1,B8,Cw7	A2,Bw41,DR3
A2,B27,Cw2	A25,B18,DR2
A30,B13,Cw6	A30,B18,DR3
A25,B18,CX	A23,B44,DR7
A3,B7,Cw7	
A26,B38,CX	
A11,Bw55,Cw3	
A2,B44,Cw5	
A1,Bw57,Cw6	
A2,Bw56,Cw1	
A11,B35,Cw4	
A29,B44,CX	

1.3 Four-locus haplotypes A/B/C/DR
A1,B8,Cw7,DR3
A3,B7,Cw7,DR2
A2,B44,Cw5,DR4
A2,Bw62,Cw3,DR4
A24,B35,Cw4,DR1
A23,B44,Cw4,DR7
A2,Bw56,Cw1,DR1

2. Orientals: Two-locus haplotypes

A/B	A/C	A/DR	B/C	B/DR	C/DR
Aw33,B44	A30,Cw6	Aw33,DRw13	Bw54,Cw1	B7,DR1	Cw6,DR7
A30,B13	A26,Cw3	Aw33,DRw14	B13,Cw6	B44,DRw13	Cw7,DR1
Aw33,Bw58	A2,Cw1	Aw33,DR3	B7,Cw7	Bw52,DR2	Cw1,DR4
A24,Bw52			Bw46,Cw1	B13,DR7	Cw4,DR4
A2,Bw46			B39,Cw7	B44,DRw14	Cw3,DR3
A11,Bw55			B35,Cw4	Bw54,DR4	
A11,Bw62			B35,Cw3	Bw61,DRw9	
Aw31,B51			Bw61,Cw3	Bw59,DR4	
A3,B7			Bw42,Cw7	Bw46,DRw8	
			Bw55,Cw1	B27,DRw12	
			Bw62,Cw4	B51,DRw8	
			B38,Cw7	B35,DR4	
			Bw59,Cw1		
			Bw58,Cw3		
			Bw56,Cw1		
			Bw62,Cw3		

3. Blacks: Two-locus haplotypes

A/B	A/C	A/DR	B/C	B/DR	C/DR
A1,B8	Aw36,Cw4		Bw58,Cw6	Bw42,DR3	
Aw36,Bw53	A28,Cw8		Bw53,Cw4	Bw64,DR7	
A30,Bw42	A11,Cw4		Bw72,Cw2	B8,DR3	
A11,B35			B35,Cw4	B13,DR7	
			Bw62,Cw3	B7,DR2	
			Bw60,Cw3		
			B7,Cw7		
			Bw57,Cw6		
			B49,Cw7		
			B27,Cw2		
			B8,Cw7		
			B44,Cw5		

ously named SB)[52] are built up by the complex of a DP1α and a DP1β chain. DP1α shows no polymorphism; DP2α and DP2β are probably pseudogenes. For the time being, six HLA-DP specificities are known (DPw1–DPw6).[16] They are routinely defined by a cellular method (PLT, or primed lymphocyte typing), but some DP factors may be detectable by serology. Another recombination hot spot probably exists between DP1β and DXβ.

The HLA-Dw specificities recognized by the mixed lymphocyte culture (MLC)[53] can be arranged in another series. It is probable that they are not coded for by other loci of the HLA-D region, but that the reactivity in the MLC is caused by differences within the whole HLA-D region. In this respect, HLA-DR differences seem to induce the highest stimulation, but differences in other factors also produce a positive MLC. Thus far, 19 HLA-Dw specificities are known.[16] A strong linkage disequilibrium exists between HLA-Dw and HLA-DR; the Dw factors are included mostly in the DR specificities.

Biological Function

The main role of the molecules governed by the MLC is to function in the immune response: individuals lacking either the expression of HLA-ABC[54] or HLA-D[55,56] alloantigens show, in general, a severe immunodeficiency. The involvement of HLA gene products in the immune response[57] has been demonstrated in many in vitro experiments which showed clearly that the class I antigens are necessary for the activity of cytotoxic effector cells, while the class II antigens play an important role in the cooperation between antigen-presenting cells and T-helper lymphocytes. It is probable that some antigens are more effective than others with respect to these immunological reactions; this possibility would explain several associations between HLA and diseases and would give some indication as to how selective forces could act on the HLA system.[36]

When different individuals possess different HLA molecules, these subjects have different blind spots in their immunological defense mechanisms. The species as a whole has a better chance of survival if these molecules exhibit a pronounced polymorphism, as some individuals of the species will show an effective immune response against any pathogen. The rapid change of the immunological make-up of the pathogens and the selective pressure caused by them enables the production of such an enormous polymorphism.[58]

The easiest explanation for the existence of the linkage disequilibrium is the assumption that selective forces are acting on some haplotypes. Without such selection, the linkage disequilibrium between two alleles should decrease with a rate of $1 - r$ (r = recombination frequency) per generation. That means that it should be reduced to 20% in 200 generations (4,000 years). Other causes for the existence of the linkage disequilibrium, though not very probable, could be recent mixtures of populations, genetic drift, or inbreeding.[59]

THE HLA SYSTEM IN PATERNITY TESTING

Bases of Its Application

In order to use a genetic system for solving questions of disputed paternity, the following criteria must be fulfilled: (1) the mode of inheritance must be known with certainty; (2) the characteristics must be developed at birth or soon thereafter; (3) the characteristics must not depend on the environment; and (4) the techniques for the detection of the characteristics must be simple and reproducible.

All of these criteria apply to the HLA system. The alloantigens coded for HLA-A, -B, -C, -DR, and -DQ are transmitted via closely-linked loci on the short arm of chromosome 6 and show a remarkable multiple allelism. The single factors have an autosomal-dominant pattern of inheritance. The HLA-ABC alloantigens already have been detected on 6 week-old embryos and they, as well as the HLA-D region factors, are fully expressed at birth.[60,61] In contrast to the characteristics of erythrocytes or plasma, transfused lymphocytes are of no importance for the definition of the HLA type of an individual (the transfusion of 6 liters of fresh whole blood during cardiac surgery produced only slight changes in the HLA reactions in 3 out of 25 cases and these alterations could be observed for only a very short period of time).[62]

Alterations of the HLA phenotype could be observed in very few cases. It was seen after therapeutic irradiation with 60Co,[63] in patients with acute myeloid leukemia[64] or severe combined immunodeficiencies,[65,66] and in patients treated with some antibiotics.[67,68] Such possible changes can be recognized easily through extensive interrogation of the individuals to be tested. Furthermore, these cases are sufficiently rare so as not to interfere with paternity testing.

Bone marrow transplantation may provide another cause of modification of the HLA phenotype. If the donor is a HLA-different individual, the phenotype of the recipient will be changed after engraftment of the donor's bone marrow. This possibility can be excluded also by interrogating the propositus.

Masking of the alloantigens on the lymphocytes of a newborn child by IgG antibodies of the mother which are able to cross the placenta could present a further difficulty.[69] If such antisera are only blocking and not complement fixing, they could mask paternal antigens. However, because paternity testing usually is not performed with the blood of a newborn, this is not a practical difficulty. In addition, it can be avoided by incubating the sensitized lymphocytes of the child for approximately 12 hours at 37°C. During this incubation, the antigen-antibody complexes are shed from the cell surface and replaced by native alloantigens which can be detected in the usual microlymphocytotoxicity assay.

The reproducibility of the microlymphocytotoxicity assay is excellent.[70] Furthermore, each specificity should be detected by at least three sera originating from different donors in order to increase the safety of the test (see section on "Sources of Error"). The excellent standardization of the procedure for definition of the alloantigens has been demonstrated in the nine international histocompatibility workshops and in many regional and national workshops.

Exclusions

Based on the formal genetics of the HLA system, two different classes of exclusion are possible[71]:

1. The child may possess an HLA alloantigen which is not present in the mother or in the putative father (e.g., mother HLA-A1 negative, child HLA-A1 positive, putative father HLA-A1 negative). This class of exclusion is based on the dominant pattern of inheritance of the HLA alloantigens.
2. The child may possess two HLA alloantigens in one locus that are lacked by the putative father, or vice versa (e.g., child HLA-A1,2 and putative father HLA-A3,23). This class of exclusion is based on the allelism of the genes of the loci HLA-A, -B, -C, -DR, and -DQ.

A third constellation which could lead to a possible exclusion is one in which the child inherited from his true father two genes which the putative father does not carry on one haplotype (e.g., mother A1,B8,Cw7/A3,B35,Cw3; child A1,B8,Cw7/A2,B44,Cw5; putative father A2,B13,Cw6/A24,B44,Cw5). For this situation, the genotype of the putative father has to be fixed by family investigations. Because of the relatively high frequency of crossing-over between HLA-A and -B (0.9%), such constellations must be evaluated with extreme caution.

The total chance of exclusion for HLA-A,B,C amounts to 96%; that means that an average of 96 out of 100 non-fathers can be excluded by HLA-A,B,C typing. This figure is increased to 98% by taking into account the gene products of the loci HLA-DR and -DQ. The use of the systems ABO, MNSs, P, Rh, Lu, K, Se, Fy, Jk, Xg, Gm, Km, acP1, PGM1, AK1, ADA, 6-PGD, EsD, GLO, GPT, PGP, Hp, Gc, C3, Bf, Tf, and Pi yields a 98.6% chance of exclusion. The use of HLA-A,B,C, raises this figure to 99.94% and the use of HLA-A,B,C,DR raises it to 99.97%.[72]

The conclusive force of HLA exclusions based on the dominant inheritance of the single HLA factors becomes very high as the number of family investigations showing no deviation from the postulated mode of transmission exceeds 10,000 informative matings. Concerning the exclusions based on allelism, some problems can arise, as "triplets" exist in HLA-C and HLA-DR. Cw1 and Cw3 are frequently transmitted by one haplotype in Oriental populations[73] and two cases have been reported in which DR1 and DR2 are coded for by one haplotype.[74,75]

Biostatistics

A method for computing the plausibility of paternity according to Essen-Möller which takes into account the linkage disequilibrium within the HLA system has been published.[76] The values obtained can be expressed as W or as PI and can be added to the values obtained by testing other marker systems. This method can be used for cases without a mother[77] and, in principle, for all possible constellations. An algorithm for the calculation of the plausibility of paternity has been described also.[78] Furthermore, formulae for the calculation of the chance of paternity exclusion have been presented[79] and a computer program is also available.[80]

Practical Application

Beginning in 1971, the HLA system (class I antigens) began to be used routinely for affiliation cases in many countries[81–89] (Bartova, personal communication; Hiller, personal communication; Curtoni, personal communication). The results are excellent, especially in problematic cases such as those with two men not excluded in non-HLA systems, those without the mother, those in which only relatives of the putative father could be tested, and those involving possible superfecundations[90–92] or the typing of fetal fibroblasts.[93]

The analysis of 1,130 affiliation lawsuits from Austria and East Germany,[94] for instance, showed that the inclusion of HLA-A,B,C could reduce the number of problematic situations from 66% to 9% in 249 cases with two accused men. In this material, the frequency of exclusions is 4% in non-HLA systems without exclusion in HLA-A,B,C. This figure corresponds well to the calculated chance of paternity exclusion of 96% for HLA-A,B,C.

The inclusion of HLA-A,B,C also has a strong effect on the biostatistical computations. In the above-mentioned material, the plausibility of paternity according to Essen-Möller reached a W value of 99.8% without HLA in only 9% of 832 cases, while with HLA a W value greater than 99.8% was observed in 56% of these cases. A similar increase could be seen in the chance of paternity exclusion. The chance of exclusion was greater than 99% without HLA in 13% of 589 cases, and with HLA in 79% of these cases.

The alloantigens coded for by the HLA-D region are included in paternity testing in a few laboratories.[95,96] Due to the strong linkage disequilibrium between the alleles of the HLA-B and HLA-D regions, the information given by DR and DQ is not very high. In a few cases, however, an exclusion could be observed only in HLA-DR/DQ and not in HLA-A,B,C.

For the practice of paternity testing, the following sequence of tests should be followed: ABO, MNSs, Rh, HLA, and then all other markers. The investigation of ABO, MNSs, and Rh, which are very simple from a technical point of view (only one marker, s, detected by indirect anti-humanglobulin test) and can be performed immediately after the bleeding, gives a 61% chance of exclusion. If no exclusion is made by these means, the exclusion chance can be increased to 98.5% by HLA typing. After this test, if the putative father still is not excluded, all other systems can be analyzed. Proceeding by this means takes into account the high chance of paternity exclusion of HLA and the relatively short lifespan of the lymphocytes used for the determination of HLA factors, and thereby avoids multiple bleedings of the involved individuals and provides all the necessary information in only one series of tests.[97]

Sources of Error

The errors in HLA typing arise in connection with the various reagents used in the microlymphocytotoxicity assay (lymphocytes, antisera, rabbit complement, and other reagents), but can be also due to atypically expressed HLA alloantigens (for an extensive discussion and further references, see reference 97).

Lymphocytes.—For the reading of the results in the microlymphocytotoxicity assay, it is necessary to obtain a cell suspension consisting mainly of lymphocytes. Contaminating granulocytes are usually killed by the rabbit serum and could be mistaken for dead lymphocytes by unexperienced workers. The presence of thrombocytes can cause false-negative reactions as the HLA-ABC alloantigens on the platelet surface are able to absorb HLA-ABC antibodies. For the determination of HLA-D region alloantigens with enriched B-lymphocytes, a contamination with T-cells brings about weak reactions, because the T-cells do not carry these antigens.

Another important factor in the lymphocytotoxicity assay is the viability of the cells. If old blood samples are tested, it is possible to already have a high percentage of killed cells in the negative control. In such cases, the use of fluorescent methods is advised, as only the living cells are able to metabolize fluorescin-diacetate to fluorescin. Therefore, only living cells are seen. The dead cells, however, can absorb HLA antibodies so that false-negative results can occur if the antisera are weak. Living cells can be kept alive in special media[98] for approximately 7 to 10 days; if cells have to be stored for a longer period of time, they have to be frozen at a rate of −1°C/minute and kept in liquid nitrogen.

Problems can arise if the blood samples are taken by another investigator and shipped by mail. If the samples contain heparin as an anticoagulant, the reactions can be much weaker than usual. The best way to send samples for HLA typing at another institution is to separate the lymphocytes at the place where the blood is taken and then ship the cells resuspended in a culture medium such as Park-Terasaki medium.[98]

Another factor influencing the lymphocytotoxicity assay for the detection of HLA-ABC is the medium in which the cells are resuspended. The use of human serum in these media should be avoided, as human serum contains soluble HLA-ABC antigens which can absorb HLA-ABC antibodies. In our experience, there is no major difference between buffered Hanks solution and culture media with fetal calf serum for resuspending the lymphocytes.

Antisera.—The sera used for HLA typing should be specific and strong. It is very difficult to find such anti-HLA sera, as cross-reactivity is very commonly observed in the HLA system (see sections on "HLA-ABC" and "The HLA-D Region"). This cross-reactivity coupled with the fact that gene-dosage and synergistic effects exist in the HLA system can cause false-positive results.[97] An anti–HLA-A28 serum containing a weak anti-A2, for example, is able to lyse the lymphocytes of a homozygous HLA-A2 individual (gene-dosage). Cells with phenotypes such as B27,w22 can be killed by an anti-B7 serum containing weak cross-reacting anti-B27 and anti-Bw22 antibodies which are not able to lyse the cells of individuals being B27+,Bw22− or B27−,Bw22+ (synergism).

The sera used for the detection of HLA-DR/DQ frequently contain antibodies against HLA-ABC factors; these must be removed by absorption with platelets. If this absorption is not sufficient, the remaining HLA-ABC antibodies can cause false-positive reactions.

A further pitfall is the presence of cytotoxic non-HLA antibodies in the HLA typing sera. Such antisera can be directed against Le^a or against antigens of the ABO blood group system. These antibodies, however, can easily be removed by absorption with erythrocytes.

As a rule, in order to overcome the difficulties caused by the antisera, the HLA alloantigens should be defined by at least three different antisera coming from different donors; the alloantigens should only be considered present if all antisera show a clear-cut positive reaction. Furthermore, before using the sera in affiliation cases, they should be tested against a large panel of cells with known HLA alloantigens and against several informative families. These stringent conditions are absolutely necessary in order to avoid incorrect HLA typings which may lead to false conclusions in affiliation cases.

Rabbit Complement.—For the lymphocytotoxicity assay, the quantity of complement as measured by the lysis of sensitized sheep red blood cells is probably less important than the presence of thermolabile IgM xenoantibodies against species-specific determinants on human lymphocytes.[99] These xenoantibodies are not yet defined sufficiently, so that it is not possible to standardize the rabbit sera to be used in the lymphocytotoxicity test. The best way to obtain a rabbit serum which shows a minimal variability between lots is to pool a large amount of serum (approximately 5 liters). The pool is divided into aliquots and stored at a maximum temperature of −80°C in order to prevent a deterioration of the xenoantibodies and some complement components (the optimal storage is in liquid nitrogen). The rabbit serum should not have been frozen more than once; for optimal reactivity, it should be thawed just before use.

Another factor influencing the reactivity of the rabbit complement is temperature, which should be between 20°C and 24°C. Temperatures higher or lower than this can produce false-negative or false-positive results. The incubation times during the test should not be changed in order to avoid incorrect reactions.

Other Reagents.—The mineral oil which is used to prevent evaporation of the small serum volume (1 μl) can be cytotoxic or anticomplementary. Because the action of the complement is pH-dependent, the pH of the reaction medium should be 7.4. This pH can be reached by adding a buffer in the medium used for the resuspension of the lymphocytes. If the antisera or the rabbit complement have been stored in dry ice, the pH of these reagents should be brought back to 7.4. Furthermore, the formaldehyde used for the fixation of the cells after the end of the test should have a pH of 7.4. If the pH is lower than 7.0, the reading of the results is very difficult in that it may become impossible to differentiate between living and dead cells.

Other Sources of Error.—Other causes of false-negative and false-positive results (see also section on "The HLA System in Paternity Testing—Bases of Its Application") are the weak expression of HLA antigens, especially factors governed by HLA-C, which can vary with time and within one family[100–104]; the in vitro action of drugs[105–107]; and blocking antibodies. In addition to these problems, errors also can be caused by the lack of expression of HLA alloantigens due to chimerism[108] or suppressor genes.[109,110]

Conclusions

The alloantigens coded for by the HLA system can be defined without difficulty and, because of their known mode of inheritance, their expression at birth, and the fact that the HLA phenotype reflects the genotype only, they can be used in affiliation cases. If the potential pitfalls associated with this technology are kept in mind, the possibility of errors occurring in experienced laboratories is minimal. Due to its prodigious polymorphism, the HLA is the most efficient marker system which can be included in routine investigations. The relatively simple method used for detection of the HLA alloantigens assures that this system will keep its enormous importance for paternity testing, even when other powerful markers, such as DNA polymorphisms, also come into use for this purpose.

REFERENCES

1. Dausset J: Iso-leuco-anticorps. *Acta Haematol* 1958; 20:156–166.
2. Rood JJv, Leeuwen Av: Leukocyte grouping. A method and its application. *J Clin Invest* 1963; 42:1382–1390.
3. Amos DB, Rood JJv (eds): *Histocompatibility Testing 1965*. Copenhagen, Munksgaard, 1965.
4. Curtoni ES, Mattiuz PL, Tosi RM (eds): *Histocompatibility Testing 1967*. Copenhagen, Munksgaard, 1967.
5. Terasaki PI (ed): *Histocompatibility Testing 1970*. Copenhagen, Munksgaard, 1970.
6. Dausset J, Colombani J (eds): *Histocompatibility Testing 1972*. Copenhagen, Munksgaard, 1973.
7. Kissmeyer-Nielsen F (ed): *Histocompatibility Testing 1975*. Copenhagen, Munksgaard, 1975.
8. Bodmer WF, Batchelor JR, Bodmer JG, et al (eds): *Histocompatibility Testing 1977*. Copenhagen, Munkgsaard, 1978.
9. Terasaki PI (ed): *Histocompatibility Testing 1980*. Los Angeles, UCLA Tissue Typing Laboratory, 1980.
10. Albert ED, Baur MP, Mayr WR (eds): *Histocompatibility Testing 1984*. Heidelberg, Springer, 1984.
11. Gorer PA, O'Gorman P: The cytotoxic activity of isoantibodies in mice. *Transplant Bull* 1956; 3:142–143.
12. Brand DL, Ray JG Jr, Hare DB, et al: Preliminary trials toward standardization of leukocyte typing, in Terasaki PI (ed): *Histocompatibility Testing 1970*. Copenhagen, Munksgaard, 1970, pp 357–367.
13. Bodmer JG, Kennedy LJ, Aizawa M, et al: HLA-D region monoclonal antibodies, in Albert ED, Baur MP, Mayr WR (eds): *Histocompatibility Testing 1984*. Heidelberg, Springer, 1984, pp 217–236.

14. Fauchet R, Bodmer JG, Kennedy LJ, et al: HLA-ABC monoclonal antibodies, in Albert ED, Baur MP, Mayr WR (eds): *Histocompatibility Testing 1984*. Heidelberg, Springer, 1984, pp 211–217.
15. Amos DB, Batchelor R, Bodmer WF, et al: Nomenclature for factors of the HLA system, in Kissmeyer-Nielsen F (ed): *Histocompatibility Testing 1975*. Copenhagen, Munksgaard, 1975, pp 5–11.
16. Bodmer WF, Albert E, Bodmer JG, et al: Nomenclature for factors of the HLA system 1984, in Albert ED, Baur MP, Mayr WR (eds): *Histocompatibility Testing 1984*. Heidelberg, Springer, 1984, pp 4–8.
17. Bodmer WF, Bodmer JG: Evolution and function of the HLA system. *Br Med Bull* 1978; 34:309–316.
18. Lamm LU, Olaisen B: Report of the committee on the genetic constitution of chromosomes 5 and 6. *Cytogenet Cell Genet* 1985; 40:128–155.
19. Campbell RD, Bentley DR: The structure and genetics of the C2 and factor B genes. *Immunol Rev* 1985; 87:19–37.
20. Carroll MC, Belt KT, Palsdottir A, et al: Molecular genetics of the fourth component of human complement and steroid 21-hydroxylase. *Immunol Rev* 1985; 87:39–60.
21. White PC, New MI, Dupont B: Adrenal 21-hydroxylase cytochrome P-450 genes within the MHC class III region. *Immunol Rev* 1985; 87:123–150.
22. Harris JP, Tegoli J, Swanson J, et al: A nebulous antibody responsible for cross-matching difficulties (Chido). *Vox Sang* 1967; 12:140–142.
23. Longster G, Giles CM: A new antibody specificity, anti-Rg[a], reacting with a red cell and serum antigen. *Vox Sang* 1976; 30:175–180.
24. O'Neill GJ, Yang SY, Tegoli J, et al: Chido and Rodgers blood groups are distinct antigenic components of human complement C4. *Nature* 1978; 273:668–670.
25. Jordan BR, Caillol D, Damotte M, et al: HLA class I genes: From structure to expression, serology and function. *Immunol Rev* 1985; 84:73–92.
26. Orr HT: The major histocompatibility complex: Analysis at the protein and DNA levels, in Parham P, Strominger J (eds): *Histocompatibility Antigens*. London, Chapman & Hall, 1982, pp 1–51.
27. Srivastava R, Duceman BW, Biro PA, et al: Molecular organization of the class I genes of human major histocompatibility complex. *Immunol Rev* 1985; 84:93–121.
28. Berah M, Hors J, Dausset J: A study of HL-A antigens in human organs. *Transplantation* 1970; 9:185–192.
29. Harris R, Zervas JD: Reticulocyte HL-A antigens. *Nature* 1969; 221:1062–1063.

30. Perrault R, Högman C: Automated red cell antibody analysis. A parallel study. II. Identification of serological specificities. *Vox Sang* 1971; 20:356–370.
31. Seaman MJ, Benson R, Jones MN, et al: The reactions of the Bennett-Goodspeed group of antibodies with the Auto-Analyser. *Br J Haematol* 1967; 13:464–473.
32. Morton JA, Pickles MM, Sutton L: The correlation of the Bg^a blood group with the HL-A7 leukocyte group: Demonstration of antigenic sites on red cells and leukocytes. *Vox Sang* 1969; 17:536–547.
33. Morton JA, Pickles MM, Sutton L, et al: Identification of further antigens on red cells and lymphocytes. Association of Bg^b with W17(Te57) and Bg^c with W28(Da15,Ba*). *Vox Sang* 1971; 21:141–153.
34. Baur MP, Neugebauer M, Deppe H, et al: Population analysis of deduced haplotypes from random families, in Albert ED, Baur MP, Mayr WR (eds): *Histocompatibility Testing 1984*. Heidelberg, Springer, 1984, pp 333–341.
35. Piazza A, Viganotti C: Evolutionary trees and HL-A polymorphism, in Dausset J, Colombani J (eds): *Histocompatibility Testing 1972*. Copenhagen, Munksgaard, 1973, pp 731–738.
36. Mayr WR: Leukozytäre und thrombocytäre Merkmale, in Prokop O, Göhler W (eds): *Die menschlichen Blutgruppen, 5. Auflage*. Jena, Fischer, 1986, pp 145–170.
37. Ferrara GB, Longo A, Tosi R, et al: HLA segregation of human T-cell subpopulation markers. *Hum Immunol* 1981; 2:213–223.
38. Gazit E, Terhorst C, Yunis EJ: The human "T" genetic region of the HLA linkage group is a polymorphism detected on lectin activated lymphocytes. *Nature* 1980; 284:275–277.
39. Leeuwen Av, Festenstein H, Rood JJv: Di-allelic alloantigenic systems on subsets of T cells. *Hum Immunol* 1982; 4:109–121.
40. Bell JI, Denny DW Jr, McDevitt HO: Structure and polymorphism of murine and human class II major histocompatibility antigens. *Immunol Rev* 1985; 84:51–71.
41. Giles RC, Capra JD: Structure, function and genetics of human class II molecules. *Adv Immunol* 1985; 37:1–71.
42. Korman AJ, Boss JM, Spies T, et al: Genetic complexity and expression of human class II histocompatibility antigens. *Immunol Rev* 1985; 85:45–86.
43. Rask L, Gustafsson K, Larhammar D, et al: Generation of class II antigen polymorphism. *Immunol Rev* 1985; 84:123–143.
44. Segall M, Cairns JS, Dahl CA, et al: DNA and protein studies of HLA class II molecules: Their relationship to T cell recognition. *Immunol Rev* 1985; 85:129–148.

45. Shackelford DA, Kaufman JF, Korman AJ, et al: HLA-DR antigens: Structure, separation of subpopulations, gene cloning and function. *Immunol Rev* 1982; 66:133–187.
46. Trowsdale J, Young JAT, Kelly AP, et al: Structure, sequence and polymorphism in the HLA-D region. *Immunol Rev* 1985; 85:5–43.
47. Natali PG, Segatto O, Ferrone S, et al: Differential tissue distribution and ontogeny of DC-1 and HLA-DR antigens. *Immunogenetics* 1984; 19:109–116.
48. Baur MP, Neugebauer M, Albert ED: Reference tables of two-locus haplotype frequencies for all MHC marker loci, in Albert ED, Baur MP, Mayr WR (eds): *Histocompatibility Testing 1984*. Heidelberg, Springer, 1984, pp 677–755.
49. Baur MP, Neugebauer M, Albert ED: Reference tables of three-locus haplotype frequencies and Delta values in Caucasians, Orientals and Negroids, in *Histocompatibility Testing 1984*. Heidelberg, Springer, 1984, pp 756–760.
50. Alper CA, Raum D, Karp S, et al: Serum complement "supergenes" of the major histocompatibility complex in man (complotypes). *Vox Sang* 1983; 45:62–67.
51. Charron DJ, Lotteau V, Turmel P: Hybrid HLA-DQ antigens: Molecular expression, in Albert ED, Baur MP, Mayr WR: *Histocompatibility Testing 1984*. Heidelberg, Springer, 1984, pp 539–543.
52. Shaw S, Johnson AH, Shearer GM: Evidence for a new segregant series of B cell antigens that are encoded in the HLA-D region and that stimulate secondary allogeneic proliferation and cytotoxic responses. *J Exp Med* 1980; 152:565–580.
53. Bach FH, Hirschhorn K: Lymphocyte interaction: A potential in vitro histocompatibility test. *Science* 1964; 143:815–817.
54. Touraine JL: The bare lymphocyte syndrome, a combined immunodeficiency associated with the lack of expression of HLA antigens and β2 microglobulin on lymphocytes, in Touraine JL, Gluckman E, Griscelli C (eds): *Bone Marrow Transplantation in Europe*, vol II. Amsterdam, Excerpta Medica, 1981, pp 190–193.
55. Hadam MR, Dopfer R, Dammer G, et al: Defective expression of HLA-D region determinants in children with congenital agammaglobulinemia and malabsorption: A new syndrome, in Albert ED, Baur MP, Mayr WR (eds): *Histocompatibility Testing 1984*. Heidelberg, Springer, 1984, pp 645–650.
56. Lisowska-Grospierre B, Charron DJ, Preval C de, et al: Defect of expression of MHC genes responsible for an abnormal HLA class I phenotype and the class II negative phenotype of lymphocytes from patients with combined immunodeficiency, in Albert ED, Baur MP,

Mayr WR (eds): *Histocompatibility Testing 1984*. Heidelberg, Springer, 1984, pp 650–655.
57. Doherty PC, Zinkernagel RM: A biological role for the major histocompatibility antigens. *Lancet* 1975; i:1406–1409.
58. Klein J: Evolution and function of the major histocompatibility complex, in Parham P, Strominger J (eds): *Histocompatibility Antigens*. London, Chapman & Hall, 1982, pp 221–239.
59. Bodmer W, Thomson G: Population genetics and evolution of the HLA system, in Dausset J, Svejgaard A (eds): *HLA and Disease*. Copenhagen, Munksgaard, 1977, pp 280–295.
60. Seigler HF, Metzgar RS: Embryonic development of human transplantation antigens. *Transplantation* 1970; 9:478–486.
61. Ceppellini R, Bonnard GD, Coppo F, et al: Mixed leukocyte cultures and HL-A antigens. I. Reactivity of young fetuses, newborns and mothers at delivery. *Transplant Proc* 1971; 3:58–63.
62. Ting A, Morris PJ, Stocker JW: Leukocyte antigens in renal transplantation. IV. The effect of blood transfusions on leukocyte typing by lymphocytotoxicity. *Transplantation* 1969; 7:424–429.
63. Bertrams J, Kuwert E, Gallmeier WM, et al: Transient lymphocyte HL-A antigen "loss" in a case of irradiated M. Hodgkin. *Tissue Antigens* 1971; 1:105–108.
64. Evans CA, Pegrum GD: The reactivity of leukaemic cells to HL-A typing sera. *Tissue Antigens* 1973; 3:454–464.
65. Sanderson AR, Gelfand EW, Rosen FS: A change in HL-A phenotype associated with a specific blocking factor in the serum of an infant with severe combined immunodeficiency disease. *Transplantation* 1972; 13:142–145.
66. Terasaki PI, Miyajima T, Sengar DPS, et al: Extraneous lymphocytic HL-A antigens in severe combined immunodeficiency disease. *Transplantation* 1972; 13:250–255.
67. Ben-David A, Orgad S, Danon Y, et al: HL-A antigen change in patients treated with chloramphenicol. *Tissue Antigens* 1973; 3:378–384.
68. Majsky A, Todorovicova H: The transient loss of HLA antigens on lymphocytes in patients following administration of penicillin and tetracyclin. *Folia Haematol (Leipzig)* 1978; 4:502–507.
69. Tiilikainen A, Schröder J, de la Chapelle A: Fetal leukocytes in the maternal circulation after delivery. II. Masking of HL-A antigens. *Transplantation* 1974; 17:355–360.
70. Mittal KK, Mickey MR, Singal DP, et al: Serotyping for homotransplantation. XVIII. Refinement of microdroplet lymphocyte cytotoxicity test. *Transplantation* 1968; 6:913–927.

71. Mayr WR: Das HL-A System in der Paternitätsserologie. *Z Rechtsmed* 1974; 75:81–103.
72. Mayr WR: HLA and other leukocyte and platelet alloantigen in paternity testing. *Referate 9. Tagung der Ges. für forensische Blutgruppenkunde*. Bern, 1981, pp 1–7.
73. Goodfellow PN, Payne R: Serological studies of Cw1 and Cw3 expressed on the same haplotype. *Tissue Antigens* 1978; 11:350–356.
74. Bontrop RE, Schreuder GMT, Elferink DG, et al: Molecular, serologic and functional evidence for an apparent HLA-DR triplet. *J Immunol* 1986; 137:211–216.
75. Brasil L, Clarke J, Cerilli J, et al: A unique family with an apparent DR triplet in three generations. *Hum Immunol* 1984; 12:106.
76. Mayr WR: Grundlagen zur Berechnung der Vaterschaftswahrscheinlichkeit im HL-A System. *Z Immun-Forsch* 1972; 144:18–27.
77. Mayr WR: Die Berechnung der Vaterschaftswahrscheinlichkeit und der Vaterschaftsausschlußchance im HLA system auf Grund der Befunde des Kindes und des Präsumtivvaters ohne Einbeziehung der Mutter. *Z Rechtsmed* 1977; 80:23–26.
78. Baur MP, Mayr WR, Rittner Ch: Algorithm for the computation of plausibilities of paternity in the HLA system. *Z Immun-Forsch* 1976; 152:209–219.
79. Mayr WR, Pausch V: Die Berechnung der Vaterschaftsausschlußchance im HLA System. *Z Immun-Forsch* 1975; 150:447–457.
80. Allen FH Jr, Mayr WR, Lee CL: RMNE (random men not excluded) calculations for two-locus systems such as HLA, in Walker RH (ed): *Inclusion Paternity Probabilities in Parentage Testing*. Arlington, AABB, 1983, pp 297–304.
81. Speiser P: Das HL-A System im Paternitätsprozeß mit Berücksichtigung des Beweiswertes. *Referate 5. Tagung der Ges. für forensische Blutgruppenkunde*. Amsterdam, 1973, pp 273–289.
82. Gürtler H, Svejgaard A, Staub-Nielsen L, et al: The HL-A system in cases of disputed paternity. Exclusions and positive evidences for paternity. *Referate 5. Tagung der Ges. für forensische Blutgruppenkunde*. Amsterdam, 1973, pp 313–324.
83. Soulier JP, Moullec J, Prou-Wartelle O: Recherches de paternite par le systeme HL-A. *Rev Fr Transfus* 1972; 15:11–35.
84. Mayerova A, Bender K, Hiller Ch: Die Verwendung des HL-A Systems in erbbiologischen Gutachten: eine Zusammenstellung von Daten. *Referate 4. Tagung der Ges. für forensische Blutgruppenkunde*. Trier, 1972, pp 111–119.
85. Spielmann W, Seidl S: Zur Anwendung des HL-A Systems in der Paternitätsserologie. *Z Rechtsmed* 1974; 74:121–140.

86. Waltz H, Prokop O: HLA in der Paternitätsbegutachtung, ein Erfahrungsbericht. *Proc 12th Congress of the Intl Academy of Forensic and Social Medicine*. Wien, 1982, pp 869–872.
87. Nijenhuis LE: Die Zweckmäßigkeit von HLA im Vaterschaftsgutachten. *Referate 6. Tagung der Ges. für forensische Blutgruppenkunde*. Innsbruck, 1975, pp 125–131.
88. Jeannet M, Hässig A, Bernheim J: Use of the HL-A antigen system in disputed paternity cases. *Vox Sang* 1972; 23:197–200.
89. Terasaki PI: Resolution by HLA testing of 1,000 paternity cases not excluded by ABO testing. *J Fam Life* 1977–78; 16:543–557.
90. Majsky A, Kout M: Another case of occurrence of two different fathers of twins by HLA typing. *Tissue Antigens* 1982; 20:305.
91. Spielmann W: Ein Zwillingsfall mit Superfecundatio. *Ärztl Lab* 1977; 23:283–284.
92. Terasaki PI, Gjertson D, Bernoco D, et al: Twins with two different fathers identified by HLA. *N Engl J Med* 1978; 299:590–592.
93. Jonasson J, Lindsten J, Lundborg R, et al: HL-A antigens and heteromorphic fluorescence characters of chromosomes in prenatal paternity investigation. *Nature* 1972; 236:312–313.
94. Mayr WR, Waltz H, Wegener R: Das HLA System in der Vaterschaftsserologie: praktische Erfahrungen bei 1130 Fällen, in Hummel K, Gerchow J (eds): *Biostatistischer Beweis der Vaterschaft - Festschrift für Erik Essen-Möller*. Berlin, Springer, 1981, pp 177–191.
95. Rittner CH, Stradmann B: HLA-DR in der Abstammungsbegutachtung. *Ärztl Lab* 1983; 29:167–170.
96. Waltz H, Prokop O, Mayr WR: HLA-DR in der Paternitätsbegutachtung. *Referate 10. Tagung der Ges. für forensische Blutgruppenkunde*. München, 1983, pp 41–44.
97. Mayr WR: Probleme bei der Anwendung des HLA Systems im Vaterschaftsgutachten. *Referate 7. Tagung der Ges. für forensische Blutgruppenkunde*. Hamburg, 1977, pp 417–441.
98. Park MS, Teraski PI: Storage of human lymphocytes at room temperature. *Transplantation* 1974; 18:520–524.
99. Ferrone S, Cooper NR, Pellegrino MA, et al: The role of complement in the HL-A antibody-mediated lysis of lymphocytes. *Transplant Proc* 1974; 6:13–19.
100. Hansen HE: Inheritance of a "weak" HLA-Bw35 antigen in a Danish family. *Tissue Antigens* 1976; 8:49–53.
101. Hansen HE, Gürtler H: Problems concerning the reliability of HLA exclusions in paternity cases. *Referate 10. Tagung der Ges. für forensische Blutgruppenkunde*. München, 1983, pp 25–29.

102. Lokki ML, Koskimies S: The usability of HLA typing in paternity problems. *Referate 10. Tagung der Ges. für forensische Blutgruppenkunde*. München, 1983, 31–33.
103. Majsky A: Incidence of a weak HLA-B27 antigen in a Czech family. *J Immunogenet* 1976; 3:211–213.
104. Mayr WR, Mayr D: Schwache Ausprägung des Merkmals HL-A2 in einer deutschen Familie. *Z Immun-Forsch* 1972; 144:404–413.
105. Claas FHJ, Ruina-van Nieuwkoop R, Berge Wvd, et al: Interaction of penicillin with HLA-A and -B antigens. *Hum Immunol* 1982; 5:83–90.
106. Majsky A, Chudomel V, Jakoubkova J: Effects of antibiotics and chemotherapeutics on the cytotoxic reaction between HLA antigens and corresponding sera. *J Immunogenet* 1976; 3:135–137.
107. Scorza-Smeraldi R, Smeraldi E, Fabio G, et al: Interference between anti-HLA antibodies and adrenergic receptor-binding drugs. *Tissue Antigens* 1977; 9:163–166.
108. Mayr WR, Pausch V, Schnedl W: Human chimera detectable only by investigation of her progeny. *Nature* 1979; 277:210–211.
109. Bias WB, Hopkins KA, Hutchinson JR, et al: Evidence for an unlinked gene which modifies HLA antigen expression. *Tissue Antigens* 1974; 4:36–41.
110. Wenk RE, Houtz TD, Brooks M, et al: Unexpressed HLA haplotype and erroneous maternal exclusion. *Referate 10. Tagung der Ges. für forensische Blutgruppenkunde*. München, 1983, pp 35–40.

Chapter 11

Forensic Applications of Enzyme-Linked Immunosorbent Assay

S.M. Fletcher, Ph.D.

Enzyme-linked immunosorbent immunoassay (ELISA) is widely used in many areas of biological science, replacing conventional immunological methods such as latex and red cell agglutination, complement fixation, and immunofluorescence, and displacing radioimmunoassay in some areas. The basic design of ELISA methods was originally derived from the immunohistochemical staining techniques, but many new variants of the method have been devised which make it much more versatile than other types of labelled immunoassay.

With very few exceptions, ELISA methods measure compounds in solution or presented to the assay in solution. Some of the conventional methods of forensic serology (e.g., absorption/elution) depend on the insolubility of the antigen they are detecting, and there clearly is a need to develop new extraction techniques for blood stains. It is fortunate that some of the agents which have proved most useful in this respect (e.g., detergents), are not as disruptive in ELISA methods as they are to red blood cells.

This review aims to provide background information on ELISA theory and practice, and to highlight the advantages and disadvantages of different protocols and reagents. In addition, it will review work on ELISA methods for use in all areas of forensic serology and discuss future prospects.

THEORETICAL AND PRACTICAL ASPECTS OF ELISA

Immunoassay Strategies

All immunoassays rely on some change in property, physical or chemical, which occurs when antigen and antibody combine. If the reaction results in precipitation it may be visible to the naked eye, or measured by light scattering in a nephelometer. If the antigen or antibody can be adsorbed onto the surface of red cells or latex, and if the other reactant causes bridging of the carriers, then agglutination is seen. This was the first type of labelled immunoassay published, and it has given good service for most of this century. Since the 1950s, however, there has been a steady development toward greater and greater method sensitivity, using radioisotopes, enzymes, spin labels, fluorophores, luminescent compounds, and heavy metal ions as labels.[1] These labels can be attached to the antigen or to the antibody. In the latter case, the assay is termed "immunometric." The scheme of reaction with a labelled antigen is:

$$\mathrm{Ag}^* + \mathrm{Ab} <-> \mathrm{Ag}^*\mathrm{Ab}$$

What is needed to make use of this system is some means of separating bound from unbound antigen. This separation may be achieved in a number of ways. The most common are (1) precipitation of the AgAb complex by a chemical reagent (e.g., polyethylene glycol; second antibody), (2) adsorption of the uncombined antigen by some solid (e.g., charcoal), or (3) attachment of the unlabelled species to a solid support (antibody absorbed onto polystyrene). After separation, either the amount of label attached to the solid or that remaining free in solution is measured.

This type of assay is termed "heterogeneous". The separation stage involves centrifugation in some assays and washing stages in others, and this has made it difficult to completely automate this type of assay. A different type of assay system has been developed, largely in the commercial sector, in which some property of the label attached to one of the reactants changes quantitatively or qualitatively upon binding to the other reactant. This type of assay is termed "homogeneous," as there is no need for the separation of bound and free labelled species. An example of this type is the proprietary EMIT system (Syva, Inc) for the detection of drugs of abuse in urine. In general, these assays are less sensitive than the heterogeneous type, but have the great advantage of being very rapid, giving a result within minutes.

Enzyme-linked immunosorbent immunoassay (ELISA) methods are of the heterogeneous type, in which one of the reactants is bound to a solid phase and may be designed to detect and quantify both antigens and antibodies. The different types may be classified in different ways: competitive/non-competitive; antigen/antibody detection; one-site/two-site; or reagent balance/reagent excess. The classification that follows is essentially pragmatic. The type of ELISA most appropriate to any particular analytical need depends on the analyte itself, the availability and nature of specific antibody, and the type of result wanted (e.g., qualitative or quantitative).

Antigen Detection Types

Five basic types of ELISA for antigen detection can be distinguished as outlined below.

Direct Antigen Immobilization.—In this type of ELISA the sample containing the substance to be assayed is allowed to bind to an adsorptive surface. Binding of the analyte is detected by a specific antibody labelled with enzyme.

Competition With Labelled Antigen.—In this type of ELISA the analyte and a constant amount of labelled antigen compete for a constant and limiting amount of specific antibody, which optimally is bound to a solid phase. This is comparable to Berson and Yalow's original radioimmunoassay (RIA) for insulin.

Competition With Labelled Antibody.—The analyte and a constant amount of solid phase antigen compete for a limiting amount of labelled antibody in this type of ELISA. The components can be added simultaneously, or the analyte and labelled antibody may be allowed to react for some time before adding the mixture to the solid phase antigen.

Immunometric Assay (Antibody Excess).—This assay has two forms as outlined below:

One-Site Assay.—The analyte is reacted with a slight and constant excess of labelled antibody in this form of the assay. Unreacted antibody is removed by an excess of solid phase antigen. Enzymic activity is measured in either the solid or liquid phase.

Two-Site or Sandwich Assay.—Here the analyte must possess at least two simultaneously available antigenic sites. It is first bound by solid phase antibody, and then another site is reacted with labelled antibody. If the second antibody is not conjugated, it may be detected by an anti-species conjugate, though in this case it should be from a different species to avoid reaction with the solid phase antibody.

In theory, the two-site immunometric assay offers better specificity than the others, but this depends on the presence of a second binding site on the antigen which is unaffected by the binding of the first. A second advantage is that it presents a selective adsorptive surface which confers greater sensitivity because the analyte of interest comprises only a small amount of the total potentially adsorptive material in the sample.

Antibody Detection Types

Double Antibody Method.—The antibody to be detected is first extracted from the sample by solid phase antigen, and then identified by a labelled anti-immunoglobulin antibody from a different species. The second antibody may be isotype-specific, allowing class determination of the detected antibody.

Reverse Sandwich Method.—Antibody is first extracted with solid phase antigen and then detected by reaction with enzyme-labelled antigen. This method requires that the antibody be able to react with a second antigen, and is practically restricted to the detection of IgM antibody.

Antibody Class Capture Assay.—Immunoglobulins of a specific class are first captured by solid phase anti-isotype antibody and then detected with labelled antigen (or with multivalent antigen and labelled antibody).

Solid Phase Considerations

Two types of interaction have been used to fix the components of the immunodetection system on solid phases. The first type, physical adsorption, is often strong enough for many proteins and polysaccharides to give adequate and reproducible binding.[2–4] Glass and various types of plastic such as polystyrene, polyvinyl chloride, polypropylene, polycarbonate, nylon, nitrocellulose, and silicones all have been used as supports. Surface charge plays a minor role in this interaction which appears to be predominantly mediated by hydrophobic bonding. Sterilization of polystyrene and polyvinyl plastics by gamma radiation substantially improves their binding capacity.

The second type of fixation is covalent attachment. Antigen or antibody has been chemically bound to a variety of derivatised solids such as activated cellulose, dextran, polyacrylamide gel, agarose, and hydrolysed nylon. Antigens or antibodies may be linked to these using carbodiimides, succinic anhydride, or glutaraldehyde. Glutaraldehyde has been used to pre-coat polystyrene microtitre plates with an "activated" layer and thereby improve their binding capacity. Interest in covalent attachment stems from the need to achieve reproducibility and stability of coated proteins.[5] The sensitivity of ELISA methods is related directly to the binding capacity of the solid phase, and also to the surface area used. The ratio of the surface to the sample volume is less critical, but still important.

The immobilization of Ig on solid phases has some negative effects.[6] The avidity of antibody, at least for large antigens, is reduced by one or two orders of magnitude, and the rate of antigen-antibody interaction is slower due to the compartmentalization of antibody. Some of the immobilized antibody also will have its binding site partially obscured, which has a distorting effect on the kinetics of association.[7]

Microtitre Plates.—These have been the most widely used solid phase for many years.[8] Their main advantages are ease of manipulation and capacity for high throughput, which have been brought about by the development of a wide range of automatic washers, dispensers, and photometers. Their reproducibility is not as good as that of solid supports such as polystyrene balls, but where this is not a prime consideration they represent the most convenient ELISA support. Intra-plate variation in the binding capacity of the best types of plate is now acceptable, but cannot be taken for granted. Economies made on microtitre plates could have catastrophic effects on assay precision.

Unwanted Adsorption (Non-Specific Binding).—This occurs when enzyme-labelled antigen or antibody binds to the solid phase (or to the adsorbed layer) unexpectedly. One widely used method of reducing this effect is to employ a "blocking agent," a protein or detergent, to blank off the unwanted adsorption sites before the labelled reagent is added.

Antiserum Considerations

In common with other immunoassays, the specificity of ELISA is determined by the antibody used, and the ultimate sensitivity is directly related to the affinity of the antibody binding site for its antigen. Conventional antiserum has been used successfully for ELISA since its inception, though it has been observed frequently that purification of serum gives much improved results, whether it be a simple immunoglobulin fraction that is taken, or an affinity-purified product. This appears to have the most effect where the purified antibody is used to coat the solid phase. Reducing the amount of potentially interfering protein in serum samples to be labelled with enzyme is an obvious precaution, though it is generally found that a crude immunoglobulin fractionation is all that is necessary. Some workers have reported further improvements in assay sensitivity by the use of Fab antibody fragments.

The achievement of Kohler and Milstein[9] in producing stable hybrids of antibody-secreting lymphocytes with tumor cells to generate monoclonal antibodies (MCA) has had a revolutionary effect on the field of immunoassay. Its potential for forensic serology has been reviewed,[10] and MCA are now beginning to be used for routine grouping in forensic science laboratories around the world. Although MCA have some limitations, these hardly apply to their use in ELISA methods. The monovalency of MCA is no disadvantage and the affinity requirements for any particular method can be satisfied by selection. Direct conjugation of IgG MCA with enzymes and other markers can be achieved by a number of reliable methods, though IgM MCA still prove difficult to conjugate. It is not however, necessary to conjugate an MCA directly, as it is possible to detect the specific binding of an MCA by a commercial anti-mouse Ig antibody enzyme conjugate. In this way, a large number of MCAs can be used in the same assay format with a single enzyme conjugate.

Conjugate Considerations

Several enzymes have been used successfully for ELISA, including alkaline phosphatase, horseradish peroxidase, glucose oxidase, and beta-galactosidase.[11] Horseradish peroxidase (HPO) is the most widely used enzyme, since it is cheap and easy to conjugate. One disadvantage is that none of the available substrates yields a simple product, and during incubation with substrate the monitored absorbance increase can reverse due to further oxidation of the primary product. Thus, it is normal to determine the optimum incubation time with substrate and to stop the reaction by the addition of dilute sulphuric acid. Alkaline phosphatase (AP) is next in order of popularity. The most common substrate used for this enzyme is p-nitrophenyl phosphate (pNP). This substance is sufficiently soluble to achieve zero-order kinetics and has a strongly absorbing product, but it requires careful storage. A fluorogenic substrate, methylumbelliferylphosphate, allows much greater sensitivity of detection, but requires a fluorimeter for measurement.[12]

The first successful conjugation of enzyme and antibody was reported by Avrameas in 1969[13] using glutaraldehyde, and this method is still in widespread use. In its simplest form, the antigen or antibody is mixed with an appropriate amount of enzyme and glutaraldehyde is added to the mixture. After a period of incubation at room temperature, any remaining active aldehyde groups are reacted with dimethylamine. Another useful method for peroxidase conjugates is the periodate method.

Recently, more sophisticated cross-linking agents have been used[14] in an attempt to gain better control of enzyme conjugation.

As mentioned earlier, where MCA is employed the same enzyme labelled anti-mouse Ig may be used as detection reagent in a number of assays. This adds another layer to the method, but it is often possible to add both MCA and conjugate at the same time, avoiding an extra incubation step.

Enzymes constitute relatively large antibody labels, and conjugation can lead to considerable loss of immunoreactivity. Smaller labels should interfere less, and this underlies the success of a recent ELISA variant which uses biotin as a label.[15] Biotin is a B complex factor with a molecular weight of 264 which can be conjugated easily to free primary amine groups of proteins. This factor is bound by avidin, a very high affinity binding protein which is isolated from egg white. Streptavidin (*Streptomyces avidinii*) is another binding protein which has even better characteristics. Avidin-enzyme conjugates bind well to biotinylated proteins, and this provides a means of detecting the retention of the protein by solid phase antibody.

Data Treatment Considerations

Some ELISA assays can be read by eye alone, but for most analytical purposes a more objective and quantitative measurement is needed.[16] A single reading of absorbance at a fixed period of incubation with substrate often is all that is needed, but some assays achieve greater sensitivity and/or selectivity by the measurement of the reaction rate. Several commercial ELISA readers also make measurements at two different wavelengths, one of which is used to correct for variations in the optics of the microtitre plate (e.g., scratched wells). The results of ELISA usually are expressed in terms of absorbance units, or in the cases of fluorogenic substrates, as arbitrary fluorescence units. The use of rapid, automated spectroscopy is now widespread and is likely to become more sophisticated in the future.

The determination of a positive/negative discrimination or cut-off value has proved to be one of the major problems in defining the sensitivity of ELISA.[17] The non-specific binding of conjugate to the solid phase, or to the protein components themselves, produces a background absorbance. The absolute level of this background is an important parameter, but it is the variability of the background that effectively decides how sensitive an assay is. If the background is unaffected by the sample matrix, then the minimum detection limit can be fixed by reference to the standard deviation of the background. For example, it might be set at mean background plus three standard deviations. Sample matrix, however, often does have some influence on results, and in this circumstance some estimate of the matrix-related effect is needed. In order to establish an even level of performance it is also essential to use, as positive control, some stable standard which will give an absorbance within a previously defined range. This ensures that a minimum level of sensitivity will be maintained.

In the direct immobilization type of ELISA the amount of competing protein in the sample is the major factor influencing the amount of analyte that is adsorbed by the solid phase. This unrelated protein has its own capacity to bind components of the immunological detection system non-specifically, and this must be estimated in some way. Where separate specific antiserum and second antibody-enzyme conjugate are used, this can be done by omitting the specific antiserum from the control. It is not a perfect control, but in practice it has proven effective. A second control, in which no sample is applied to the microtitre plate well (a "no-sample" control), will give the relevant non-specific background of the assay for the limiting case where sample dilution approaches infinity (i.e., where the sample is vanishingly small). This control is independent of sample matrix effects, and is one of the assay parameters which should be checked in each run. The sample absorbance value should be corrected by subtracting the value for the first type of control rather than the "no-sample" control, unless the latter is higher (which it rarely is). Where the specific antiserum is itself labelled with enzyme, there is no easy way to estimate the effect of sample matrix on individual samples. The usual approach followed is to estimate a large enough number of representative negative samples to establish the range of matrix effect.

An alternative way of treating data is to relate the sample absorbance to the absolute background absorbance level. This is comparable to the signal:noise ratio concept of electronic communication. If the sample background variability is known, then mathematically-derived confidence limits may be calculated to allow minimum detection limits to be set as, for example, double the background absorbance level.

It is also difficult to measure the effect of sample matrix in capture and competitive ELISA, but one effective way is to analyze a second portion of sample to which a known amount of standard analyte has been added. The increase in absorbance related to the amount of analyte added then can be used to calculate the amount of analyte in the sample itself. This adds more complexity to the assay than most workers are prepared to accept, so the same approach as described above is usually taken; many representative negative samples are run in order to establish confidence limits for minimum detection levels.

The use of sandwich and competitive/inhibition ELISA protocols provides a basis for quantitation of analyte in a way not possible by the direct immobilization of analyte. The reproducibility and accuracy of these types of ELISA are comparable to those of RIA and are used widely for the measurement of proteins of clinical importance. Quantitation is achieved using a range of assay standards to generate a standard curve against which sample results may be read. There is a wide variety of practice in constructing assay and reference standards, in sample dilution and parallel dose-response curve interpretation, and in data processing (e.g., transformation to permit linear curve-fitting) of results which have been reviewed elsewhere.[18–20]

FORENSIC APPLICATIONS

Table 11–1 shows the trend in published work on ELISA applications in forensic serology. As might have been predicted, much of the work has employed MCA, and the history of ELISA in this field is closely linked to the isolation of MCA with appropriate specificities. Since 1983 there has been a steady stream of publications on ELISA methods for most of the serological specificities currently tested for in casework. Most

TABLE 11–1.
ELISA Methods in Forensic Science

Year	Number of Reports
1978	2
1983	7
1984	13
1985	12
1986	17

are research reports which reveal a progressive increase in method sensitivity and sophistication, but some are applicable as they stand. There is also a large amount of work relating to the application of methods to evidentiary material which is yet unpublished, and some attempt has been made below to indicate the extent of this.

Species Identification

A number of ELISA methods have been developed for the speciation of bloodstains. Tamaki and Kishida[21] utilized anti-human albumin and hemoglobin sera in an inhibition assay, with good specificity and sensitivity. Anti-hemoglobin sera (rabbit) were also used by Oshima et al[22–25] in an inhibition configuration with hemoglobin-coated activated polystyrene beads. Cross-reactivity was observed with hemolysates from a range of mammals (including dog, cat, and pig), which indicates that a careful choice of antiserum is essential for this protein.

MCA was used first for the speciation of bloodstains by Fletcher et al.[26] The MCA was directed against a determinant on the light (lambda) chains of immunoglobulin. Blood and secretion stain extracts were immobilized directly into microtitre plate wells and then detected by incubation with MCA, and subsequently by incubation with anti-mouse Ig-alkaline phosphatase conjugate (AMIAP). Cross-reactivity was observed with chimpanzee and some other simian and prosimian sera, but not with a wide range of domestic mammals, fish, and birds. For stains up to 1 year old the sensitivity was adequate, but beyond this, variable results were obtained. Results with saliva stains were variable, some stains giving strong positive reactions and others no reaction at all. Results with semen stains were very poor. A much more rapid version (4.5 hours) of this assay was developed subsequently[27] using a commercial alkaline phosphatase–labelled anti-human IgG (clone CG-5: Miles) reagent. Sera from 40 domestic and 6 simian/prosimian species were tested, of which only chimpanzee and eel sera cross-reacted to any extent. The assay performed well with blood stains up to 3 years old, but failed with older stains.

Tsutsumi et al[28] used rabbit antiserum to human serum protein in an inhibition ELISA with human plasma protein-coated microtitre plates. Large amounts of blood stain (5 mm × 5 mm per test) were used to evaluate the system, so no indication of its ultimate sensitivity is available. However, the method did differentiate between human and chimpanzee serum to a much greater degree than did other methods.

On the basis of findings obtained with the above methods, speciation of human blood stains requires careful choice and testing of antisera to establish levels of cross-reactivity. Undoubtedly, MCA offer the best long-term prospect for ELISA, as they do for most assays. Indeed, one MCA against a human albumin determinant recently has been found to discriminate absolutely between human serum and other primate serum (Dr. Benjamin, University of Virginia, School of Medicine, personal communication; a commercial kit based on this MCA is available from Humagen Inc, Charlottesville, Virginia, 22901, USA). Both direct and inhibition protocols appear to offer adequate sensitivity for recent blood stains. Older blood stains will present problems for all types of ELISA which require a soluble extract, as progressive denaturation reduces the amount of target antigen and its extractability with the passage of time. Speciation of other types of body fluid stains is rarely needed, and no adequate ELISA or other method is available. Some types of anti-albumin or anti-immunoglobulin speciation methods for blood stains also may prove suitable for exocrine secretions.

Fetal Blood Identification

ELISA methods for the measurement of alpha-fetoprotein[29,30] (AFP) were developed originally as potential cancer screening methods. This protein is present in fetal blood, maternal blood, and amniotic fluid, but only at very low concentrations in normal individuals at 1 month post-partum. Kurucz et al[31] evaluated the use of a double antibody sandwich ELISA for AFP on stains of fetal blood, amniotic fluid, and adult blood. Two MCA were used, one to coat microtitre plates and the other to be conjugated directly with horseradish peroxidase. AFP was extracted from stains with a recovery rate of 10% to 40%, and was detectable in stains of fetal, but not adult, blood. The sensitivity of the method was quoted as 50 μl of blood. Better recoveries than this were reported by Tsao et al,[32] who applied a double antibody sandwich assay to dried blood samples on filter paper for clinical purposes. This assay used MCA-coated polystyrene beads and alkaline-phosphatase conjugated anti-AFP.

Katsumata et al[33] used a similar assay configuration with goat anti-human AFP-coated plates and rabbit anti-human AFP with an anti-rabbit Ig-enzyme conjugate to detect AFP binding. Approximately 2 mm^2 of blood stain was added to each microtitre plate well with buffer. Excellent discrimination of fetal blood stains from adult and maternal blood stains was obtained.

AFP levels are raised in primary hepatoma, which is fortunately rare. The marker is stable in blood stains for many months. The ELISA methods described above are minor modifications of published assays for clinical use and it is probable that commercial assays for AFP could be adapted easily for forensic use.

Semen Identification

ELISA methods have been developed for two established semen markers (prostatic acid phosphatase and gamma-seminoprotein), and three new markers (p30, prostate-specific antigen, and seminal vesicle antigen) have been investigated largely by means of ELISA. Three of these markers, gamma-seminoprotein (gSM; 23,000 daltons), prostate-specific antigen (PSA; 34,000 daltons), and p30 (30,000 daltons), appear to be parts of the same protein, or at least to share the same epitopes. Much work in this area has been instigated by the search for a diagnostic marker of prostatic carcinoma,[34] and many MCA have been isolated with specificity for components of prostatic fluid.

Gamma-seminoprotein was identified by Hara et al[35] in 1966, who demonstrated its usefulness as a semen marker in forensic practice in a series of publications. The first report of an ELISA method for PSA came in 1980[36] from a group at Roswell Park Memorial Institute (Buffalo, New York) which was looking for a prostate cancer marker. The assay used rabbit antiserum immobilized on Sepharose 4B (Pharmacia) and the same antiserum conjugated with peroxidase. It detected PSA at low levels in serum from healthy men, but not from women. Several groups since have reported the application of gSM/p30 ELISA to the identification of semen in forensic work.

Tsuda et al[37,38] produced assays using rabbit IgG or Fab' antibody conjugated with peroxidase and seminal protein-coated polystyrene beads. Stain material was incubated with labelled antibody, and the excess unbound antibody was captured by the coated beads. The beads then were placed in enzyme substrate and color development was noted. The same labelled antibody was used to detect semen on stain material immobilized on cellophane tape in a histochemical-type technique. These methods were specific but not particularly sensitive. A more sensitive assay was achieved by the use of a monoclonal anti-gSM bound to acrylbutadiene-styrene beads for antigen capture, followed by detection with peroxidase-conjugated rabbit anti-gSM. This detected semen in stain extracts diluted to the equivalent of 1:512 of original semen,[39] and diluted to 1:25,600 in liquid seminal plasma (cut-off level 8 ng/ml). However, an acid phosphatase color test performed on the same samples gave identical sensitivities.

Commercial assays based on the Kuriyama[36] and Tsuda[39] methods are available from Hybritech (TANDEM-R PSA; San Diego, California, 92121, USA) and Chugai Pharmaceutical Co (Tokyo, Japan), respectively. A recent comparison of these two kits[34] showed good correlation of results.

Graves et al[40] used an affinity-purified rabbit anti-p30 antiserum both for capture (in polystyrene microtitre plate wells) and as alkaline phosphatase conjugate for antigen detection. The assay was evaluated with timed post-coital samples and detected the presence of semen in vaginal swabs up to 27 hours after intercourse, on the average. By comparison, the mean cut-off for acid phosphatase detection was 14 hours post-coitus, using the same samples. The marker also was found at moderate levels in adult male urine, and might conceivably be useful for the sexing of urine stains.

A number of anti-p30 MCA are now available, including the Hybritech MCA used in the kit referred to above. An ELISA using microtitre plates coated with Hybritech anti-PSA MCA, with detection of bound p30 by rabbit anti-p30 (SERI, Emeryville, California, USA) and anti-mouse Ig-alkaline phosphatase has been evaluated by Baechtel[41] on more than 2,000 casework samples. Compared with methods currently in use, the anti-p30 ELISA detected seminal traces in 50% more samples. There was also some correlation between the detectability of semen donor ABO group and p30 level.

Recently, another semen-specific protein has been identified by Herr and co-workers.[42] This is a basic protein (SVA; seminal vesicle antigen) secreted by seminal vesicle epithelium, which undergoes proteolytic degradation as the seminal coagulum liquifies, yielding peptides weighing 10,500 to 13,500 daltons. An MCA (MHS-5) with specificity for these products of degradation has been isolated and used for semen identification in casework samples.[43] Extracts of stains are immobilized directly in microtitre plate wells and SVA is detected using biotinylated MHS-5 followed by streptavidin-peroxidase conjugate. A simplified assay based on this procedure is available in kit form (SEMA) from Humagen Inc (Charlottesville, Virginia, 22901, USA). The total assay time is 2 hours, and endpoint detection is by visual inspection.

A comparison of p30 and SVA ELISA on casework samples indicates similar levels of sensitivity. Most positive samples react in both assays, with a few samples giving positive results in one or the other (Dr. FS Baechtel, personal communication). Premixing biotinylated MHS-5 and streptavidin-enzyme conjugate eliminates potential interference by endogenous biotin in saliva; in a study of more than 1,000 samples of all types of body fluids and common contaminants no interfering reactions have been observed (B. Parkin, personal communication). High backgrounds were seen with vaginal swabs contaminated with menstrual blood, possibly as a result of its peroxidase activity, but this was identified clearly by the sample control.

Prostatic acid phosphatase (PAP) is still used by the majority of workers to identify semen, though dissatisfaction with its limitations is increasing. Radioimmunoassay methods[44] and monoclonal antibodies have been investigated with a view to improving the sensitivity and specificity of detection of this marker. However, these efforts have met with little success, and have largely been abandoned by research workers in forensic science. The conclusion reached by most workers is that vaginal secretion contains low levels of phosphatase with sufficient cross-reactivity with anti-prostatic phosphatase as to set an unacceptably high background level, and thereby limit the sensitivity of detection of intercourse to a maximum of 24 hours post-coitus. However, interest in PAP as a cancer marker has spurred developments in the clinical field, and a commercial ELISA method for this has been marketed recently.[45] This assay uses two MCA, one coated on microtitre plates and the other conjugated with alkaline phosphatase. The assay uses NADP as substrate, and the NAD produced by enzyme action is linked to an oxido-reductase cycle which converts INT to formazan. This makes the assay very sensitive, and allows it to be used for the detection of PAP in serum, in the presence of large amounts of other phosphatases. The sensitivity and specificity is thus considerably better than any assay for PAP currently used in forensic work. To date, this assay has not been evaluated on casework samples.

The existence of semen-specific prostaglandin derivatives has been known of for some time, but exploitation of these markers has been hindered by the difficulty of producing antisera of adequate specificity. Recently, however, a suitable rabbit antiserum to 19-hydroxy prostaglandins F)1(a and F)2(a has been raised which was used to develop a radioimmunoassay for the detection of semen.[46] This detected semen on vaginal swabs up to 72 hours post-coitus, and gave no cross-reaction with other body fluids. The same antiserum has been used to develop an ELISA method in which microtitre plates are coated with prostaglandins and stain extracts are used to inhibit the binding of labelled antibody to the immobilized antigen (Dr. J Sutton, personal communication). Based on preliminary studies, the specificity and sensitivity of this appears to be comparable to the RIA method.

The amount of active research being performed on semen identification reflects its crucial importance in serological casework. The commercial kits available for prostatic or seminal vesicle markers, or minor modifications of these, represent a significant advance in both sensitivity and specificity over current methods of identifying prostatic acid phosphatase. The sensitivity increase is probably on the order of a doubling in the post-coital period over which semen can be detected. Recent improvements in prostatic acid phosphatase assays, however, might re-establish this marker as a viable competitor of the gSM/PSA/p30/SVP group. Although the prostaglandin assay appears to offer even greater sensitivity of semen detection, the assay is currently based on polyclonal rabbit serum and will not be widely used until this, or preferably an MCA, is available commercially.

Saliva Identification

Identification methods for saliva have focused largely on salivary amylase as marker, and on its reaction with dyed starch substrates. Immunological methods are not widely used due to the difficulty of obtaining absolutely specific sera. Most anti-saliva sera are, in fact, anti-amylase sera, and since salivary amylase shares much of its structure with pancreatic amylases, cross-reactions are inevitable with polyclonal sera.

A specific anti-salivary amylase MCA (27–4–1) has been reported by Ito et al.[47] This MCA was used to coat polystyrene balls and to prepare a conjugate with beta-galactosidase. The ELISA method was specific for the salivary isoenzyme, giving no reaction with 10 μg/ml of purified pancreatic enzyme. The method has not been applied to crime samples. Other anti-amylase MCA have been produced (Dr. J Herr, personal communication), and ELISA methods based on two of these are being evaluated for use on crime samples (F Gdowski, personal communication).

A preliminary report of an ELISA using anti-human immunoglobulin sera for the identification of human saliva has been published also.[48]

The potential of near-absolute specificity for salivary amylase offered by MCA makes this marker the best prospect for future developments in saliva detection.

Urine Identification

The use of anti-urinary protein serum in the identification of urine stains was first reported by Lee et al[49] in 1977. A similar approach has been taken by Tsutsumi and Katsumata[50] who have reported preliminary findings with a direct immobilization ELISA using a commercial polyclonal anti-human uromucoid serum.

ABO Grouping of Bloodstains

The development of ELISA grouping methods for blood stains has proved problematic. Current grouping methods rely to a large extent on the stable attachment of erythrocyte antigens to the stain substrate (e.g., cloth). The main exception to this is the ammonia extraction technique of Kind and Cleevely,[51] in which strong alkali is needed to disrupt the consolidated and denatured protein in a blood stain. In this method, the extract is subsequently dried down on plastic or glass slides, or even on clean cotton threads, where it adheres strongly. This characteristic insolubility of erythrocyte antigens has important consequences for the development of ELISA methods for blood stain grouping. Either the antigens of interest must be extracted and stabilized in solution by complexing with detergents or other compounds, or they must be extracted and immobilized on a suitable surface.

The extraction of ABO substances from blood stains by dilute salt solutions is very inefficient. The use of aqueous ammonia is a considerable improvement, but even better results are achieved with detergents in alkaline solution. A number of detergents are effective, but best results are obtained with non-ionic detergents with a high critical micelle concentration.[52] There is, however, a limitation to the use of detergents since an excess of detergent interferes with subsequent stages of ELISA. Some detergents inhibit the reaction of antigen with antibody, and the detergent molecules themselves may compete with antigen for adsorption sites on whatever solid phase is used. The ratio of the amount of detergent used to the protein content of a blood stain is the important factor here. Provided this ratio can be kept within reasonable limits, however, ABO grouping of blood stains is possible.[53] A second essential requirement for immobilization of blood group substance from erythrocytes, though not from body fluids, is the adjustment of the pH of the diluted extracts down to pH8 or lower.[54]

Reliable detection of H substance by ELISA in blood stains was reported first by Harris-Smith and Fletcher[55, 56] using an alkaline phosphatase conjugate of *Ulex europaeus* lectin I. The method was not very sensitive, but did provide a model with which to study the extraction of blood group substances from blood stains. A large number of MCA to A, B, and H substance were investigated subsequently in a direct immobilization ELISA employing several alkaline-phosphatase anti-mouse Ig conjugates,[57] and the effects of adding the conjugate either as a separate stage or at the same time as MCA were determined.[58] Several useful MCA were identified, and some were observed to give reactions with blood stain extracts but not with body fluid stain extracts. Such specificity is extremely desirable for the grouping of blood stains on dirty clothing. This work highlighted the need to choose anti-mouse Ig-enzyme conjugates carefully. Most MCA performed well when added simultaneously with anti-mouse-Ig enzyme conjugate.

The performance of this ABO grouping ELISA system for blood stains was adequate for group O, A_1, A_2, and B stains, but did not work reliably for A_2B stains.[53] There appeared to be competition for adsorption sites, or a sensitivity imbalance which resulted in the loss of A substance detectability in some, though not all, A_2B stains. On prepared blood stains it was possible to distinguish A_1 and A_2 stains on the basis of the detection of substantial amounts of H substance in A_2 stains. The method required approximately 0.2 microliters of blood for a strong grouping reaction.

Greater sensitivity is needed for blood stain grouping than for body fluid stains. This might be achieved with an inhibition/competition ELISA in which stain extracts compete with solid phase blood group substances for specific MCA. The other possibility is an antibody sandwich method. However, at least part of the blood group active substance in blood is monovalent, which could severely limit the sensitivity of the latter approach. Both alternatives would rely on the stabilization of extracted antigens in solution, without interfering with their immunoreactivity.

MN Grouping

Attempts to develop an ELISA method for MN grouping have been only partially successful. Monoclonal antibodies specific for both N and M antigens have been reported by Messeter.[59] Only the anti-M MCA, however, retained its specificity in ELISA. The ELISA method reported was an inhibition assay, with purified MN glycoproteins immobilized in microtitre plate wells. The specificity of these two antibodies also showed considerable pH dependence, which has been noted elsewhere.[60] This ELISA method was not applied to crime samples. Anti-MN MCA have also been reported by Fraser et al,[61] Allen et al,[62] and Bigbee et al.[63]

Sensabaugh et al[64] used butanol to selectively extract from blood stains the erythrocyte glycophorins which bear the MN determinants. The extracts were immobilized directly in microtitre plate wells and detected with MCA to M antigen or glycophorin A. The second MCA was used to provide evidence that negative reactions were not due simply to insufficient material. A minimum of 5 μl of dried blood was needed for reliable results, and more than 100 blood stains were examined with no unexpected results. Preliminary work on detergent extraction of stains suggested that this may offer some improvements in sensitivity.

One of the problems in applying the MN system to blood stains is that the basic polymorphism rests on two amino-acid substitutions which subsequently produce different patterns of post-translational glycosylation with N-acetyl neuraminic acid (NANA). In blood stains there is a progressive loss of these NANA residues with time. Antisera to M and N determinants rarely express their specificity independent of the presence of NANA; usually they have an absolute requirement for their presence or absence.[65] In order to cope with stains of all ages, a mixture of these types is needed. However, a more pragmatic solution is to treat extracts with neuraminidase to remove the NANA residues, and use the appropriate MCA. This does not seem to be a difficult problem to resolve, and leaves the identification of reliable anti-N MCA as the main objective in this area.

Rhesus Grouping

A form of ELISA has been reported for the detection and quantitation of Rhesus D antigen,[66] but this was developed for and applied to intact red cells. A number of human MCA to D antigen have been produced by transformation of human peripheral lymphocytes with Epstein-Barr virus. These have generally been low-yield clones with low affinities, though their specificity appears adequate for grouping purposes. One of these has been used with good results in an absorption-elution method for blood stain typing.[67] A true hybridoma MCA to Rhesus antigens has been isolated only recently (Dr. D Voak, personal communication) and has not yet been applied to casework samples.

The main obstacle to the development of an anti-D ELISA is the need to extract the antigen and preserve its immunoreactivity. A number of detergents may be used to extract the antigen, and it appears to retain some of its specific structure in the presence of SDS. Some workers have investigated immunoblotting[68,69] as a potential technique for blood stain analysis, but the sensitivity of the methods reported is not yet adequate. The extraction technique used for ABO grouping of blood stains reported by Fowler et al[57] has been used together with two human anti-D MCA (from Dr. P Rouger and Dr. H Lee, CNTS, Paris, France) and an anti-human IgG-alkaline phosphatase conjugate (Fletcher and Dolton, unpublished results). This was unsuccessful, but it was unclear which element had failed, the extraction stage or the detection stage.

Detection of Isohemagglutinins

In the transfusion field, various enzyme-linked antibody methodologies have been used to detect and quantify red cell antibodies,[66,70] most of which require unhemolyzed blood as starting material. However, attempts by Watson and Thorpe[71] to develop ELISA methods for use on blood stains and for non-secretor saliva (S Ameno, Kagawa Medical School, personal communication) have been unsuccessful.

ABO Grouping of Secretions

The first published application of an enzyme-linked antibody method in the forensic field was by Inoue and Okada in 1978.[72] These workers employed human anti-A and anti-B serum and rabbit anti-human Ig conjugated peroxidase to identify a group of immobilized stained threads. The method was evaluated on saliva stains, but also worked with semen stains and a few blood stains. The sensitivity of the method was not quite as good as that of an elution test, but was better than that of an inhibition test.

In the same year results with a direct immobilization ELISA for liquid saliva were reported by Werrett and Dolton.[73] Human anti-A and anti-B sera were used together with alkaline phosphatase conjugated anti-human Ig, in a four-stage assay. Sensitivity was comparatively poor and no satisfactory anti-H reagent was identified. These authors also experienced some problems with non-specific binding.

The methods described above relied on the use of human antisera and anti-human Ig conjugates. One problem with this approach is that stains contain endogenous human IgG which tends to produce a high background. Satisfactory assays developed subsequently with polyclonal antisera have been those which employ animal antisera as the capture antibody in a double antibody sandwich assay.

The lack of good antisera to group H substance has been a traditional problem for forensic serologists and delayed the further development of ABO ELISA for several years. Eventually, a direct immobilization ELISA method for H using alkaline phosphatase conjugates of *Ulex europaeus* lectin I was reported by Harris-Smith and Fletcher[56] in 1983, which gave very good sensitivity for semen and saliva stains from secretors. Low H activity was detectable also in secretions from some non-secretors, using more concentrated conjugates.

A similar ELISA using monoclonal antibodies to A, B, and H substances, and anti-mouse Ig alkaline phosphatase conjugate was published by the same workers in 1984.[52] A large number of MCA and anti-mouse Ig enzyme conjugates have subsequently been tested in this assay format,[57] and some modifications have been made to reduce the time taken to perform the assay.[58] Trials with the method on saliva and semen stains gave considerably better results than conventional grouping methods.[53] Post-coital and semen-free vaginal swabs also have been grouped successfully (Fletcher and Skaramauskas, unpublished observations), and the salivary blood group substance from the suspected assailant has been detected on vaginal swabs in two cases of sexual assault involving oral intercourse (Bolton and Sayce, personal communication). An extensive parallel study of this ELISA method with conventional techniques on case-work samples is under way in the UK Forensic Science Service. Results to date indicate that the method is more sensitive than current methods by at least one order of magnitude.

Anti-blood group MCA tend to have a narrower range of specificity than polyclonal sera, and this has led to the identification of MCA which exhibit specificity for different structural types of A, B, and H substances.[74,75] One such anti-A (supplied by Dr. H Lee, CNTS, Paris, France) was found to react with A substance from blood stains, but not from semen or saliva stains.[52,57] Another MCA (an anti-H MCA from Chembiomed), despite being a good hemagglutinating antibody, was found to give positive reactions with exocrine secretion stain extracts but no reactions with blood stain extracts.[57] This type of specificity should make possible the typing of individual components of mixed blood/secretion stains without resorting to more complicated procedures such as immunoaffinity chromatography.

A method designed to distinguish between AB saliva and mixtures of A and B saliva was reported by Katsumata et al in 1984.[76] This method was based on the assumption that in AB individuals the carriers of ABH activity would have both A and B determinants on the same molecule. Microtitre plates were coated with *Dolichos biflorus* lectin (anti-A_1) or goat anti-B serum, and extracts of saliva stains were allowed to react. After washing, human anti-A or -B antiserum was added and the bound antibody detected by the addition of alkaline phosphatase labelled anti-human IgM. The detection limit of the method for liquid saliva was approximately 1:10,000 dilution for group A saliva, but the sensitivity for group B was poor, owing to low binding efficiency of the immobilized anti-B serum. Sensitivities for saliva stains were not reported, but a group ABSe stain was clearly distinguished from mixed A and B saliva stains.

The same assay was applied by Sato and co-workers[77] to liquid semen mixtures. Detection limits similar to those of saliva were obtained, with the anti-B system again proving to be rather insensitive. Mixtures of A and B liquid semens were easily distinguished from AB semen.

Bolton and Thorpe[78] used affinity columns in an attempt to separate saliva mixtures, after failing to reproduce the method reported by Katsumata et al (SL Bolton, personal communication). Monoclonal anti-A, -B, and -H were bound to Sepharose 4B, and mixtures of A, B, and AB saliva were passed down the columns. Only anti-A columns gave reproducible results, but with these the activity retained from AB saliva demonstrated only a small amount of B activity compared with much higher A activity. This suggests that there may be considerable heterogeneity in the composition of blood group activity on carriers in saliva. However, the methods reported to date have not been sufficiently sensitive or reproducible to allow firm conclusions to be drawn about the feasibility of this approach to mixed stain grouping.

In 1985 Katsumata and co-workers reported[79] an anti-H ELISA for saliva in which chicken anti-H was coated on polystyrene and used to capture H substance. The H substance then was detected by a combination of *Ulex europaeus* lectin I(UEA-I), rabbit anti-UEA-I, and enzyme-labelled anti-rabbit serum. Liquid group O saliva gave positive results to approximately 1:10,000 dilution; H substance was also detectable in group A (secretor) saliva. Saliva stains (5 mm × 5 mm filter paper stain was used per microtitre plate well) from secretors gave moderately positive results, while those from non-secretors were marginal or negative. Extended incubation with substrate produced some increase in sensitivity.

Rukavishnikova et al[80] tried unsuccessfully to immobilize saliva and stain extracts in microtitre plates and detect A and B substances with poly- and monoclonal antisera. Some specific performance was obtained for group A stains (up to a dilution of 1:1280) in an ELISA in which *Phaseolus lunatis* anti-A lectin was used as a precoating capture agent, but no anti-B or anti-H system was achieved. This latter method also gave weak results with an aqueous extract of a blood stain.

A direct immobilization assay for saliva substances was reported by Bolton and Thorpe[81] in which MCA were shown to give much better performance than polyclonal sera. Liquid saliva (not stain) dilutions were coated on microtitre plates at pH 12, and A and B substances were detected by incubation with MCA followed by incubation with anti-mouse Ig-peroxidase conjugate. Positive reactions were obtained for saliva diluted up to 1:100,000.

The biotin-avidin system was used by Takatori and Tsutsubuchi[82] to detect ABH substances in liquid saliva samples immobilized directly in microtitre plates. Polyclonal antisera and UEA-I were used, together with biotinylated antiglobulin, avidin, and biotinylated peroxidase. The assay involved six incubation stages and five layers of reactants. It detected A, B, and H substance in dilutions of saliva up to 1:4096. This was a four- to eightfold increase in sensitivity over a hemagglutination-inhibition test performed on the same samples. Some weak but specific reactions were obtained with non-secretor salivas.

A very similar avidin-biotin scheme was used by Kitagawa and co-workers in a dot-ELISA system for grouping liquid saliva.[83] Saliva was spotted on a nitrocellulose membrane, blocked with gelatin, and then incubated successively with polyclonal anti-A or -B (or UEA-I), biotinylated antiglobulin, avidin, biotinylated peroxidase, and substrate. The six incubations occupied a total of 170 minutes. The enzyme substrate used was 4-chloro-1-naphthol, which is converted to a blue-colored product. The reaction was assessed by eye. Positives were obtained with liquid saliva diluted to 1:1,000,000 for secretors, and to 1:100 for non-secretors.

Recently, Mudd[84] reported results with a direct immobilization ELISA in which 10 microlitres of semen stain extract is added to wells and allowed to evaporate to dryness. Using MCA, the method proved to be much more sensitive than A/E and

A/I methods for blood group substances A and H, but only marginally better for substance B.

The extensive research carried out in this area of application has shown that direct immobilization of secretory antigens yields assays with considerably more sensitivity than do hemagglutination methods. The capture assays reported have not offered any greater sensitivity, but they do have a potential for precise quantitation, and for the development of routine assays capable of grouping the individual components of mixed stains. However, much more work is needed on capture assays for ABH substances before their potential can be realized. The direct ELISA, on the other hand, is likely to be in routine use within a short time.

Lewis Grouping

In 1983 Steplewski and co-workers reported the isolation of several specific MCA for Lewis antigens, and they used these to develop RIA and ELISA methods for saliva grouping.[85,86] Saliva dilutions were coated onto polystyrene beads and then incubated with MCA, followed by detection with biotinylated anti-mouse Ig and avidin-biotinyl-horseradish peroxidase, or (125)I-labelled anti-mouse Ig. A full evaluation of the methods was not published, but saliva dilutions up to 1:10,000 gave good results.

The same group of workers subsequently developed the RIA method further and used other MCA to show that part of the Le(a) antigen in saliva in sialylated (N-acetyl-neuraminic acid linked alpha 2–3 to the terminal galactose residue).[87] Immobilized salivary substance was treated with sialidase to remove the additional sugar residue, which thus generated the simple Le(a) determinant. Picard et al[88] confirmed that sialylated Le(a) also occurs on the erythrocyte. He regenerated the original determinant, again using sialidase. Similar effects with sialidase treatment have been observed with semen stains and vaginal secretions (unpublished observations). Thus, it is very important to ensure that the antibodies used for Lewis grouping react with the parent determinant and its subsequent derivatives, or that some enzyme treatment is used to remove the interfering sugar residues.

The studies of Steplewski et al and other groups of workers form part of a wider investigation of carbohydrate determinants on glycoproteins which attempts to understand the surface antigens of tumor cells. Many MCA have been generated by immunization with tumor cells, and many of these have potentially useful specificities within the ABO, secretor, and Lewis grouping systems.[89] ELISA has been used extensively in the characterization of the specificity of these MCA. In particular, Woodward and co-workers[90] used purified natural glycolipids and synthetic Lewis(a)-BSA conjugates to precoat polystyrene in order to identify MCA with relevant specificities. Some MCA have been identified which react with groups of closely-related structures, whereas others distinguish between structures with only small differences. This has made it difficult to find MCA which exactly mirror the type of reactivity commonly associated with "good" polyclonal anti-Lewis sera.

The first anti-Lewis MCA to be made available commercially came from Chembiomed. These were used successfully by Lang[91] in a direct immobilization ELISA for saliva and saliva stains. However, it was found that they gave reactions with saliva from eight Lewis-negative individuals at dilutions up to 1:1,000 of liquid saliva. The cross-reactivity was consistent with secretor status (i.e., secretors gave Le(b) reactions and non-secretors gave Le(a) reactions). When the same reagents were used in a slightly different ELISA method[53] to group 143 saliva stain extracts, only one Lewis negative secretor saliva gave a reaction with anti-Le(b). Some results from this latter study are shown in Table 11–2; saliva stain extracts were diluted to give the equivalent of 1:1,000 dilution of original saliva. The difference between the two methods may be simply a quantitative effect, but it also might reflect some alteration in the specificity of the Lewis antisera when anti-mouse Ig conjugate is allowed to react with the MCA before it binds to Lewis determinants.

Table 11–2 also shows results obtained with an anti-X MCA. This determinant is present in simple or sialylated form in all secretions, from virtually all secretors and non-secretors. Interest in this antigen arises from its potential use as a positive control to enable non-secretor stains to be reliably interpreted. Unfortunately, the anti-X MCA used in our laboratory (clone $D_1$56–45 supplied by Dr. Steplewski, Wistar Institute, Philadelphia) gave positive reactions in only 24 of 36 non-secretor stains, and in 12 of 107 secretor stains. The incidence and strength of positive reactions with seminal material is higher, but very few positive reactions have been obtained with uncontaminated vaginal swabs (Fletcher and Skaramauskas, unpublished observations). It is possible that other anti-X MCA may perform better in this respect.

In 1985 Baechtel and Henning[92] described an inhibition ELISA method which was based on the ability of body fluids to inhibit the binding of anti-Lewis MCA to Lewis substance (Ortho Diagnostics) previously immobilized in microtitre plates. The method was specific and rapid, and had the same sensitivity as did conventional grouping methods. Much higher levels of activity were detected in saliva than in semen. Some vaginal tampon samples were grouped successfully by the method.

Currently, Lewis grouping is used to clarify negative findings in ABO grouping, and to establish "secretor" status. With this latter objective in view, it seems likely that classical Lewis grouping will be replaced in the future by a more comprehensive

TABLE 11–2.
ELISA Results for Secretor Saliva Stains*

		Percentage of Samples Giving Positive Results†							
		Monoclonal Antibodies							
Blood Group	No. Stains	CBM A	CLT B	BRIC 39 (H)	CBM H	CBM Lea	CBM Leb	LUND Leb	WIST X
O	45	0	0	58	73	62	100	93	13
A1	42	100	0	26	19	55	88	48	12
A2	8	88	0	25	25	50	100	88	13
B	9	0	78	0	11	44	89	11	0
AB	3	100	67	0	0	67	100	0	0

*Extracts diluted to give 1:1,000 dilution of the original saliva volume. CBM = Chembiomed; CLT = Celtech (UK) Ltd. BRIC 39, nominally anti-H, was supplied by Dr. Anstee, Bristol Blood Transfusion Lab, UK; LUND Le b was supplied by Dr. Messeter, Lund University, Sweden; and WIST X was clone $D_1$45-56, from Dr. Steplewski, Wistar Institute.
†A positive-negative threshold of 0.1 absorption units was used.

system which employs MCA specific for groups of related precursor substances which are present in secretions from all individuals, not just in Lewis-positives, as at present. This will provide the basis upon which positive identification of ABO non-secretor stains can be made. Several likely candidate specificities are known, but a discussion of their relative merits would be too lengthy for inclusion in this review.

The use of the Lewis system as a discriminating system in its own right has been impracticable in the absence of a Lewis-negative marker, and of little interest in view of its poor population split. There is, however, a possibility that suitable MCA could be used to establish "secretor" status and Lewis status with very little extra effort. This would give four phenotypes with the approximate ratio 72:18:8:2, though in black populations the higher incidence of Lewis-negative individuals would produce a more useful split.

Gm Allotype ELISA

ELISA methods have not found wide application for clinical allotyping, largely because MCA with precise allotype specificity have proven difficult to isolate. MCA with specificity for G1m(1/a),[93] G1m(3/f),[94,95] G1m(17/z),[93] G3m(16),[96] and G3m(21/g)[96] have been reported, but not all of these express their specificity in ELISA assays.

An ELISA for G1m(3) was reported by Fletcher, Dorrill, and Dolton in 1983, based on direct immobilization of blood stain extracts in microtitre plates with detection by MCA and anti-mouse Ig conjugate.[97] The method was much more sensitive than hemagglutination-inhibition, giving good results with blood stain extracts diluted 1 in 10,000. Very weak results were obtained for saliva stains, and no success was achieved with semen stains. The method took approximately 40 hours to complete. A similar assay was reported by Newall using the same MCA and giving similar results.[98] The MCA used in these studies is now available commercially as clone BAM T14 from Unipath (Bedford, UK).

Francois-Gerard and Hoste[99] developed a double antibody sandwich ELISA in which rabbit anti-human IgG (gamma chain) immunoglobulin was used as capture antibody, and BAM T14 was used to detect G1m(3) in samples. Initial coating with antibody was performed by overnight incubation, and the subsequent assay stages took another 30 hours to complete. The sensitivity of the method for blood stains was similar to the direct immobilization methods described above, but it appeared to give better results for semen and saliva stains.

In 1984, Kishida and Tamaki[96] reported an inhibition ELISA based on polyclonal rabbit anti-G1m(3). In this test, the specific antiserum and test sample were added simultaneously to wells precoated with human IgG1. Binding was subsequently detected with anti-rabbit Ig-HRP conjugate. The total assay time, excluding precoating, was approximately 2 hours. Complete discrimination was reported for serum samples diluted 1:10. The same workers[96] also reported similar ELISA assays based on MCA specific for G3m(16) and G3m(21). For both of these, tests with 1:10 dilutions of serum gave complete discrimination. None of these assays were used for blood stain typing.

In 1985, de Lange and co-workers reported the performance of MCA specific for

G1m(1) and G1m(17) in ELISA[93] using serum samples. In a direct immobilization ELISA, the G1m(1) clone(1C2) was non-specific, reacting with all sera tested. The G1m(17) clone(5A1) gave allotype-specific reactions with IgG1 fractions, but also showed reactivity with IgG3. In contrast, when used in inhibition mode ELISA with plates coated with G1m(1,17) IgG, the MCA reacted with the same specificity as in hemagglutination. In this mode, the serum samples were incubated with MCA before being added to the wells.

Recently, Tahir and Thorpe[100] also reported a direct immobilization ELISA for Gm(1) typing using commercial human antiserum (Molter, Heidelberg, West Germany) and anti-IgM-HRP conjugate. The protocol involved overnight immobilization followed by separate incubations with specific antiserum and conjugate. A fourfold difference was observed between positives and negatives up to a dilution of 1:30,000 of serum, and satisfactory discrimination was reported for blood stain typing.

All of the MCA referred to above, except the anti-G3m(16), have been compared in three different ELISA modes by Nelson.[101] These modes were direct immobilization, inhibition, and class capture protocols. G1m(3) and G3m(21) MCA expressed their specificity in all three modes, whereas G1m(1) and G1m(17) were only specific in the inhibition mode. In general terms, capture assays were the most sensitive and direct immobilization assays were the least. However, these results were obtained using myeloma and paraproteins as samples, which may give a false picture of performance with blood stain extracts.

An ELISA method also has been reported by Newall for Km(3) typing[102] for use as a control for Km(1 −) results. Blood stain extracts were immobilized directly in microtitre plate wells and Km(3) was detected with polyclonal rabbit anti-Km(3) serum. The assay took approximately 24 hours to complete. Only 1 mm of blood-stained thread was needed to provide reliable results, and stains up to 17 months old were typed successfully. Semen stains, however, could not be typed by the method.

The future of ELISA application in this area is less certain than in many other areas. Problems clearly exist with the production of suitable MCA, and among the polyclonal-based assays, only the Km(3) assay of Newall has approached the convenience and sensitivity achieved in other areas. There is considerable advantage in the clinical field in switching to an MCA-based methodology, and much work has been carried out to produce suitable clones. Most workers in this area screen hybridomas by ELISA, and these screening methods would require only minor modifications for forensic application. However, the comparative lack of success in establishing anti-allotype MCA suggests some fundamental difficulty in generating or identifying suitable clones (e.g., lack of appropriate murine response genes), and useful ELISAs in this field may not materialize for some years.

Miscellaneous Applications

Some enzyme immunoassay methods (most of which are homogeneous assays) have been developed for the identification of drugs in evidentiary material. Probably the largest series of assays are those marketed by Syva Inc (Palo Alto, California, USA) for the detection of drugs of abuse in urine. Other true ELISA methods have been reported for the detection and quantification of ricin,[103] methamphetamine,[104] phenobarbital,[105] and paraquat.[106]

TABLE 11–3.

Summary of Types of ELISA Methods Reported for Serological Specificities of Forensic Importance

Characteristic	Types of ELISA Used: Direct	Competitive	Sandwich	Success With Stains
Species id.*	+	+	−	+
Foetal blood	−	−	+	+
Semen id.	+	−	+	+
Saliva id.	−	−	+	−
Urine id.	+	−	−	+
ABO group—				
Blood	+	−	−	+
Body fluid	+	+	+	+
Lewis group	+	+	−	+
MN group	+	+	−	+
Gm allotype	+	+	+	+

*id. = identification.

In the field of legal medicine, clinical assays have been adapted for the identification of fatal bovine cytochrome C allergy,[107] and the determination of post-mortem thyroglobulin levels (and their relation to death by asphyxia).[108] ELISA methods for HLA typing[109] and H-Y typing[110] have been reported also, but these have not yet been applied to evidentiary material.

Immunoblotting

The technique of immobilizing biological fluids on cellulose acetate or nitrocellulose sheet (with or without electrophoresis), followed by detection with specific antibody-enzyme conjugate, is very close in principle to ELISA.[111] The only element missing is quantitation, and even this is a feature of some "dot-ELISA" methods in which the diameter or intensity of the reactive spot is measured. This is an expanding technique with forensic applications in Gm,[112] Gc,[113] alpha-2HS glycoprotein,[114] haptoglobin,[115] C3, C4, and coagulation factor 13B.[116] The special features of the method derive from the reactivity of the solid support used, and from the enzyme substrate (4-chloro-1-naphthol), which yields an insoluble product. Fluorogenic substrates also can be used[116] to give enhanced sensitivity.

Conclusions

The introduction of ELISA methods into forensic serology has been delayed by problems with sensitivity, the non-availability of suitable antisera, and difficulties in making stain antigens soluble. These problems have now been overcome for several antigens, and progressively better and more extensively tested methods are being reported in the literature (Table 11–3). There is also a trend towards simpler and more rapid assays. As yet, there is little routine use of ELISA in casework, but the next year should see the widespread adoption of ELISA methods for semen detection and ABO grouping of body fluid stains. Other assays will take a little longer to develop. Developments in the field of DNA typing will have a profound effect on the approach to stain analysis over the next few years, and it is not yet clear which immunological methods will disappear and which will grow in importance. Thus, it would be premature to make any prediction about the ultimate extent of ELISA application, but there is little doubt that it will replace hemagglutination methods within a few years' time.

REFERENCES

1. Butt WR (ed): *Practical Immunoassay: The State of the Art.* Marcel Dekker, New York, 1984.
2. Cantarero LA, Butler JE, Osborne JW: The adsorptive characteristics of protein for polystyrene and their significance in solid-phase immunoassays. *Anal Biochem* 1980; 105:375–382.
3. Norde W, Lyklema J: Thermodynamics of protein adsorption. Theory with special reference to the adsorption of human plasma albumin and bovine pancreas ribonuclease at polystyrene surfaces. *J Colloid Interface Sci* 1979; 71:350–366.
4. Ansari AA, Hattikudur NS, Joshi SR, et al: ELISA solid phase: Stability and binding characteristics. *J Immunol Methods* 1985; 84:117–124.
5. Wood WG, Gadow A: Immobilization of antibodies and antigens on macro solid phases - A comparison between adsorptive and covalent binding. *J Clin Chem Clin Biochem* 1983; 21:789–797.
6. Dierks SE, Butler JE, Richerson HB: Altered recognition of surface-adsorbed compared to antigen-bound antibodies in the ELISA. *Mol Immunol* 1986; 23:403–411.
7. Nygren H, Stenberg M: Kinetics of antibody-binding to surface-immobilized antigen: Influence of mass transport on the enzyme-linked immunosorbent assay (ELISA). *J Colloid Interface Sci* 1985; 107:560–566.
8. Kricka LJ, Carter TJN, Burt SM, et al: Variability in the adsorption properties of microtitre plates used as solid supports in enzyme immunoassay. *Clin Chem* 1980; 26:741.
9. Kohler G, Milstein C: Continuous cultures of fused cells secreting antibody of predefined specificity. *Nature* 1975; 256:495–496.
10. Fletcher SM, Davie MJ: Monoclonal antibody: A major new development in immunology. *J Forensic Sci Soc* 1980; 20:163–167.
11. Porstmann B, Porstmann T, Nugel E, et al: Which of the commonly used marker enzymes gives best results in colorimetric and fluori-

metric enzyme immunoassays: Horseradish peroxidase, alkaline phosphatase or beta-galactosidase? *J Immunol Methods* 1985; 79:27–37.

12. Shalev A, Greenberg AH, McAlpine PJ: Detection of attograms of antigen by a high-sensitivity enzyme-linked immunoabsorbent assay (HS-ELISA) using a fluorogenic substrate. *J Immunol Methods* 1980; 38:125–139.
13. Avrameas S: Coupling of enzymes to proteins with glutaraldehyde. Use of the conjugates for the detection of antigens and antibodies. *Immunochemistry* 1969; 5:43.
14. Schrenk WJ, Kurzinger K: Purpose-made enzyme conjugates for quantitative immunoassays. *Med Lab Sci* 1986; 43:269–276.
15. Guesdon J, Ternynck T, Avrameas S: The use of avidin-biotin interaction in immunoenzymatic techniques. *J Histochem Cytochem* 1979; 27:1131.
16. Savigny Dde, Voller A: The communication of ELISA data from laboratory to clinician. *J Immunoassay* 1980; 1:105–128.
17. Sutula CL, Gillett JM, Morrissey SM, et al: Interpreting ELISA data and establishing the positive-negative threshold. *Plant Disease* 1986; 70:722–726.
18. Caulfield MJ, Schaffer D: A computer program for the evaluation of ELISA data obtained using an automated Microtiter Plate Absorbance Reader. *J Immunol Methods* 1984; 74:205–215.
19. Lehtonen O, Viljanen MK: A binding function for curve-fitting in ELISA and its use in estimating the amounts of total and high affinity antibody. *Int J Biomed Comput* 1982; 13:471–479.
20. Spitalnik S, Cowler J, Cox MT, et al: A new technique in quantitative immunohaematology: Solid-phase kinetic enzyme-linked immunosorbent assay. *Vox Sang* 1983; 45:440–448.
21. Tamaki Y, Kishida T: Identification of human blood stains by enzyme-linked immunosorbent assay (ELISA). *Jpn J Legal Med* 1983; 37:84–87.
22. Oshima M, Hara M: Identification of human hemoglobin by enzyme-linked immunosorbent assay (ELISA) using hemoglobin-coated polystyrene beads. Forensic immunological studies on human specificity. Paper XVI. *Jpn J Legal Med* 1984; 38:170–176.
23. Oshima M, Hara M: Identification of human hemoglobin by enzyme-linked immunosorbent assay (ELISA) using hemoglobin-coated polystyrene beads. Forensic immunological studies on human specificity. Paper XVII. *Jpn J Legal Med* 1984; 38:403–409.
24. Oshima M, Hara M: Cross reaction between animal haemoglobins and anti-human haemoglobin sera using ELISA. *Jpn J Legal Med* 1986; 40:80.

25. Oshima M, Takenaka O, Hara M: Comparative studies of human and animal hemoglobins by ELISA method - Forensic immunological studies on human specificity. Paper XVII. *Jpn J Legal Med* 1986; 40:287–292.
26. Fletcher SM, Dolton P, Harris-Smith PW: Species identification of blood and saliva stains by ELISA using monoclonal antibody. *J Forensic Sci* 1984; 29:67–74.
27. King SJ, Fletcher SM: A direct ELISA for the identification of human blood stains. *CRE Report 610,* 1986.
28. Tsutsumi H, Sato M, Nakamura S, et al: Differentiation between human and chimpanzee in bloodstains by enzyme-linked immunosorbent assay (ELISA) using antihuman serum. *Z Rechtsmed* 1986; 97:99–103.
29. Maiolini R, Masseyeff R: A sandwich method of enzyme immunoassay. I. Application to rat and human alpha-fetoprotein. *J Immunol Methods* 1975; 8:223–234.
30. Belanger L, Hamel D, Dufour D: Double-antibody enzyme immunoassay applied to human alpha-1-foetoprotein. *Clin Chem* 1976; 22:198–204.
31. Kurucz E, Kosa F, Monostori E, et al: A new method in criminology: Use of ELISA to detect AFP on different materials with monoclonal anti-alpha-fetoprotein. *Z Rechtsmed* 1984; 93:117–121.
32. Tsao D, Kwang-Jen Hsiao, Jaw-Ching Wu, et al: Two-site immunoassay for alpha-fetoprotein in dried-blood samples collected on filter paper. *Clin Chem* 1986; 32:2079–2082.
33. Katsumata Y, Sato M, Tamaki K, et al: Identification of fetal bloodstains by enzyme-linked immunosorbent assay for human alpha-fetoprotein. *J Forensic Sci* 1985; 30:1210–1215.
34. Sidall JK, Shetty SD, Cooper EH: Measurements of serum gamma-seminoprotein and prostate-specific antigen evaluated for monitoring carcinoma of the prostate. *Clin Chem* 1986; 32:2040–2043.
35. Hara M, Inoue T, Koyanagi Y, et al: Preparation and immunoelectrophoretic assessment of antisera to human seminal plasma. *Jpn J Legal Med* 1966; 20:356–362.
36. Kuriyama M, Wang MC, Papsidero LD, et al: Quantitation of prostate specific antigen in serum by a sensitive enzyme immunoassay. *Cancer Res* 1980; 40:4658–4662.
37. Tsuda R, Hara M, Inoue T: Determination of seminal stains by enzyme immunoassay using anti-gamma-Sm serum and polystyrene beads coated with seminal plasma. *Jpn J Legal Med* 1983; 37:336–341.
38. Tsuda R, Iki H, Kamachi S, et al: Demonstration of seminal stains by

enzyme immunoassay using peroxidase conjugated anti-gamma-seminoprotein Fab' serum. Forensic immunological studies of body fluids and secretions. Paper XXIV. *Jpn J Legal Med* 1985; 39:30–34.
39. Tsuda R, Hara M, Sagawa K: Demonstration of seminal stains by sandwich ELISA using monoclonal gamma-seminoprotein antibody bound to acrylbutadienestyrene beads. Forensic immunological studies of body fluids and secretion. Paper XXIII. *Jpn J Legal Med* 1984; 38:83–87.
40. Graves HCB, Sensabaugh GF, Blake ET: Post-coital detection of a male-specific semen protein: Application to the investigation of rape. *N Engl J Med* 1985; 312:338–343.
41. Baechtel FS, Jung JM, Terrell LD: Use of an enzyme-linked immunosorbent assay (ELISA) for the detection of p30 in questioned semen stains. Presented at an International Symposium on Forensic Immunology. FBI Academy, Quantico, June 1986.
42. Herr JC, Summers TA, McGee RS, et al: Characterisation of a monoclonal antibody to a conserved epitope on human seminal vesicle specific peptides: A novel probe/marker system for semen identification. *Biol Reprod* 1986; 35:773–784.
43. Herr JC, Woodward MP: An ELISA assay for human semen based on a biotinylated monoclonal antibody to a seminal vesicle-specific antigen. *J Forensic Sci* 1987; 32:346–356.
44. Vikho P, Mattila K, Ehnholm C: Radioimmunoassay of human prostate-specific acid phosphatase. A sensitive and specific assay for semen detection in forensic medicine. *Am J Clin Pathol* 1981; 75:219–220.
45. Moss DW, Self CH, Whitaker KB, et al: An enzyme amplified monoclonal immunoassay for prostatic acid phosphatase. *Clin Chim Acta* 1985; 152:85–94.
46. Sutton JG, Kelly RW, Morris BA: Evaluation of the 190H analogues of prostaglandins E)1(, E)2(, F)1(a and F)2(a as specific markers for the identification of human semen in body fluid mixtures. *Forensic Sci Int* 1987; 33:103–116.
47. Ito K, Katayama M, Minamiura N, et al: Preparation of human salivary alpha-amylase specific monoclonal antibody. *J Biochem (Tokyo)* 1985; 97:1357–1362.
48. Sasaki K, Kimura T, Yokosawa K, et al: The detection of saliva by ELISA. *Jpn J Legal Med* 1985; 39:667.
49. Lee HC, Voll S, Illuminati M: An immunological technique for identification of human urine stains. *Northeastern Assoc Forensic Sci Newsletter (USA)* 1977; 2:2.
50. Tsutsumi H, Katsumata Y: An enzyme-linked immunosorbent assay

for detection of human urinary stains using commercially available anti-human uromucoid. *Jpn J Legal Med* 1986; 40:189.
51. Kind SS, Cleevely RM: The use of ammoniacal bloodstain extracts in blood grouping. *J Forensic Sci Soc* 1969; 9:131–134.
52. Fletcher SM: Developments in ABH grouping by ELISA. *J Forensic Sci Soc* 1984; 24:384.
53. Fletcher SM: Applications and implications of ELISA in forensic serology. Presented at an International Symposium on Forensic Immunology. FBI Academy, Quantico, June 1986.
54. Fletcher SM: Applications and implications of ELISAs in forensic immunology. *Proc Int Symp Forensic Immunol.* FBI Academy, Quantico, Virginia, 1986.
55. Harris-Smith PW, Fletcher SM: Affinity purified *Ulex europaeus* lectin: Preparation and serological characteristics. *J Forensic Sci Soc* 1983; 23:225–231.
56. Harris-Smith PW, Fletcher SM: The synthesis of alkaline phosphatase conjugates of *Ulex europaeus* anti-H lectin suitable for ELISA methods. *Proceedings of the 10th International Congress of the Society for Forensic Haemogenetics*. Munich, October 1983, pp 203–208.
57. Fowler SJ, Gadd SC, Sheehan CP, et al: ABO grouping by ELISA I. An evaluation of monoclonal antisera and commercial enzyme conjugates. *CRE Report 579,* 1985.
58. Fowler SJ, Parry G, Sheehan CP, et al: ABO grouping by ELISA: A comparison of premixing, and simultaneous and sequential addition of antibody and conjugate on assay sensitivity. *CRE Report 612,* 1986.
59. Messeter L, Lisowska E, Lundblad A: Monoclonal antibodies against M and N antigens, in Brinkmann B, Henningsen K (eds): *Advances in Forensic Haemogenetics 1*. Berlin, Springer–Verlag, 1986, pp 8–12.
60. Munro AC, Fraser RH, Barrie EK, et al: Specificity and behaviour of monoclonal antibodies in the MN system. *Biotest Bulletin* 1983; 4:309–314.
61. Fraser RH, Munro AR, Williamson AR, et al: Mouse monoclonal anti-N: Production and serological characterisation. *J Immunogenet* 1982; 9:295–301.
62. Allen RW, Nunley N, Kimmeth ME, et al: Isolation and serological characterisation of a monoclonal antibody recognising the N blood group antigen. *Transfusion* 1984; 24:136–140.
63. Bigbee W, Langlois RG, Vanderlaan M, et al: Binding specificities of eight monoclonal antibodies to human glycophorin A - Studies with M(c), and M(k)En(UK) variant human erythrocytes and M- and MN(v)-type chimpanzee erythrocytes. *J Immunol* 1984; 133:3149–3155.

64. Sensabaugh GF, Kochenburger RJ, Calandro L: Enzyme immunoassay for M antigen in bloodstains. Presented at an International Symposium on Forensic Immunology. FBI Academy, Quantico, June 1986.
65. Judd WJ, Issit PD, Pavone BG, et al: Antibodies that define NANA-independent MN system antigens. *Transfusion* 1978; 18:645.
66. Makler MT, Pesce AJ, Campbell JA, et al: Application of ELISA and ELADA assay (double substrate immunoassay) to red blood cell antigens. *Transfusion* 1981; 21:303–312.
67. Aoki Y, Yokoi T, Funayama M, et al: The use of monoclonal anti-Rh)o((D) antibody for blood typing of blood stains. *Acta Crim Jpn* 1986; 52:85–87.
68. Yokoi T, Funayama M, Sagisaka K: Investigation of Rh)o((D) antigen of human erythrocyte membrane by HPLC, enzyme immunoassay and immunoelectrophoresis. *Jpn J Legal Med* 1985; 39:628.
69. Fukushima H, Segawa M, Ota M, et al: Study on the detection of Rh erythrocyte group antigen using immunoblotting. *Jpn J Legal Med* 1986; 40:196.
70. Reppun T, McIlravy D, Sherman LA: Enzyme-linked immunosorbent microtiter assay for red cell serology. *Transfusion* 1983; 23:305–309.
71. Watson ND, Thorpe JW: Inherent unreliability of the Lattes technique demonstrated by enzyme immunoassay. *Proc Int Symp Forensic Immunol* FBI Academy, Quantico, Virginia, 1986.
72. Inoue T, Okada K: ABO grouping of medico-legal materials by enzyme-labelled antibody test. *Jpn J Legal Med* 1978; 32:66–71.
73. Werrett DJ, Dolton P: Enzyme linked immunosorbent assay: Its application in forensic serology. *Proceedings of the 8th Int. Assoc. Forensic Science*. Wichita, 1978.
74. Abe K, Levery SB, Hakomori S-I: The antibody specific for type 1 chain blood group A determinant. *J Immunol* 1984; 132:1951–1954.
75. Chen H-T, Kabat EA. Immunological studies of blood groups. The combining site specificities of mouse monoclonal hybridoma anti-A and anti-B. *J Biol Chem* 1985; 260:13208–13217.
76. Katsumata Y, Sato M, Sato K, et al: A novel method for ABO grouping of mixed stains of saliva using ELISA. *Acta Crim Med Legal Jpn* 1984; 50:167–172.
77. Sato M, Tamaki K, Okajima H, et al: Differentiation of group ABSe semen from mixtures of group ASe and BSe semens by enzyme-linked immunosorbent assay (ELISA). *Jpn J Legal Med* 1986; 40:293–298.
78. Bolton SL, Thorpe JW: Separation of blood group substances ABH and Lewis in mixtures of body fluids. Presented at an International Symposium on Forensic Immunology. FBI Academy, Quantico, June 1986.

79. Katsumata Y, Sato M, Tamaki K, et al: A sensitive method for detection of blood group H substance in human saliva and semen using enzyme linked immunosorbent assay (ELISA). *Jpn J Legal Med* 1985; 39:15–18.
80. Rukavishnikova GY, Potapov MI, Sigal YR: The detection of soluble ABH blood group antigens by means of ELISA. *Zh Mikrobiol Epidemiol Immunol* 1985; 1:69–73.
81. Bolton SL, Thorpe JW: Enzyme-linked immunosorbent assay for A and B water soluble blood group substances. *J Forensic Sci* 1986; 31:27–35.
82. Takatori T, Tsutsubuchi Y: An ELISA using avidin-biotin complex for the determination of ABH group from saliva. *Forensic Sci Int* 1986; 31:61–68.
83. Kitagawa A, Komura S, Irizawa Y, et al: Immunodetection of blood group ABH substances in human saliva using avidin-biotin-peroxidase complex in a dot-ELISA system. *IRCS Med Sci* 1986; 14:47–86.
84. Mudd JL: Detection of semen blood group substances by absorption-inhibition, absorption-elution and enzyme linked immunosorbent assay. Presented at an International Symposium on Forensic Immunology. FBI Academy, Quantico, June 1986.
85. Steplewski Z, Herlyn M, Blaszczyk M, et al: A simple procedure for determining Lewis phenotypes in human saliva. *J Immunol Methods* 1983; 62:73–78.
86. Steplewski Z, Koprowski H, Herlyn M: Lewis blood group phenotype assay. US Patent Application SN 532,891 1983 [European Patent Application No 84306201.0 1984].
87. Brockhaus M, Wysocka M, Magnani JL, et al: Normal salivary mucin contains gastrointestinal cancer-associated antigen detected by monoclonal antibody 19–9 in the serum mucin of patients. *Vox Sang* 1985; 48:34–38.
88. Picard JK, Loveday D, Fiezi T: Evidence for sialylated type 1 blood group chains on human erythrocyte membranes revealed by agglutination of neuraminidase-treated erythrocytes with Waldenstrom's macroglobulin IgM^{woo} and hybridoma antibody FC10.2. *Vox Sang* 1985; 48:26–33.
89. Thurin J: Binding sites of monoclonal anti-carbohydrate antibodies. *Curr Top Microbiol Immunol* 1987; 18:75–109.
90. Woodward MP, Young WW, Bloodgood RA: Detection of monoclonal antibodies specific for carbohydrate epitopes using periodate oxidation. *J Immunol Methods* 1985; 78:143–153.
91. Lang BG: Lewis typing of body fluids by ELISA. *CRE Report 636,* 1987.

92. Baechtel FS, Henning FC: An ELISA method for detecting Lewis antigens in body fluids, in Brinkmann B, Henningsen K (eds): *Advances in Forensic Haemogenetics 1*. Berlin, Springer-Verlag, 1986, pp 317–322.
93. de Lange GG, van Leeuwen FM, van Eede PH, et al: Monoclonal antibodies to immunoglobulin allotypes: Specificity and reactivity in haemagglutination and ELISA techniques, in Brinkmann B, Henningsen K (eds): *Advances in Forensic Haemogenetics 1*. Berlin, Springer–Verlag, 1986, pp 157–162.
94. Bird P, Lowe J, Jefferis R, et al: Monoclonal antibodies to an immunoglobulin allotype marker G1m(f). *Vox Sang* 1984; 47:366–372.
95. Tamaki Y, Takahashi N, Kishida T, et al: Production and characterization of monoclonal anti-G3m(g) antibody. *Jpn J Legal Med* 1984; 38:152–154.
96. Kishida T, Tamaki Y: Gm typing by enzyme-linked immunosorbent assay (ELISA). *Z Rechtsmed* 1984; 93:23–27.
97. Fletcher SM, Dorrill MJ, Dolton P: Bloodstain allotyping: An ELISA method for G1m(3). International Symposium on Monoclonal Antibodies, Paris, July 1983. *Dev Biol Stand* 1984; 57:381–384.
98. Newall P: Advantages of monoclonal antiserum and ELISA in the identification of bloodstains, in: *Proceedings of 10th International Congress Society Forensic Haemogenetics*. Berlin, Springer–Verlag, 1984, pp 227–232.
99. Francois-Gerard C, Hoste B: A double-sandwich ELISA test for G1m(3) phenotyping of bloodstains with a mouse monoclonal antibody. *J Forensic Sci Soc* 1987; 27:31–38 .
100. Tahir MA, Thorpe JW: Enzyme-linked immunosorbent assay for Gm typing. Presented at an International Symposium on Forensic Immunology. FBI Academy, Quantico, June 1986.
101. Nelson PN: Monoclonal antibodies to human IgG allotypes. (thesis). Birmingham University UK, 1986.
102. Newall P: An enzyme linked immunosorbent assay (ELISA) for the identification of the Km (3) in dried bloodstains. *Can Soc Forensic Sci J* 1984; 17:99.
103. Griffiths GD, Newman H, Gee DJ: Identification and quantification of ricin toxin in animal tissues using ELISA. *J Forensic Sci Soc* 1986; 26:349–358.
104. Tamaki Y, Fukuda M, Kishida T, et al: Solid-phase micro ELISA for methamphetamine. *Jpn J Legal Med* 1983; 37:417–420.
105. Takatori T, Tsutsubuchi Y, Kanamori M: An ELISA using avidin-biotin complex for the determination of phenobarbital. *Jpn J Clin Chem* 1985; 14:180–184.

106. Van Emon J, Hammock B, Seiber JN: Enzyme-linked immunosorbent assay for paraquat and its application to exposure analysis. *Anal Chem* 1986; 58:1866–1873.
107. Takatori T, Terazawa K, Mizukami K: Evidence for human IgE antibodies specific for exogenous and endogenous cytochrome C in postmortem serum induced by bovine cytochrome C allergy: Detection by ELISA using avidin-biotin complex. *Jpn J Legal Med* 1986; 40:119–123.
108. Tamaki K, Katsumata Y, Yada S: Determination of thyroglobulin levels in blood by ELISA. *Jpn J Legal Med* 1985; 39:625.
109. Bishara A, Grautbar G, Marbach A, et al: Enzyme linked immunosorbent assay for HLA determination on fresh and dried lymphocytes. *J Immunol Methods* 1983; 62:265–271.
110. Brunner M, Moreira-Filho C, Wachtel G, et al: H-Y typing in the ELISA. *J Immunol Methods* 1984; 75:203–209.
111. Huisman JG: Immunoblotting: An emerging technique in immunohaematology. *Vox Sang* 1986; 50:129–136.
112. Kishida T, Tamaki Y, Takahashi N: Application of monoclonal antibodies in forensic science practice. II. Immunoblotting for Gm typing. *Jpn J Legal Med* 1985; 39:623.
113. Hoste BM: Advantages of enzyme immunoassay after blotting in blood stain grouping. Application to the Gc subtypes, in Brinkmann B, Henningsen K (eds): *Advances in Forensic Haemogenetics 1*. Berlin, Springer–Verlag, 1986, pp 382–385.
114. Tamaki Y: Application of immunoblotting to serum protein phenotyping with reference to alpha-2HS Glycoprotein (AHS) typing of bloodstains, in Brinkmann B, Henningsen K (eds): *Advances in Forensic Haemogenetics 1*. Berlin, Springer–Verlag, 1986, pp 401–404.
115. Teige B, Olaisen B, Pedersen L: Subtyping of haptoglobin, in Brinkmann B, Henningsen K (eds): *Advances in Forensic Haemogenetics 1*. Berlin, Springer–Verlag, 1986, pp 136–140.
116. Teige B, Olaisen B, Jonassen R: Fluorescent stains in protein detection on immunoblots, in Brinkmann B, Henningsen K (eds): *Advances in Forensic Haemogenetics 1*. Berlin, Springer–Verlag, 1986, pp 60–64.

Index